鷹野常雄

Tsuneo Takano

I take pride in the fact that this portrait looks exactly like me.

Tsuneo Takano

Born in Tokyo.
No hobbies.
No expression.
No interests.
No harm.
Nothing to say.

Takeshi Obata was born in 1969 in Niigata, Japan, and is the artist of the wildly popular SHONEN JUMP title *Hikaru no Go*, which won the 2003 Tezuka Shinsei "New Hope" award and the Shogakukan Manga award. Obata is also the artist of *Arabian Majin Bokentan Lamp Lamp*, *Ayatsuri Sakon*, *Cyborg Jichan G*, and the smash hit manga *Death Note*.

RalΩGrad

Vol. 3

The SHONEN JUMP ADVANCED
Manga Edition

Story By **TSUNEO TAKANO**
Art By **TAKESHI OBATA**

English Adaptation/Jake Forbes
Translation/Labaamen, HC Language Solutions, Inc.
Touch-up Art & Lettering/HudsonYards
Design/King Clovis
Editor/Yuki Murashige

Editor in Chief, Books/Alvin Lu
Editor in Chief, Magazines/Marc Weidenbaum
VP, Publishing Licensing/Rika Inouye
VP, Sales & Product Marketing/Gonzalo Ferreyra
VP, Creative/ Linda Espinosa
Publisher/Hyoe Narita

Printed in Canada

Published by VIZ Media, LLC
P.O. Box 77010
San Francisco, CA 94107

SHONEN JUMP ADVANCED Manga Edition
10 9 8 7 6 5 4 3 2 1
First printing, February 2009

THE WORLD'S MOST
CUTTING-EDGE MANGA

www.viz.com

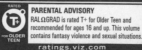

RalΩGrad

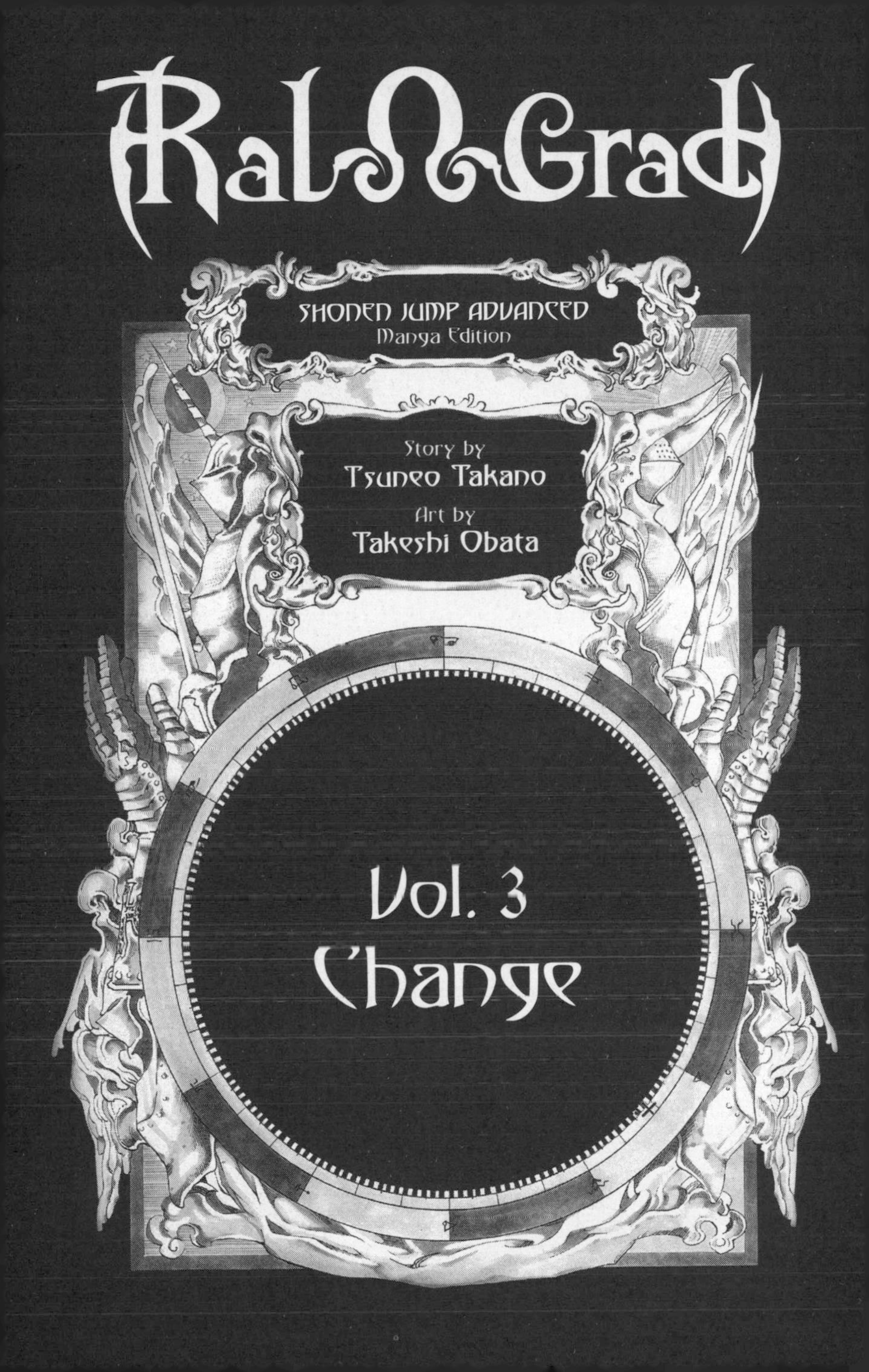

SHONEN JUMP ADVANCED
Manga Edition

Story by
Tsuneo Takano
Art by
Takeshi Obata

Vol. 3
Change

Story & Characters

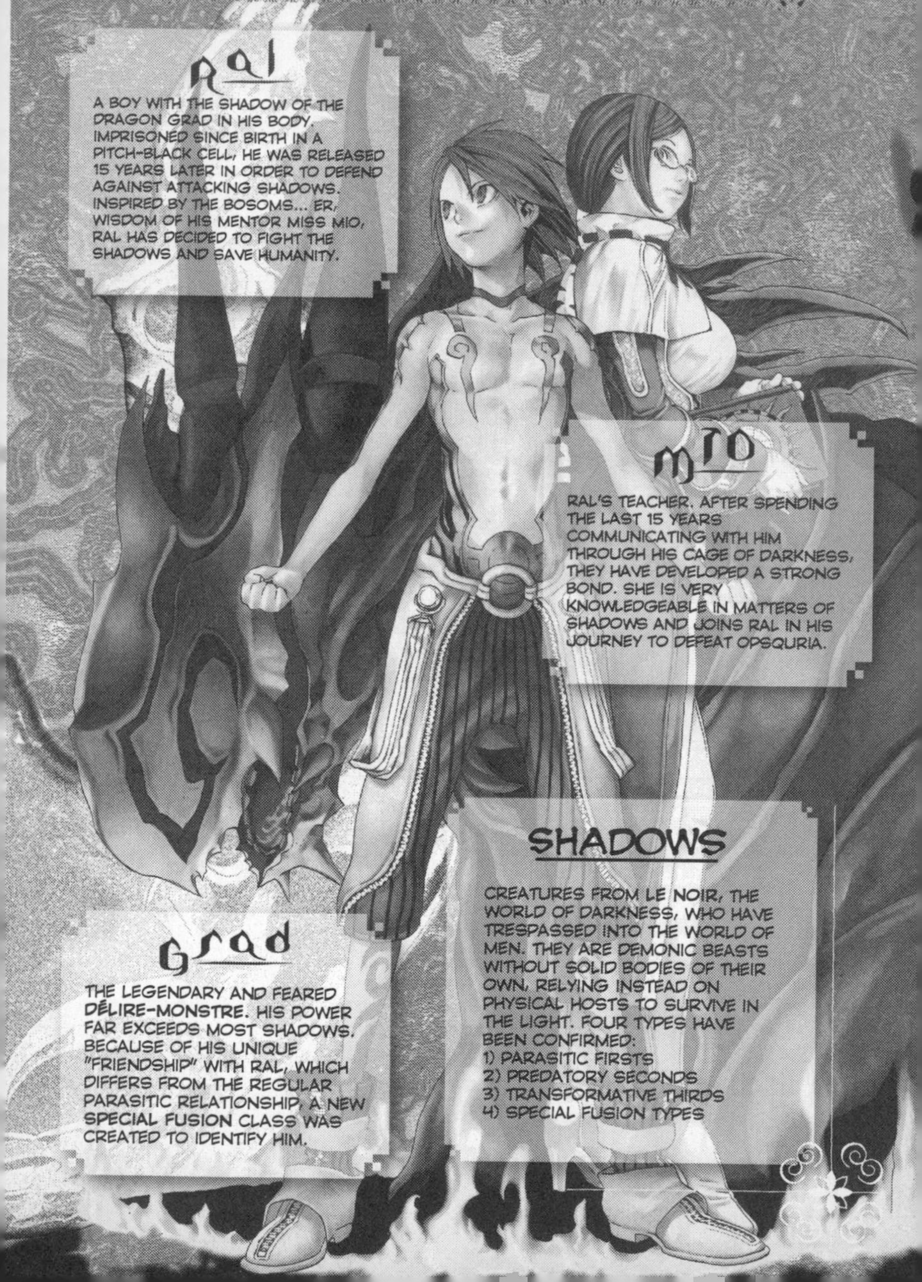

Ral

A BOY WITH THE SHADOW OF THE DRAGON GRAD IN HIS BODY. IMPRISONED SINCE BIRTH IN A PITCH-BLACK CELL, HE WAS RELEASED 15 YEARS LATER IN ORDER TO DEFEND AGAINST ATTACKING SHADOWS. INSPIRED BY THE BOSOMS... ER, WISDOM OF HIS MENTOR MISS MIO, RAL HAS DECIDED TO FIGHT THE SHADOWS AND SAVE HUMANITY.

Mio

RAL'S TEACHER. AFTER SPENDING THE LAST 15 YEARS COMMUNICATING WITH HIM THROUGH HIS CAGE OF DARKNESS, THEY HAVE DEVELOPED A STRONG BOND. SHE IS VERY KNOWLEDGEABLE IN MATTERS OF SHADOWS AND JOINS RAL IN HIS JOURNEY TO DEFEAT OPSQURIA.

Grad

THE LEGENDARY AND FEARED **DÉLIRE-MONSTRE**. HIS POWER FAR EXCEEDS MOST SHADOWS. BECAUSE OF HIS UNIQUE "FRIENDSHIP" WITH RAL, WHICH DIFFERS FROM THE REGULAR PARASITIC RELATIONSHIP, A NEW **SPECIAL FUSION** CLASS WAS CREATED TO IDENTIFY HIM.

SHADOWS

CREATURES FROM LE NOIR, THE WORLD OF DARKNESS, WHO HAVE TRESPASSED INTO THE WORLD OF MEN. THEY ARE DEMONIC BEASTS WITHOUT SOLID BODIES OF THEIR OWN, RELYING INSTEAD ON PHYSICAL HOSTS TO SURVIVE IN THE LIGHT. FOUR TYPES HAVE BEEN CONFIRMED:

1) PARASITIC FIRSTS
2) PREDATORY SECONDS
3) TRANSFORMATIVE THIRDS
4) SPECIAL FUSION TYPES

STORY THUS FAR...

RAL AND COMPANY ARE ON A QUEST TO DEFEAT OPSQURIA, THE QUEEN OF SHADOWS. THE JOURNEY BECOMES A RACE WHEN RAL LEARNS OF ANOTHER HERO OUT TO SLAY HER AS WELL—GANETTE, THE INVINCIBLE SWORDSMAN. JOINED BY TWO NEW SHADOW-WIELDING ALLIES, KAFKA AND SUNSU, THE GROUP SET SAIL FOR THE KASABIA CONTENT. UPON LANDING, THEY FIND A YOUNG WOMAN UNDER ATTACK, AND RAL RUSHES TO HER RESCUE. WHEN RAL COZIES UP TO THE GIRL TO COLLECT HIS "REWARD," HE LEARNS TOO LATE THAT IT'S A TRAP! THE GIRL'S SHADOW PARALYZES RAL WITH ITS VENOMOUS BITE, LEAVING GRAD UNABLE TO COME OUT.

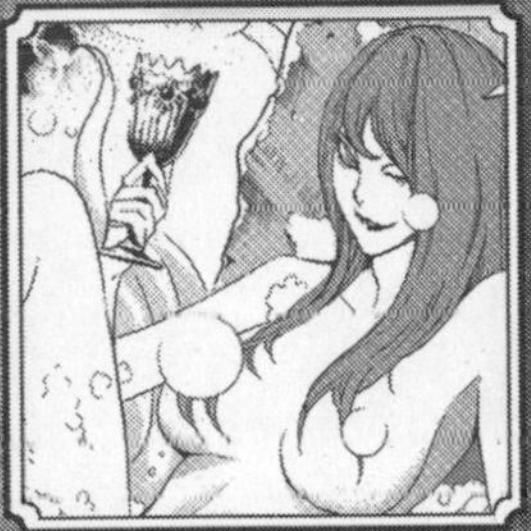

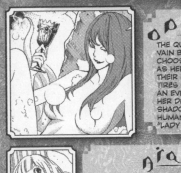

Opsquria

THE QUEEN OF THE SHADOWS. VAIN BEYOND MEASURE, SHE CHOOSES ONLY BEAUTIFUL GIRLS AS HER HOSTS, FEEDING OFF THEIR LIFE ENERGY UNTIL SHE TIRES OF HER LOOKS AND FINDS AN EVEN MORE BEAUTIFUL HOST. HER DESIRES LED HER AND THE SHADOWS FROM LE NOIR INTO THE HUMAN REALM. SHE IS CALLED "LADY BIRA" BY HER KIND.

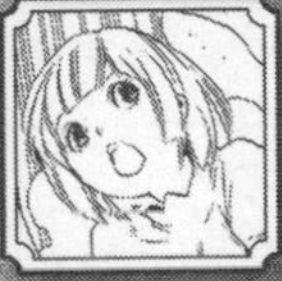

Aia

A YOUNG GIRL AND SHADOW HOST WHO WAS ALSO IMPRISONED IN THE SAME DUNGEON AS RAL.

Garudara

AIA'S SHADOW. IT IS GOOD AT RECONNAISSANCE.

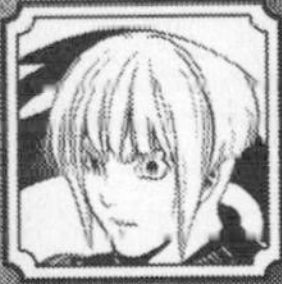

Kafka

THE BRAVE KNIGHT KNOWN AS "KAFKA OF THE CHAIN OF ROSES."

Riz

KAFKA'S SHADOW. THE CHAINE LORD, IT IS PARTICULARLY WELL SUITED FOR DEFENSE.

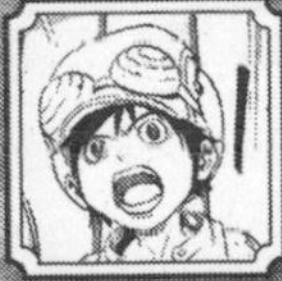

Sunsu

A BOY WHO TOOK IN A SHADOW TO JOIN RAL'S QUEST, WITH THE HOPES OF RESCUING HIS SISTER.

Gensai

SUNSU'S SHADOW. IT ALLOWS ITS HOST TO BREATH UNDERWATER.

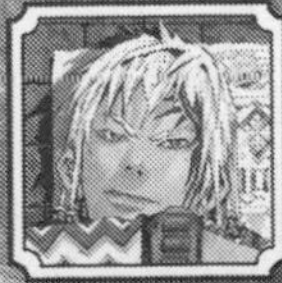

Ganette

THE "INVINCIBLE SWORDSMAN." HE HAS A HEAD START ON RAL ON THE MISSION TO DESTROY OPSQURIA.

Garla

THE LEGENDARY WHITE TIGER. IN ITS SEARCH FOR A COURAGEOUS HOST, IT CHOSE GANETTE.

Genol

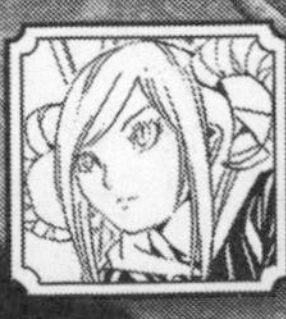

Cela

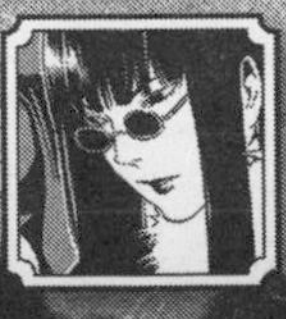

Ral Ω Grad

Vol. 3
Change

Contents

TALE 16 Vexation

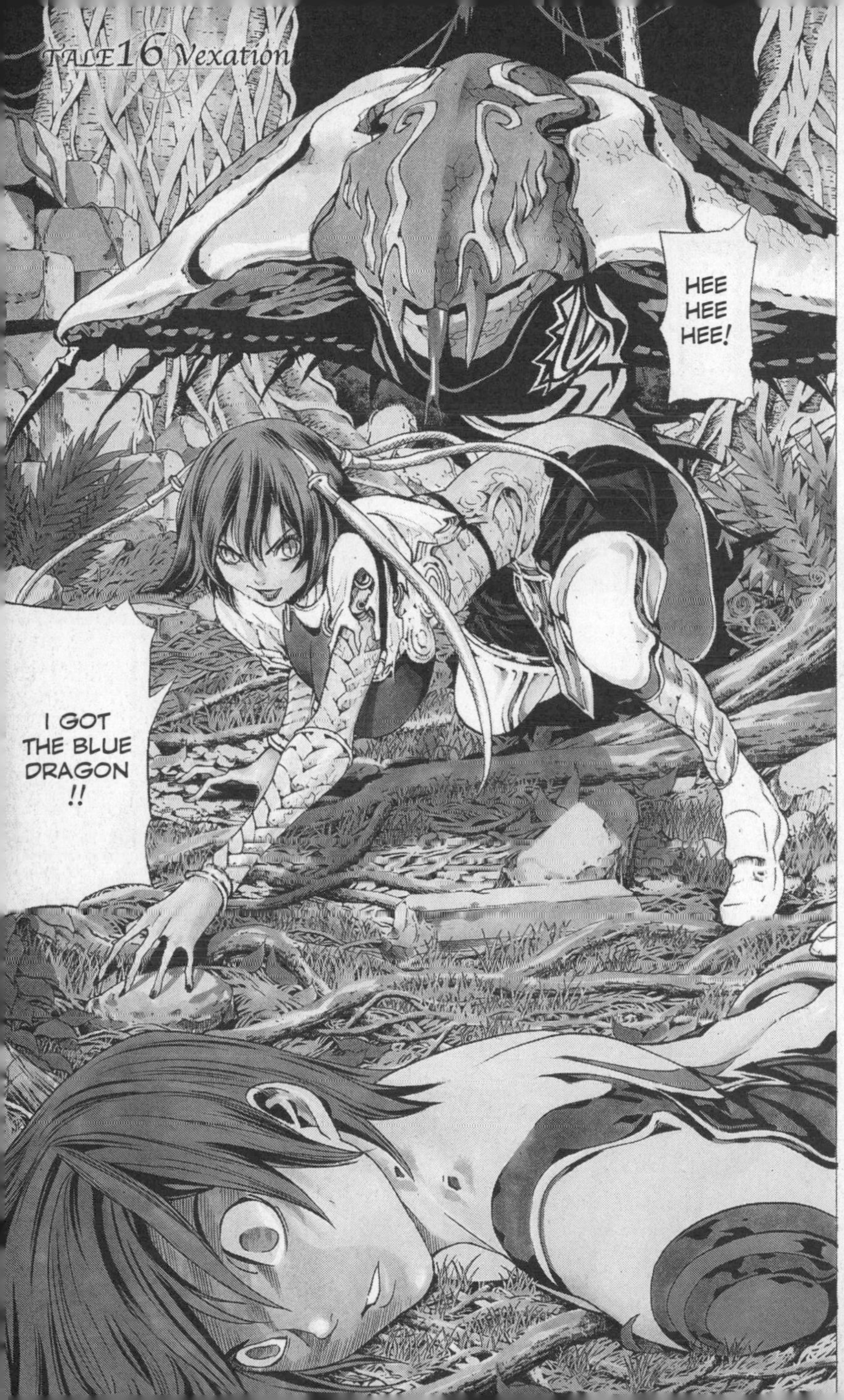
HEE HEE HEE!
I GOT THE BLUE DRAGON !!

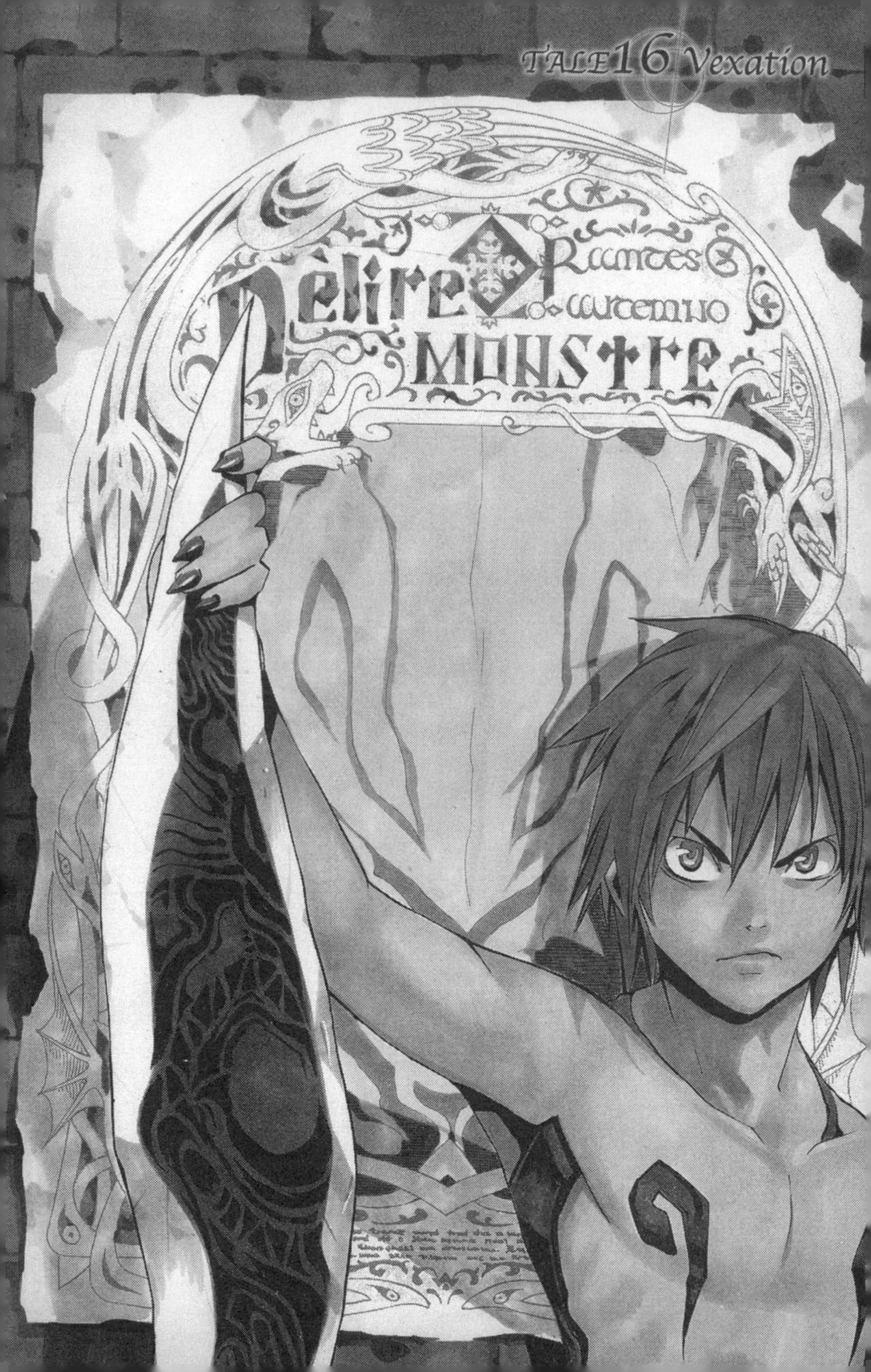
TALE16 Vexation

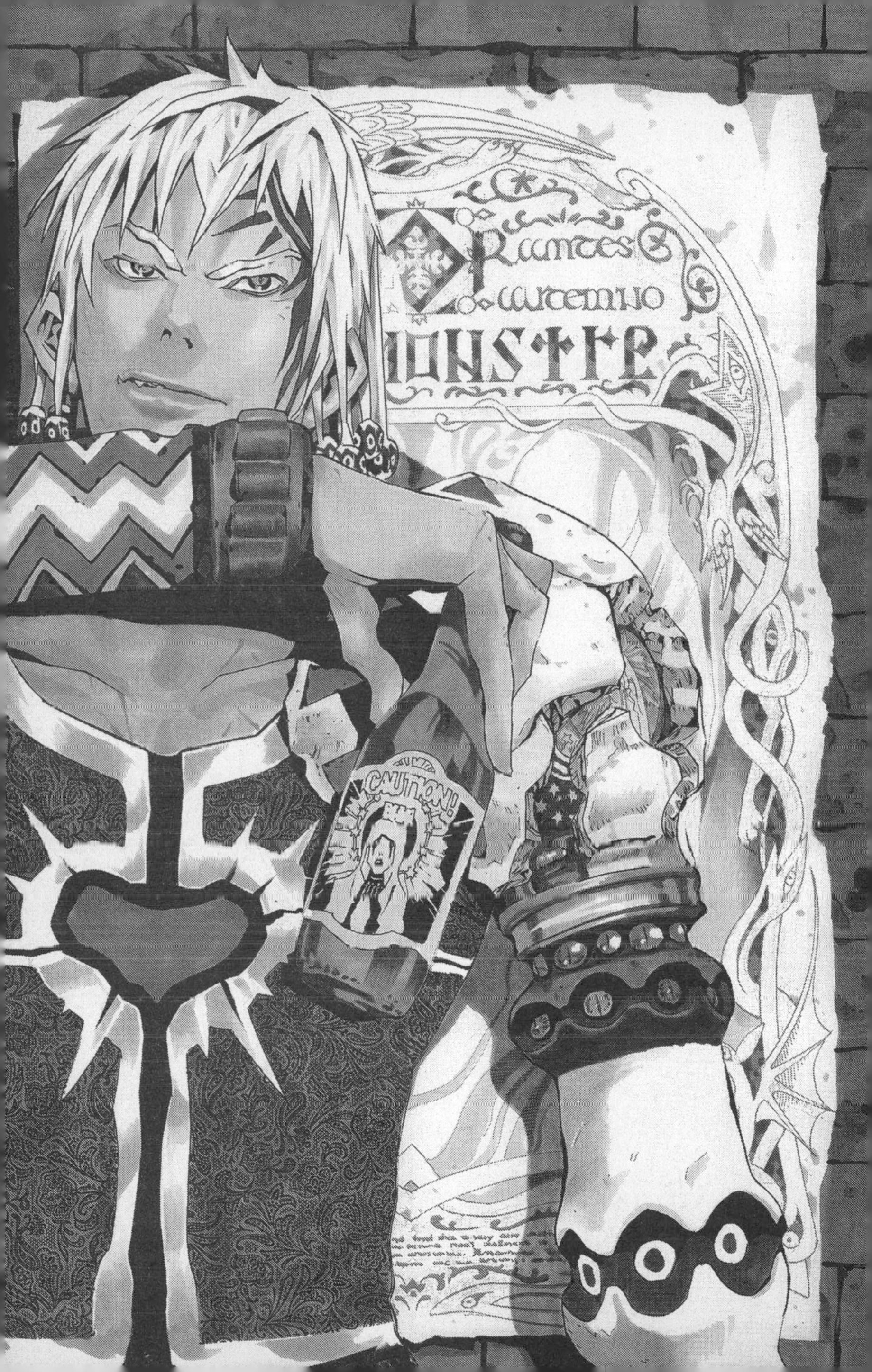
CAUTION!

Ral Ω Grad

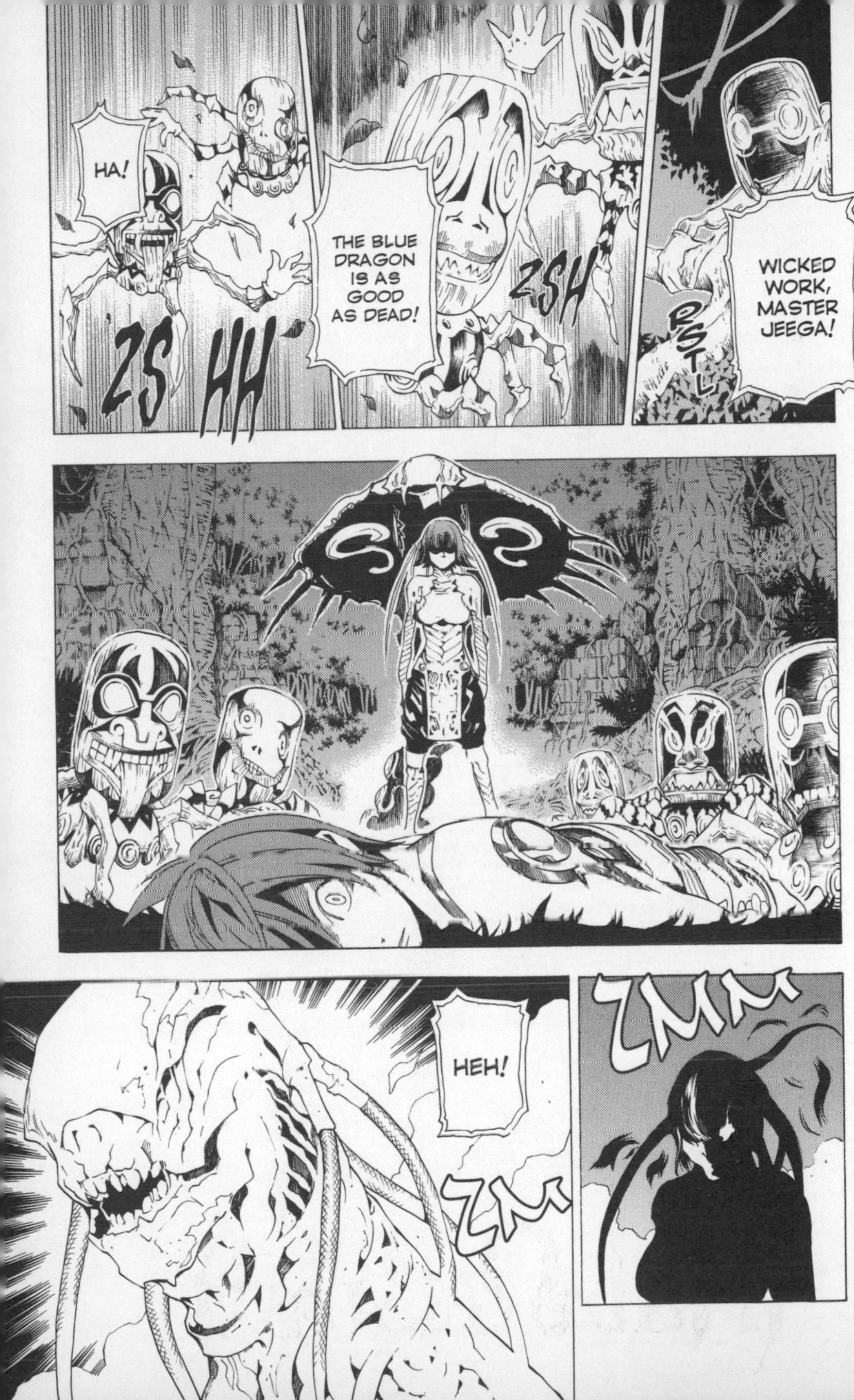
WICKED WORK, MASTER JEEGA!
RSTL
THE BLUE DRAGON IS AS GOOD AS DEAD!
ZSH
HA!
ZSHH
ZMM
HEH!
ZM

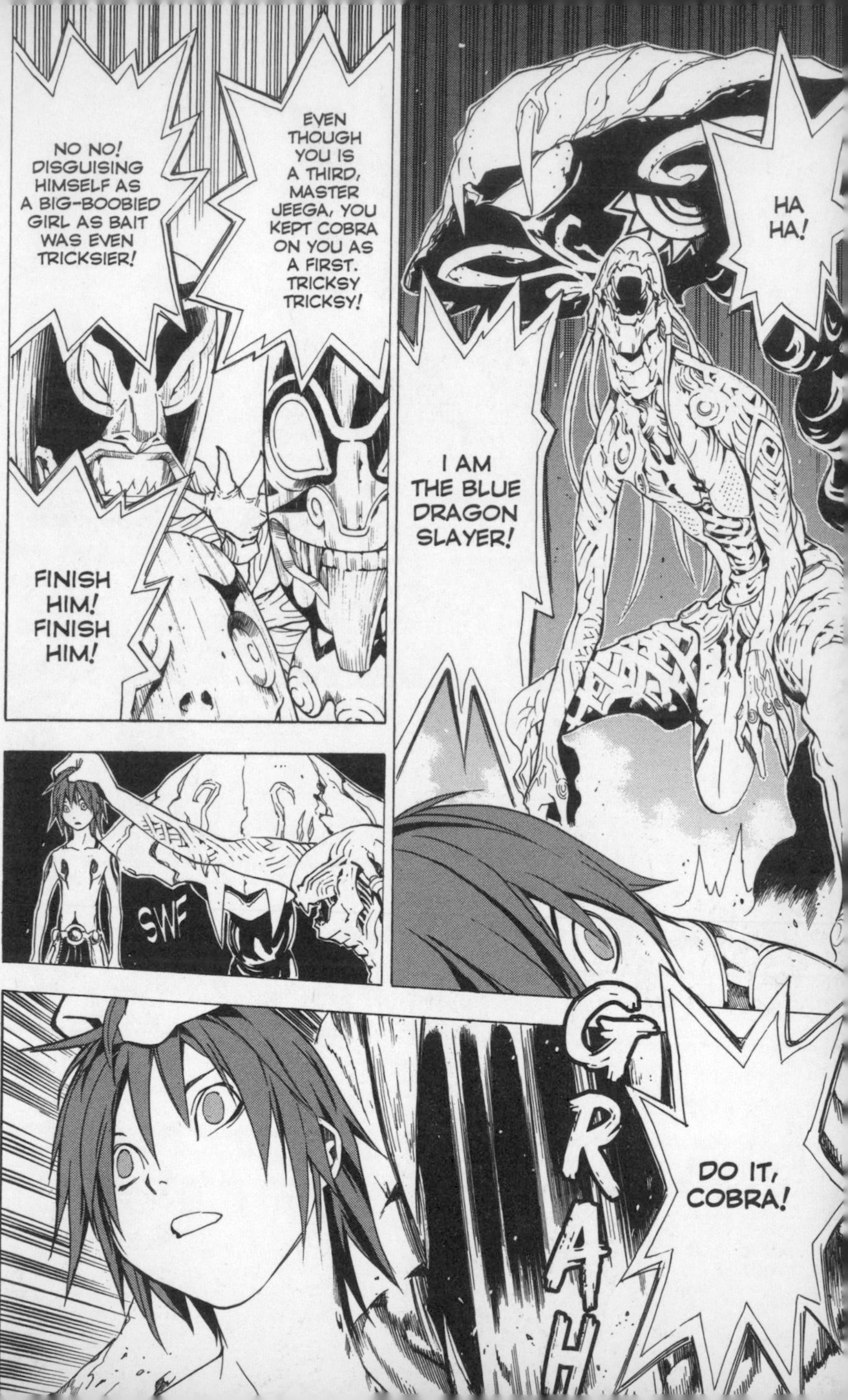
HA HA!
I AM THE BLUE DRAGON SLAYER!
EVEN THOUGH YOU IS A THIRD, MASTER JEEGA, YOU KEPT COBRA ON YOU AS A FIRST. TRICKSY TRICKSY!
NO NO! DISGUISING HIMSELF AS A BIG-BOOBIED GIRL AS BAIT WAS EVEN TRICKSIER!
FINISH HIM! FINISH HIM!
SWF
DO IT, COBRA!
GRAAH

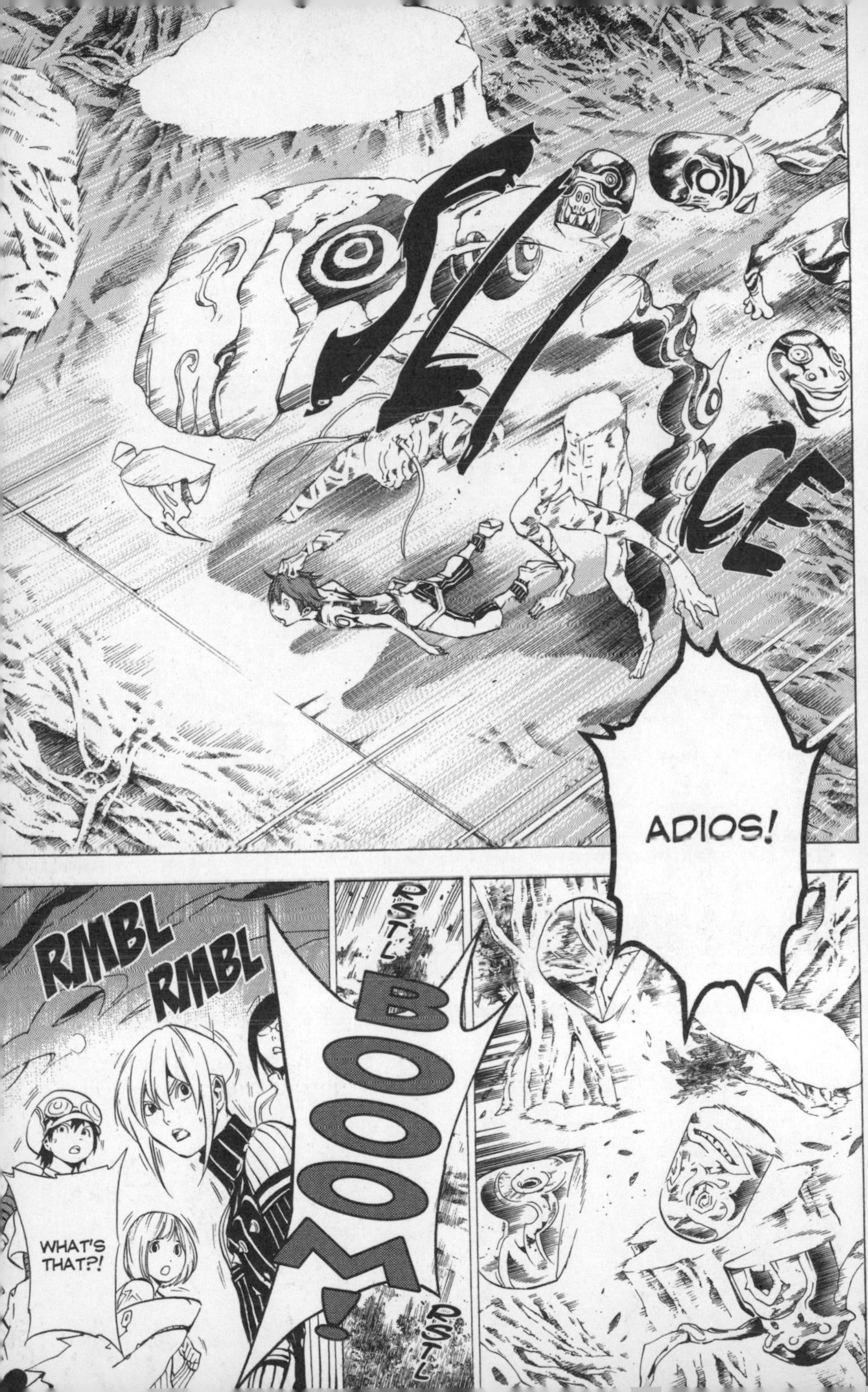
SLICE
ADIOS!
RSTL
BOOOOM!
RSTL
RMBL RMBL
WHAT'S THAT?!

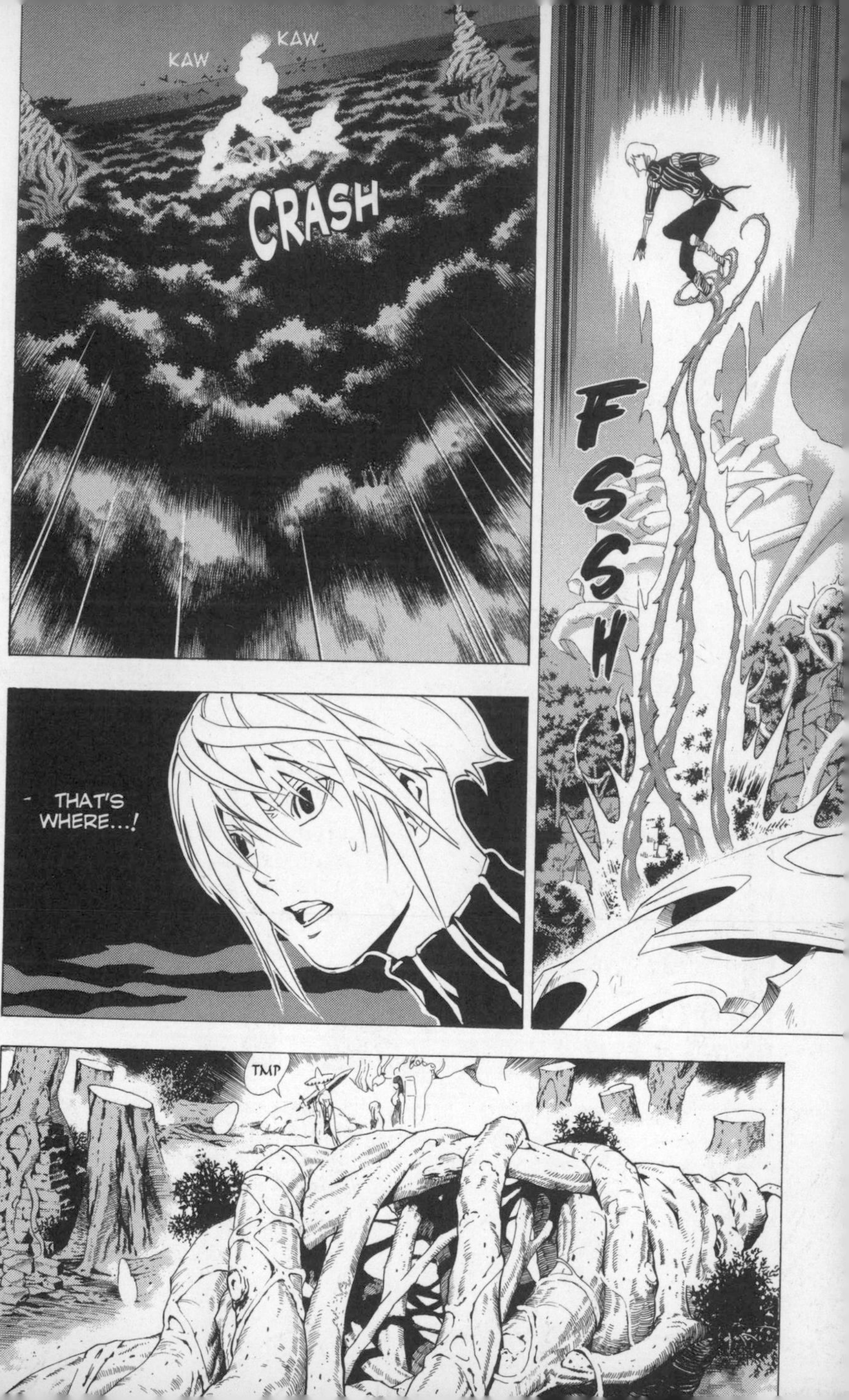
FSSSH
KAW KAW
CRASH
- THAT'S WHERE...!
TMP

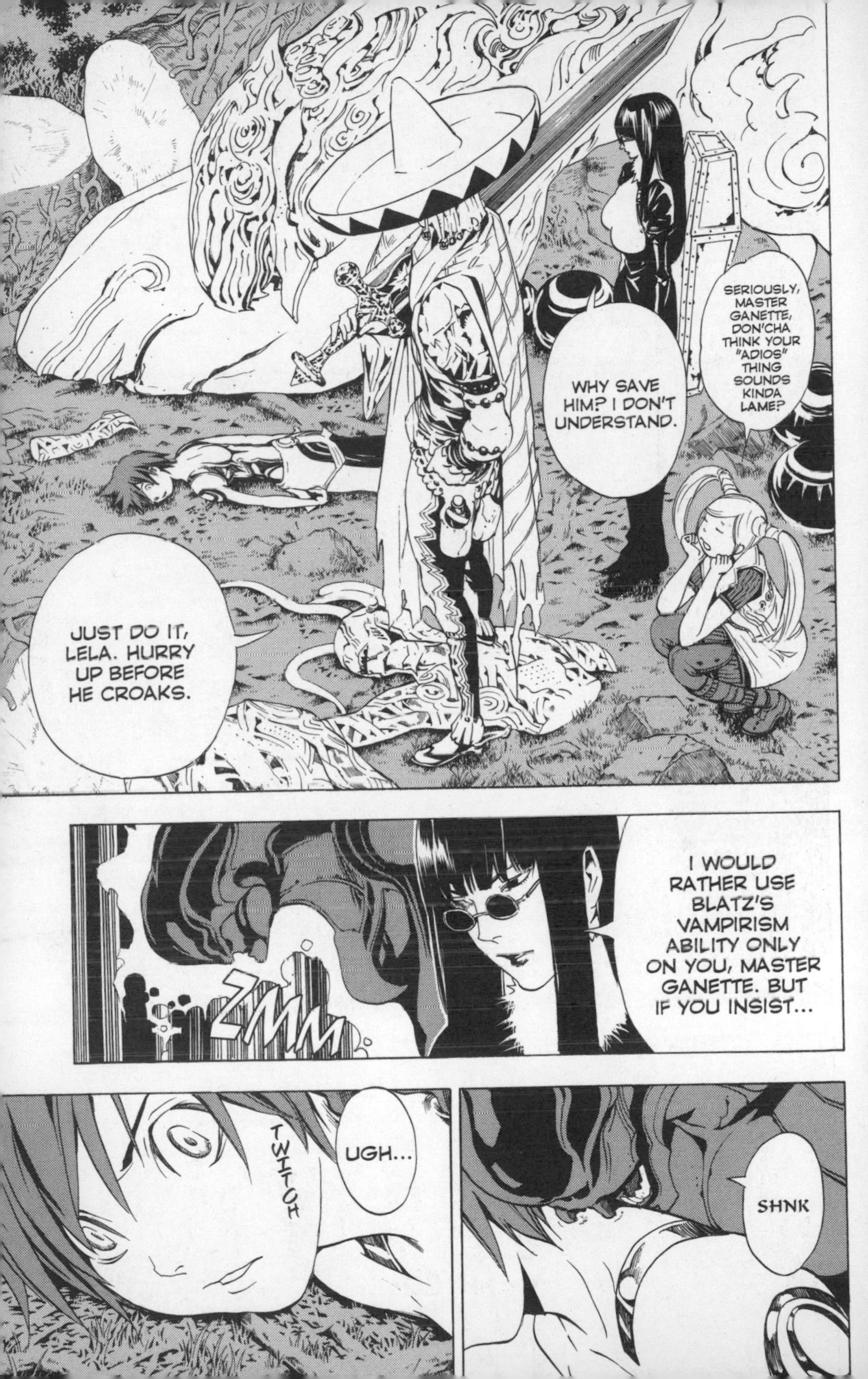
SERIOUSLY, MASTER GANETTE, DON'CHA THINK YOUR "ADIOS" THING SOUNDS KINDA LAME?
WHY SAVE HIM? I DON'T UNDERSTAND.
JUST DO IT, LELA. HURRY UP BEFORE HE CROAKS.
I WOULD RATHER USE BLATZ'S VAMPIRISM ABILITY ONLY ON YOU, MASTER GANETTE. BUT IF YOU INSIST...
ZMM
SHNK
UGH...
TWITCH

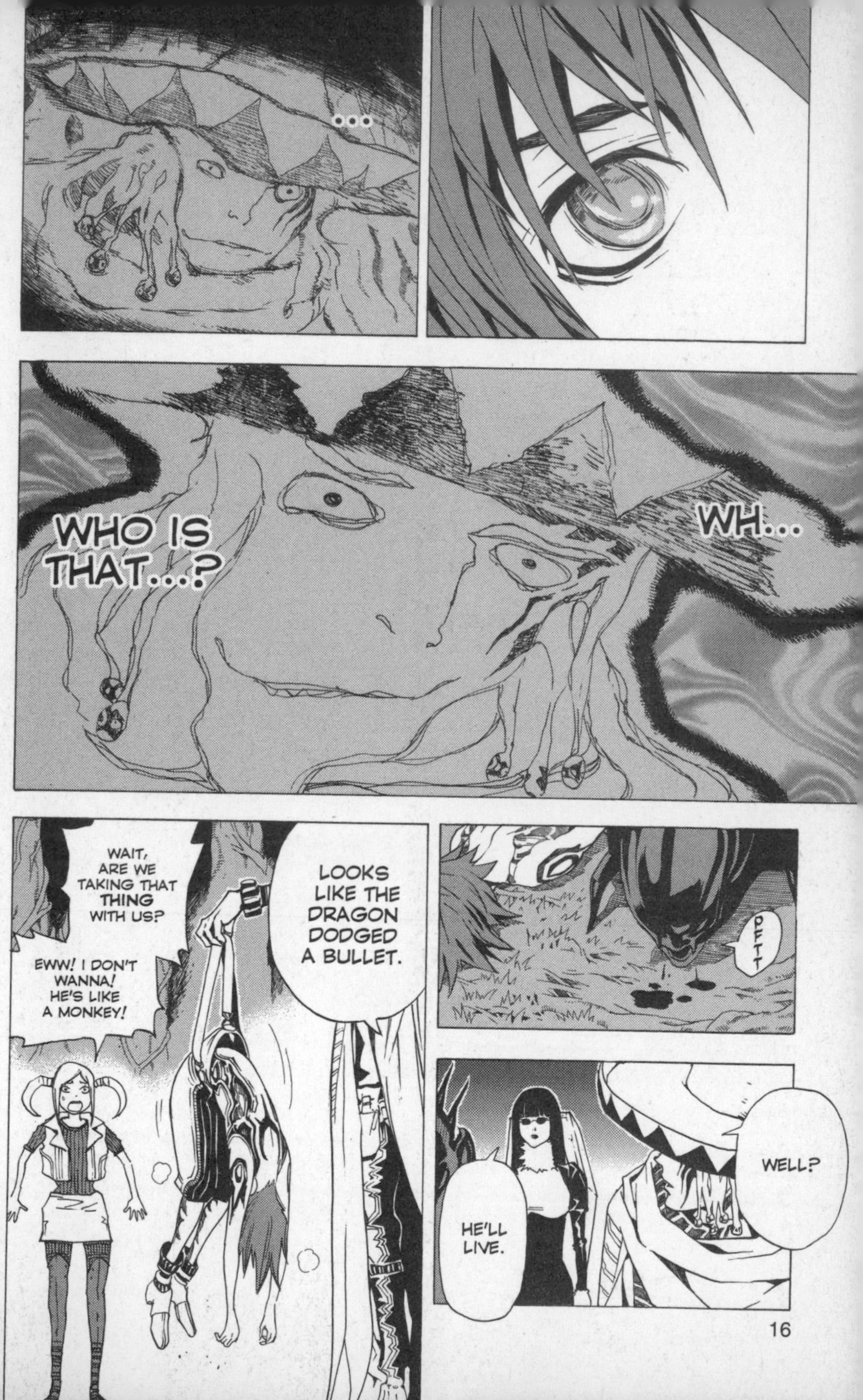
...
WH...
WHO IS THAT...?
PFFT
WELL?
HE'LL LIVE.
LOOKS LIKE THE DRAGON DODGED A BULLET.
WAIT, ARE WE TAKING THAT THING WITH US?
EWW! I DON'T WANNA! HE'S LIKE A MONKEY!

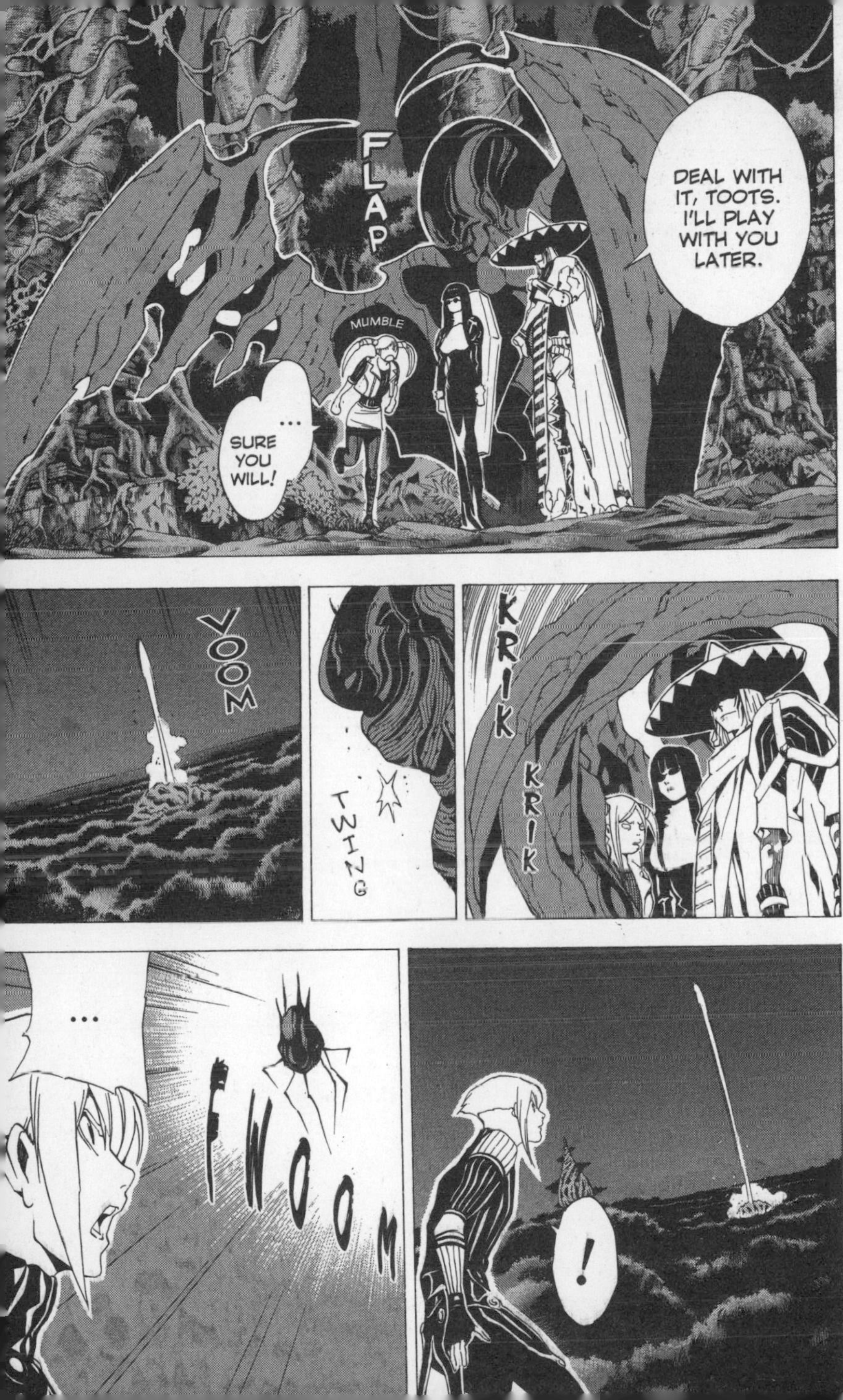
DEAL WITH IT, TOOTS. I'LL PLAY WITH YOU LATER.
FLAP
MUMBLE
... SURE YOU WILL!
KRIK
KRIK
TWING
VOOM
!
...
FWOOM

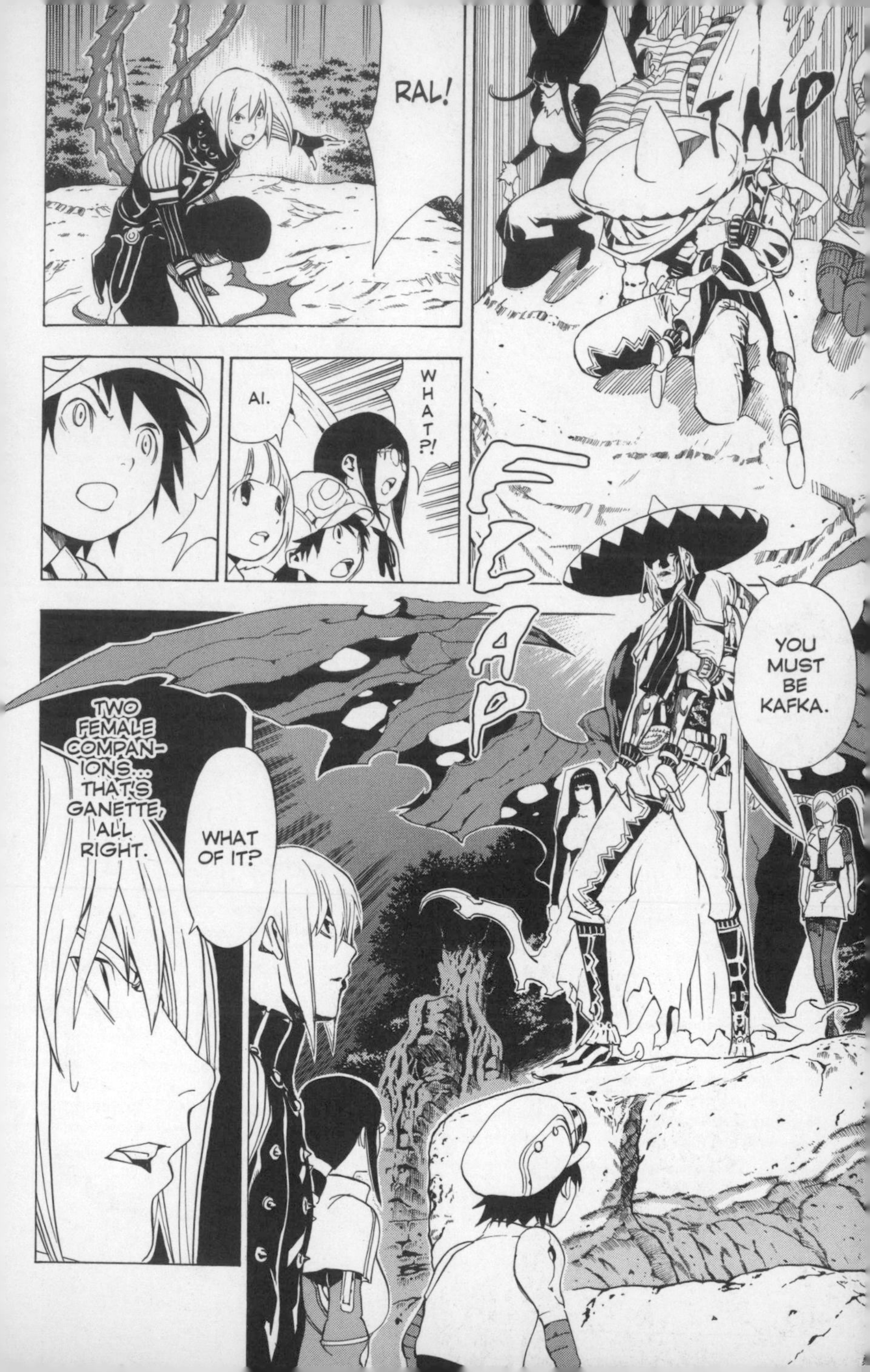
TMP
FZAP
RAL!
WHAT?!
AI.
YOU MUST BE KAFKA.
WHAT OF IT?
TWO FEMALE COMPANIONS... THAT'S GANETTE, ALL RIGHT.

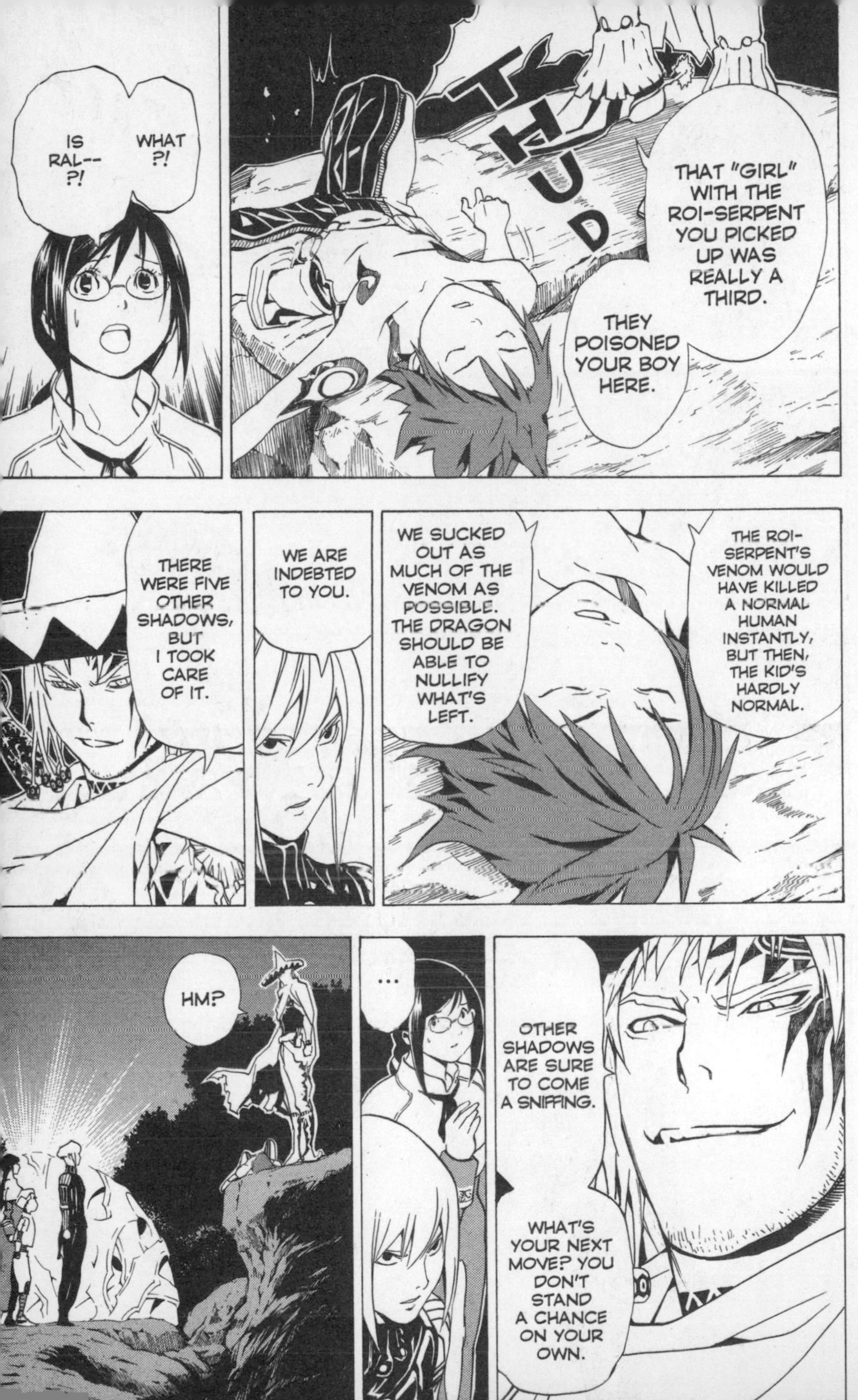
THUD
THAT "GIRL" WITH THE ROI-SERPENT YOU PICKED UP WAS REALLY A THIRD.
THEY POISONED YOUR BOY HERE.
WHAT?!
IS RAL--?!
THE ROI-SERPENT'S VENOM WOULD HAVE KILLED A NORMAL HUMAN INSTANTLY, BUT THEN, THE KID'S HARDLY NORMAL.
WE SUCKED OUT AS MUCH OF THE VENOM AS POSSIBLE. THE DRAGON SHOULD BE ABLE TO NULLIFY WHAT'S LEFT.
WE ARE INDEBTED TO YOU.
THERE WERE FIVE OTHER SHADOWS, BUT I TOOK CARE OF IT.
OTHER SHADOWS ARE SURE TO COME A SNIFFING.
WHAT'S YOUR NEXT MOVE? YOU DON'T STAND A CHANCE ON YOUR OWN.
...
HM?

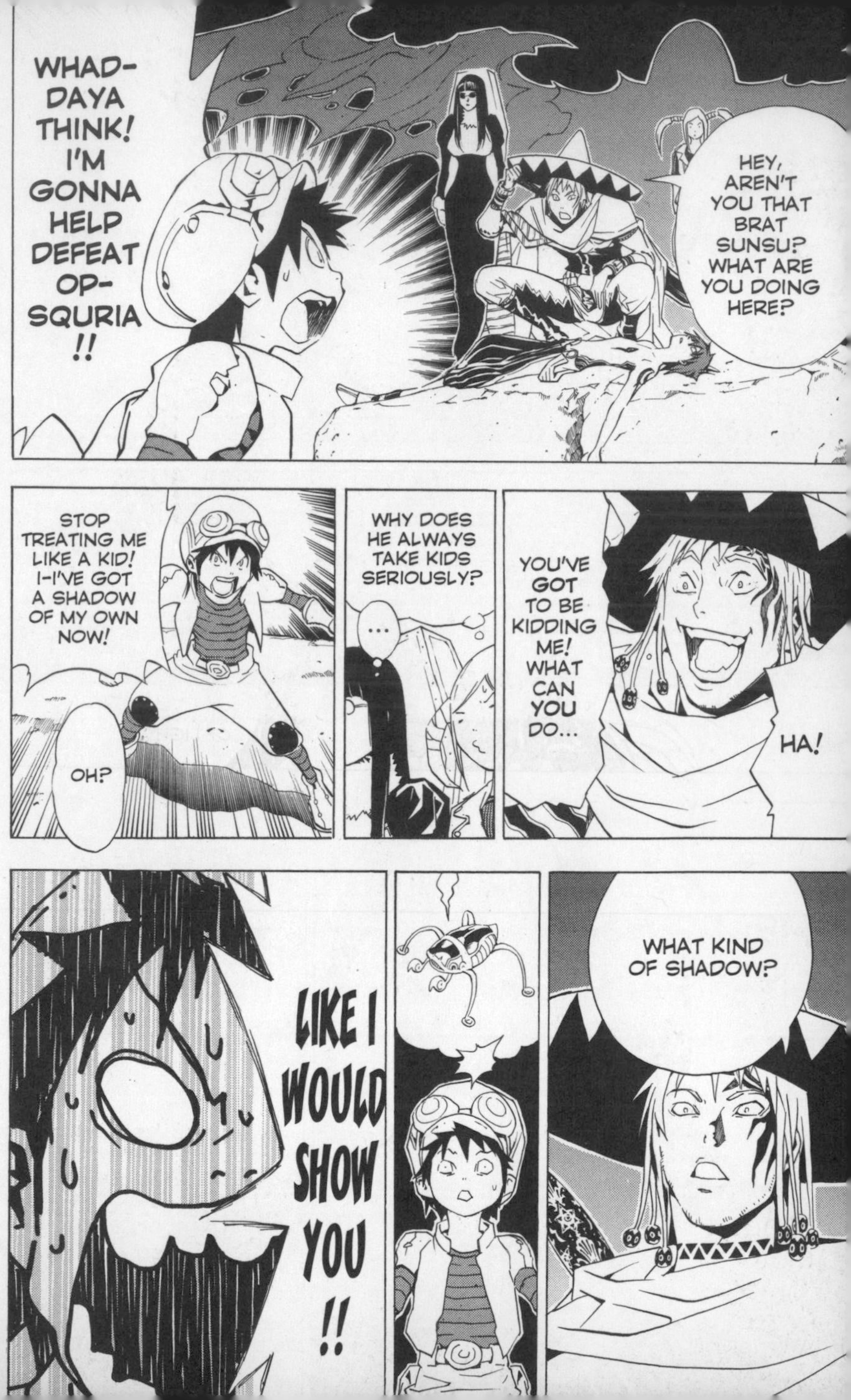
HEY, AREN'T YOU THAT BRAT SUNSU? WHAT ARE YOU DOING HERE?
WHAD-DAYA THINK! I'M GONNA HELP DEFEAT OP-SQURIA !!
YOU'VE GOT TO BE KIDDING ME! WHAT CAN YOU DO...
HA!
WHY DOES HE ALWAYS TAKE KIDS SERIOUSLY?
...
STOP TREATING ME LIKE A KID! I-I'VE GOT A SHADOW OF MY OWN NOW!
OH?
WHAT KIND OF SHADOW?
LIKE I WOULD SHOW YOU !!

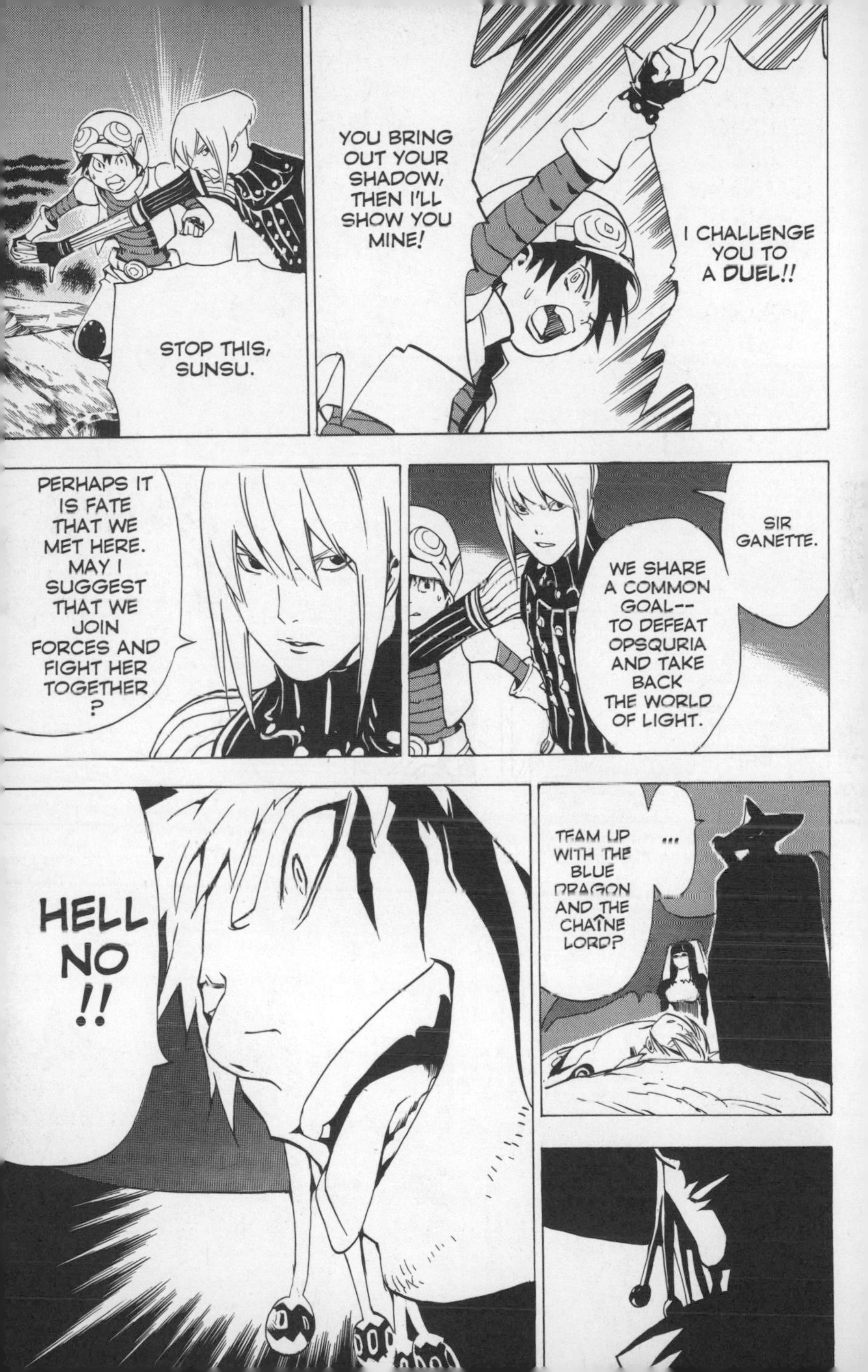
YOU BRING OUT YOUR SHADOW, THEN I'LL SHOW YOU MINE!
I CHALLENGE YOU TO A DUEL!!
STOP THIS, SUNSU.
SIR GANETTE.
WE SHARE A COMMON GOAL-- TO DEFEAT OPSQURIA AND TAKE BACK THE WORLD OF LIGHT.
PERHAPS IT IS FATE THAT WE MET HERE. MAY I SUGGEST THAT WE JOIN FORCES AND FIGHT HER TOGETHER?
...
TEAM UP WITH THE BLUE DRAGON AND THE CHAÎNE LORD?
HELL NO!!

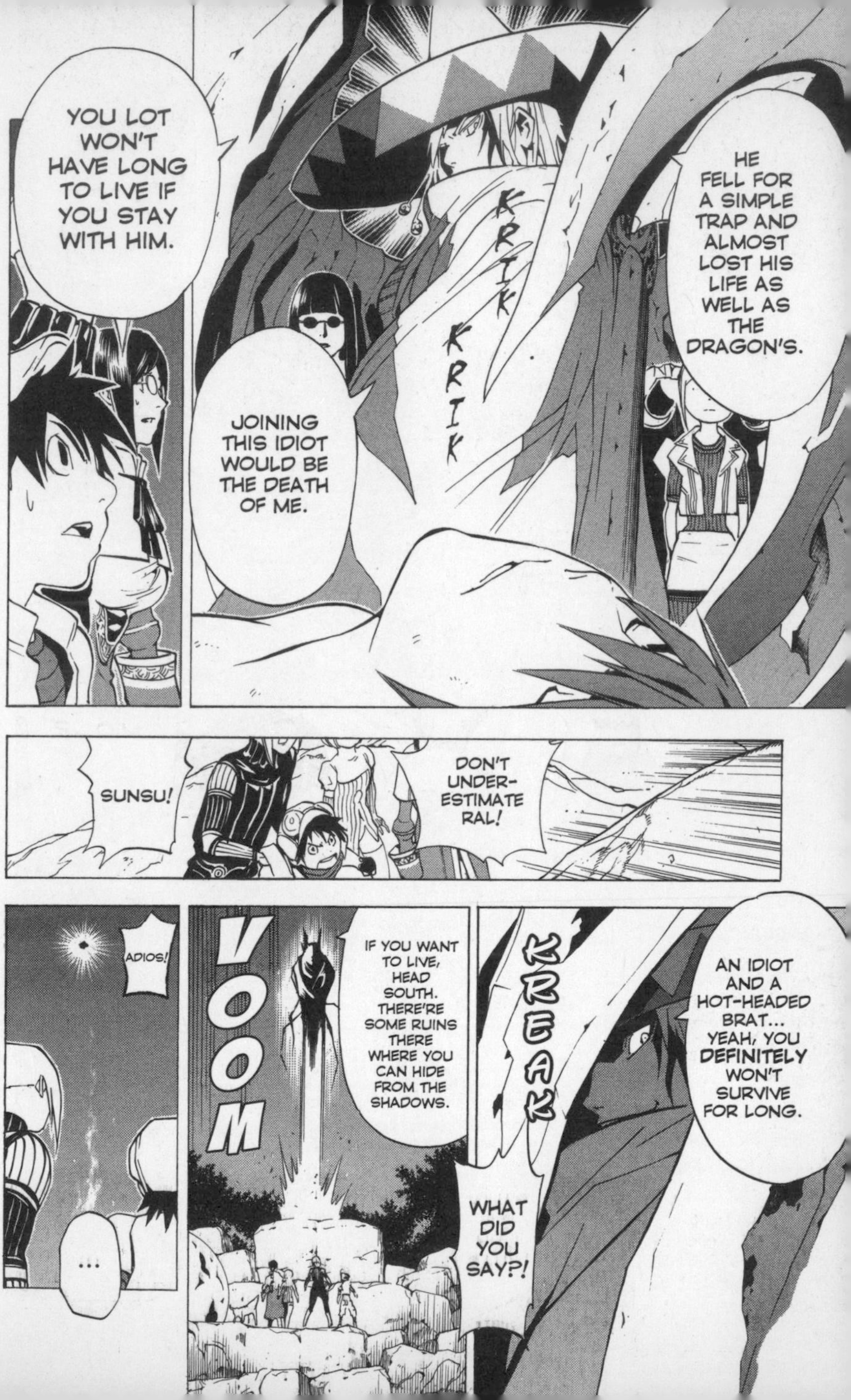
HE FELL FOR A SIMPLE TRAP AND ALMOST LOST HIS LIFE AS WELL AS THE DRAGON'S.
KRIK KRIK
JOINING THIS IDIOT WOULD BE THE DEATH OF ME.
YOU LOT WON'T HAVE LONG TO LIVE IF YOU STAY WITH HIM.
DON'T UNDER-ESTIMATE RAL!
SUNSU!
AN IDIOT AND A HOT-HEADED BRAT... YEAH, YOU **DEFINITELY** WON'T SURVIVE FOR LONG.
KREAK
WHAT DID YOU SAY?!
VOOM
IF YOU WANT TO LIVE, HEAD SOUTH. THERE'RE SOME RUINS THERE WHERE YOU CAN HIDE FROM THE SHADOWS.
ADIOS!
...

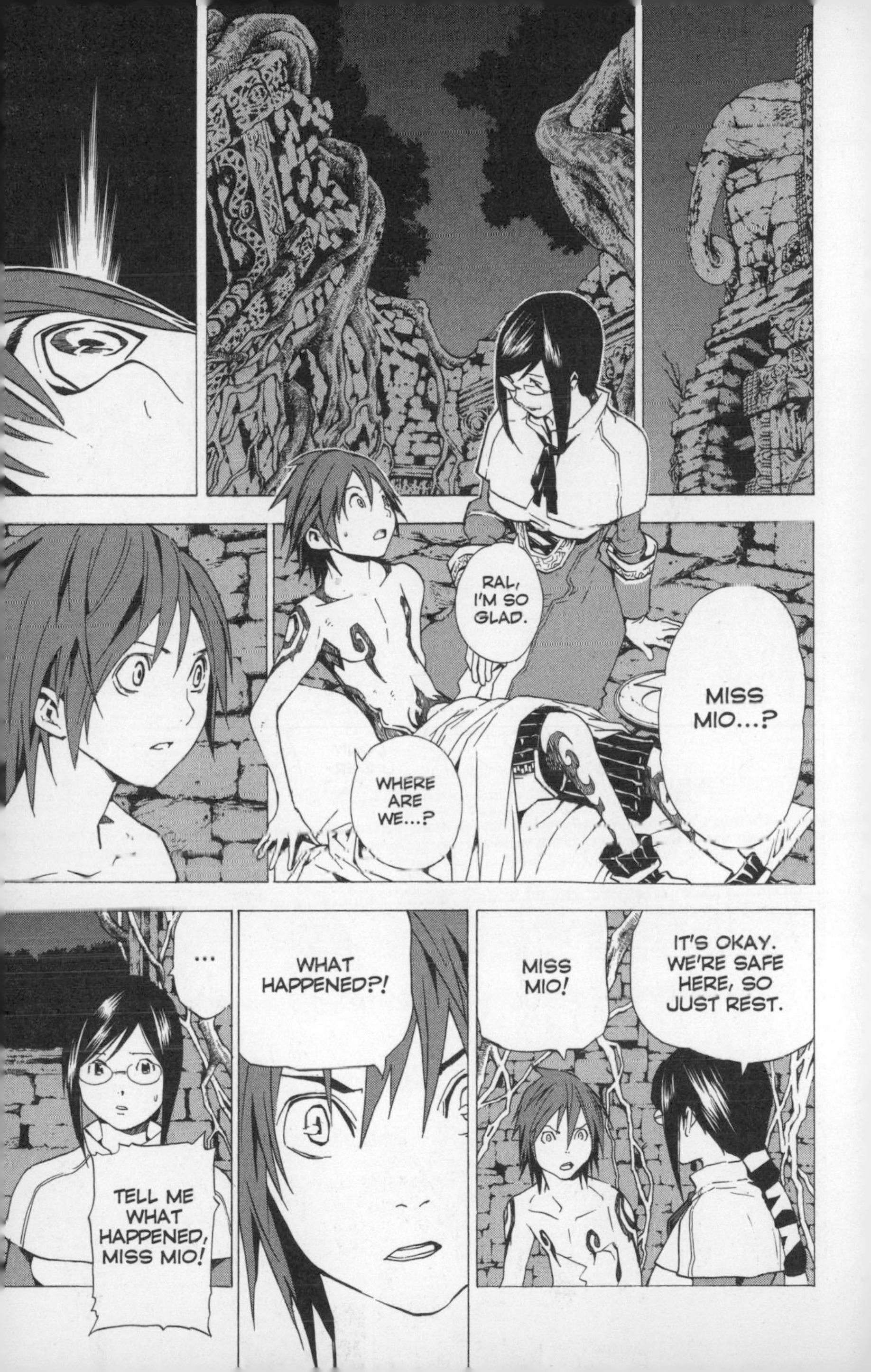
MISS MIO...?
RAL, I'M SO GLAD.
WHERE ARE WE...?
IT'S OKAY. WE'RE SAFE HERE, SO JUST REST.
MISS MIO!
WHAT HAPPENED?!
...
TELL ME WHAT HAPPENED, MISS MIO!

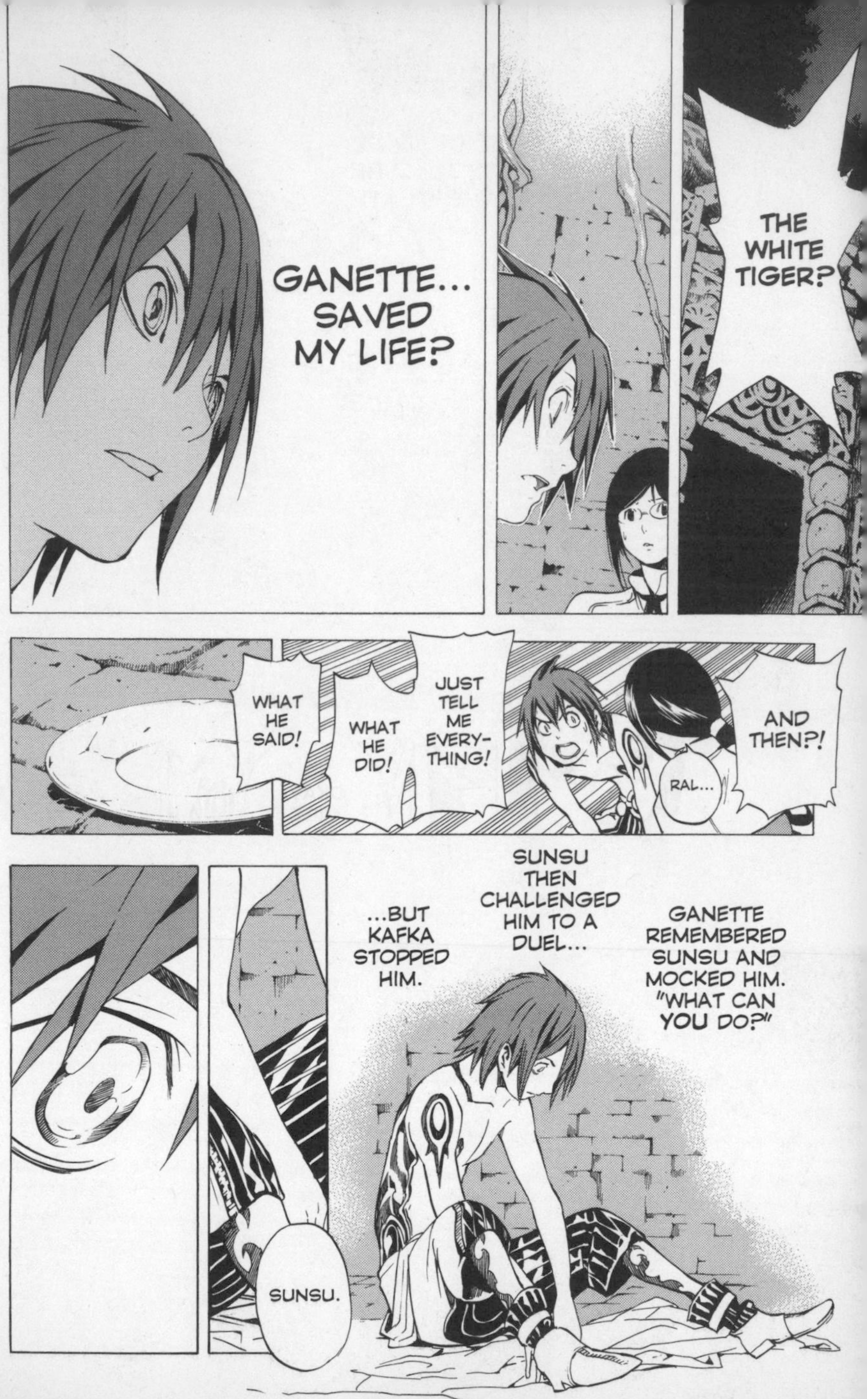
THE WHITE TIGER?
GANETTE... SAVED MY LIFE?
AND THEN?!
RAL...
JUST TELL ME EVERYTHING!
WHAT HE DID!
WHAT HE SAID!
GANETTE REMEMBERED SUNSU AND MOCKED HIM. "WHAT CAN YOU DO?"
SUNSU THEN CHALLENGED HIM TO A DUEL...
...BUT KAFKA STOPPED HIM.
SUNSU.

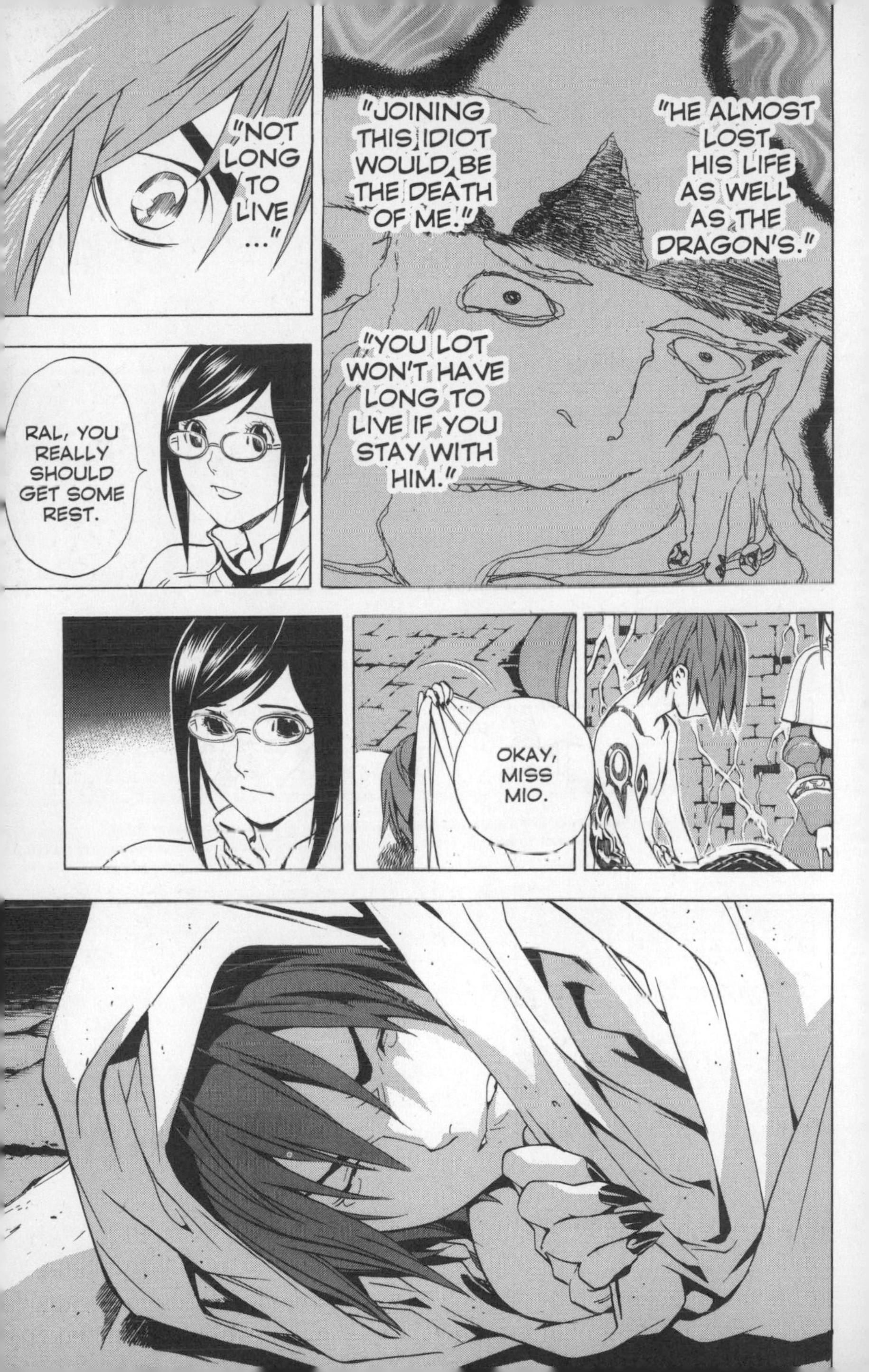
"HE ALMOST LOST HIS LIFE AS WELL AS THE DRAGON'S."
"JOINING THIS IDIOT WOULD BE THE DEATH OF ME."
"YOU LOT WON'T HAVE LONG TO LIVE IF YOU STAY WITH HIM."
"NOT LONG TO LIVE..."
RAL, YOU REALLY SHOULD GET SOME REST.
OKAY, MISS MIO.

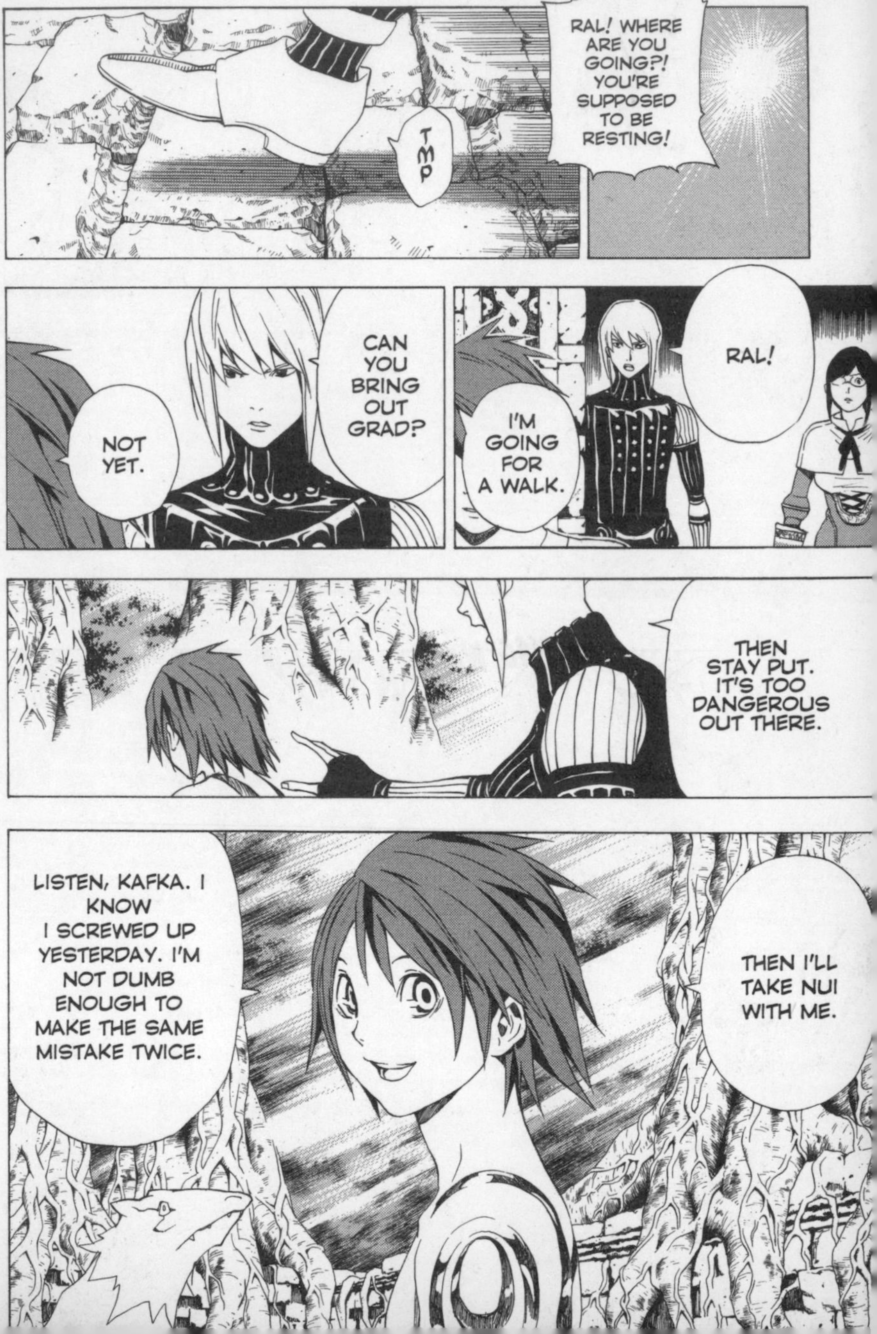
RAL! WHERE ARE YOU GOING?! YOU'RE SUPPOSED TO BE RESTING!
TMP
RAL!
I'M GOING FOR A WALK.
CAN YOU BRING OUT GRAD?
NOT YET.
THEN STAY PUT. IT'S TOO DANGEROUS OUT THERE.
THEN I'LL TAKE NUI WITH ME.
LISTEN, KAFKA. I KNOW I SCREWED UP YESTERDAY. I'M NOT DUMB ENOUGH TO MAKE THE SAME MISTAKE TWICE.

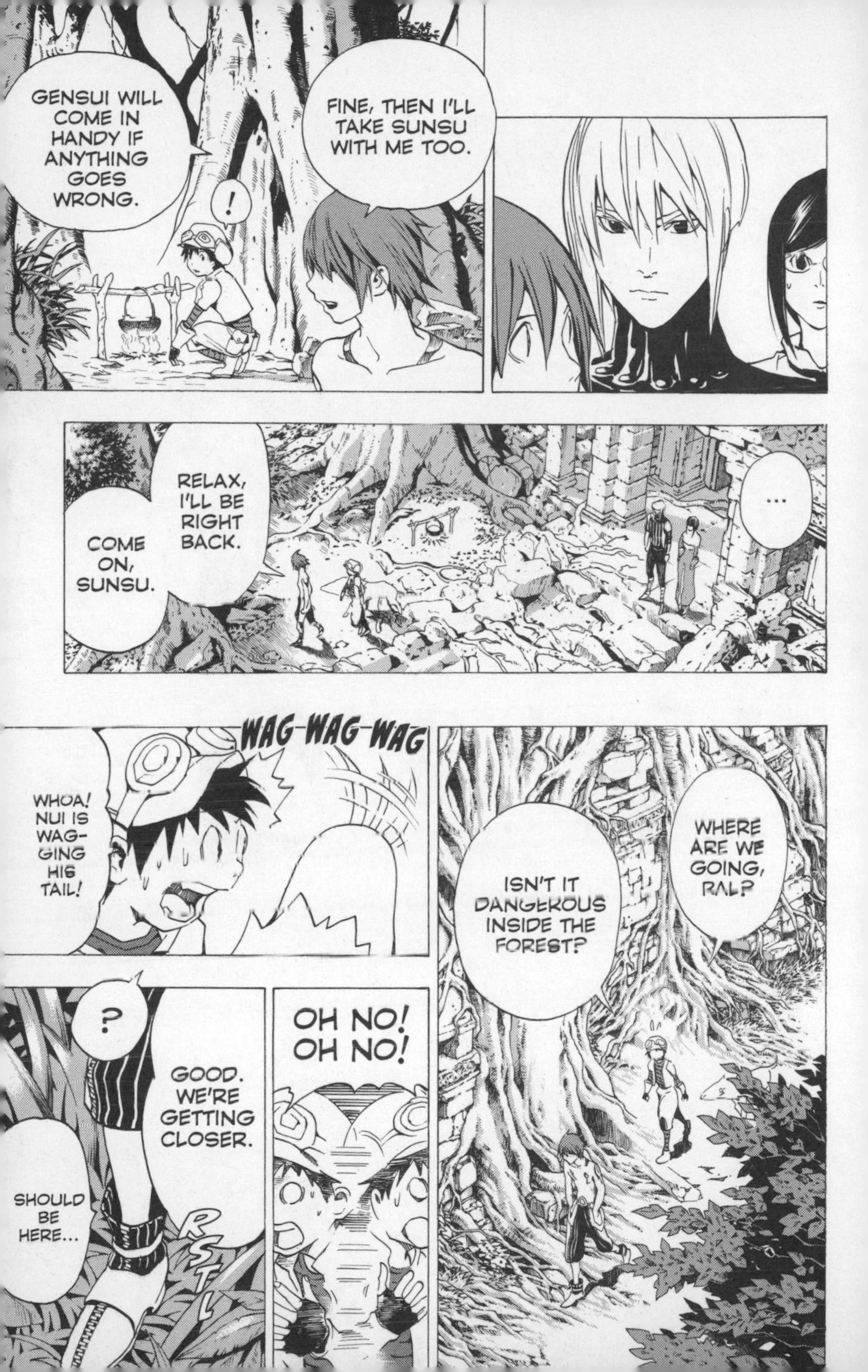
FINE, THEN I'LL TAKE SUNSU WITH ME TOO.
GENSUI WILL COME IN HANDY IF ANYTHING GOES WRONG.
!
...
RELAX, I'LL BE RIGHT BACK.
COME ON, SUNSU.
WHERE ARE WE GOING, RAL?
ISN'T IT DANGEROUS INSIDE THE FOREST?
WAG-WAG-WAG
WHOA! NUI IS WAG-GING HIS TAIL!
OH NO! OH NO!
?
GOOD. WE'RE GETTING CLOSER.
SHOULD BE HERE...
RSTL

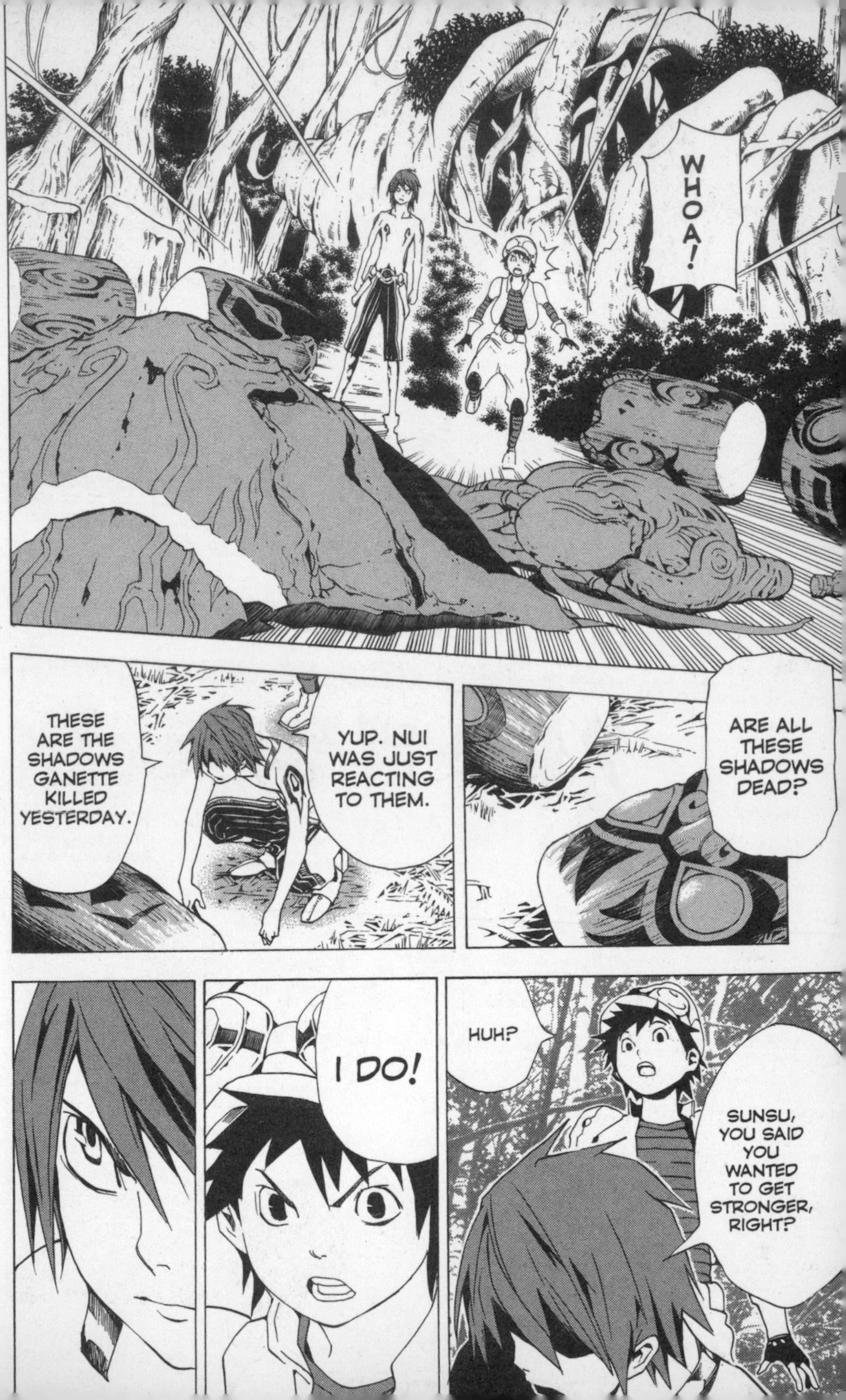
WHOA!
ARE ALL THESE SHADOWS DEAD?
YUP. NUI WAS JUST REACTING TO THEM.
THESE ARE THE SHADOWS GANETTE KILLED YESTERDAY.
SUNSU, YOU SAID YOU WANTED TO GET STRONGER, RIGHT?
HUH?
I DO!

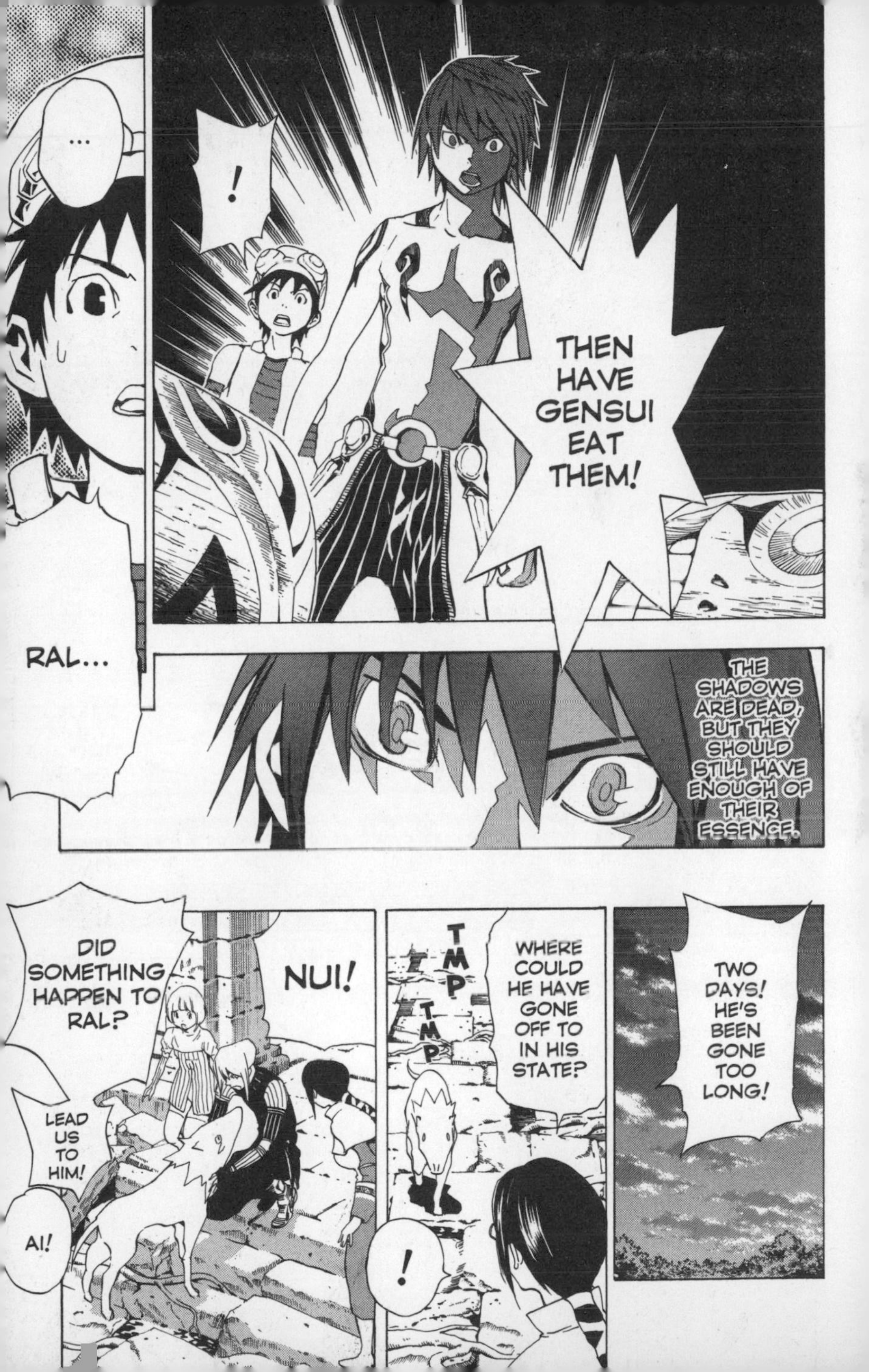
!
THEN HAVE GENSUI EAT THEM!
THE SHADOWS ARE DEAD, BUT THEY SHOULD STILL HAVE ENOUGH OF THEIR ESSENCE.
...
RAL...
TWO DAYS! HE'S BEEN GONE TOO LONG!
WHERE COULD HE HAVE GONE OFF TO IN HIS STATE?
TMP TMP
!
NUI!
DID SOMETHING HAPPEN TO RAL?
LEAD US TO HIM!
AI!

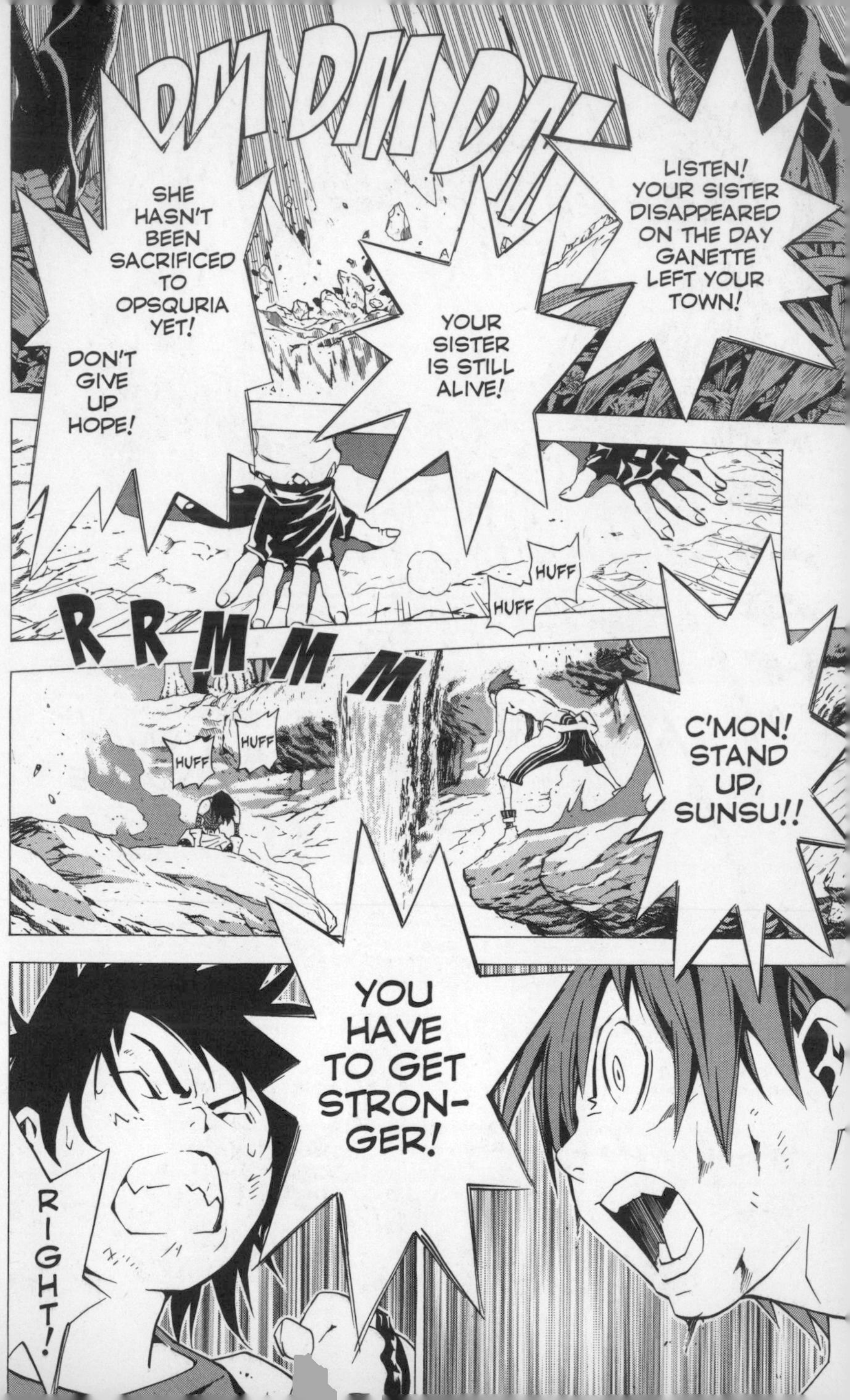
DM DM DM
LISTEN! YOUR SISTER DISAPPEARED ON THE DAY GANETTE LEFT YOUR TOWN!
YOUR SISTER IS STILL ALIVE!
SHE HASN'T BEEN SACRIFICED TO OPSQURIA YET!
DON'T GIVE UP HOPE!
HUFF
HUFF
RRMMMM
C'MON! STAND UP, SUNSU!!
HUFF
HUFF
YOU HAVE TO GET STRON-GER!
RIGHT!

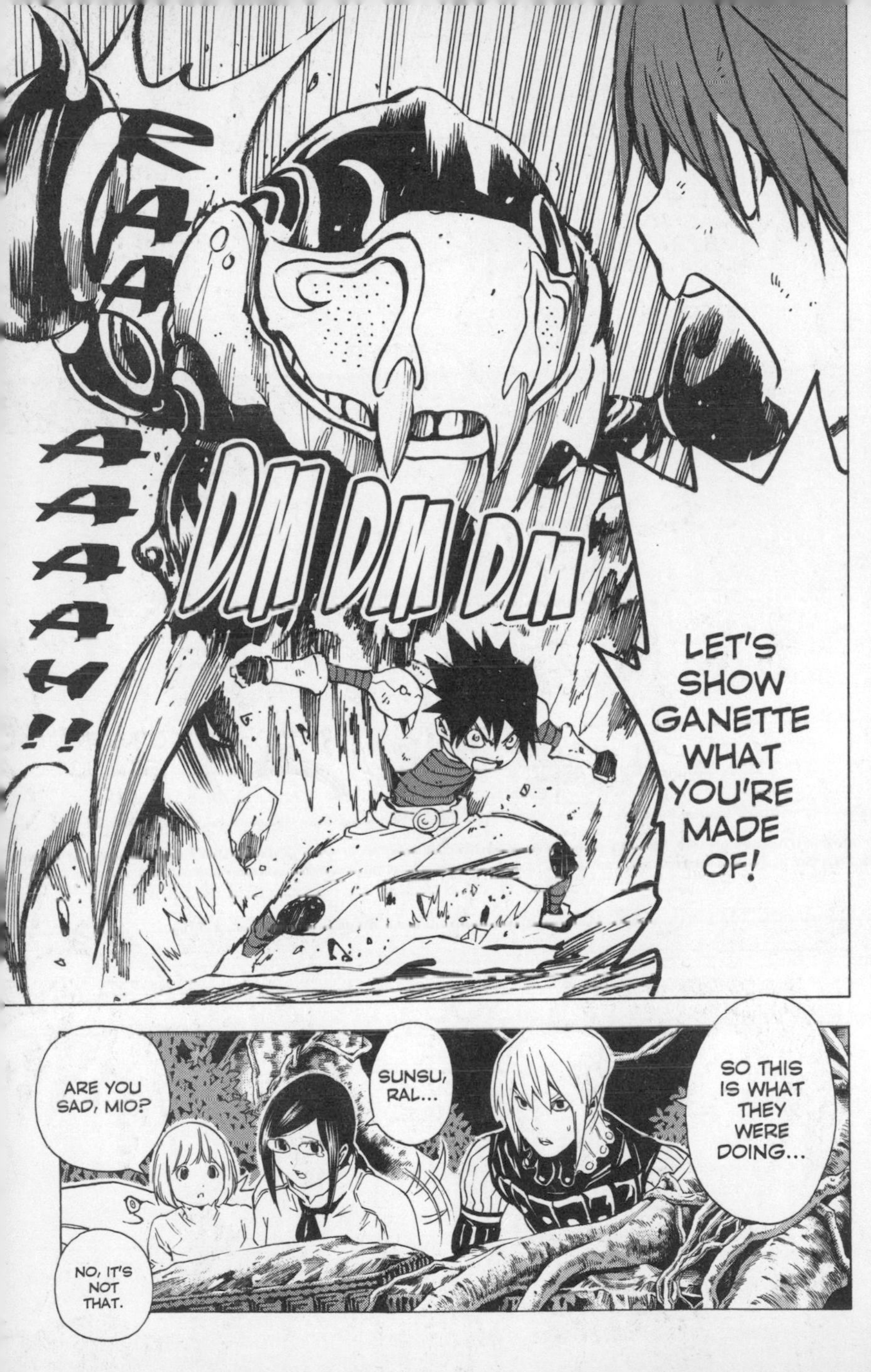
LET'S SHOW GANETTE WHAT YOU'RE MADE OF!
DM DM DM
RAAAAAAAH!!
SO THIS IS WHAT THEY WERE DOING...
SUNSU, RAL...
ARE YOU SAD, MIO?
NO, IT'S NOT THAT.

RalΩGradı

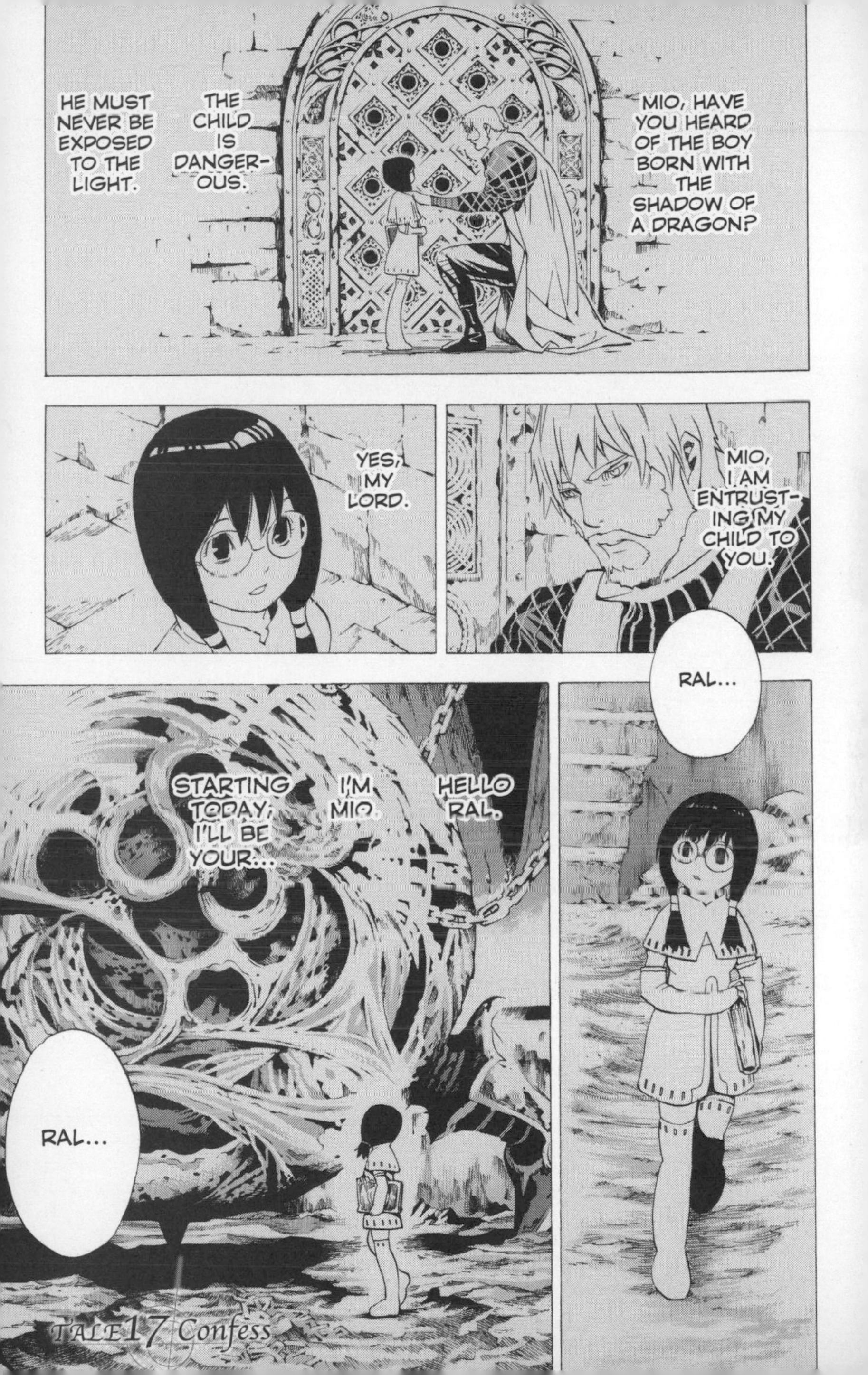
MIO, HAVE YOU HEARD OF THE BOY BORN WITH THE SHADOW OF A DRAGON?
THE CHILD IS DANGEROUS.
HE MUST NEVER BE EXPOSED TO THE LIGHT.
MIO, I AM ENTRUSTING MY CHILD TO YOU.
YES, MY LORD.
RAL...
HELLO RAL.
I'M MIO.
STARTING TODAY, I'LL BE YOUR...
RAL...
TALE 17 Confess

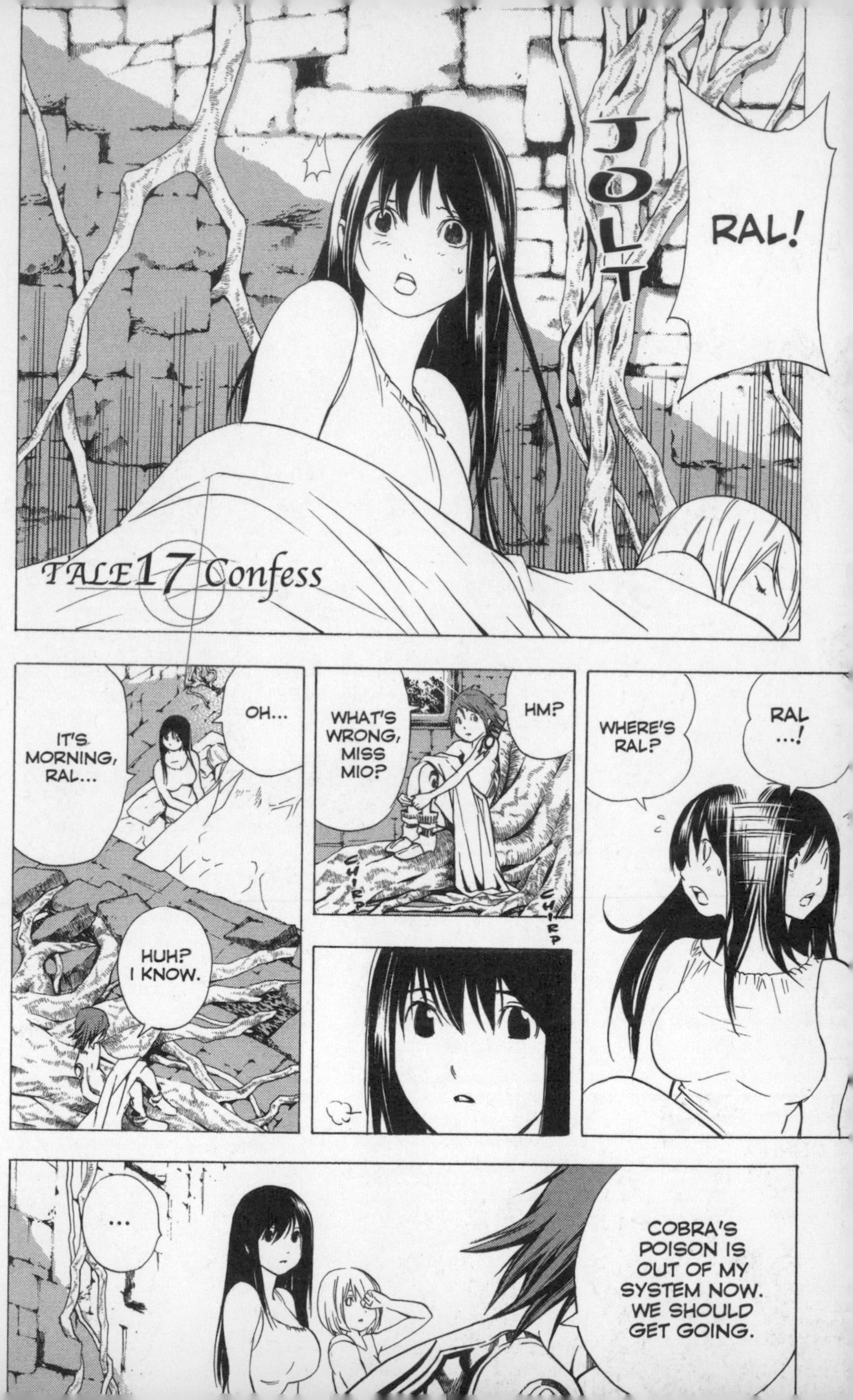
RAL!
JOLT
TALE 17 Confess
RAL ...!
WHERE'S RAL?
HM?
WHAT'S WRONG, MISS MIO?
CHIRP
CHIRP
OH...
IT'S MORNING, RAL...
HUH? I KNOW.
COBRA'S POISON IS OUT OF MY SYSTEM NOW. WE SHOULD GET GOING.
...

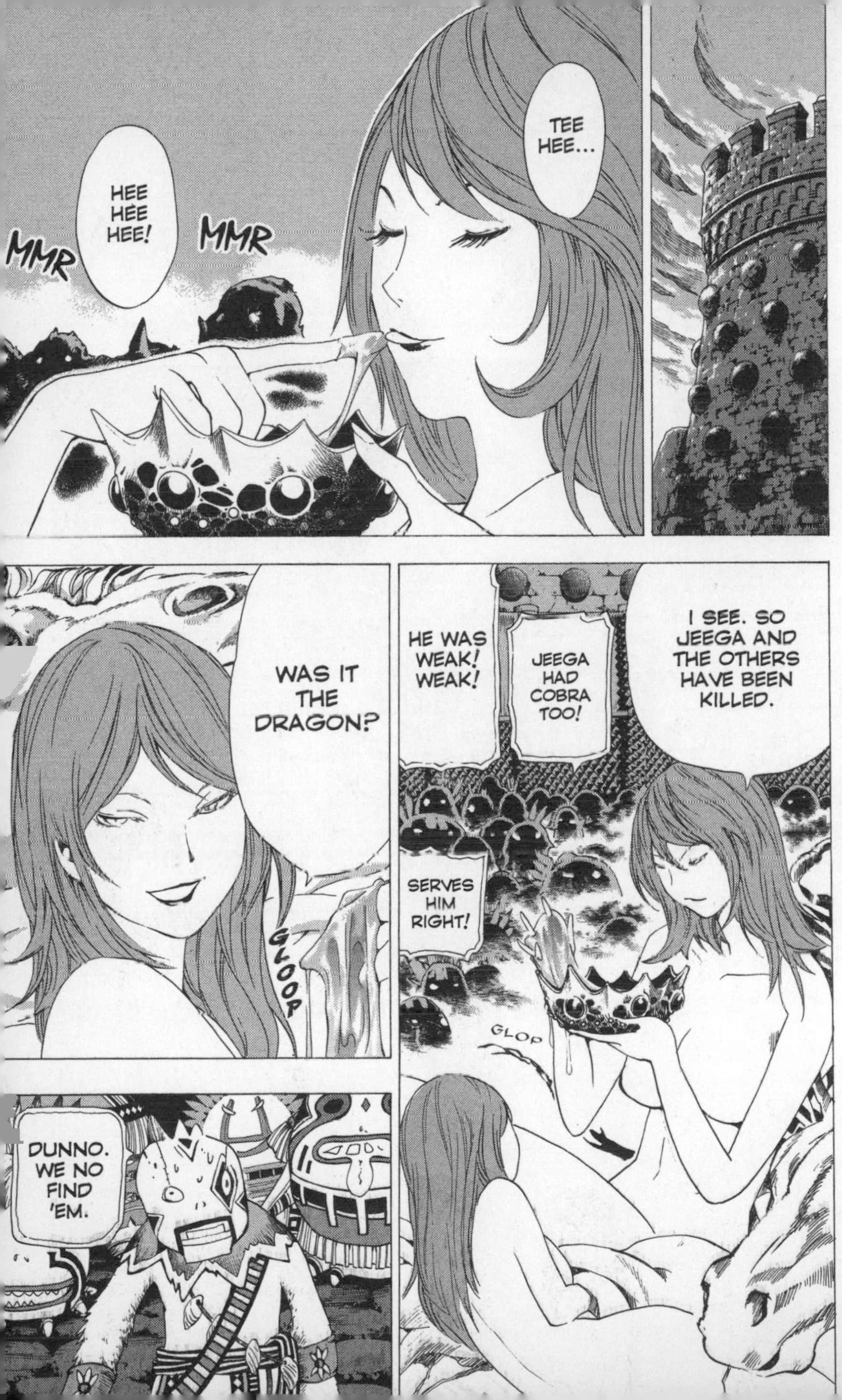
TEE HEE...
HEE HEE HEE!
MMR
MMR
I SEE. SO JEEGA AND THE OTHERS HAVE BEEN KILLED.
JEEGA HAD COBRA TOO!
HE WAS WEAK! WEAK!
SERVES HIM RIGHT!
GLOP
WAS IT THE DRAGON?
GLOOOP
DUNNO. WE NO FIND 'EM.

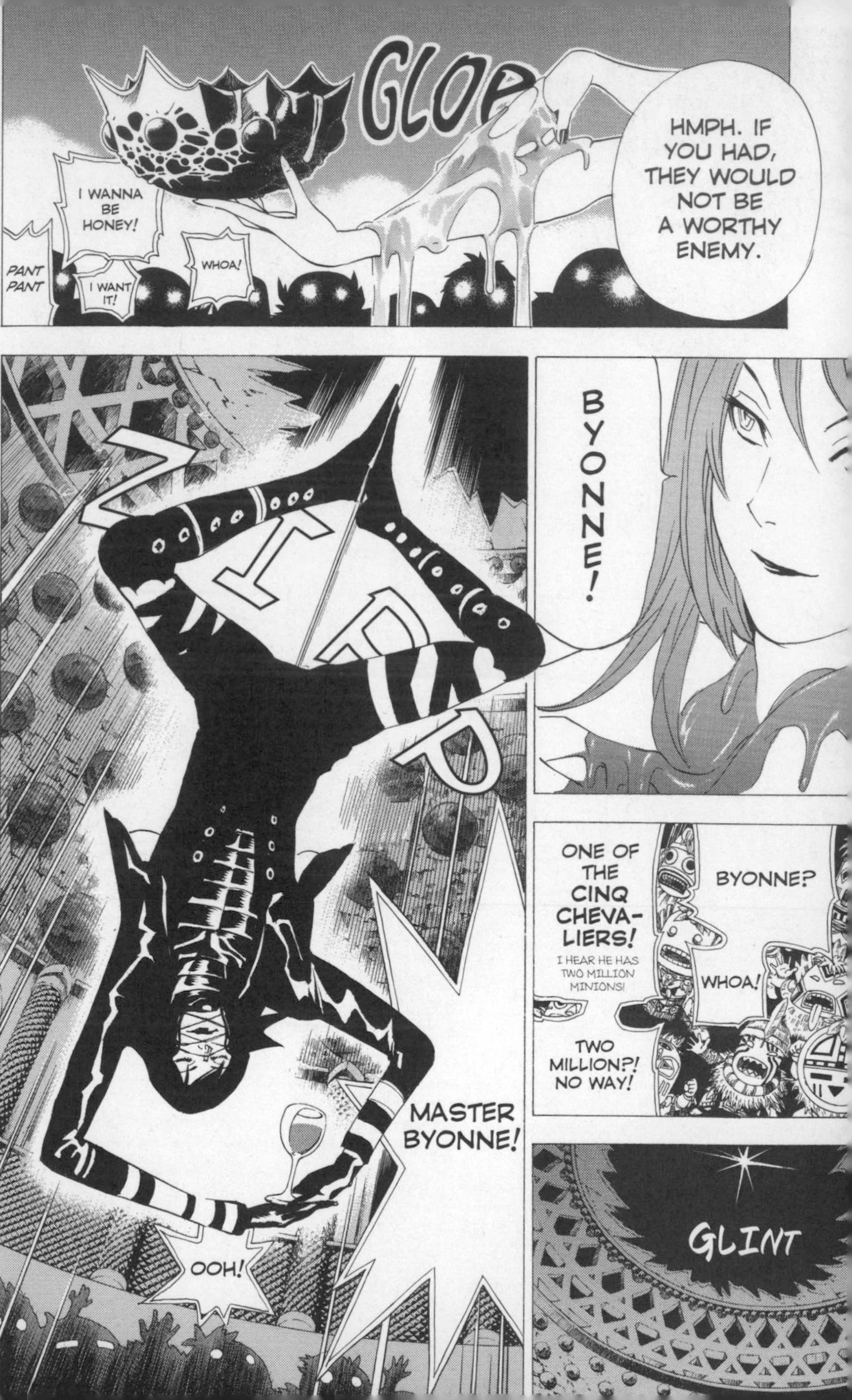
HMPH. IF YOU HAD, THEY WOULD NOT BE A WORTHY ENEMY.
GLOP
I WANNA BE HONEY!
WHOA!
I WANT IT!
PANT PANT
BYONNE!
BYONNE?
ONE OF THE CINQ CHEVALIERS!
I HEAR HE HAS TWO MILLION MINIONS!
WHOA!
TWO MILLION?! NO WAY!
GLINT
ZIP
MASTER BYONNE!
OOH!

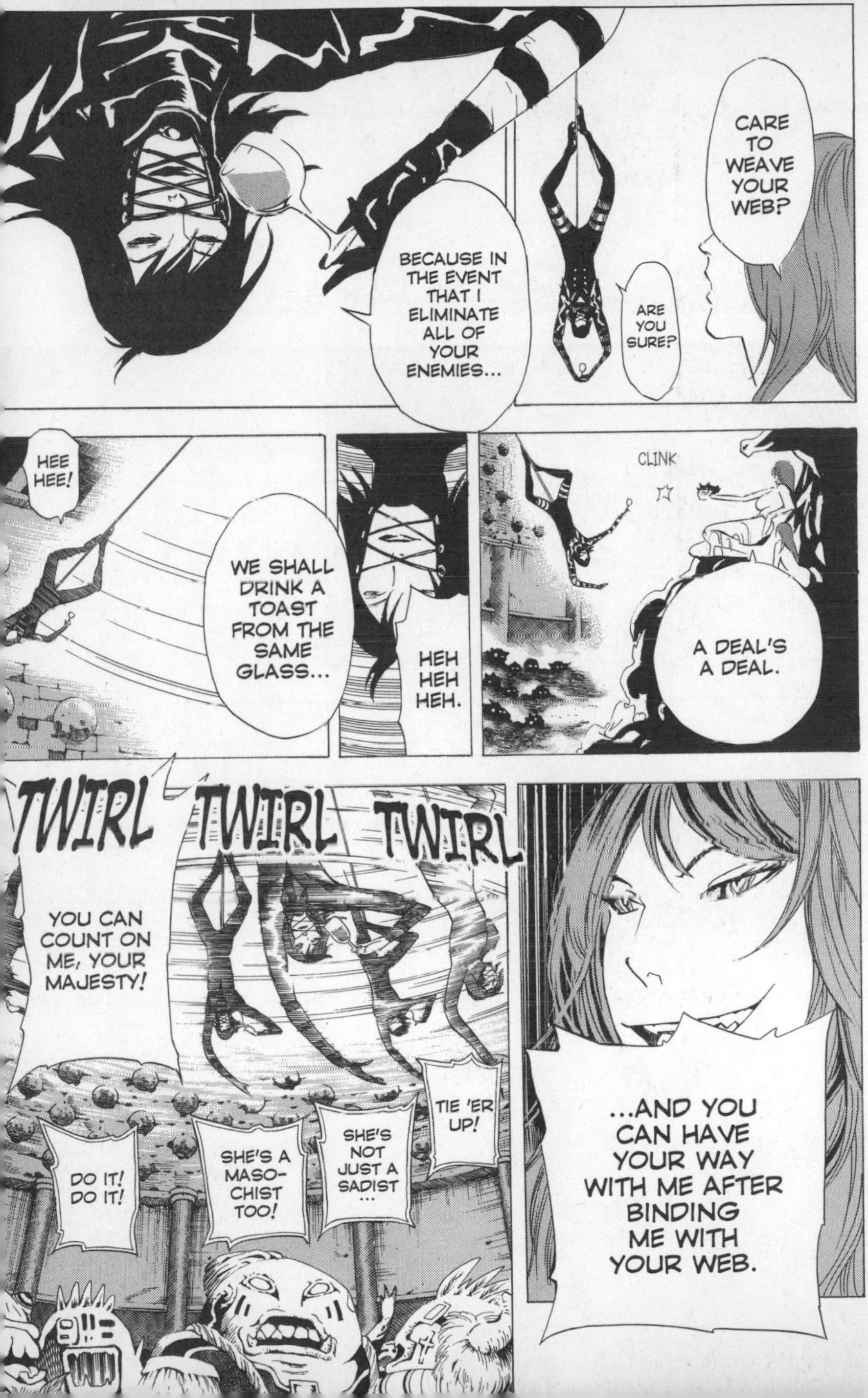
CARE TO WEAVE YOUR WEB?
ARE YOU SURE?
BECAUSE IN THE EVENT THAT I ELIMINATE ALL OF YOUR ENEMIES...
CLINK
A DEAL'S A DEAL.
HEH HEH HEH.
HEE HEE!
WE SHALL DRINK A TOAST FROM THE SAME GLASS...
...AND YOU CAN HAVE YOUR WAY WITH ME AFTER BINDING ME WITH YOUR WEB.
TWIRL TWIRL TWIRL
YOU CAN COUNT ON ME, YOUR MAJESTY!
TIE 'ER UP!
SHE'S NOT JUST A SADIST...
SHE'S A MASOCHIST TOO!
DO IT! DO IT!

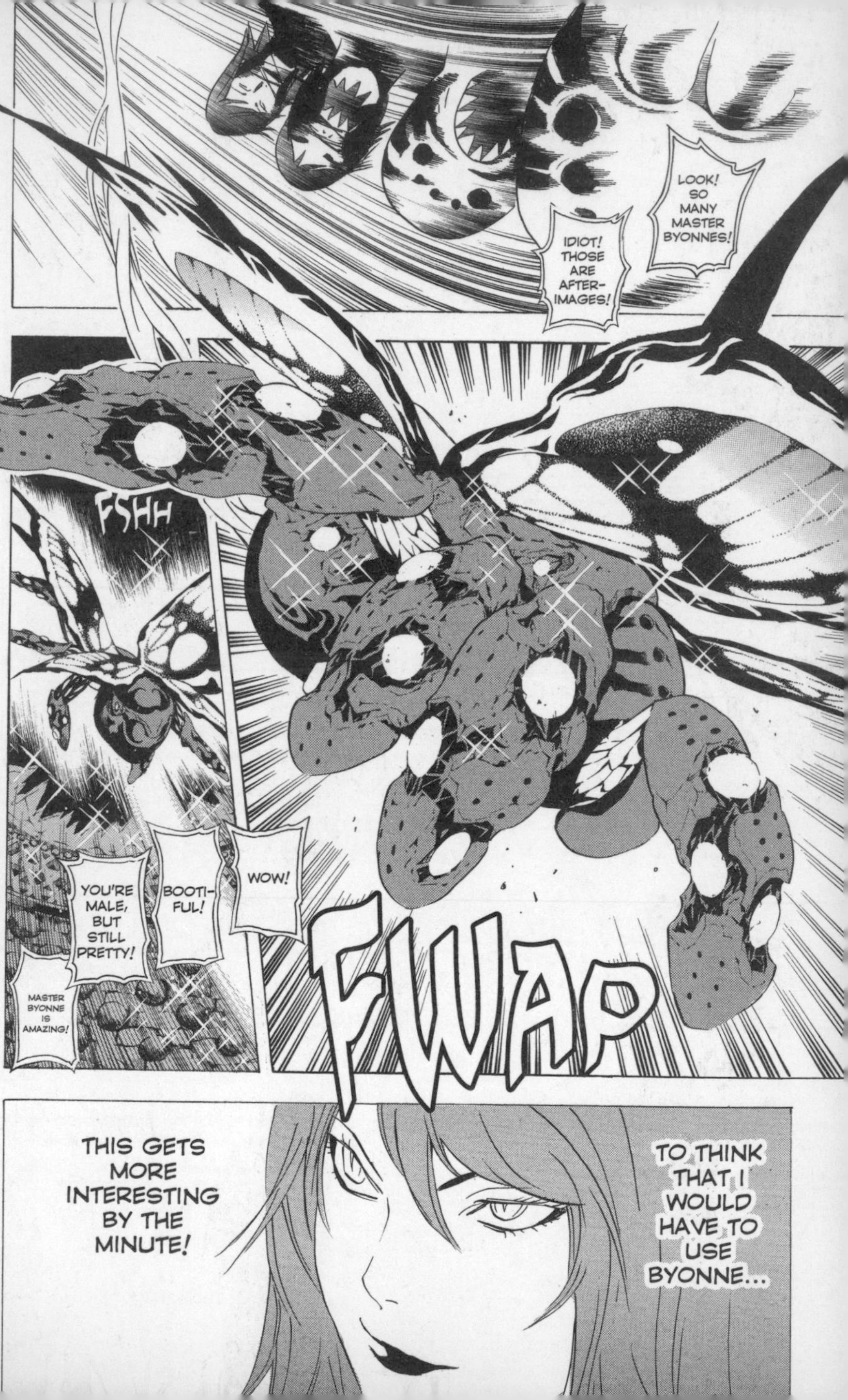
LOOK! SO MANY MASTER BYONNES!
IDIOT! THOSE ARE AFTER-IMAGES!
FWAP
FSHH
WOW!
BOOTI-FUL!
YOU'RE MALE, BUT STILL PRETTY!
MASTER BYONNE IS AMAZING!
TO THINK THAT I WOULD HAVE TO USE BYONNE...
THIS GETS MORE INTERESTING BY THE MINUTE!

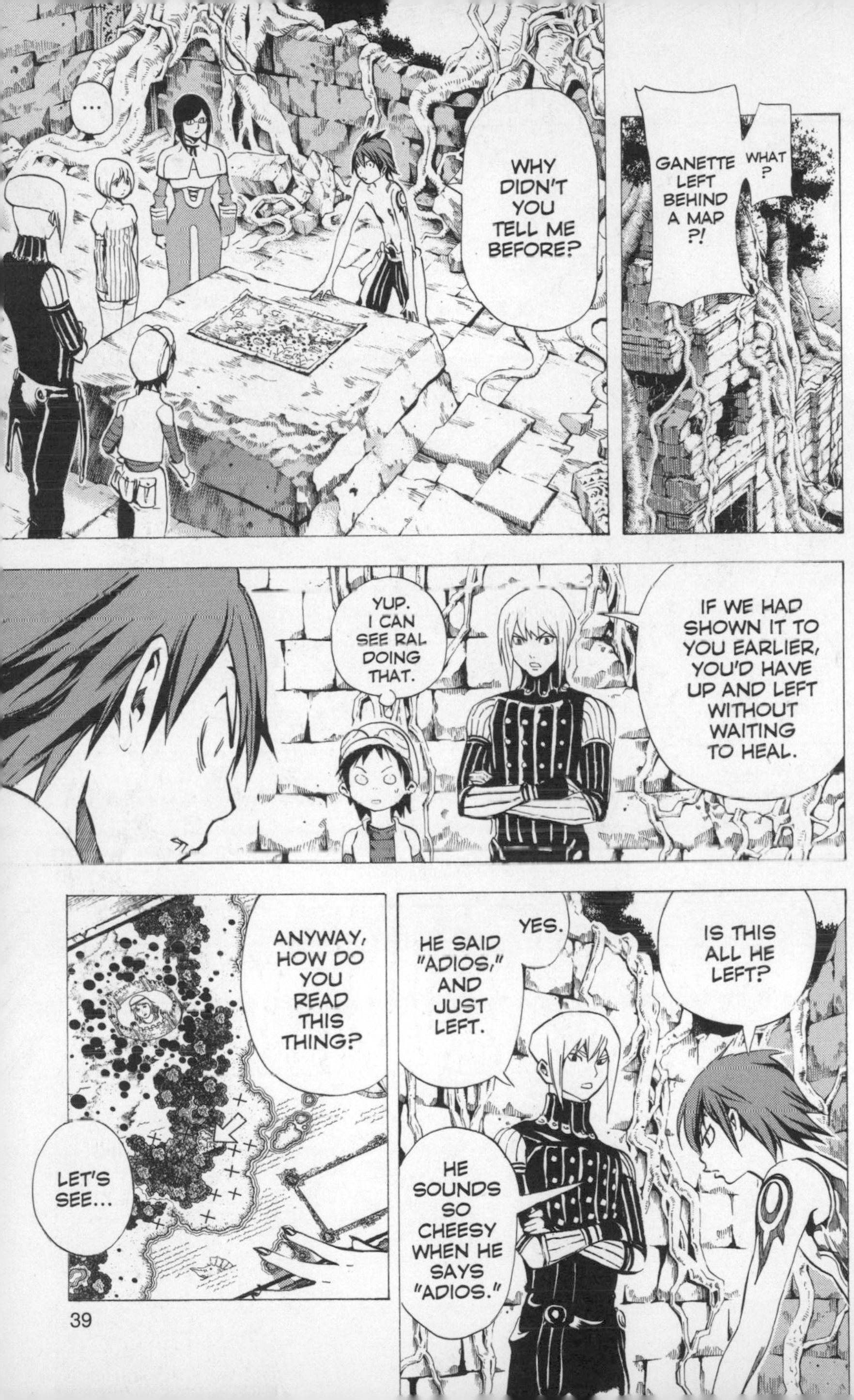
WHAT?
GANETTE LEFT BEHIND A MAP?!
WHY DIDN'T YOU TELL ME BEFORE?
...
IF WE HAD SHOWN IT TO YOU EARLIER, YOU'D HAVE UP AND LEFT WITHOUT WAITING TO HEAL.
YUP. I CAN SEE RAL DOING THAT.
IS THIS ALL HE LEFT?
YES.
HE SAID "ADIOS," AND JUST LEFT.
HE SOUNDS SO CHEESY WHEN HE SAYS "ADIOS."
ANYWAY, HOW DO YOU READ THIS THING?
LET'S SEE...

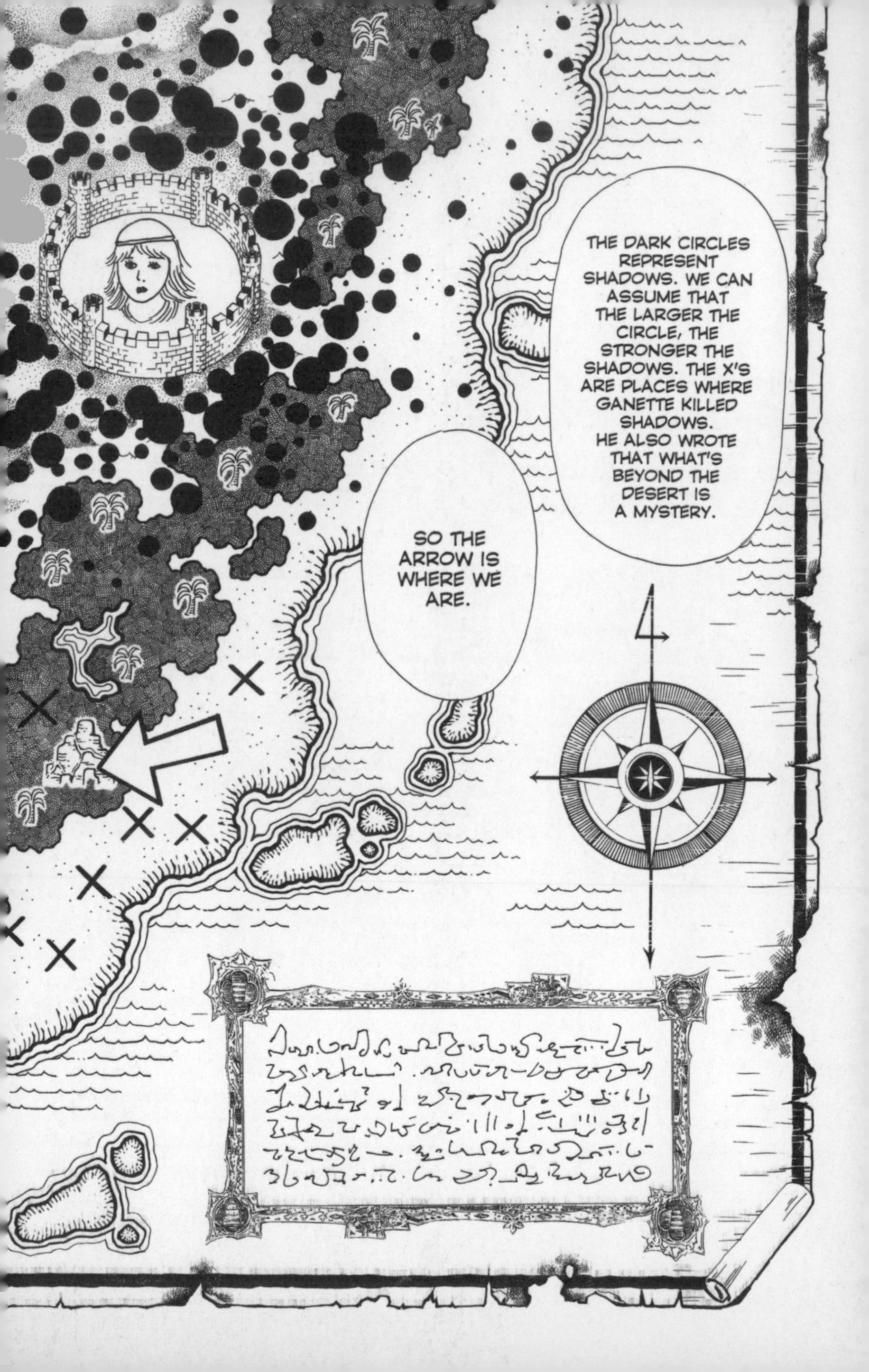
THE DARK CIRCLES REPRESENT SHADOWS. WE CAN ASSUME THAT THE LARGER THE CIRCLE, THE STRONGER THE SHADOWS. THE X'S ARE PLACES WHERE GANETTE KILLED SHADOWS. HE ALSO WROTE THAT WHAT'S BEYOND THE DESERT IS A MYSTERY.
SO THE ARROW IS WHERE WE ARE.

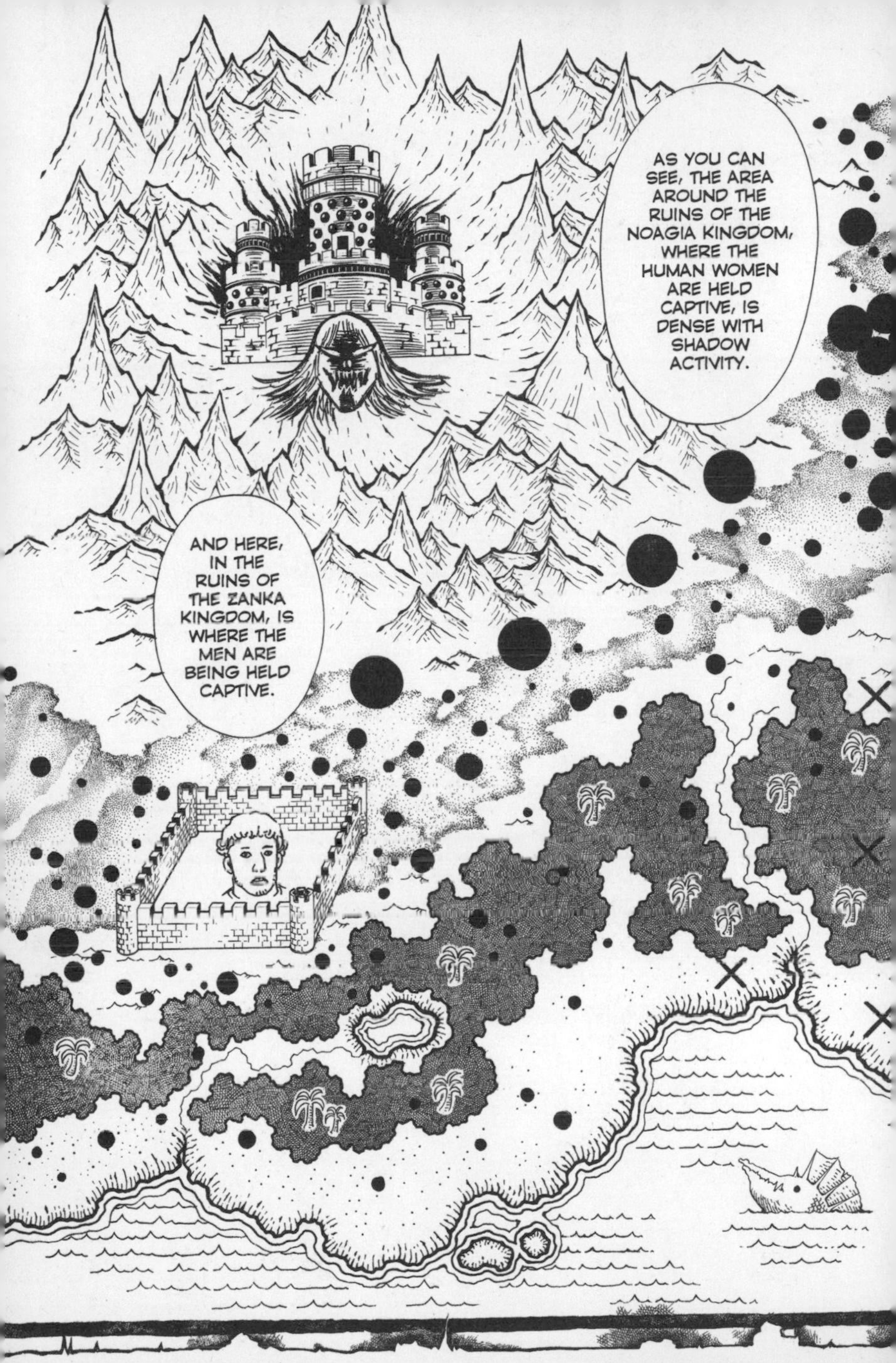
AS YOU CAN SEE, THE AREA AROUND THE RUINS OF THE NOAGIA KINGDOM, WHERE THE HUMAN WOMEN ARE HELD CAPTIVE, IS DENSE WITH SHADOW ACTIVITY.
AND HERE, IN THE RUINS OF THE ZANKA KINGDOM, IS WHERE THE MEN ARE BEING HELD CAPTIVE.

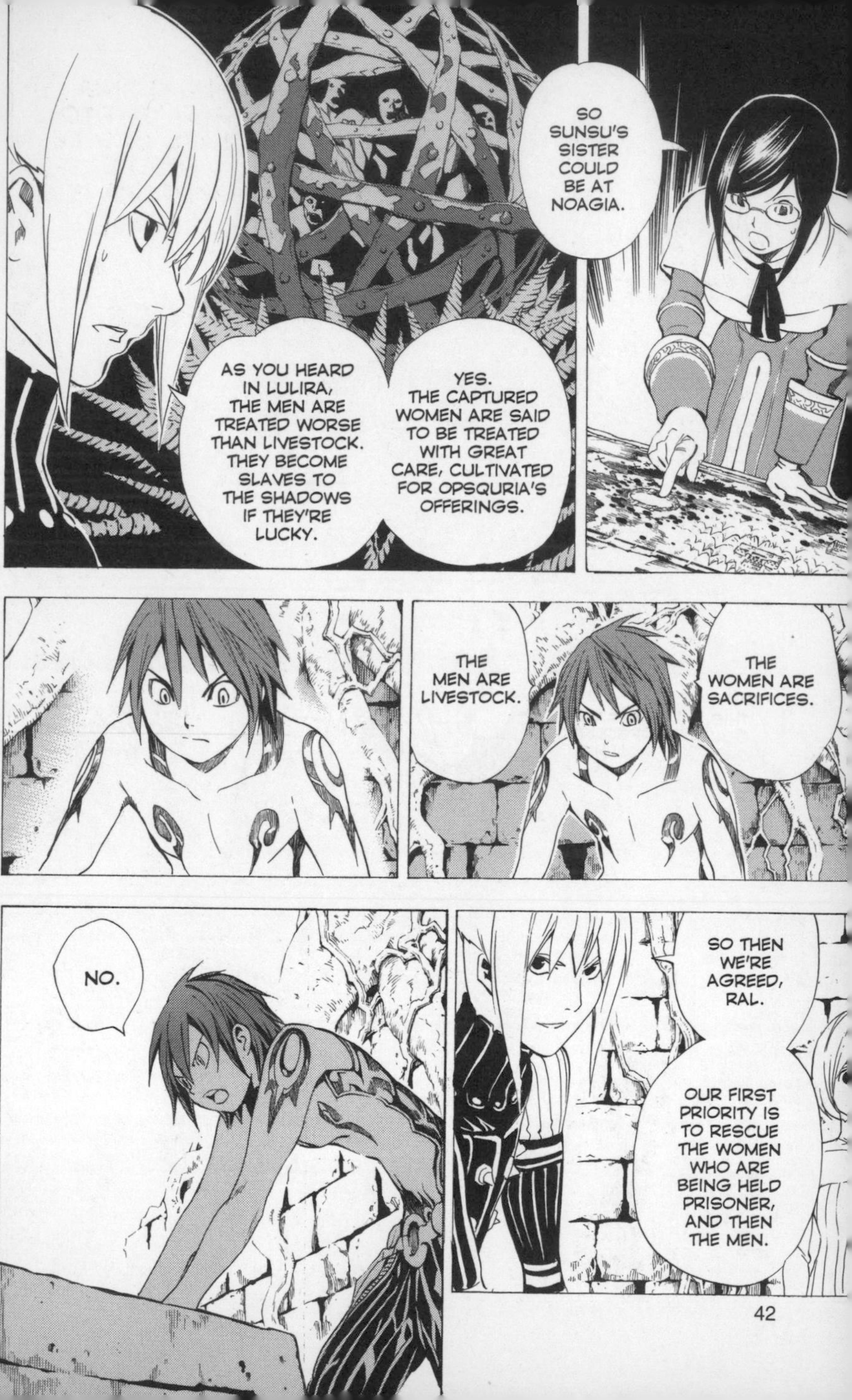

SO SUNSU'S SISTER COULD BE AT NOAGIA.
YES. THE CAPTURED WOMEN ARE SAID TO BE TREATED WITH GREAT CARE, CULTIVATED FOR OPSQURIA'S OFFERINGS.
AS YOU HEARD IN LULIRA, THE MEN ARE TREATED WORSE THAN LIVESTOCK. THEY BECOME SLAVES TO THE SHADOWS IF THEY'RE LUCKY.
THE WOMEN ARE SACRIFICES.
THE MEN ARE LIVESTOCK.
SO THEN WE'RE AGREED, RAL.
OUR FIRST PRIORITY IS TO RESCUE THE WOMEN WHO ARE BEING HELD PRISONER, AND THEN THE MEN.
NO.

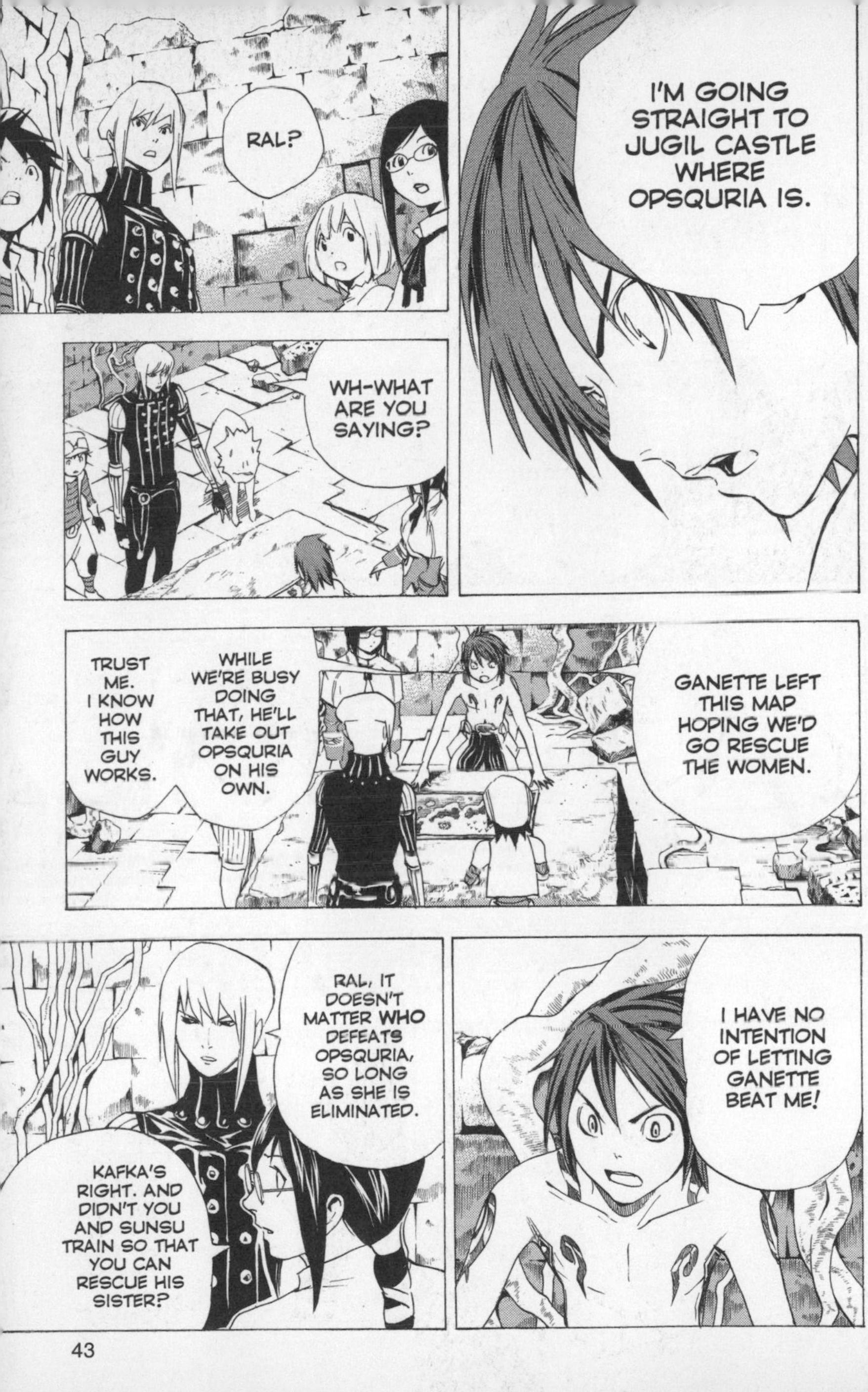
I'M GOING STRAIGHT TO JUGIL CASTLE WHERE OPSQURIA IS.
RAL?
WH-WHAT ARE YOU SAYING?
GANETTE LEFT THIS MAP HOPING WE'D GO RESCUE THE WOMEN.
WHILE WE'RE BUSY DOING THAT, HE'LL TAKE OUT OPSQURIA ON HIS OWN.
TRUST ME. I KNOW HOW THIS GUY WORKS.
I HAVE NO INTENTION OF LETTING GANETTE BEAT ME!
RAL, IT DOESN'T MATTER WHO DEFEATS OPSQURIA, SO LONG AS SHE IS ELIMINATED.
KAFKA'S RIGHT. AND DIDN'T YOU AND SUNSU TRAIN SO THAT YOU CAN RESCUE HIS SISTER?

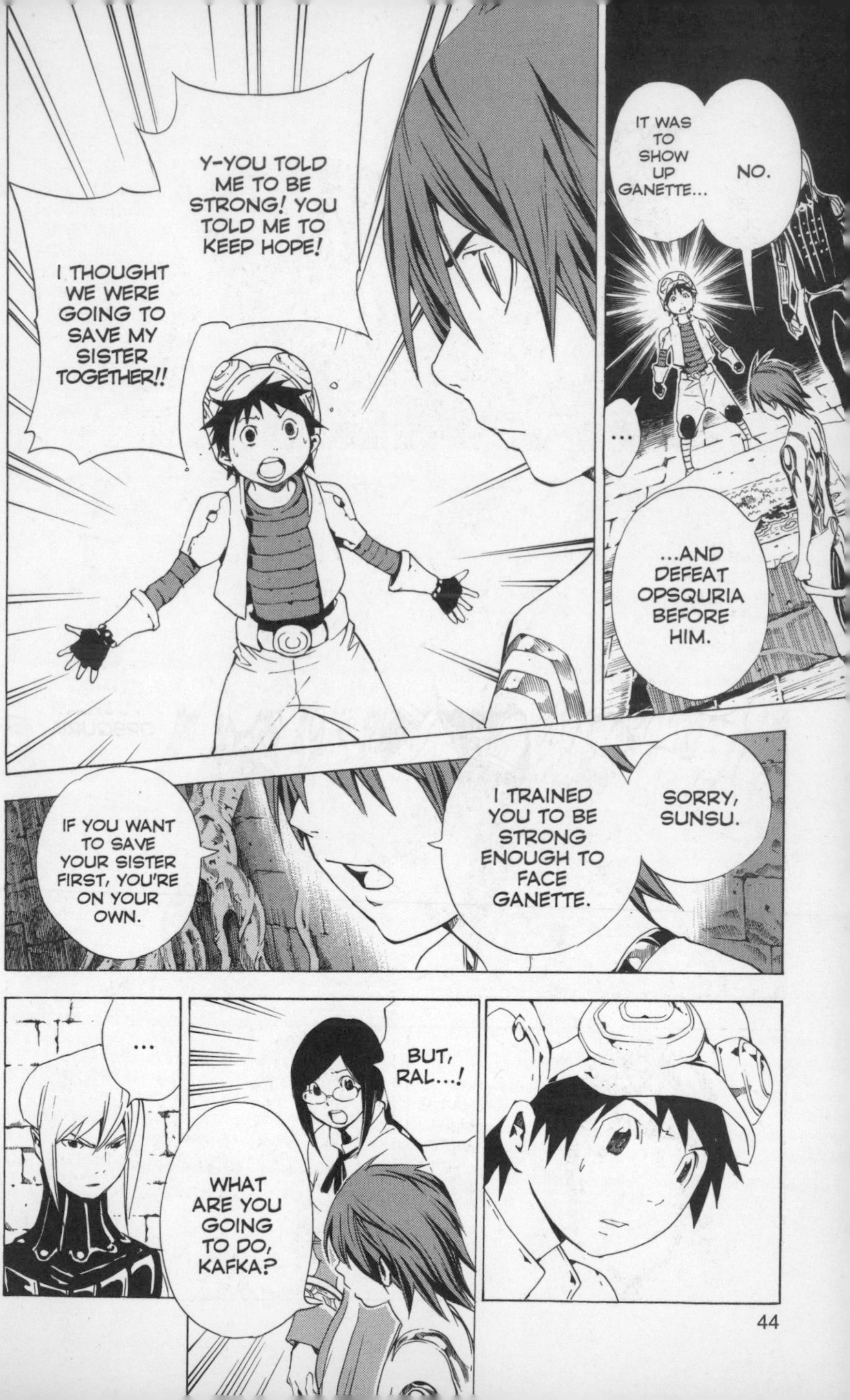
NO.
IT WAS TO SHOW UP GANETTE...
...
...AND DEFEAT OPSQURIA BEFORE HIM.
Y-YOU TOLD ME TO BE STRONG! YOU TOLD ME TO KEEP HOPE!
I THOUGHT WE WERE GOING TO SAVE MY SISTER TOGETHER!!
SORRY, SUNSU.
I TRAINED YOU TO BE STRONG ENOUGH TO FACE GANETTE.
IF YOU WANT TO SAVE YOUR SISTER FIRST, YOU'RE ON YOUR OWN.
BUT, RAL...!
WHAT ARE YOU GOING TO DO, KAFKA?
...

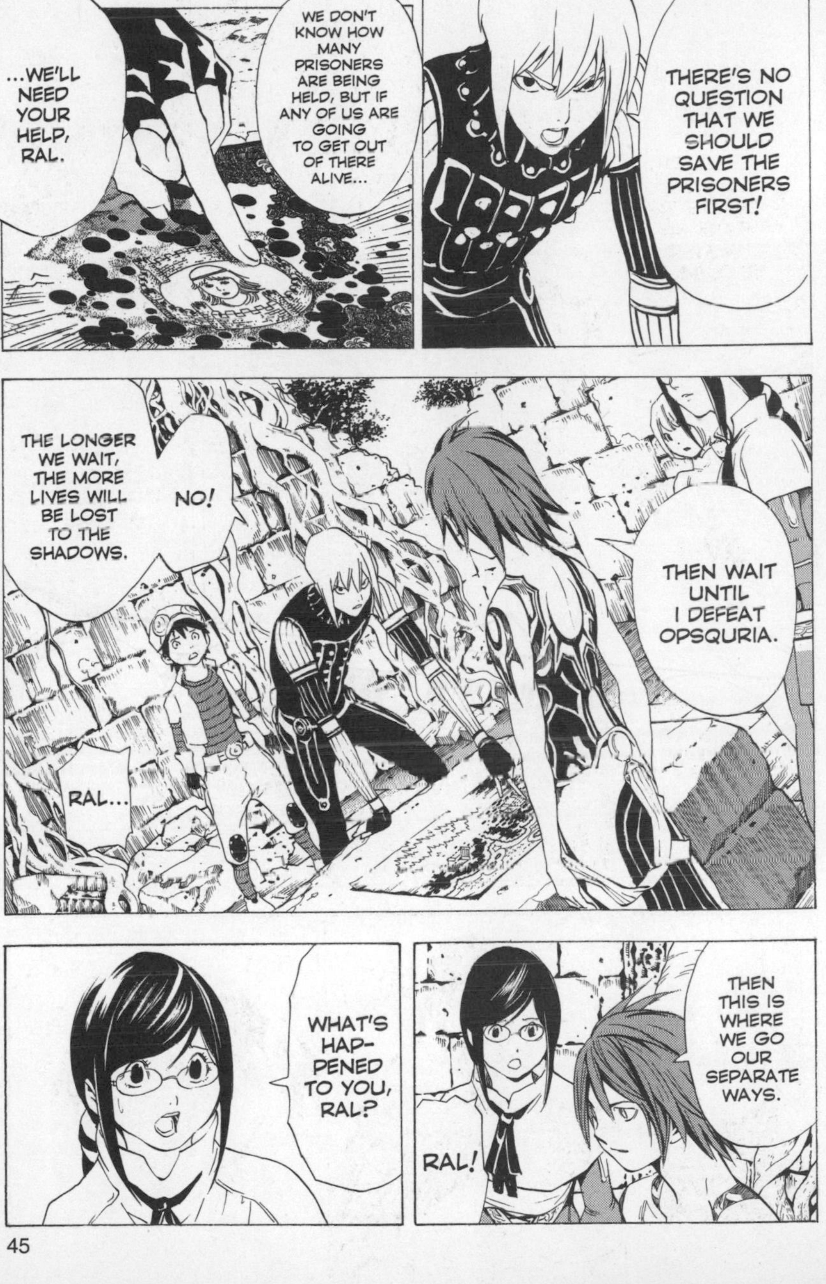
THERE'S NO QUESTION THAT WE SHOULD SAVE THE PRISONERS FIRST!
WE DON'T KNOW HOW MANY PRISONERS ARE BEING HELD, BUT IF ANY OF US ARE GOING TO GET OUT OF THERE ALIVE...
...WE'LL NEED YOUR HELP, RAL.
THEN WAIT UNTIL I DEFEAT OPSQURIA.
NO!
THE LONGER WE WAIT, THE MORE LIVES WILL BE LOST TO THE SHADOWS.
RAL...
THEN THIS IS WHERE WE GO OUR SEPARATE WAYS.
RAL!
WHAT'S HAP-PENED TO YOU, RAL?

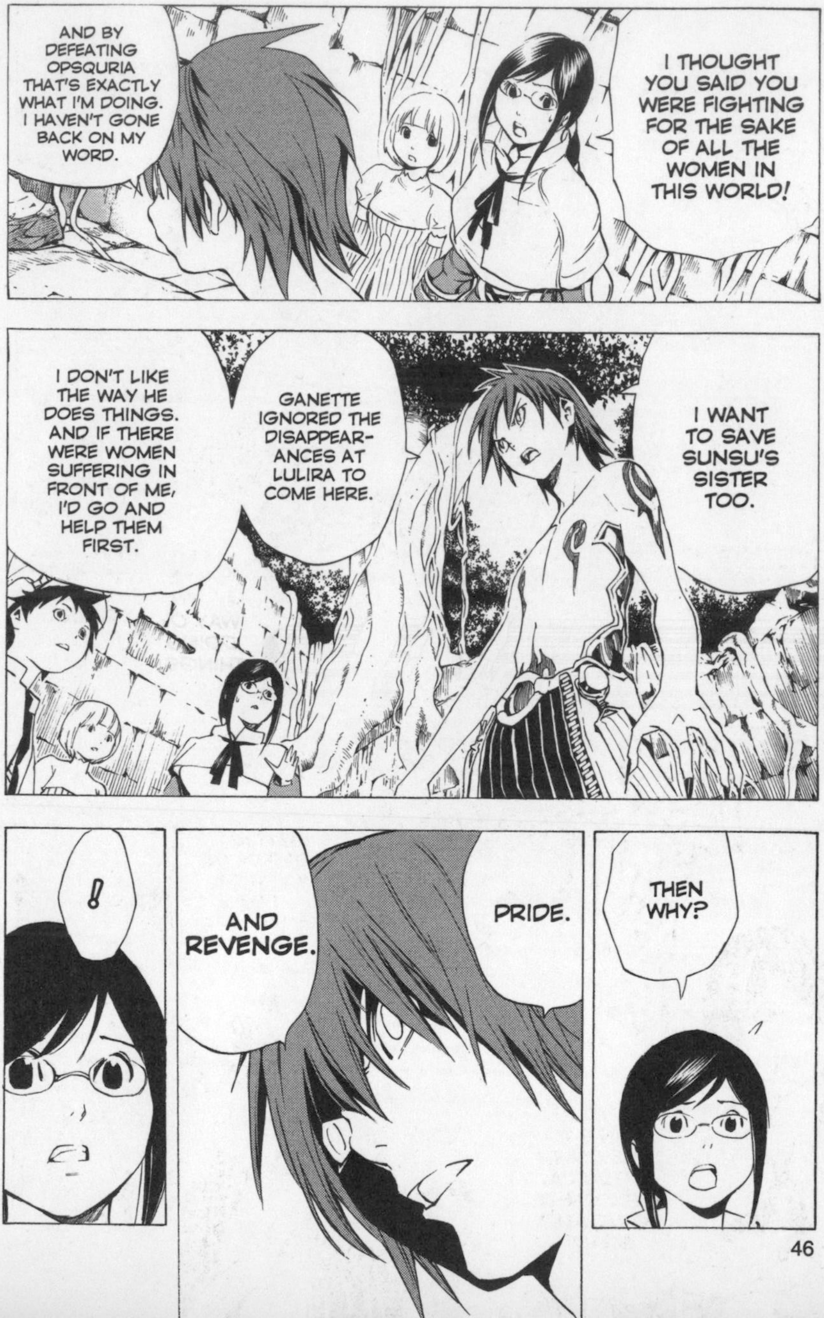
I THOUGHT YOU SAID YOU WERE FIGHTING FOR THE SAKE OF ALL THE WOMEN IN THIS WORLD!
AND BY DEFEATING OPSQURIA THAT'S EXACTLY WHAT I'M DOING. I HAVEN'T GONE BACK ON MY WORD.
I WANT TO SAVE SUNSU'S SISTER TOO.
GANETTE IGNORED THE DISAPPEAR-ANCES AT LULIRA TO COME HERE.
I DON'T LIKE THE WAY HE DOES THINGS. AND IF THERE WERE WOMEN SUFFERING IN FRONT OF ME, I'D GO AND HELP THEM FIRST.
THEN WHY?
PRIDE.
AND REVENGE.
!

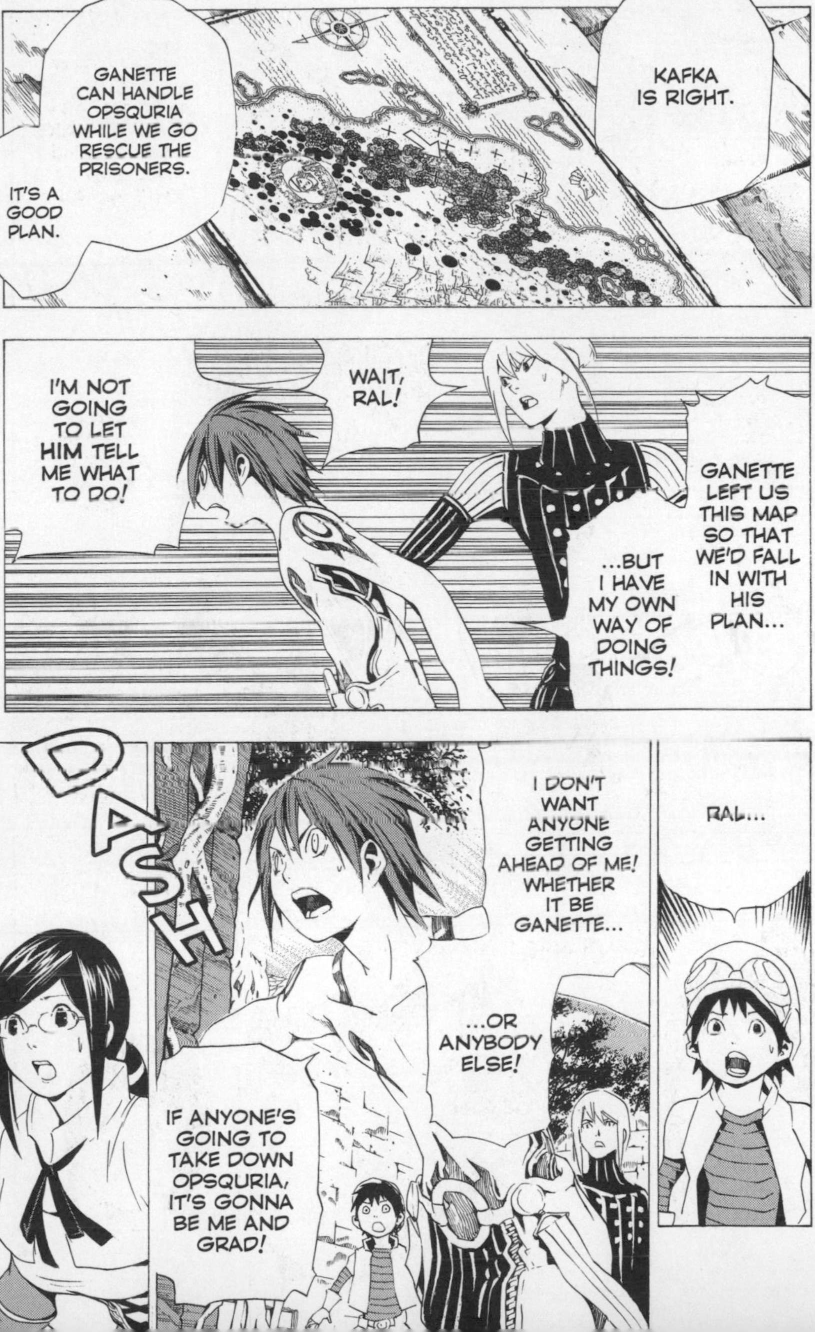
KAFKA IS RIGHT.
GANETTE CAN HANDLE OPSQURIA WHILE WE GO RESCUE THE PRISONERS.
IT'S A GOOD PLAN.
GANETTE LEFT US THIS MAP SO THAT WE'D FALL IN WITH HIS PLAN...
...BUT I HAVE MY OWN WAY OF DOING THINGS!
WAIT, RAL!
I'M NOT GOING TO LET HIM TELL ME WHAT TO DO!
RAL...
I DON'T WANT ANYONE GETTING AHEAD OF ME! WHETHER IT BE GANETTE...
...OR ANYBODY ELSE!
DASH
IF ANYONE'S GOING TO TAKE DOWN OPSQURIA, IT'S GONNA BE ME AND GRAD!

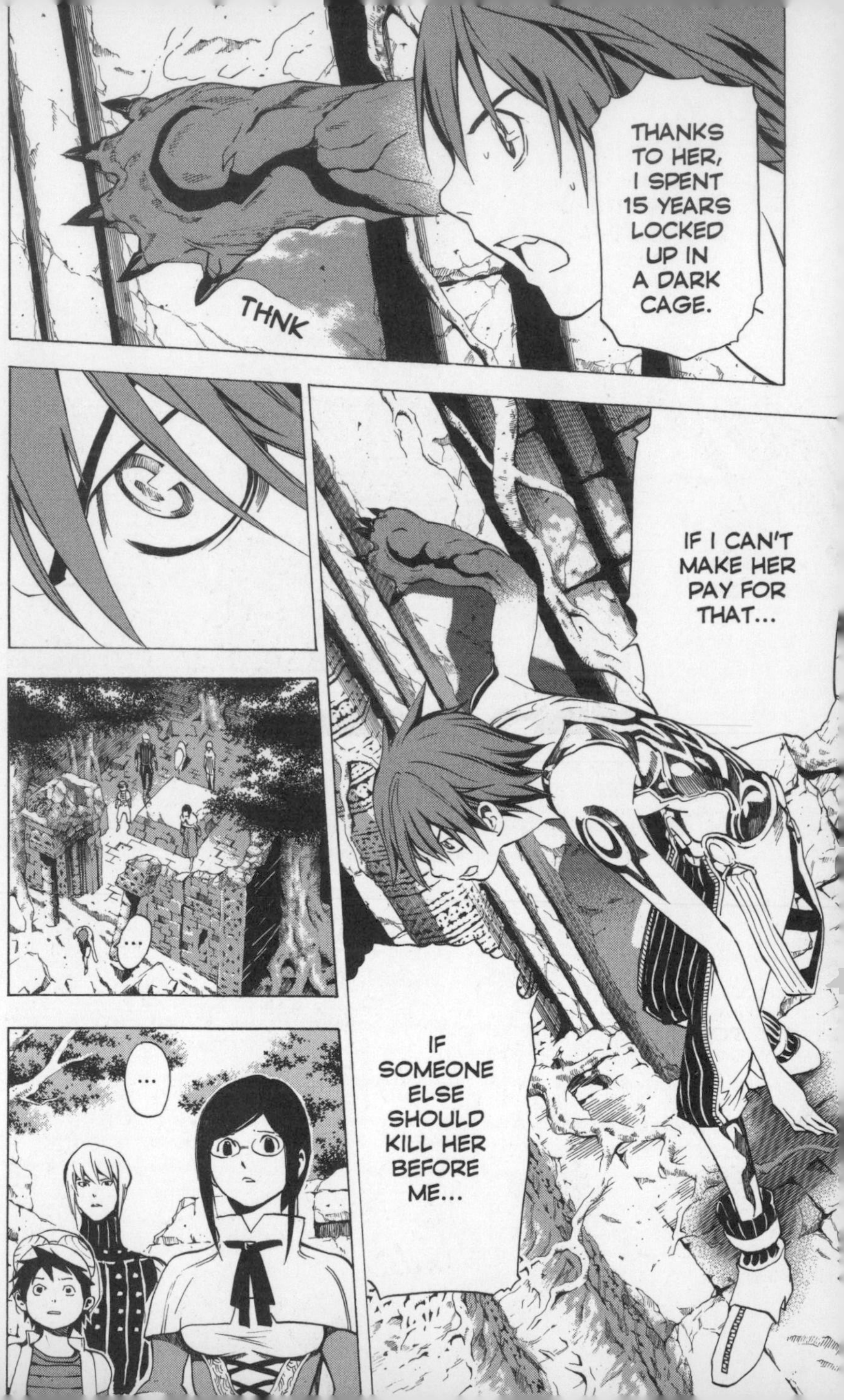
THANKS TO HER, I SPENT 15 YEARS LOCKED UP IN A DARK CAGE.
THNK
IF I CAN'T MAKE HER PAY FOR THAT...
IF SOMEONE ELSE SHOULD KILL HER BEFORE ME...
...
...

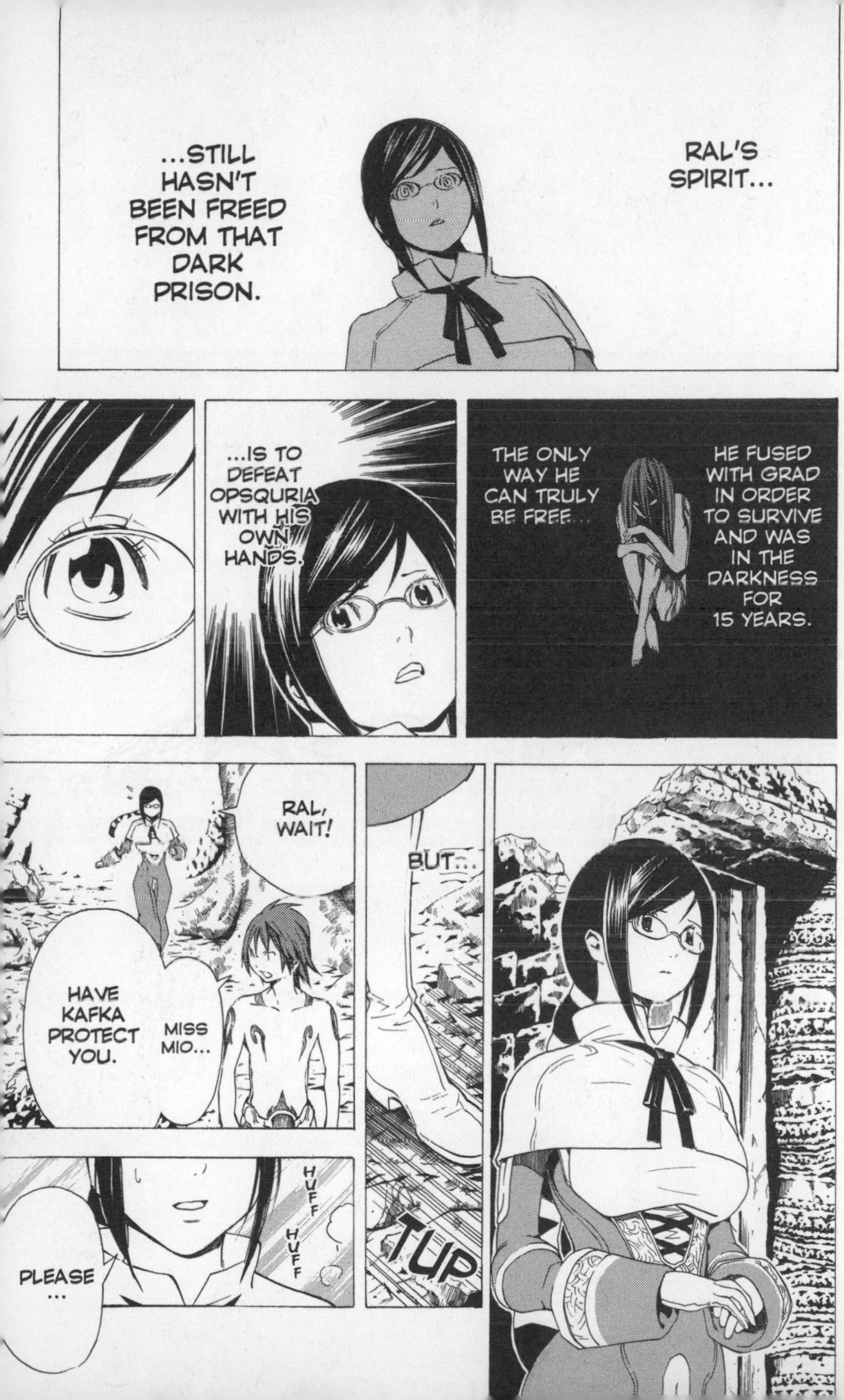
RAL'S SPIRIT...
...STILL HASN'T BEEN FREED FROM THAT DARK PRISON.
HE FUSED WITH GRAD IN ORDER TO SURVIVE AND WAS IN THE DARKNESS FOR 15 YEARS.
THE ONLY WAY HE CAN TRULY BE FREE...
...IS TO DEFEAT OPSQURIA WITH HIS OWN HANDS.
BUT...
TUP
RAL, WAIT!
MISS MIO...
HAVE KAFKA PROTECT YOU.
HUFF
HUFF
PLEASE ...

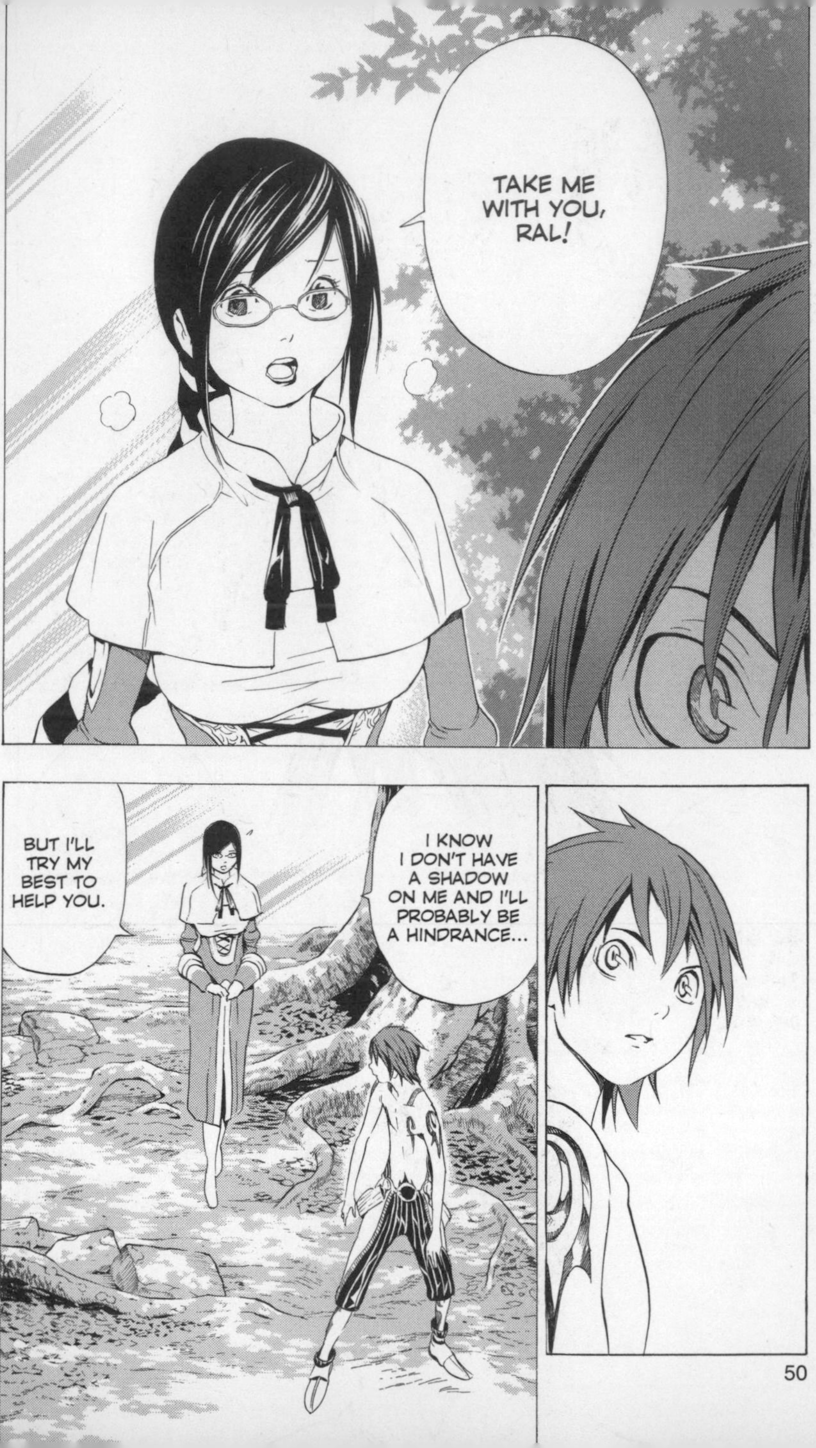
TAKE ME WITH YOU, RAL!
I KNOW I DON'T HAVE A SHADOW ON ME AND I'LL PROBABLY BE A HINDRANCE...
BUT I'LL TRY MY BEST TO HELP YOU.

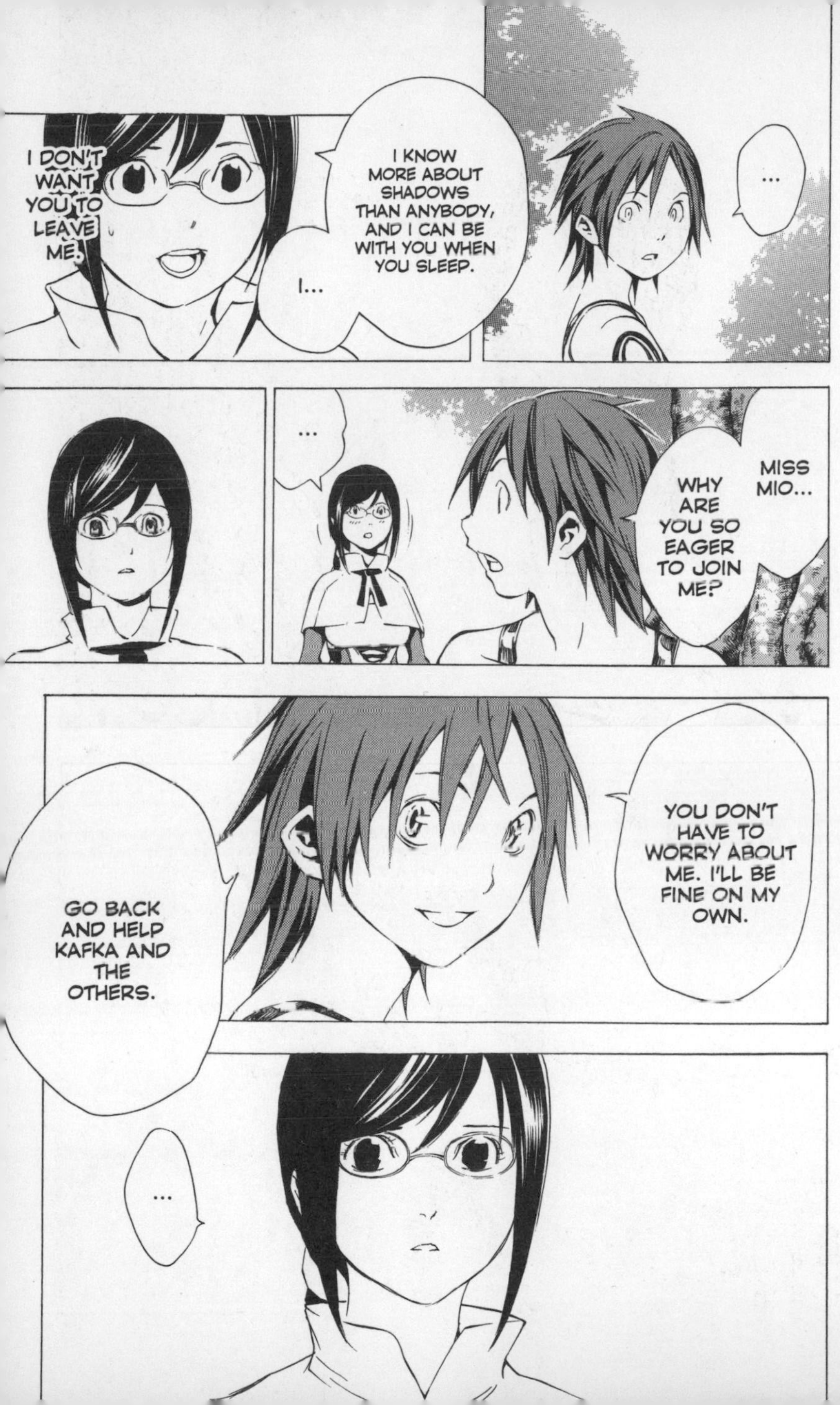
...
I KNOW MORE ABOUT SHADOWS THAN ANYBODY, AND I CAN BE WITH YOU WHEN YOU SLEEP.
I...
I DON'T WANT YOU TO LEAVE ME.
MISS MIO...
WHY ARE YOU SO EAGER TO JOIN ME?
...
YOU DON'T HAVE TO WORRY ABOUT ME. I'LL BE FINE ON MY OWN.
GO BACK AND HELP KAFKA AND THE OTHERS.
...

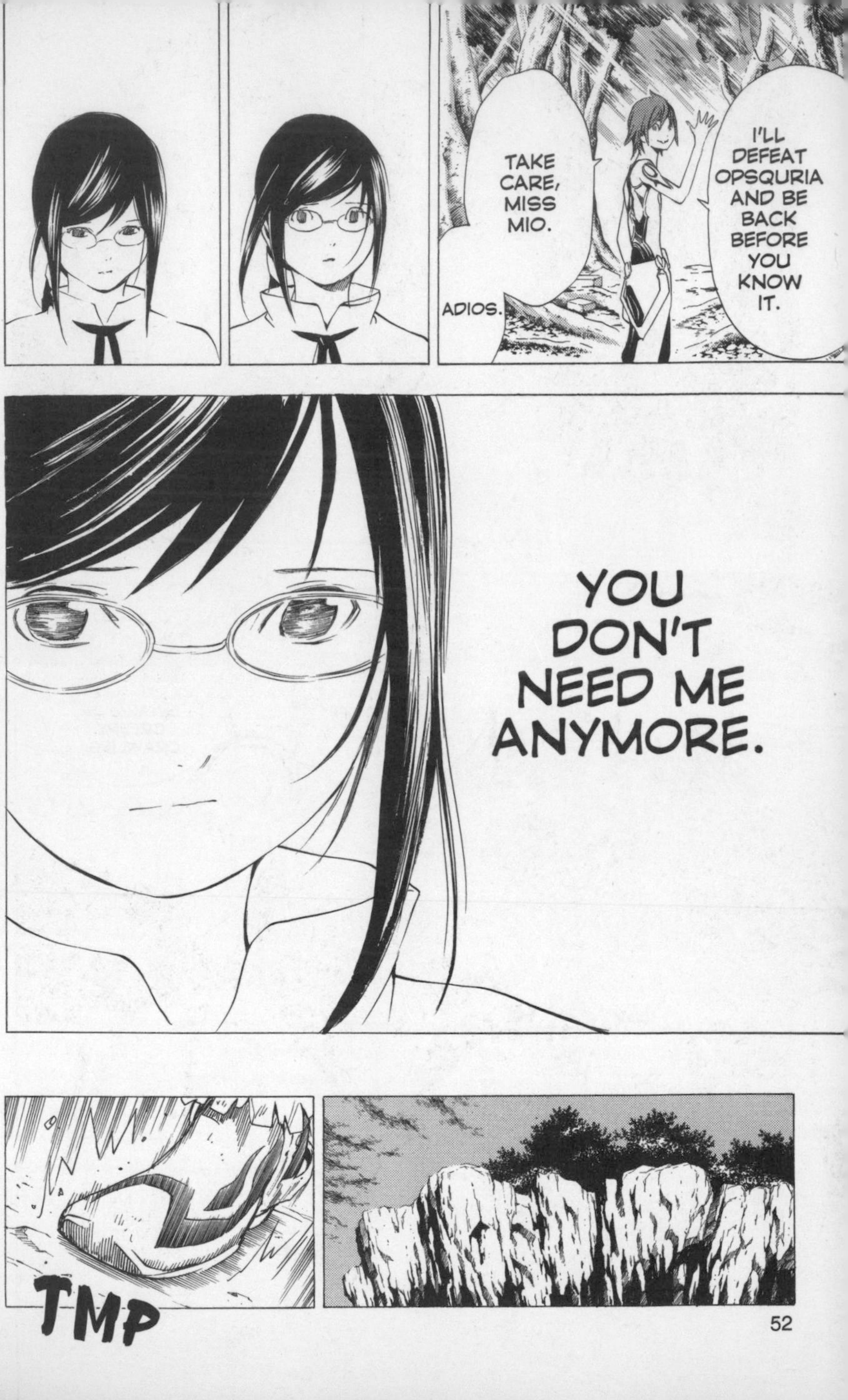
I'LL DEFEAT OPSQURIA AND BE BACK BEFORE YOU KNOW IT.
TAKE CARE, MISS MIO.
ADIOS.
YOU DON'T NEED ME ANYMORE.
TMP

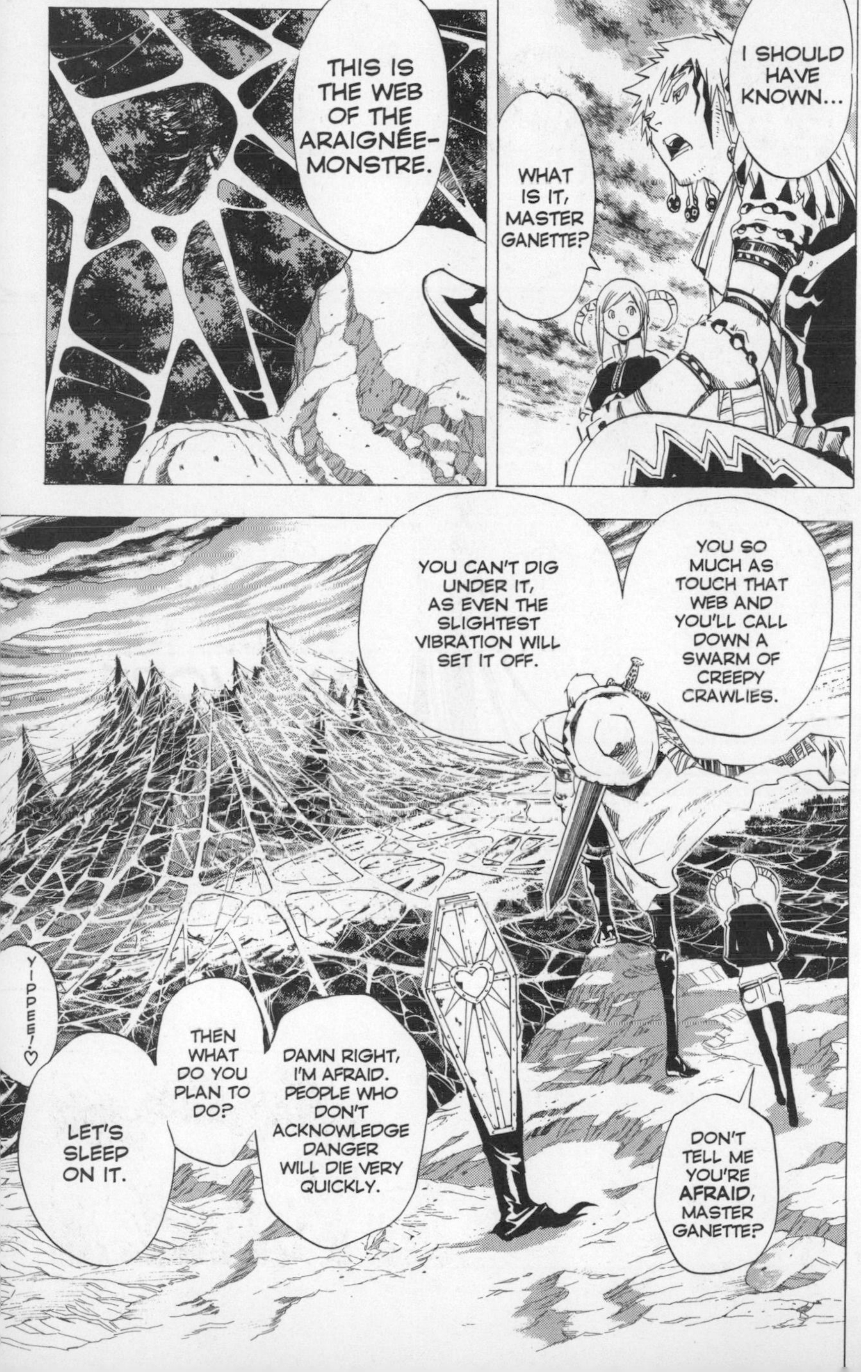
I SHOULD HAVE KNOWN...
WHAT IS IT, MASTER GANETTE?
THIS IS THE WEB OF THE ARAIGNÉE-MONSTRE.
YOU SO MUCH AS TOUCH THAT WEB AND YOU'LL CALL DOWN A SWARM OF CREEPY CRAWLIES.
YOU CAN'T DIG UNDER IT, AS EVEN THE SLIGHTEST VIBRATION WILL SET IT OFF.
DON'T TELL ME YOU'RE **AFRAID**, MASTER GANETTE?
DAMN RIGHT, I'M AFRAID. PEOPLE WHO DON'T ACKNOWLEDGE DANGER WILL DIE VERY QUICKLY.
THEN WHAT DO YOU PLAN TO DO?
LET'S SLEEP ON IT.
YIPPEE!♡

Ral Ω Grad

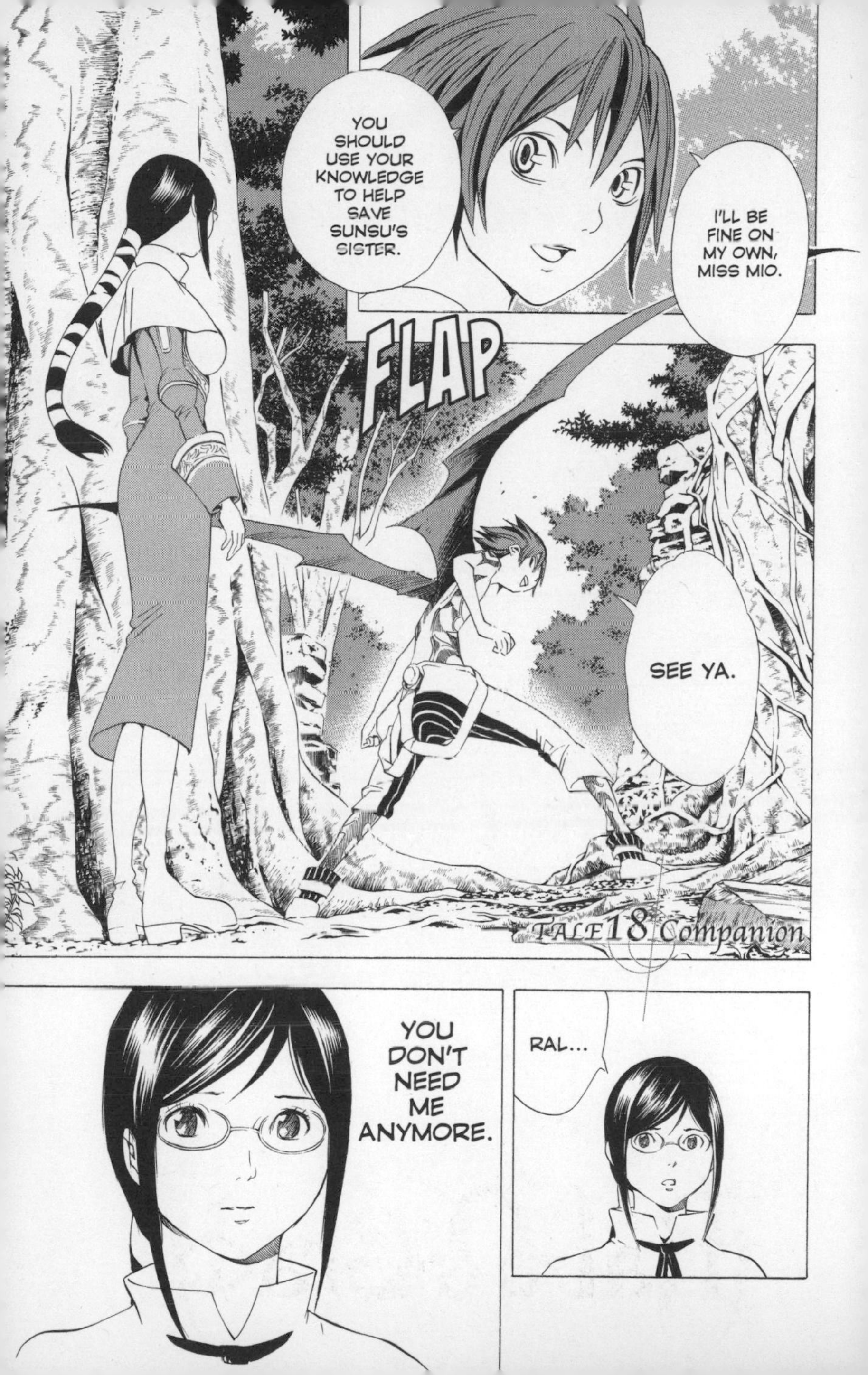
I'LL BE FINE ON MY OWN, MISS MIO.
YOU SHOULD USE YOUR KNOWLEDGE TO HELP SAVE SUNSU'S SISTER.
FLAP
SEE YA.
TALE 18 Companion
RAL...
YOU DON'T NEED ME ANYMORE.

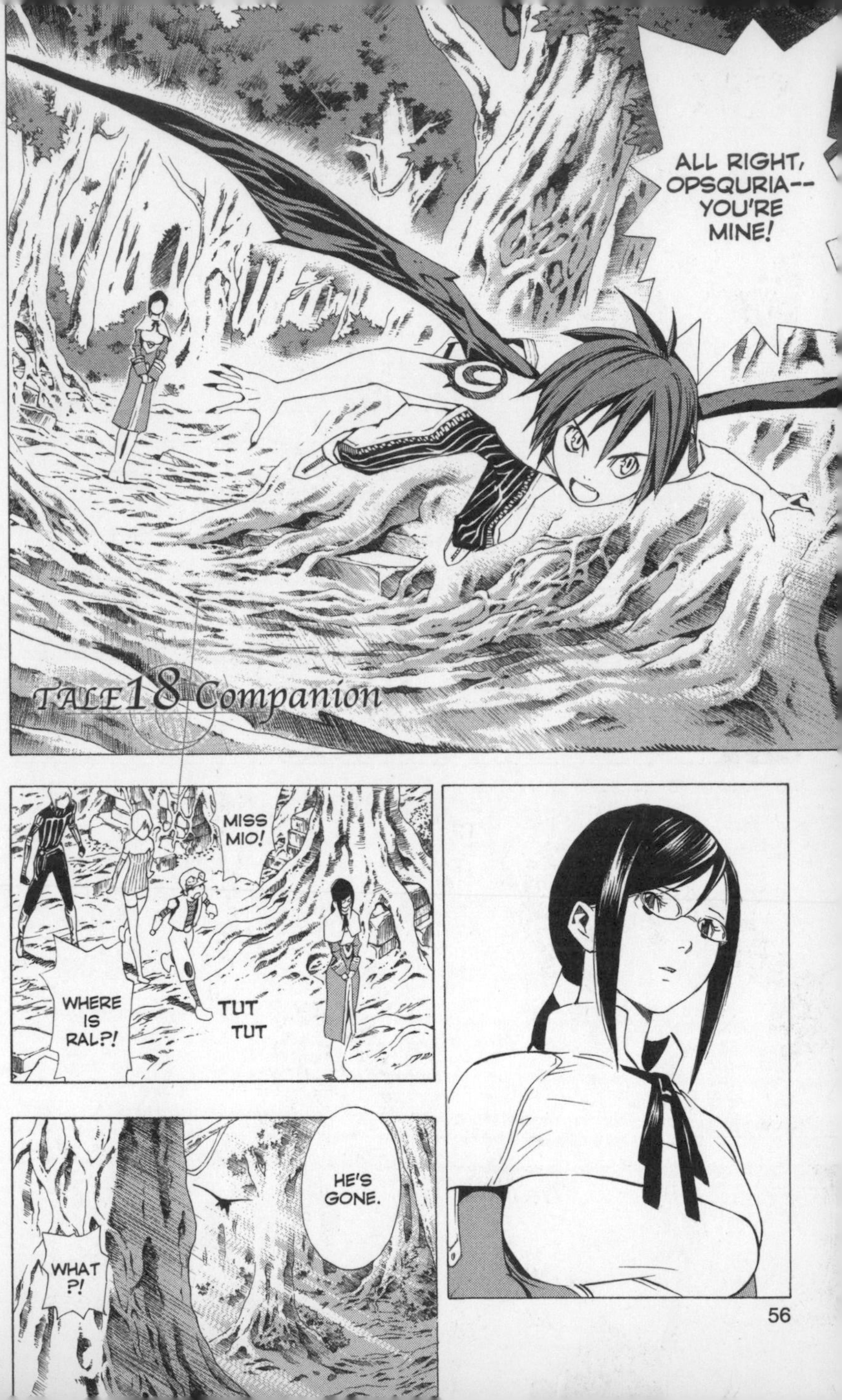
ALL RIGHT, OPSQURIA-- YOU'RE MINE!
TALE 18 Companion
MISS MIO!
WHERE IS RAL?!
TUT TUT
HE'S GONE.
WHAT ?!

READ THIS WAY

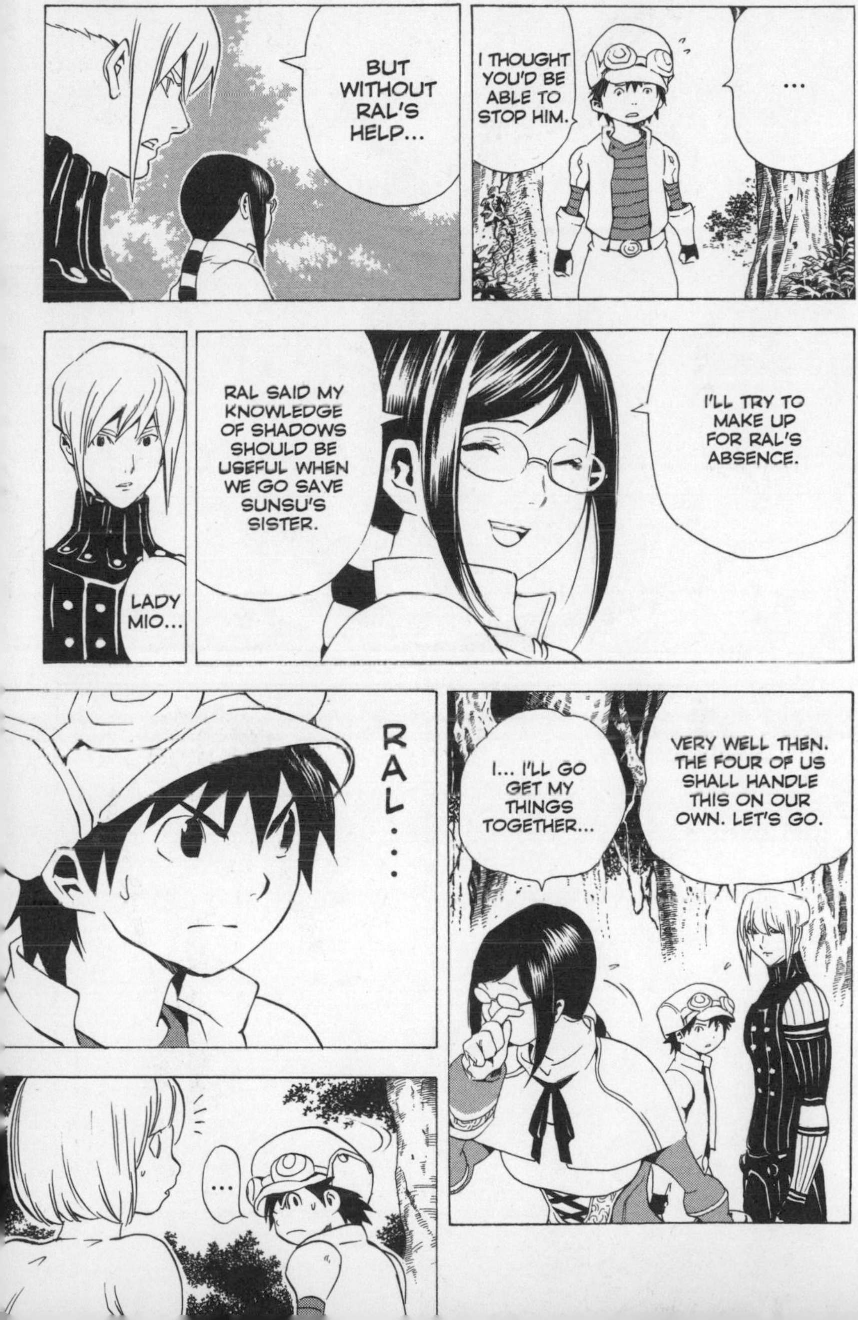
...
I THOUGHT YOU'D BE ABLE TO STOP HIM.
BUT WITHOUT RAL'S HELP...
I'LL TRY TO MAKE UP FOR RAL'S ABSENCE.
RAL SAID MY KNOWLEDGE OF SHADOWS SHOULD BE USEFUL WHEN WE GO SAVE SUNSU'S SISTER.
LADY MIO...
VERY WELL THEN. THE FOUR OF US SHALL HANDLE THIS ON OUR OWN. LET'S GO.
I... I'LL GO GET MY THINGS TOGETHER...
RAL...
...

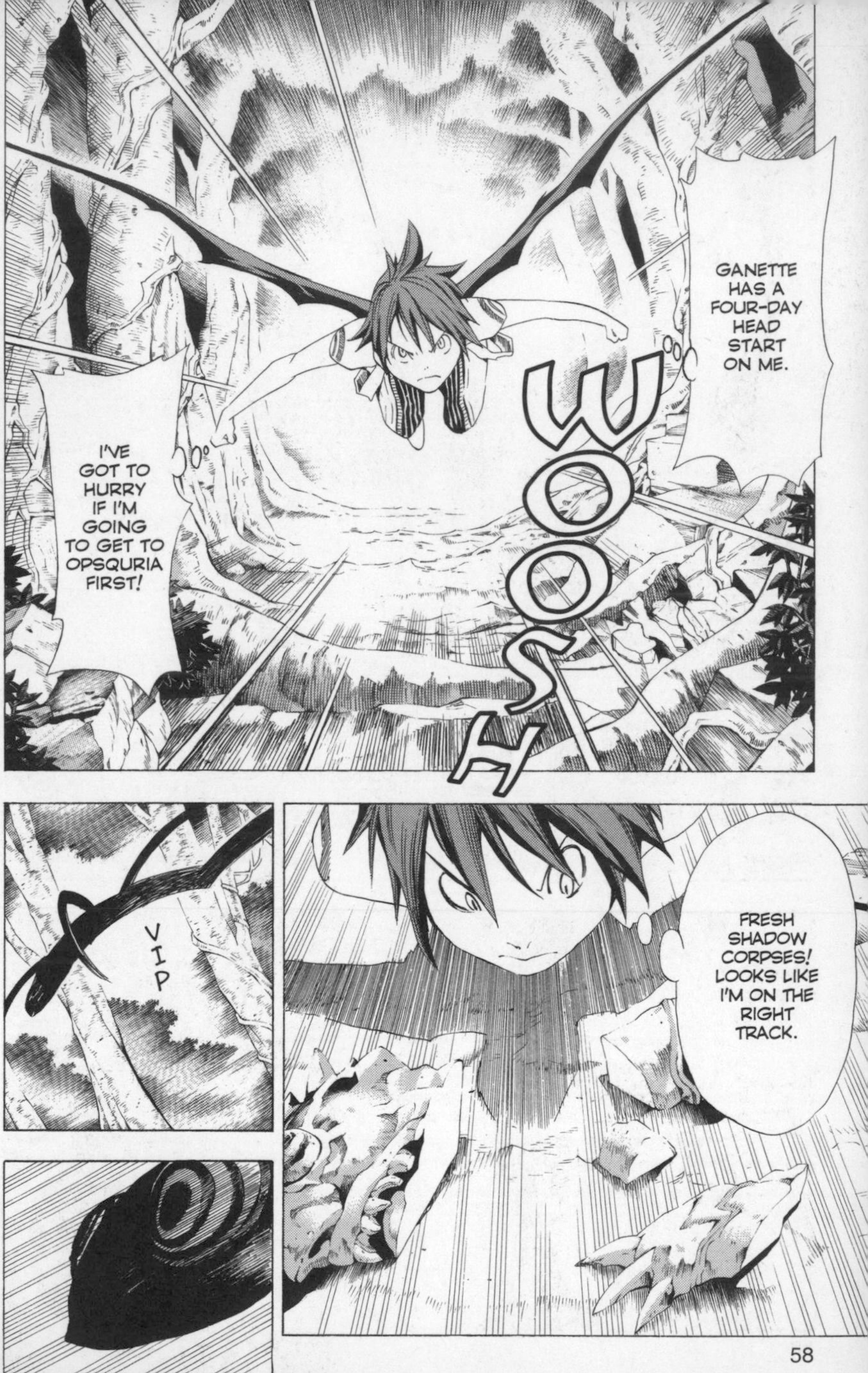
GANETTE HAS A FOUR-DAY HEAD START ON ME.
I'VE GOT TO HURRY IF I'M GOING TO GET TO OPSQURIA FIRST!
WOOOSH
FRESH SHADOW CORPSES! LOOKS LIKE I'M ON THE RIGHT TRACK.
VIP

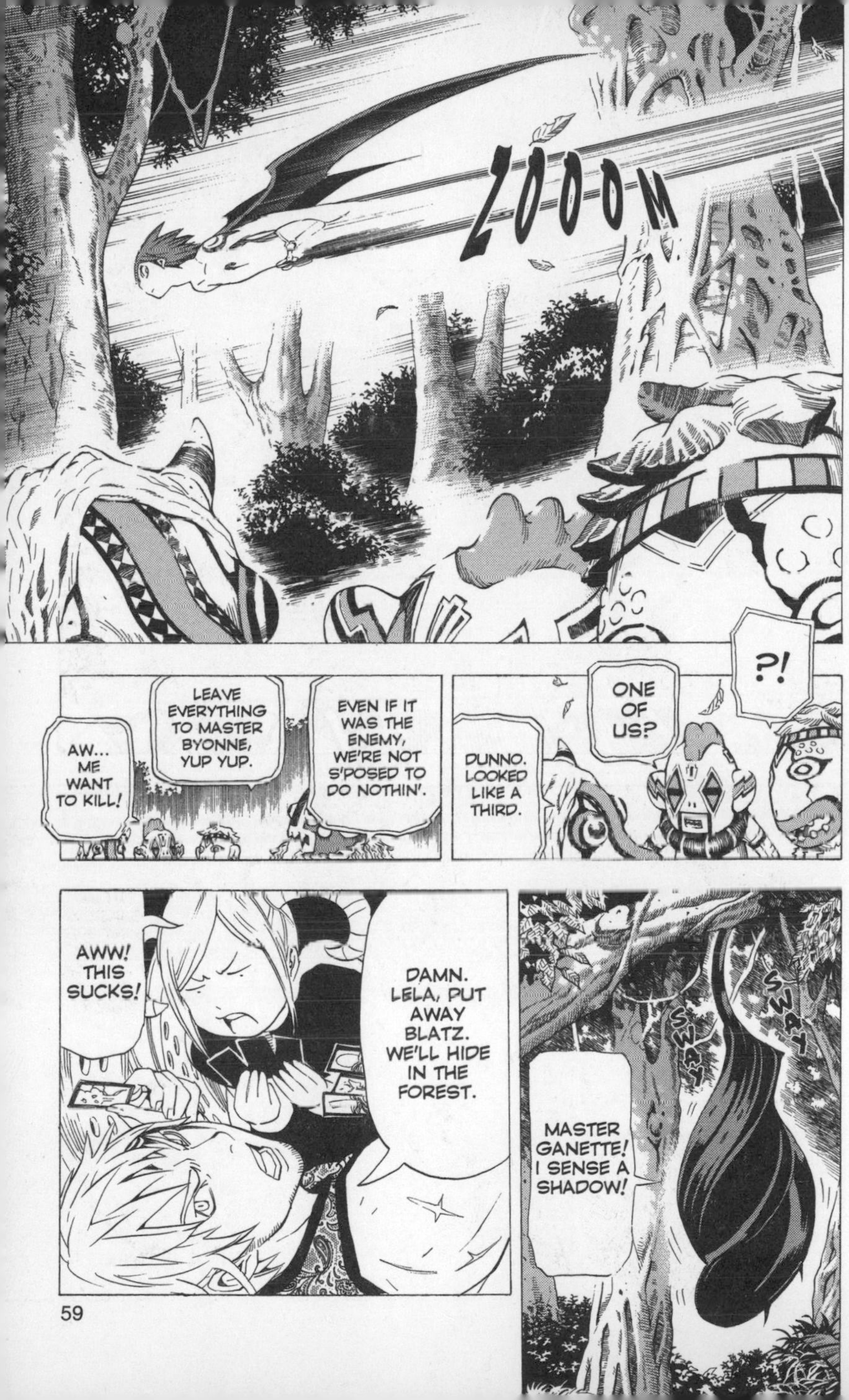
ZOOOM
?!
ONE OF US?
DUNNO. LOOKED LIKE A THIRD.
EVEN IF IT WAS THE ENEMY, WE'RE NOT S'POSED TO DO NOTHIN'.
LEAVE EVERYTHING TO MASTER BYONNE, YUP YUP.
AW... ME WANT TO KILL!
SWAY
SWAY
MASTER GANETTE! I SENSE A SHADOW!
DAMN. LELA, PUT AWAY BLATZ. WE'LL HIDE IN THE FOREST.
AWW! THIS SUCKS!

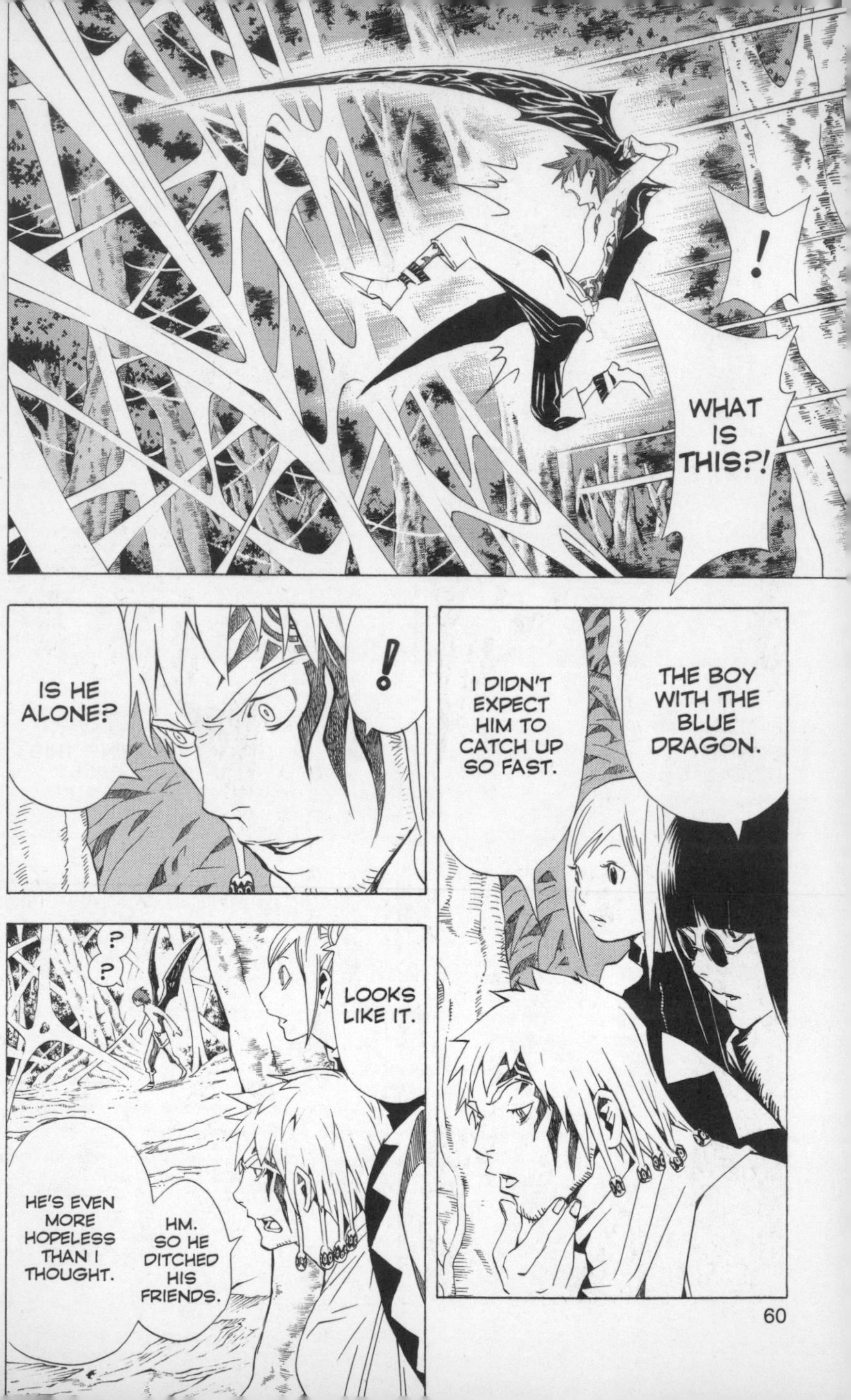
!
WHAT IS THIS?!
THE BOY WITH THE BLUE DRAGON.
I DIDN'T EXPECT HIM TO CATCH UP SO FAST.
!
IS HE ALONE?
? ?
LOOKS LIKE IT.
HM. SO HE DITCHED HIS FRIENDS.
HE'S EVEN MORE HOPELESS THAN I THOUGHT.

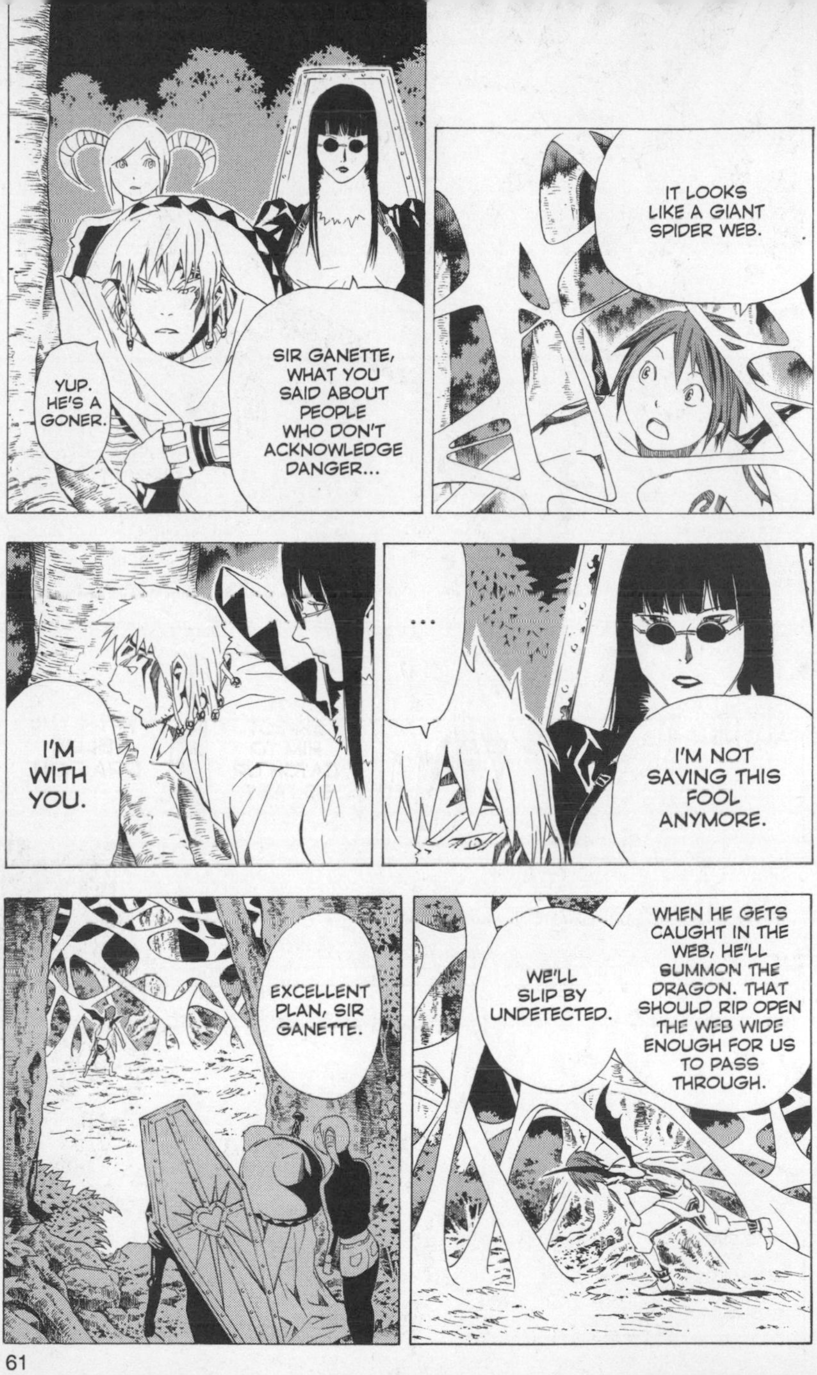
IT LOOKS LIKE A GIANT SPIDER WEB.
SIR GANETTE, WHAT YOU SAID ABOUT PEOPLE WHO DON'T ACKNOWLEDGE DANGER...
YUP. HE'S A GONER.
...
I'M NOT SAVING THIS FOOL ANYMORE.
I'M WITH YOU.
WHEN HE GETS CAUGHT IN THE WEB, HE'LL SUMMON THE DRAGON. THAT SHOULD RIP OPEN THE WEB WIDE ENOUGH FOR US TO PASS THROUGH.
WE'LL SLIP BY UNDETECTED.
EXCELLENT PLAN, SIR GANETTE.

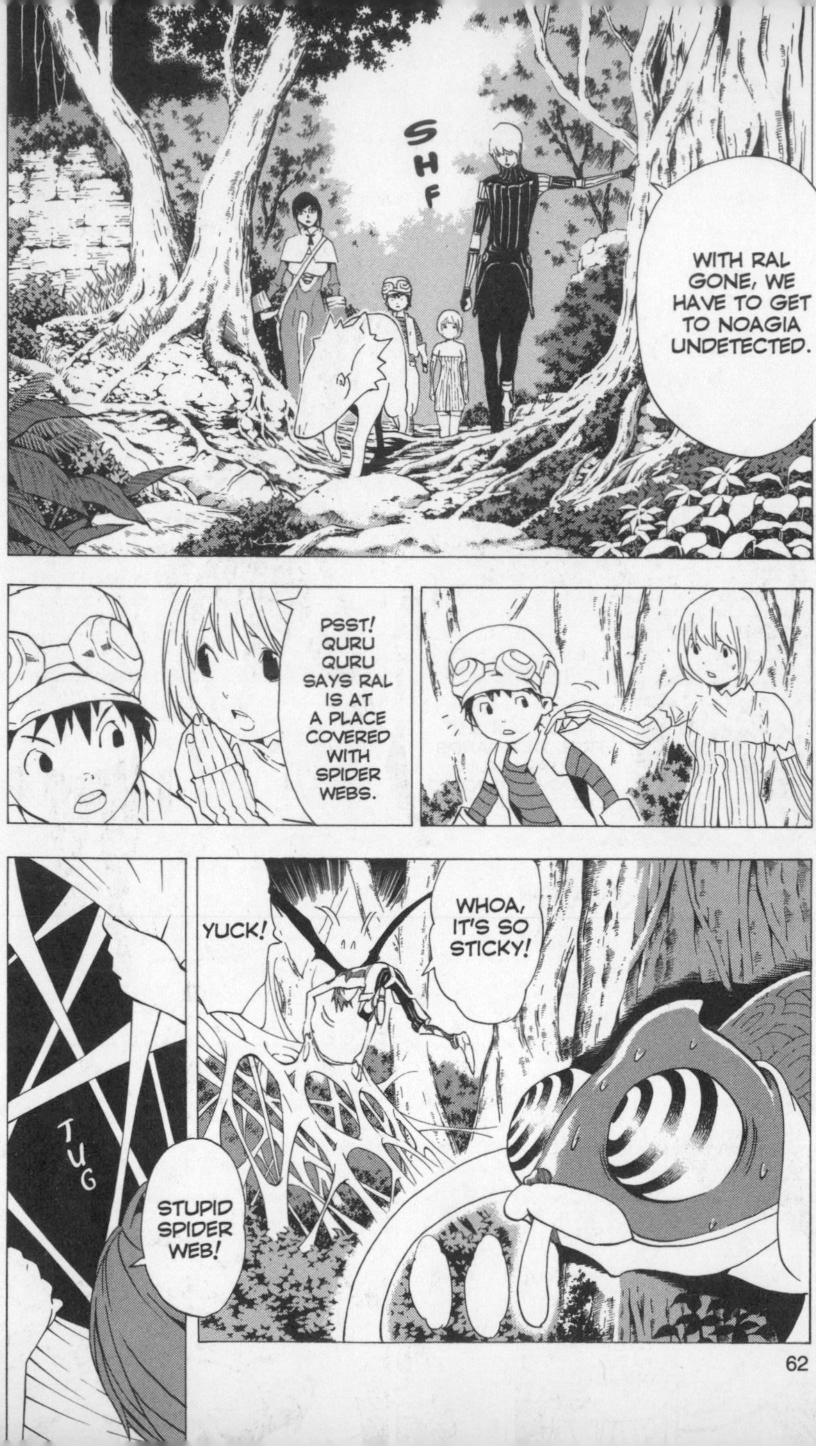
SHF
WITH RAL GONE, WE HAVE TO GET TO NOAGIA UNDETECTED.
PSST! QURU QURU SAYS RAL IS AT A PLACE COVERED WITH SPIDER WEBS.
WHOA, IT'S SO STICKY!
YUCK!
TUG
STUPID SPIDER WEB!

READ THIS WAY

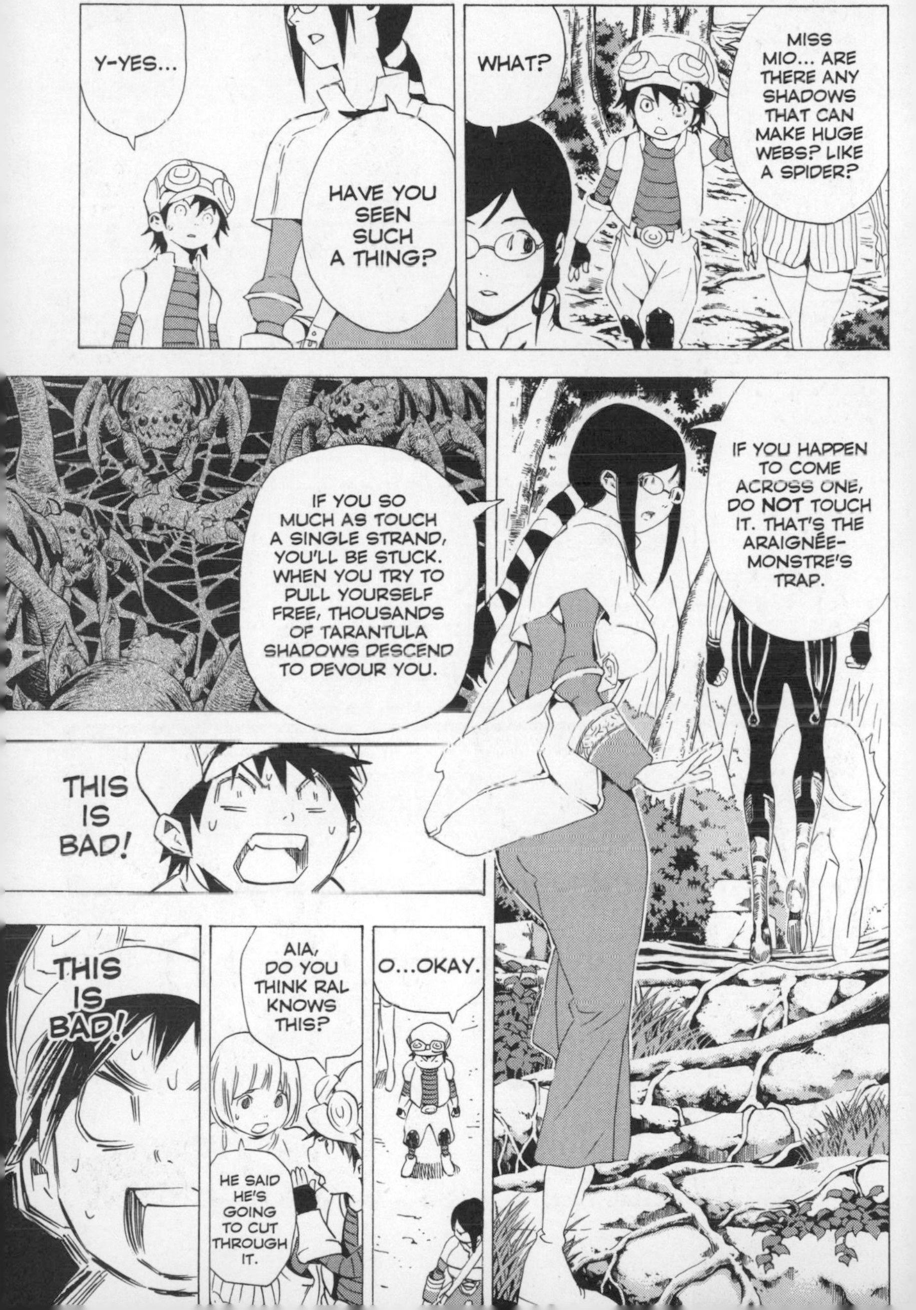
MISS MIO... ARE THERE ANY SHADOWS THAT CAN MAKE HUGE WEBS? LIKE A SPIDER?
WHAT?
HAVE YOU SEEN SUCH A THING?
Y-YES...
IF YOU HAPPEN TO COME ACROSS ONE, DO NOT TOUCH IT. THAT'S THE ARAIGNÉE-MONSTRE'S TRAP.
IF YOU SO MUCH AS TOUCH A SINGLE STRAND, YOU'LL BE STUCK. WHEN YOU TRY TO PULL YOURSELF FREE, THOUSANDS OF TARANTULA SHADOWS DESCEND TO DEVOUR YOU.
THIS IS BAD!
O...OKAY.
AIA, DO YOU THINK RAL KNOWS THIS?
HE SAID HE'S GOING TO CUT THROUGH IT.
THIS IS BAD!

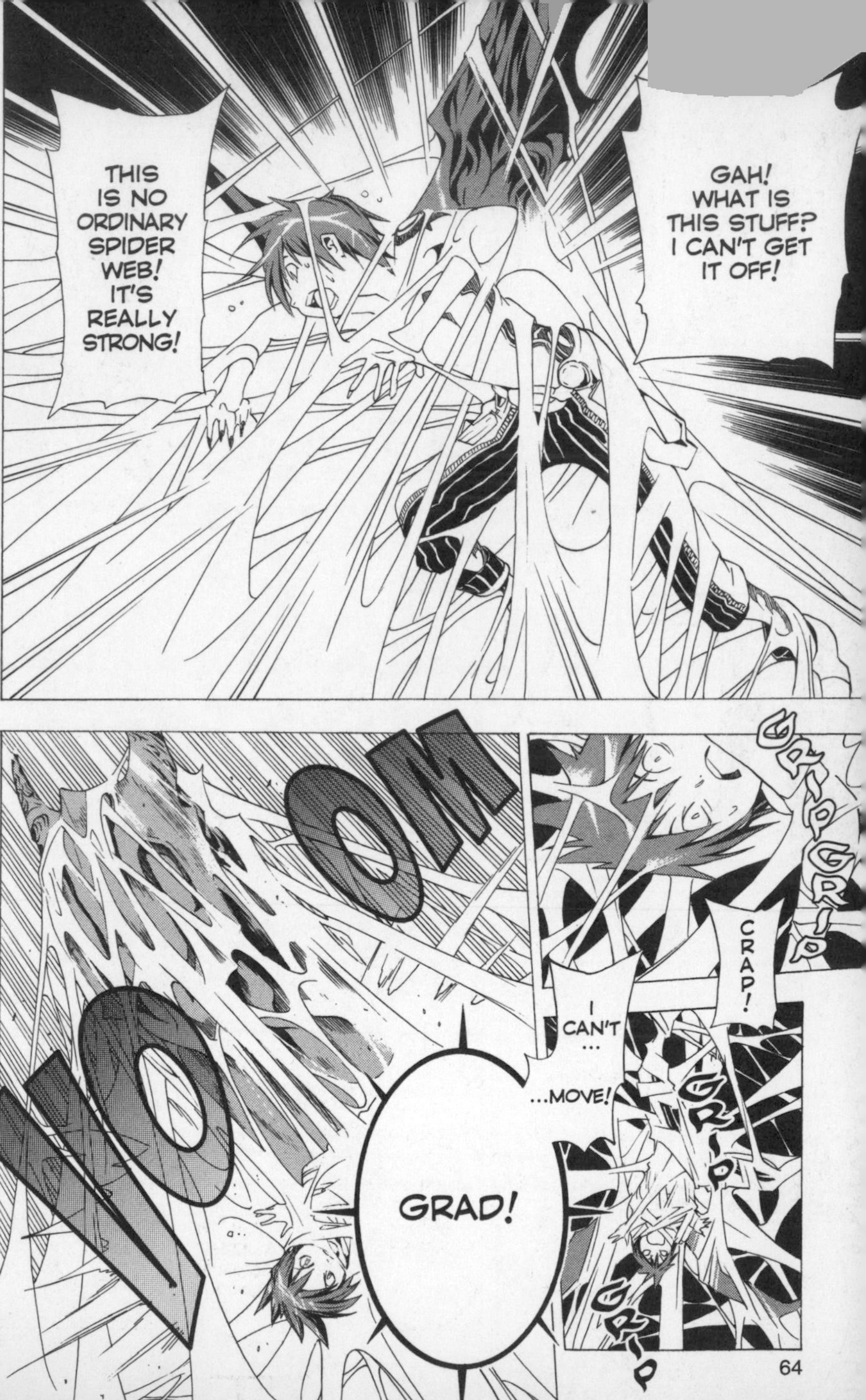
GAH! WHAT IS THIS STUFF? I CAN'T GET IT OFF!
THIS IS NO ORDINARY SPIDER WEB! IT'S REALLY STRONG!
GRIP GRIP
CRAP!
I CAN'T ...
...MOVE!
GRIP GRIP
VOOM
GRAD!

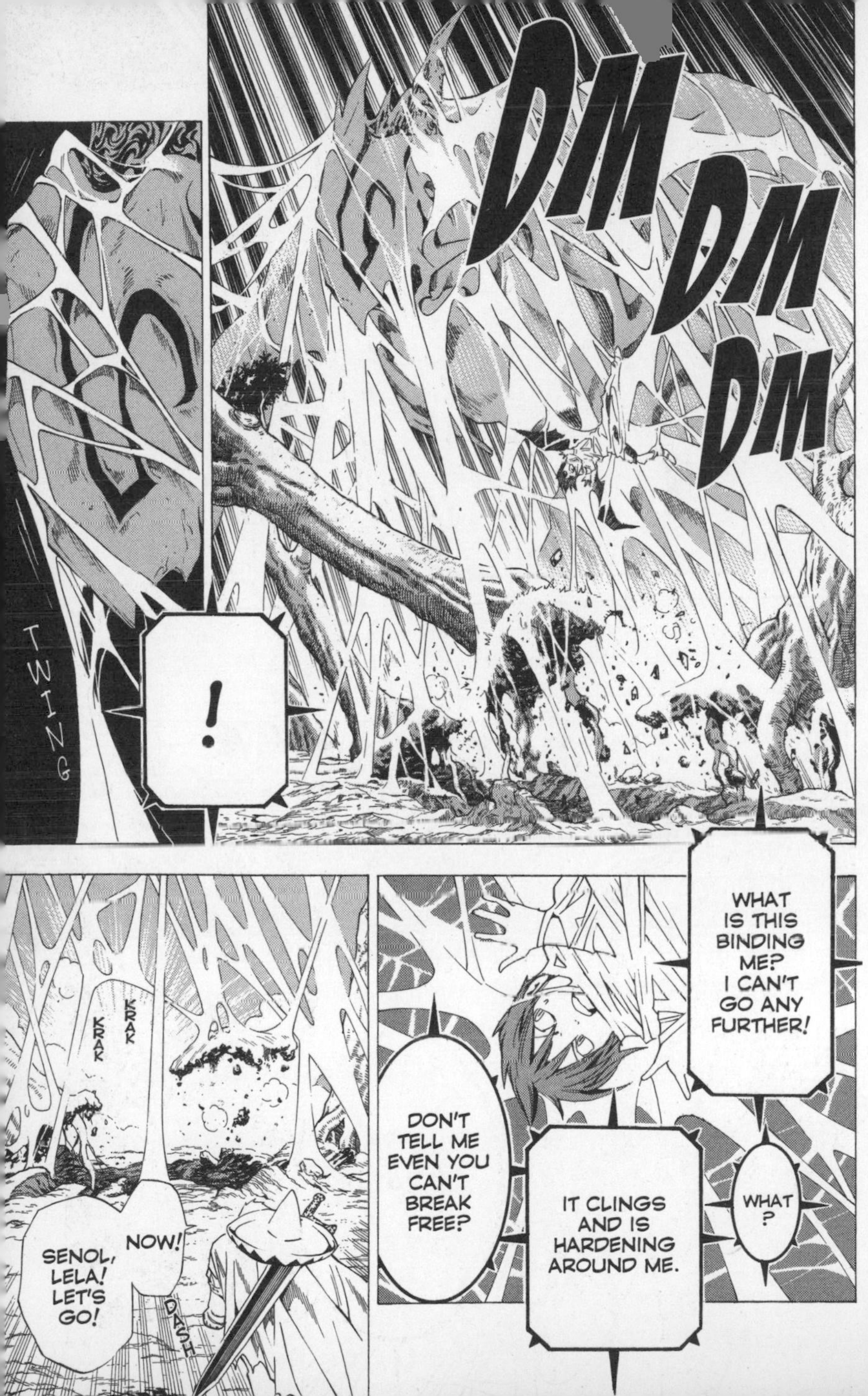
DM DM DM DM
TWING
!
WHAT IS THIS BINDING ME? I CAN'T GO ANY FURTHER!
WHAT?
IT CLINGS AND IS HARDENING AROUND ME.
DON'T TELL ME EVEN YOU CAN'T BREAK FREE?
KRAK KRAK
NOW!
SENOL, LELA! LET'S GO!
DASH

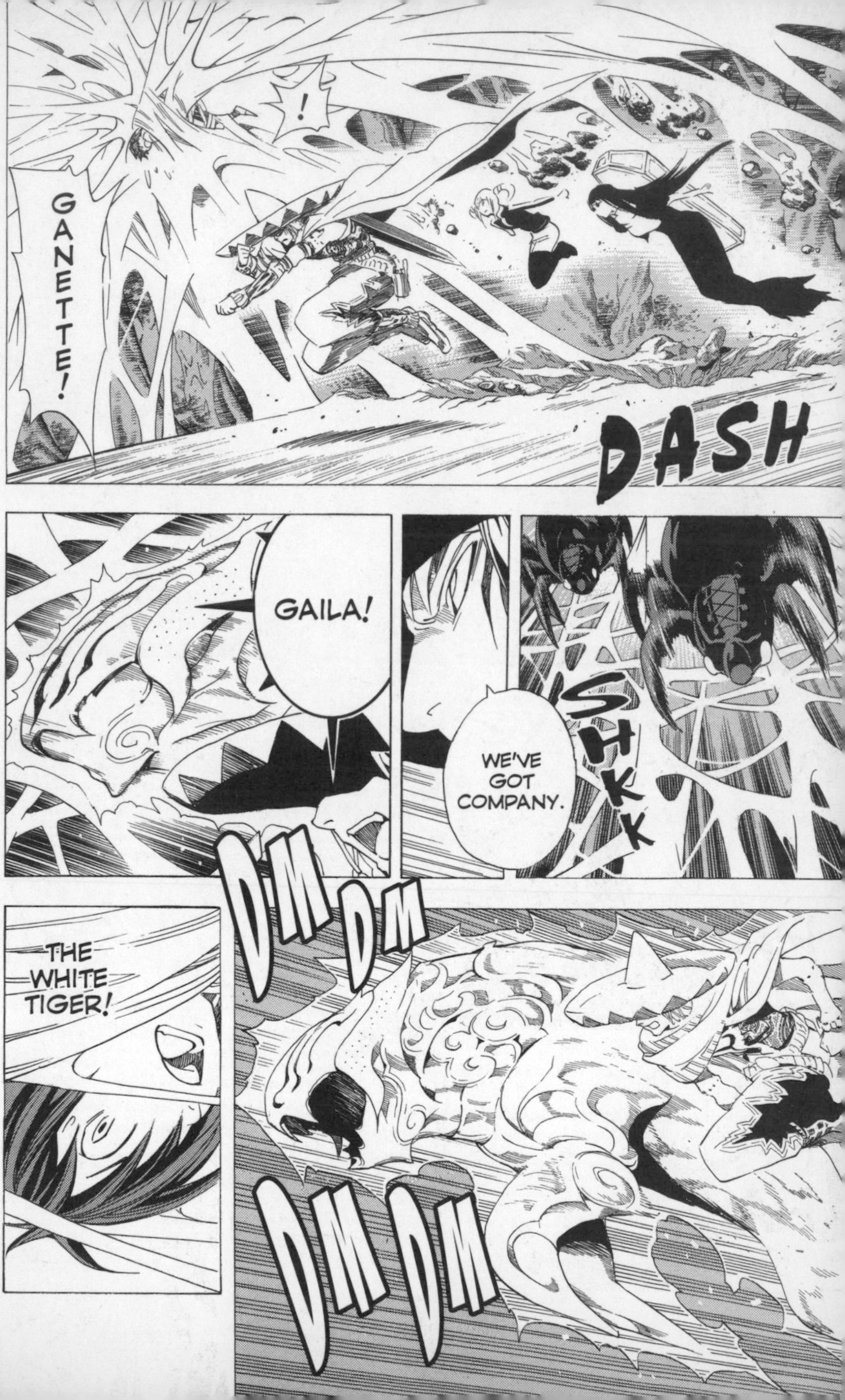
!
GANETTE!
DASH
SHKK
WE'VE GOT COMPANY.
GAILA!
D-M DM
DM DM
THE WHITE TIGER!

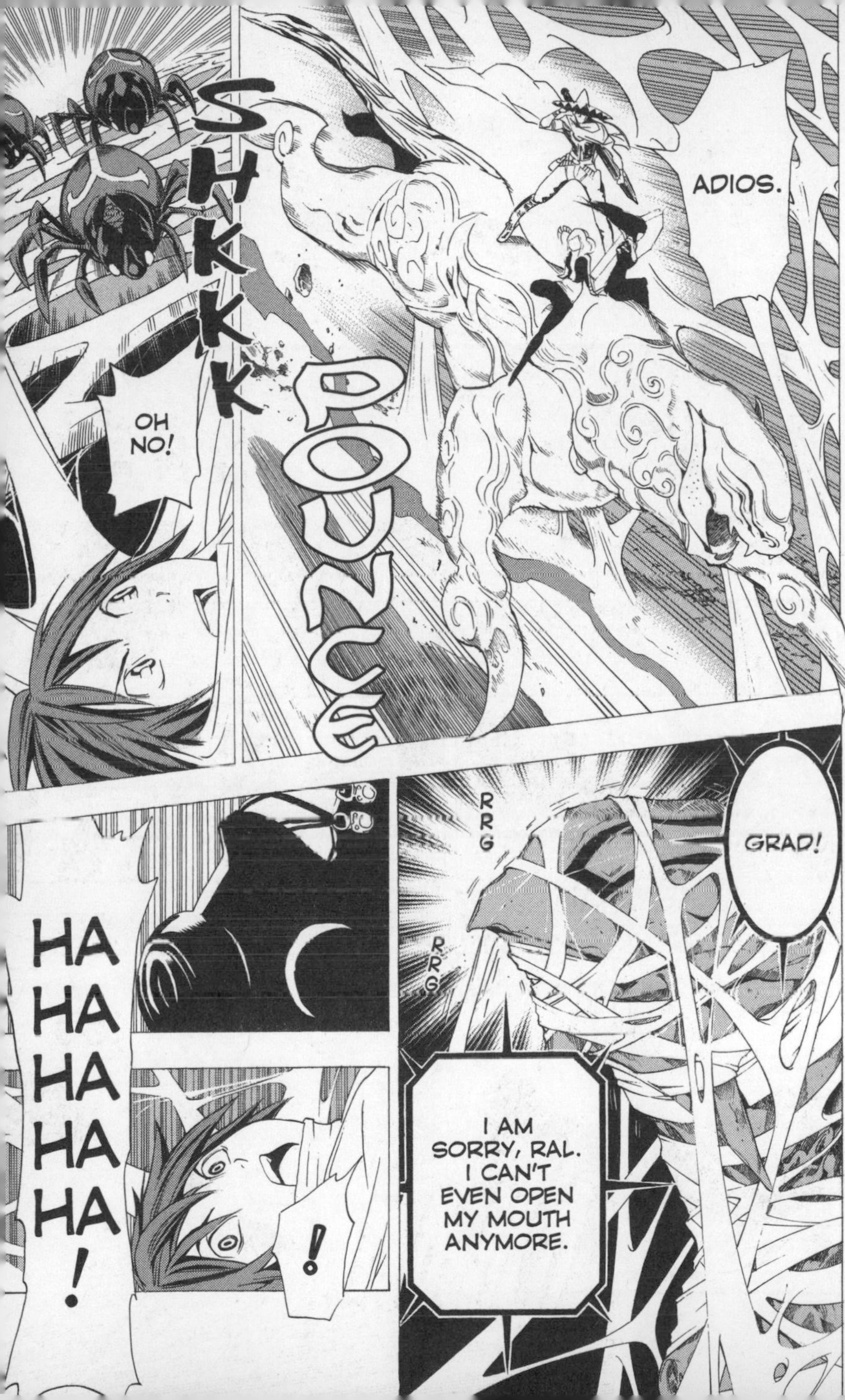
ADIOS.
POUNCE
SHKKKK
OH NO!
GRAD!
RRG
RRG
I AM SORRY, RAL. I CAN'T EVEN OPEN MY MOUTH ANYMORE.
HA HA HA HA HA!
!

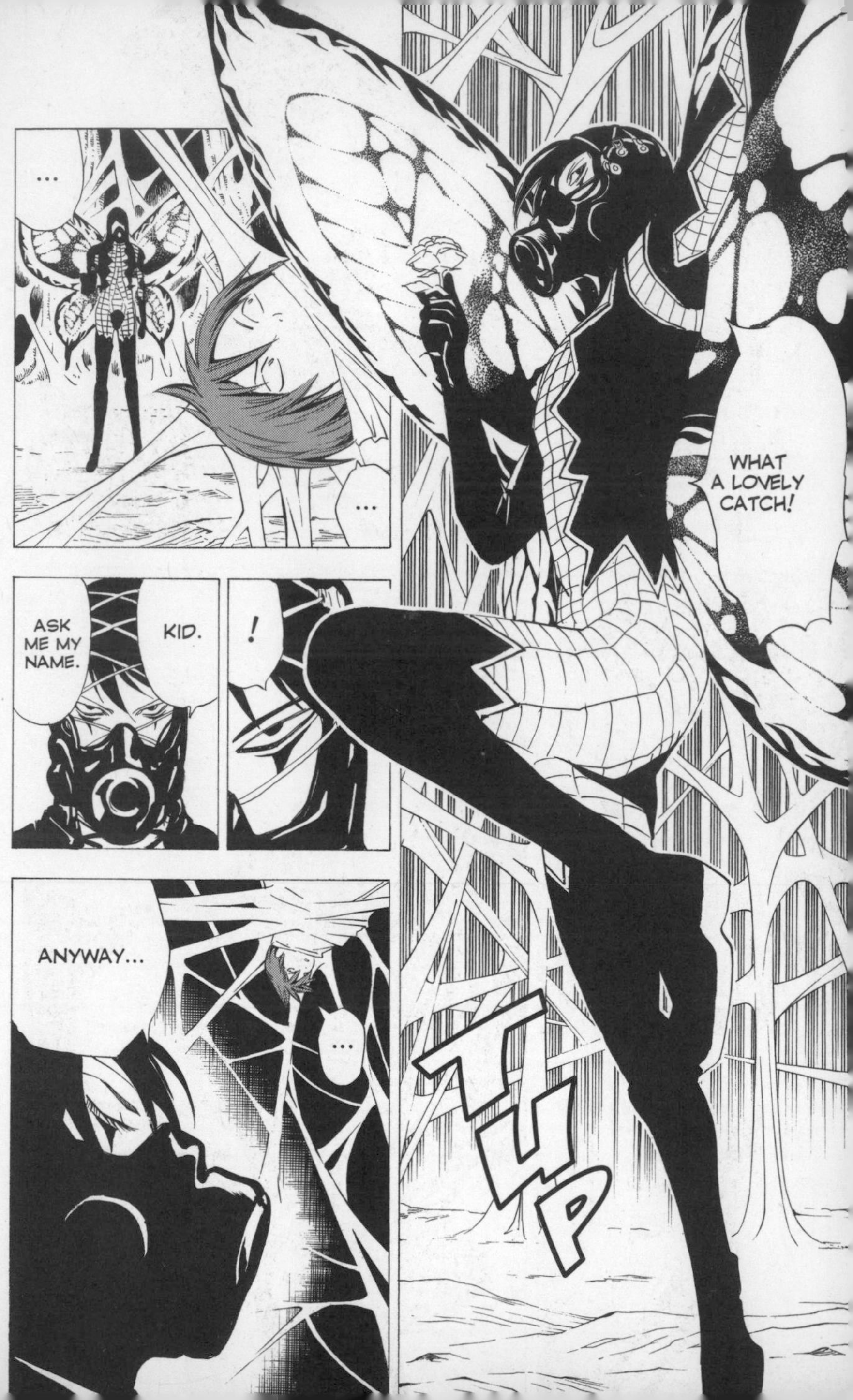
WHAT A LOVELY CATCH!
THUP
...
...
!
KID.
ASK ME MY NAME.
ANYWAY...
...

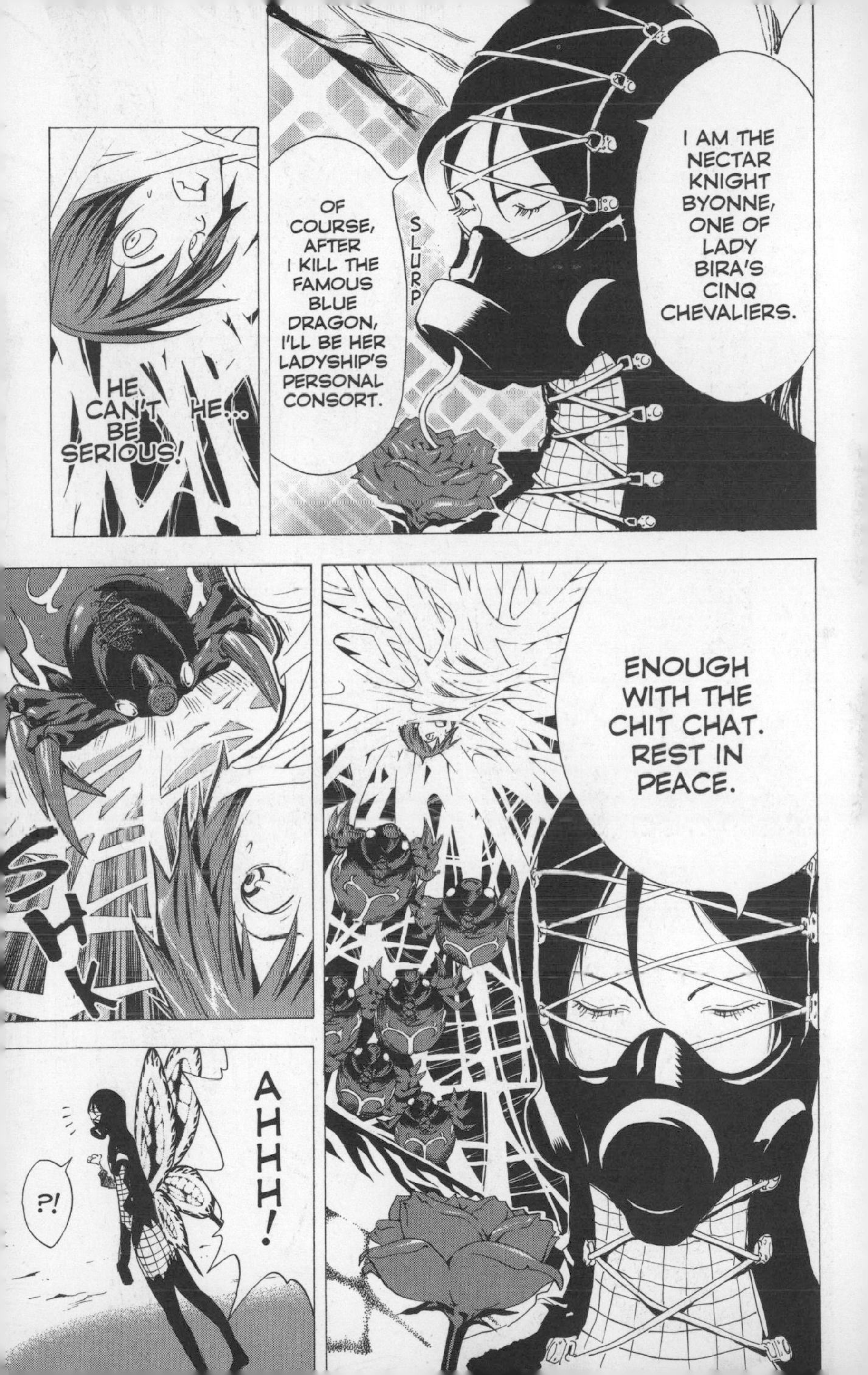
I AM THE NECTAR KNIGHT BYONNE, ONE OF LADY BIRA'S CINQ CHEVALIERS.
OF COURSE, AFTER I KILL THE FAMOUS BLUE DRAGON, I'LL BE HER LADYSHIP'S PERSONAL CONSORT.
SLURP
HE...
HE CAN'T BE SERIOUS!
ENOUGH WITH THE CHIT CHAT. REST IN PEACE.
SHK
AHHH!
?!

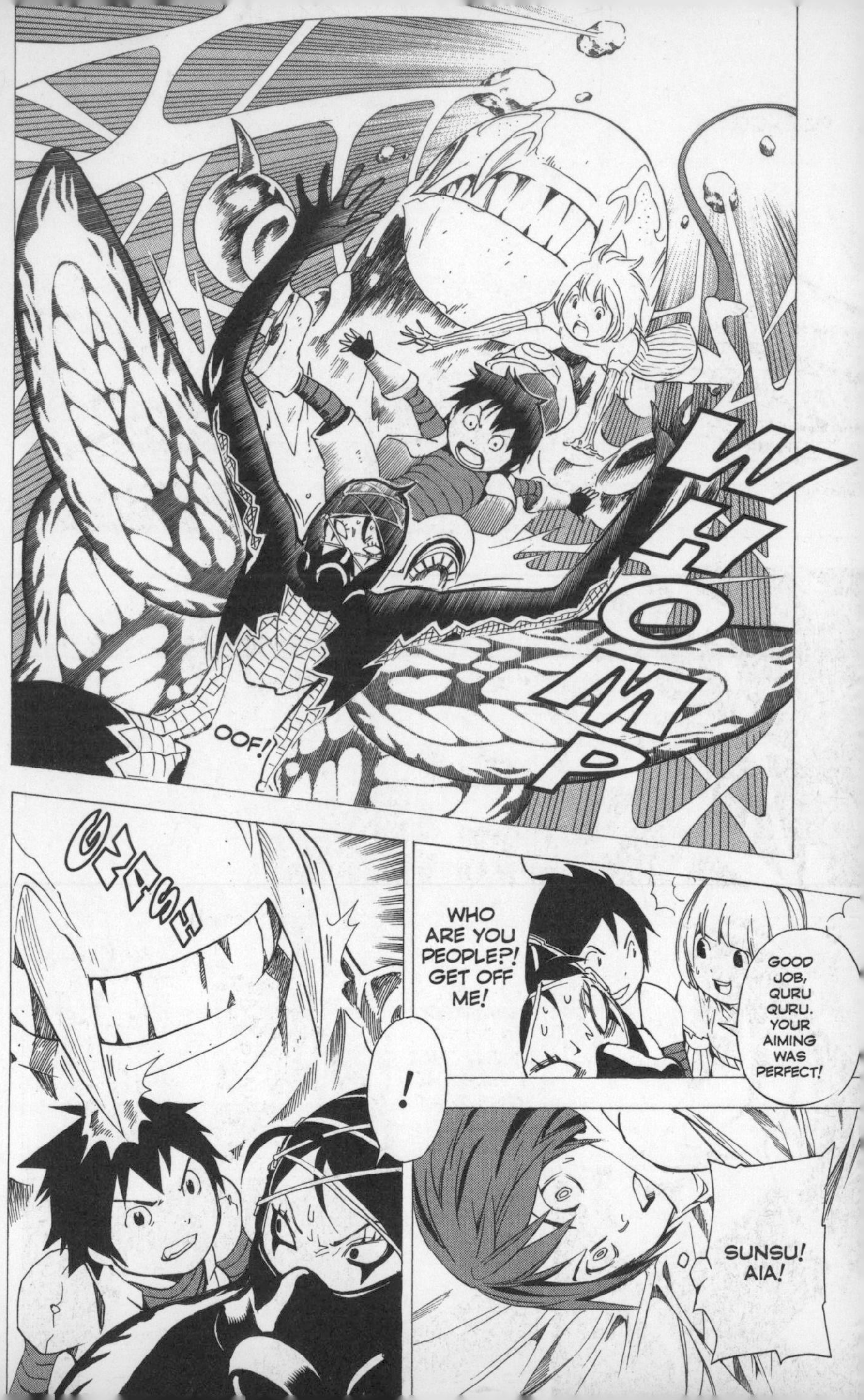
WHOMP
OOF!
GOOD JOB, QURU QURU. YOUR AIMING WAS PERFECT!
WHO ARE YOU PEOPLE?! GET OFF ME!
SUNSU! AIA!
GNASH
!

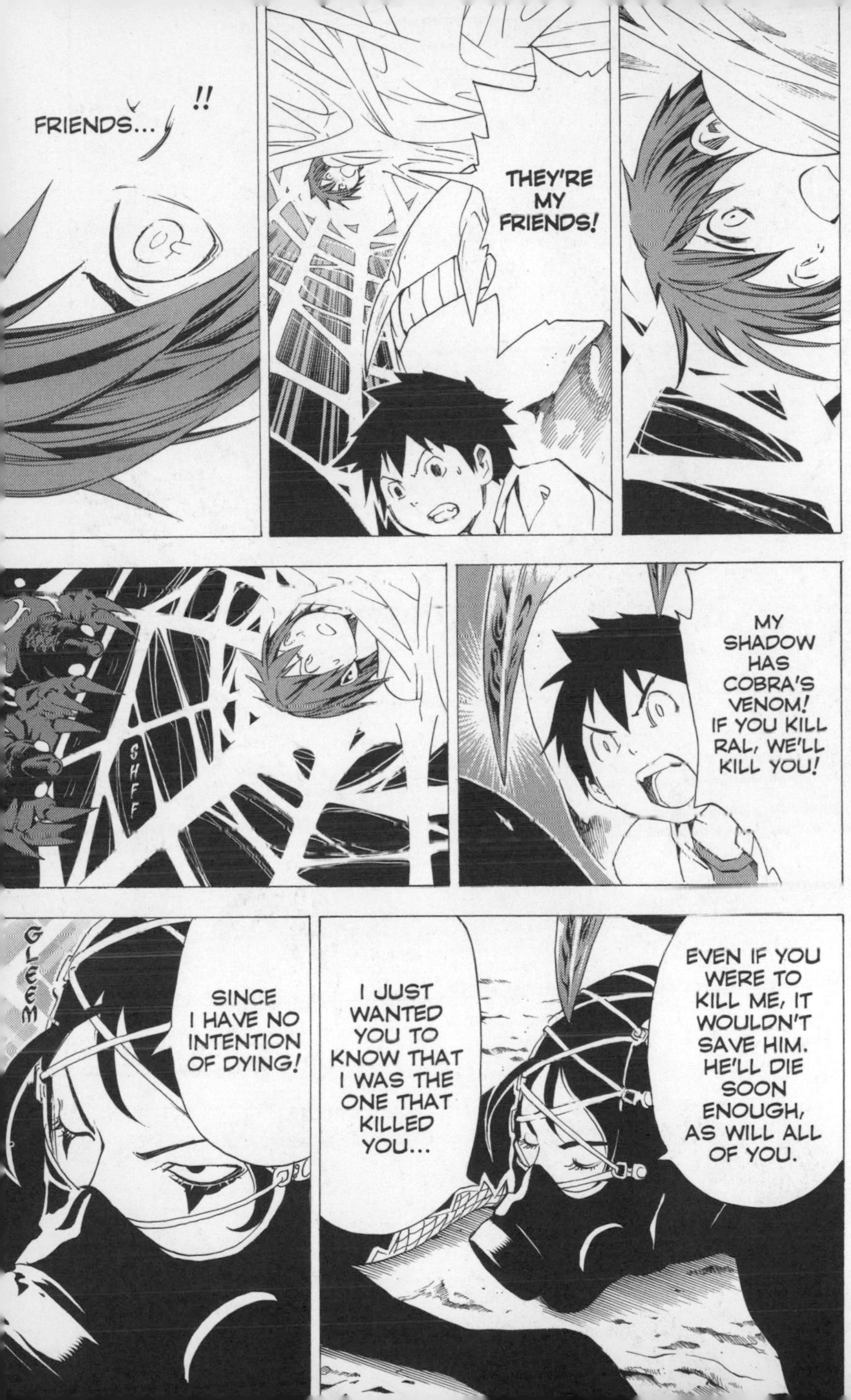
THEY'RE MY FRIENDS!
FRIENDS...
!!
MY SHADOW HAS COBRA'S VENOM! IF YOU KILL RAL, WE'LL KILL YOU!
SHFF
EVEN IF YOU WERE TO KILL ME, IT WOULDN'T SAVE HIM. HE'LL DIE SOON ENOUGH, AS WILL ALL OF YOU.
I JUST WANTED YOU TO KNOW THAT I WAS THE ONE THAT KILLED YOU...
GLEEM
SINCE I HAVE NO INTENTION OF DYING!

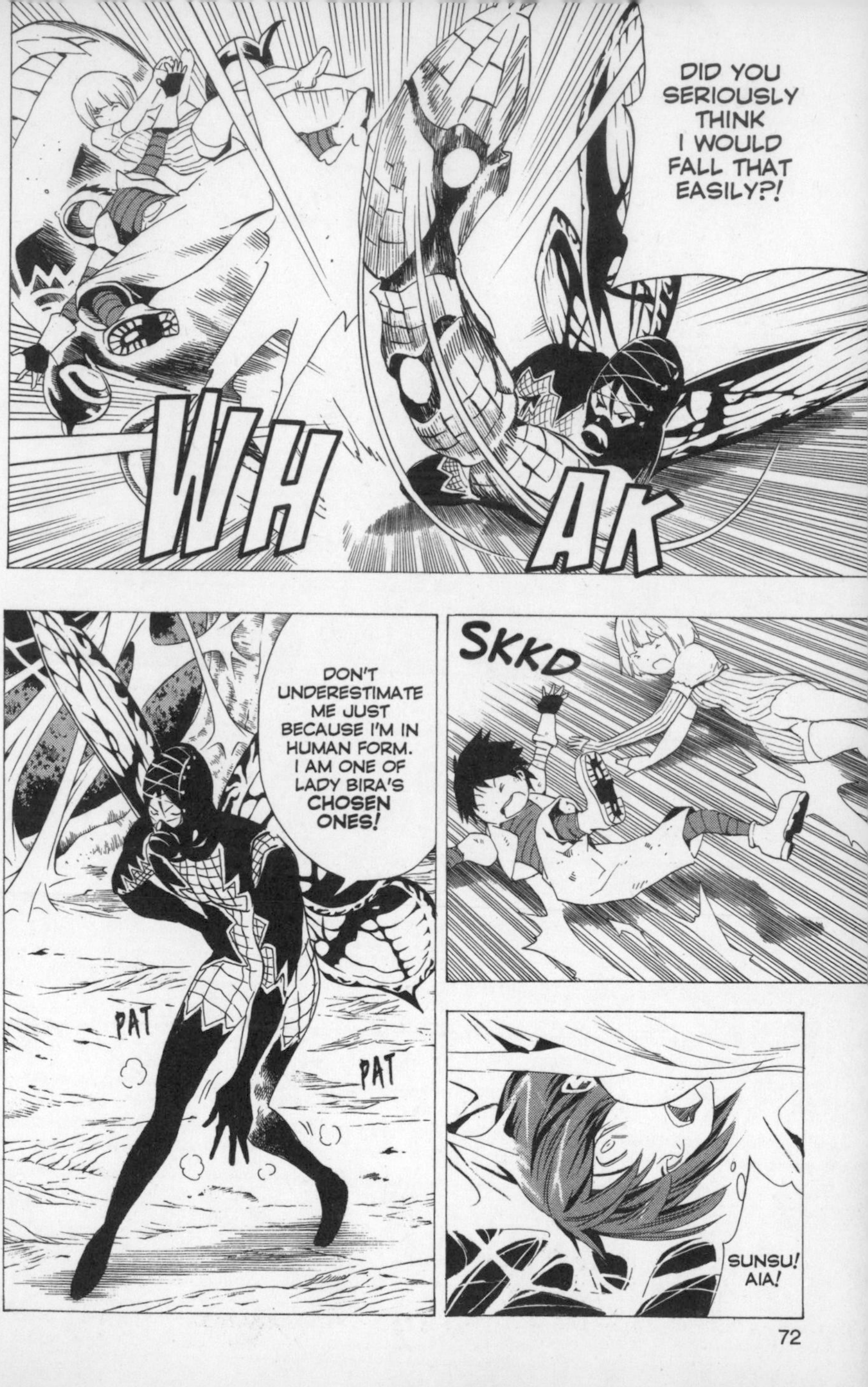
DID YOU SERIOUSLY THINK I WOULD FALL THAT EASILY?!
WHAK
SKKD
SUNSU! AIA!
DON'T UNDERESTIMATE ME JUST BECAUSE I'M IN HUMAN FORM. I AM ONE OF LADY BIRA'S CHOSEN ONES!
PAT
PAT

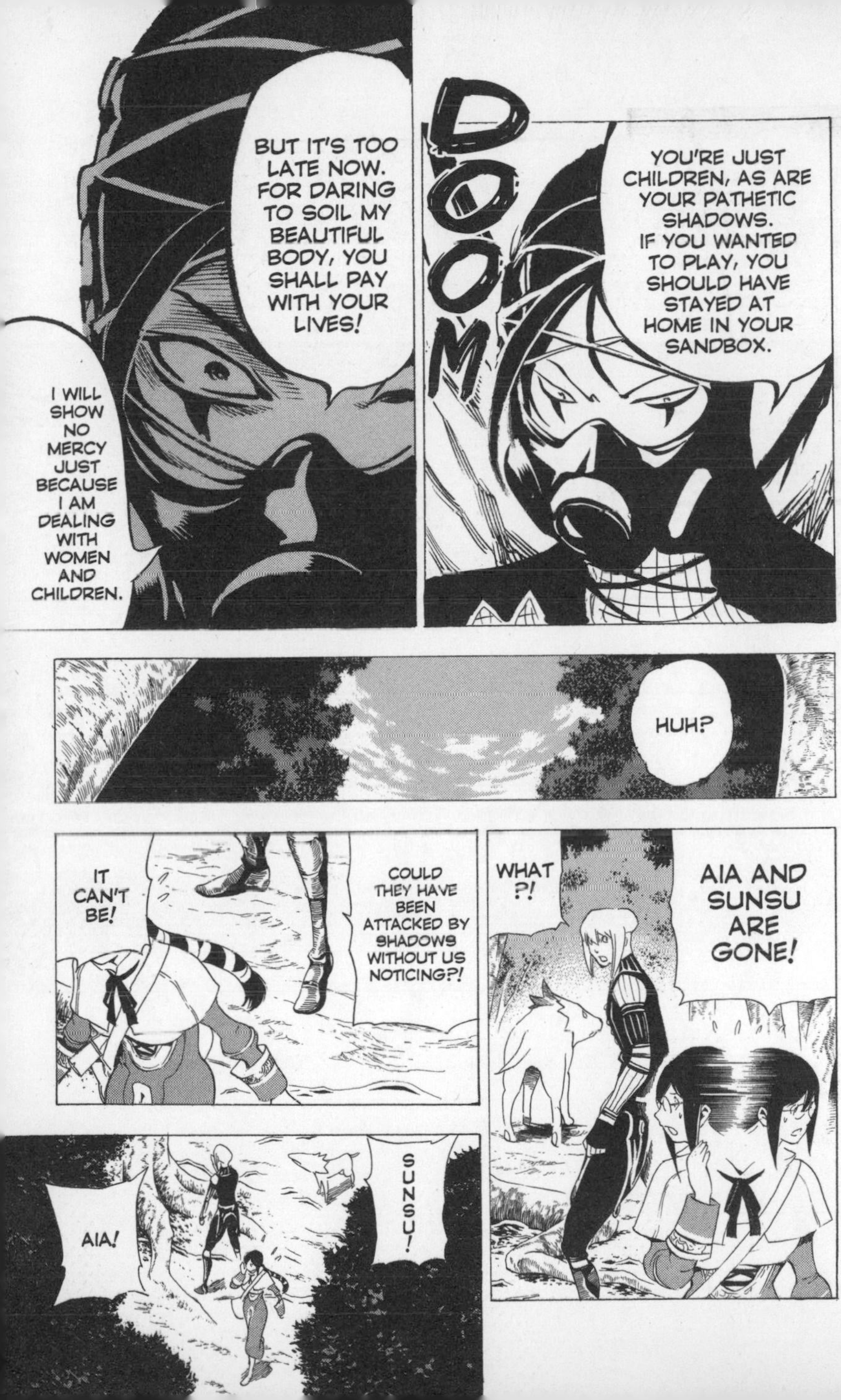
YOU'RE JUST CHILDREN, AS ARE YOUR PATHETIC SHADOWS. IF YOU WANTED TO PLAY, YOU SHOULD HAVE STAYED AT HOME IN YOUR SANDBOX.
DOOM
BUT IT'S TOO LATE NOW. FOR DARING TO SOIL MY BEAUTIFUL BODY, YOU SHALL PAY WITH YOUR LIVES!
I WILL SHOW NO MERCY JUST BECAUSE I AM DEALING WITH WOMEN AND CHILDREN.
HUH?
AIA AND SUNSU ARE GONE!
WHAT?!
COULD THEY HAVE BEEN ATTACKED BY SHADOWS WITHOUT US NOTICING?!
IT CAN'T BE!
SUNSU!
AIA!

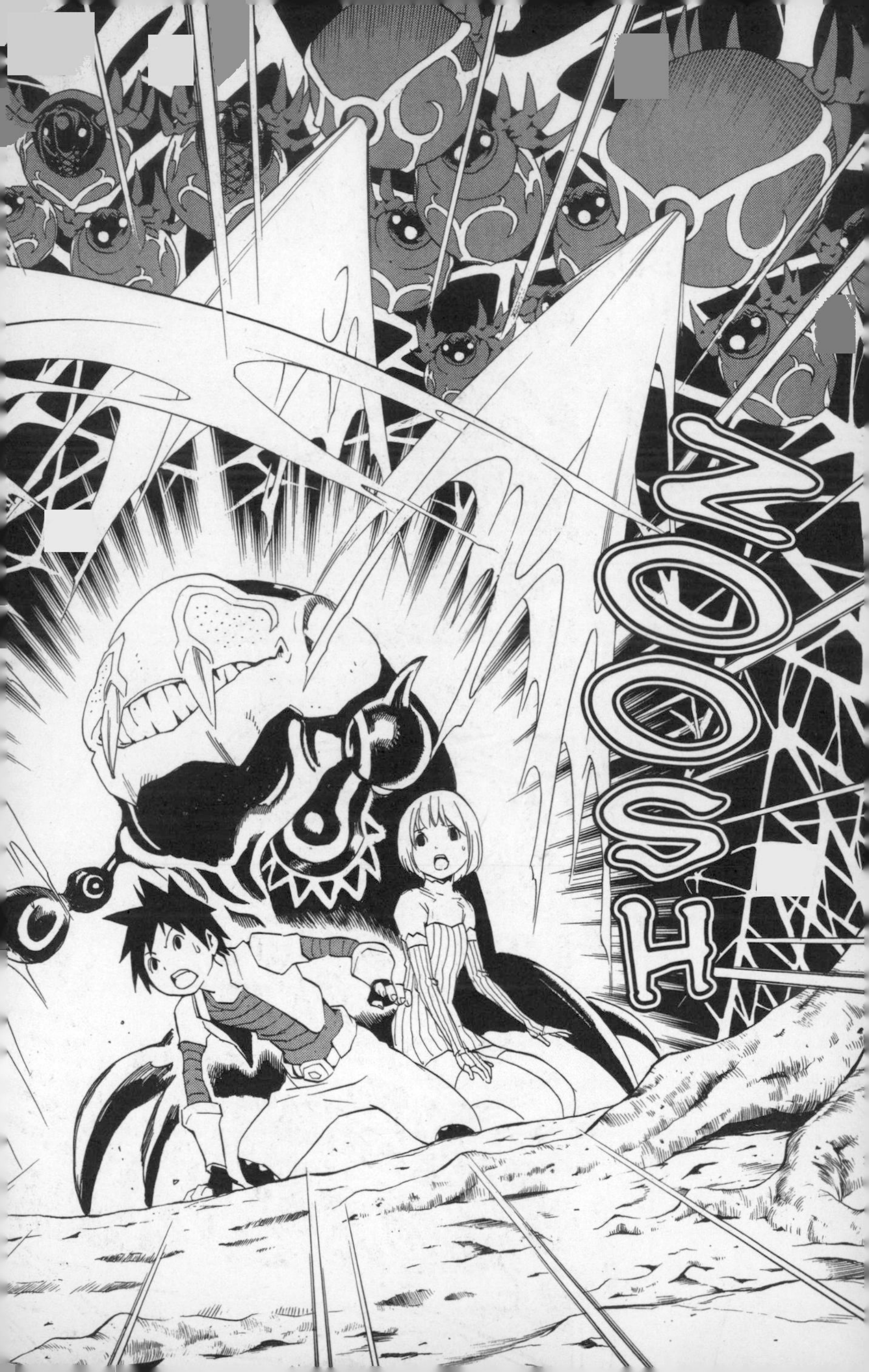
WOOSH

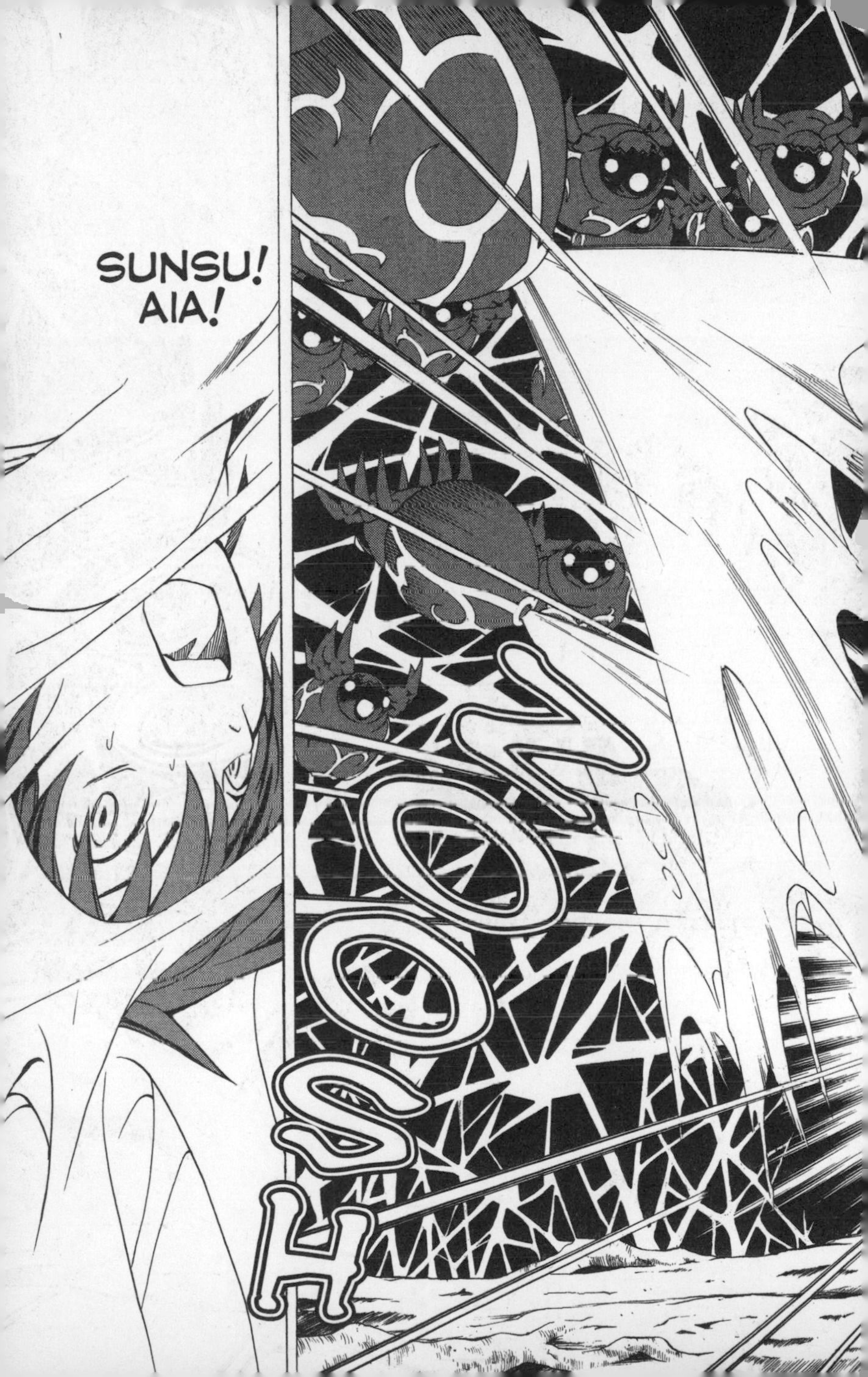
WOOSH
SUNSU! AIA!

RalΩGrad

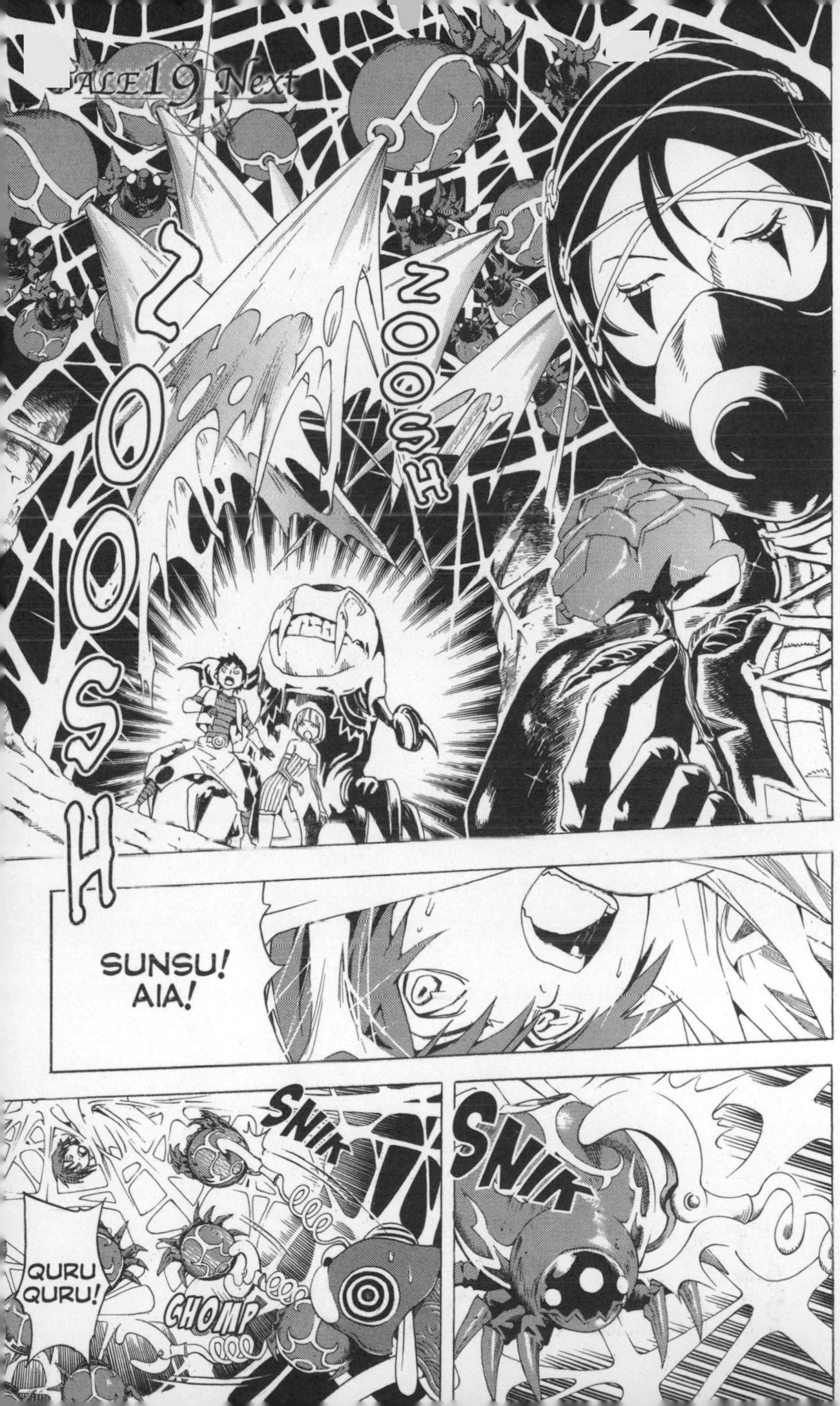
ALE 19 Next
ZOOSH
WHOOSH
SUNSU! AIA!
SNIK
SNIK
QURU QURU!
CHOMP

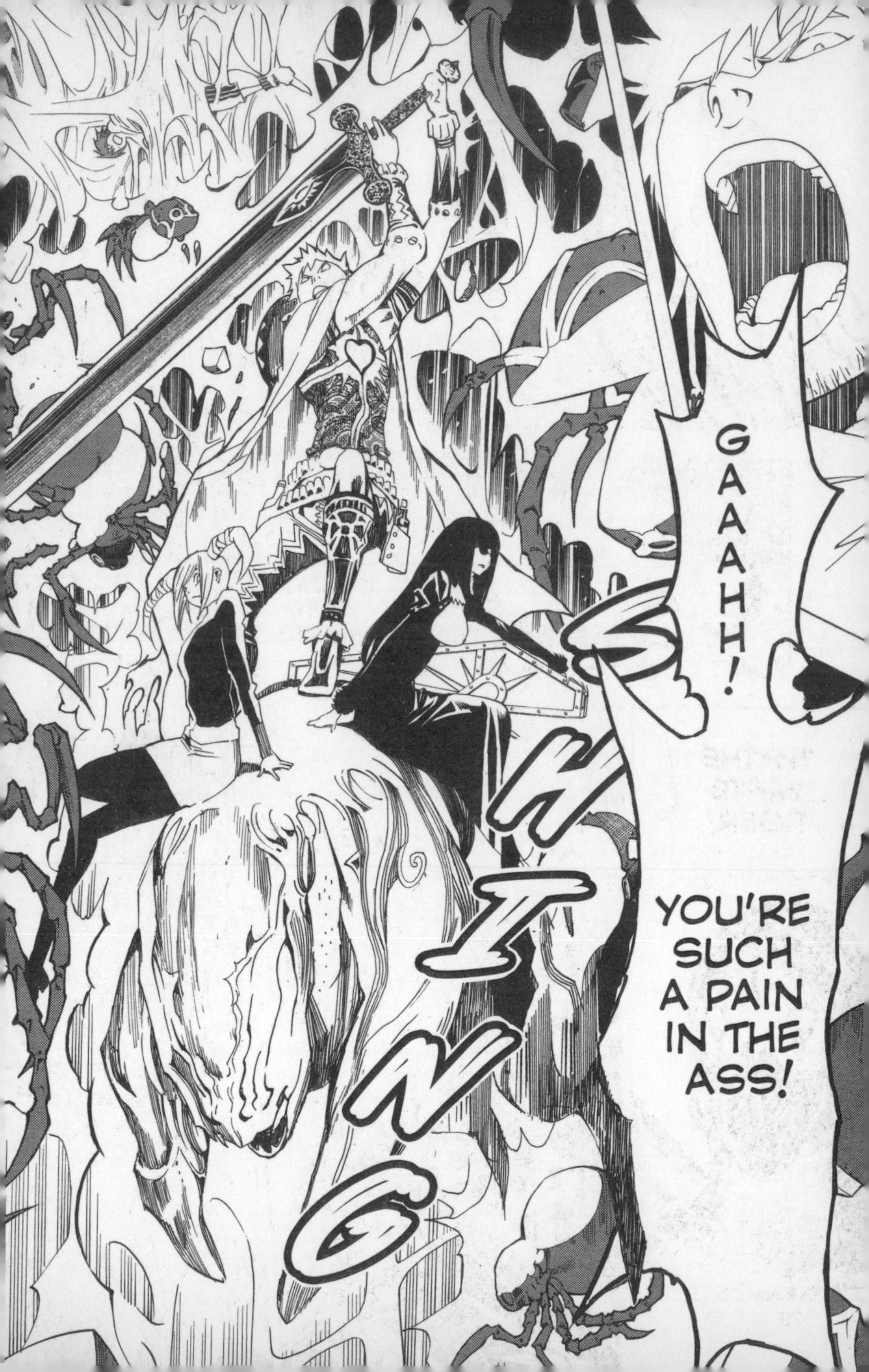
GAAAHH!
SHING
YOU'RE SUCH A PAIN IN THE ASS!

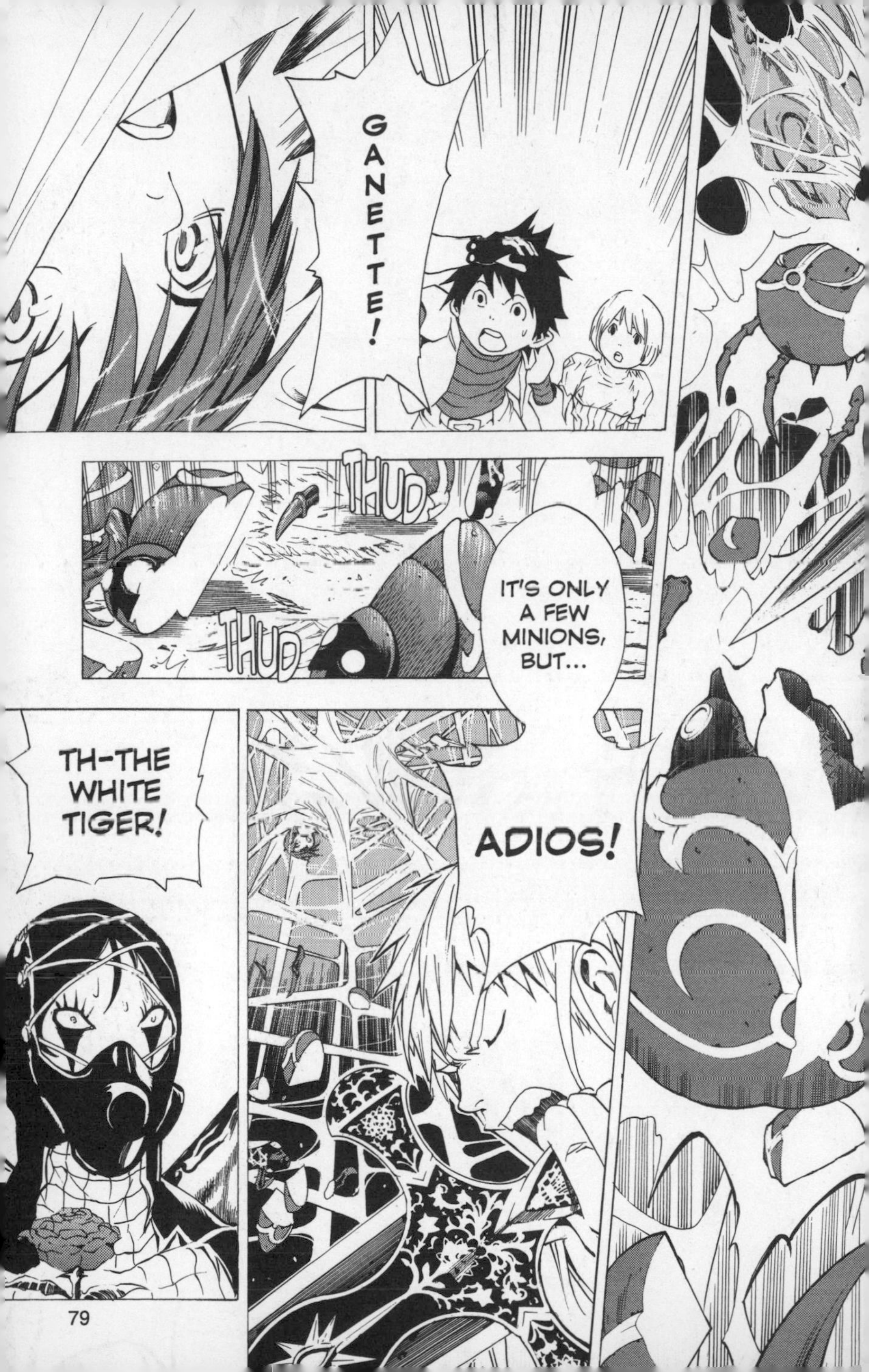
GANETTE!
THUD
THUD
IT'S ONLY A FEW MINIONS, BUT...
ADIOS!
TH-THE WHITE TIGER!

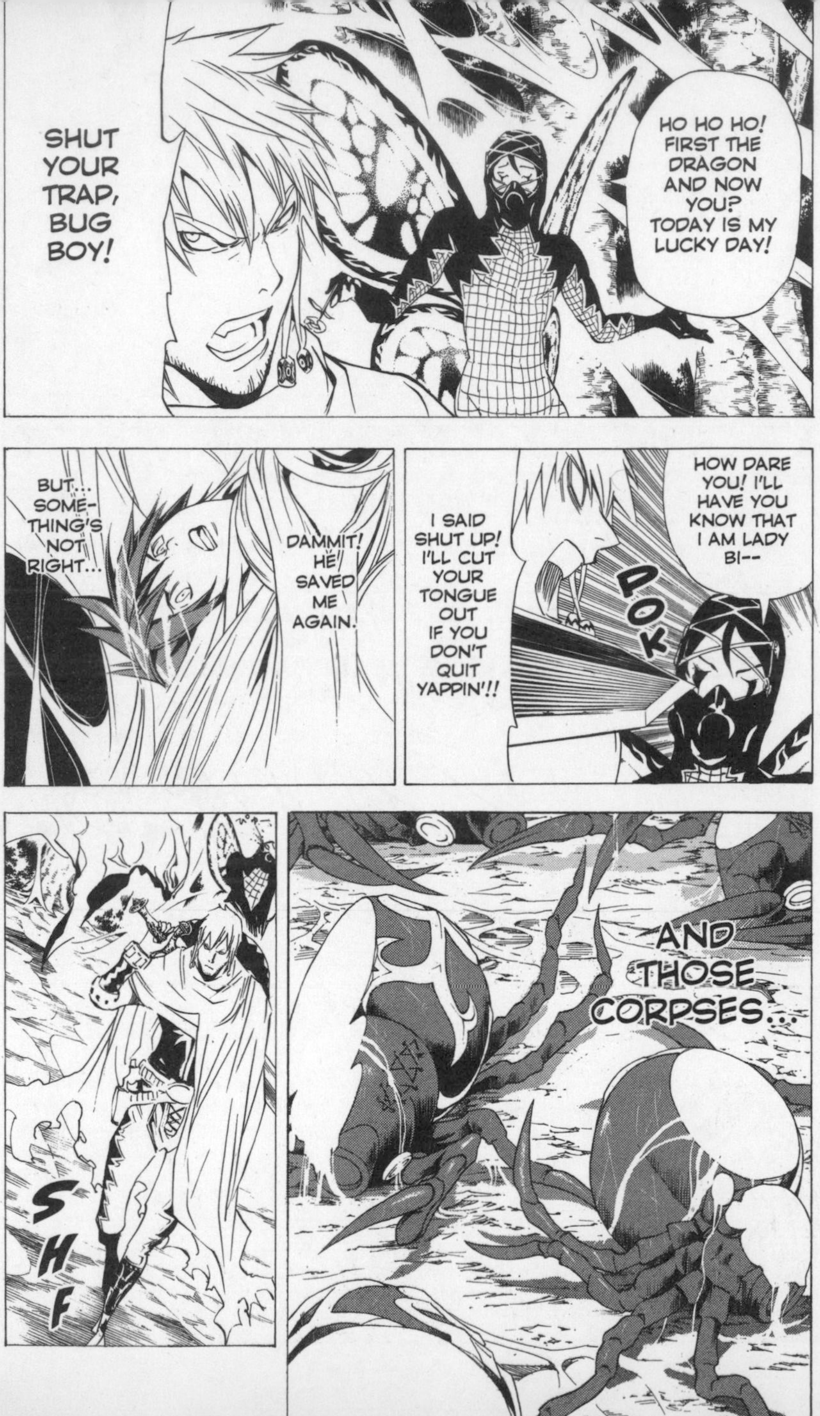
HO HO HO! FIRST THE DRAGON AND NOW YOU? TODAY IS MY LUCKY DAY!
SHUT YOUR TRAP, BUG BOY!
HOW DARE YOU! I'LL HAVE YOU KNOW THAT I AM LADY BI--
POK
I SAID SHUT UP! I'LL CUT YOUR TONGUE OUT IF YOU DON'T QUIT YAPPIN'!!
DAMMIT! HE SAVED ME AGAIN.
BUT... SOME-THING'S NOT RIGHT...
AND THOSE CORPSES...
SHF

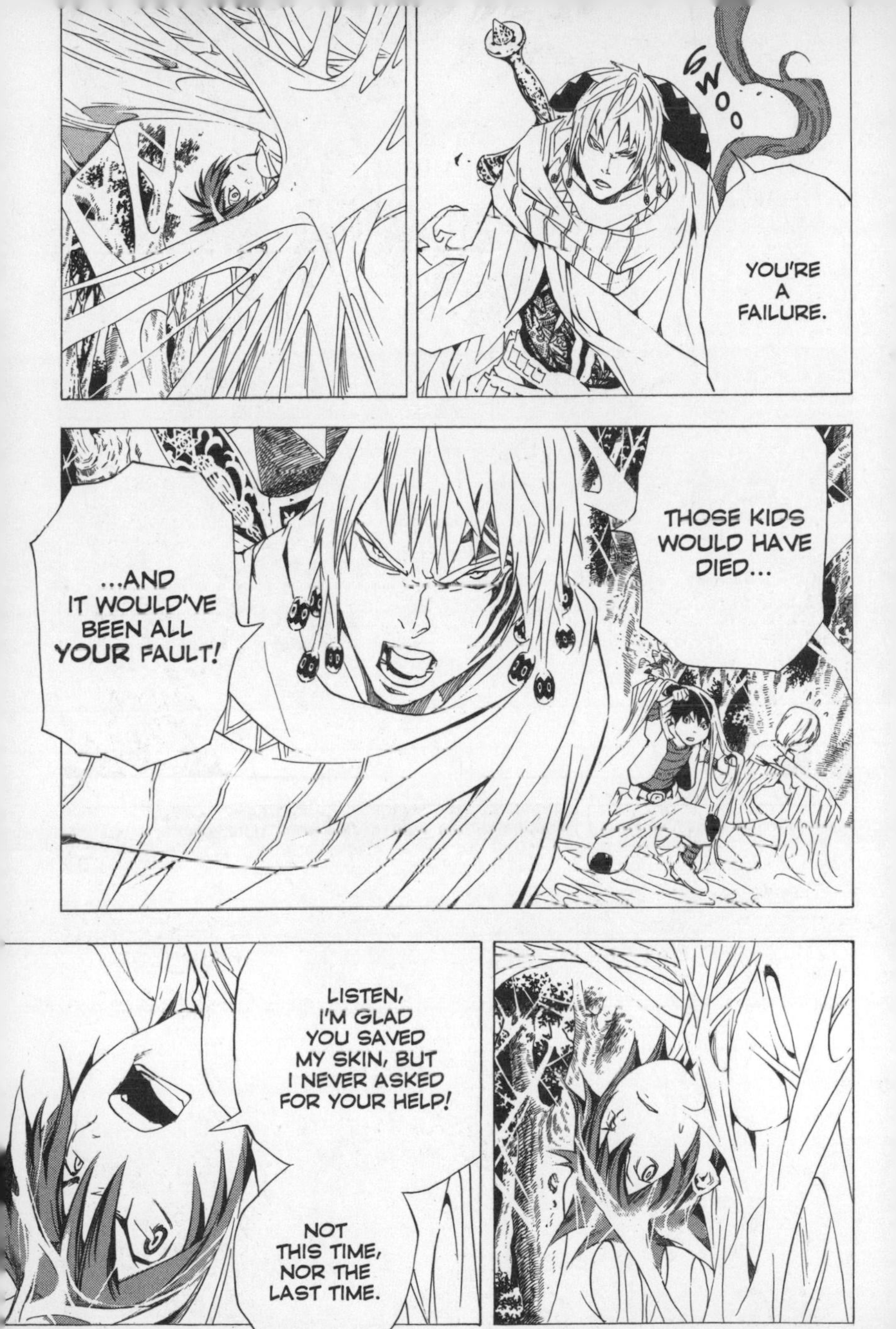
SWOO
YOU'RE A FAILURE.
THOSE KIDS WOULD HAVE DIED...
...AND IT WOULD'VE BEEN ALL YOUR FAULT!
LISTEN, I'M GLAD YOU SAVED MY SKIN, BUT I NEVER ASKED FOR YOUR HELP!
NOT THIS TIME, NOR THE LAST TIME.

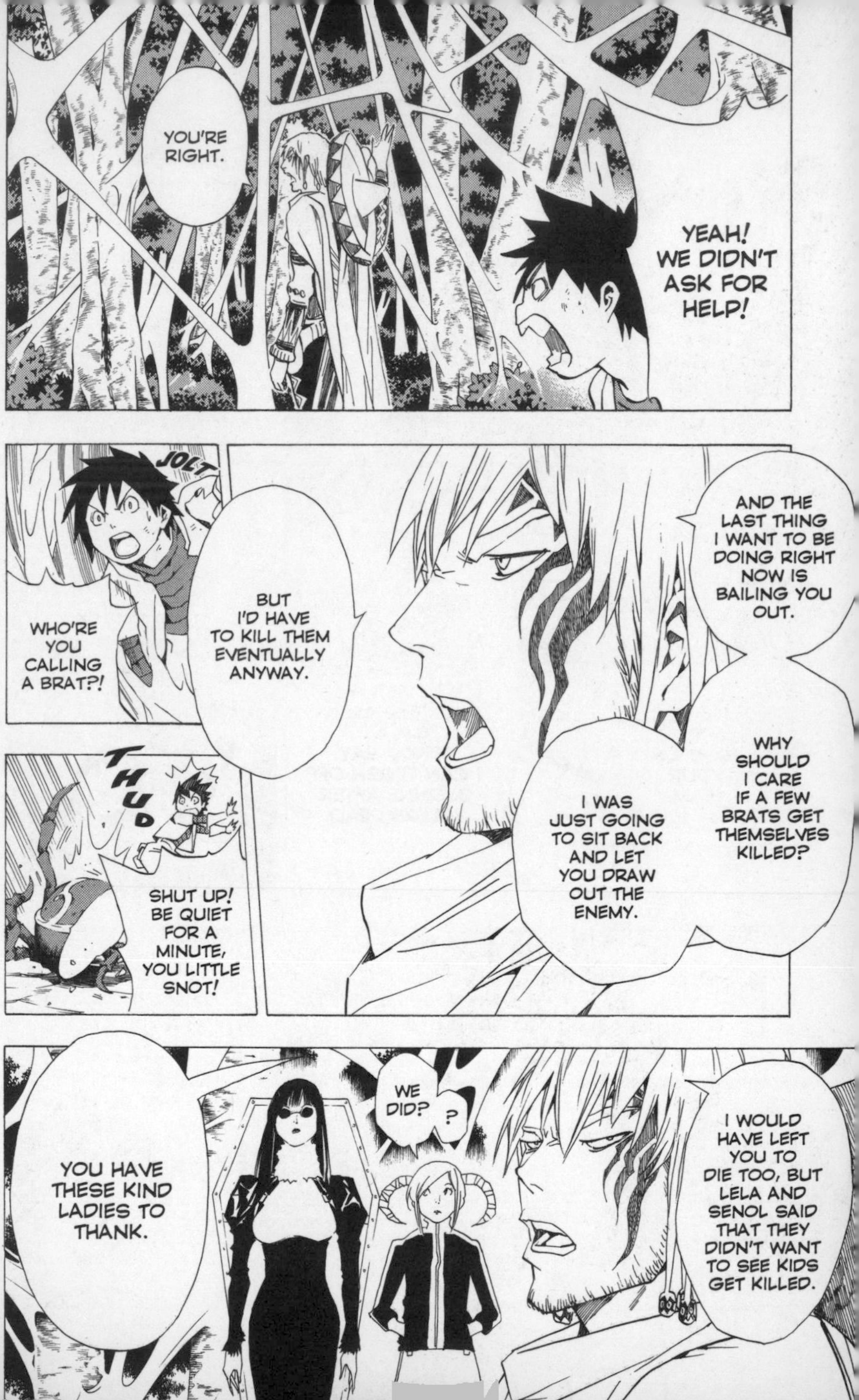
YEAH! WE DIDN'T ASK FOR HELP!
YOU'RE RIGHT.
AND THE LAST THING I WANT TO BE DOING RIGHT NOW IS BAILING YOU OUT.
WHY SHOULD I CARE IF A FEW BRATS GET THEMSELVES KILLED?
I WAS JUST GOING TO SIT BACK AND LET YOU DRAW OUT THE ENEMY.
BUT I'D HAVE TO KILL THEM EVENTUALLY ANYWAY.
JOLT
WHO'RE YOU CALLING A BRAT?!
THUD
SHUT UP! BE QUIET FOR A MINUTE, YOU LITTLE SNOT!
I WOULD HAVE LEFT YOU TO DIE TOO, BUT LELA AND SENOL SAID THAT THEY DIDN'T WANT TO SEE KIDS GET KILLED.
WE DID?
?
YOU HAVE THESE KIND LADIES TO THANK.

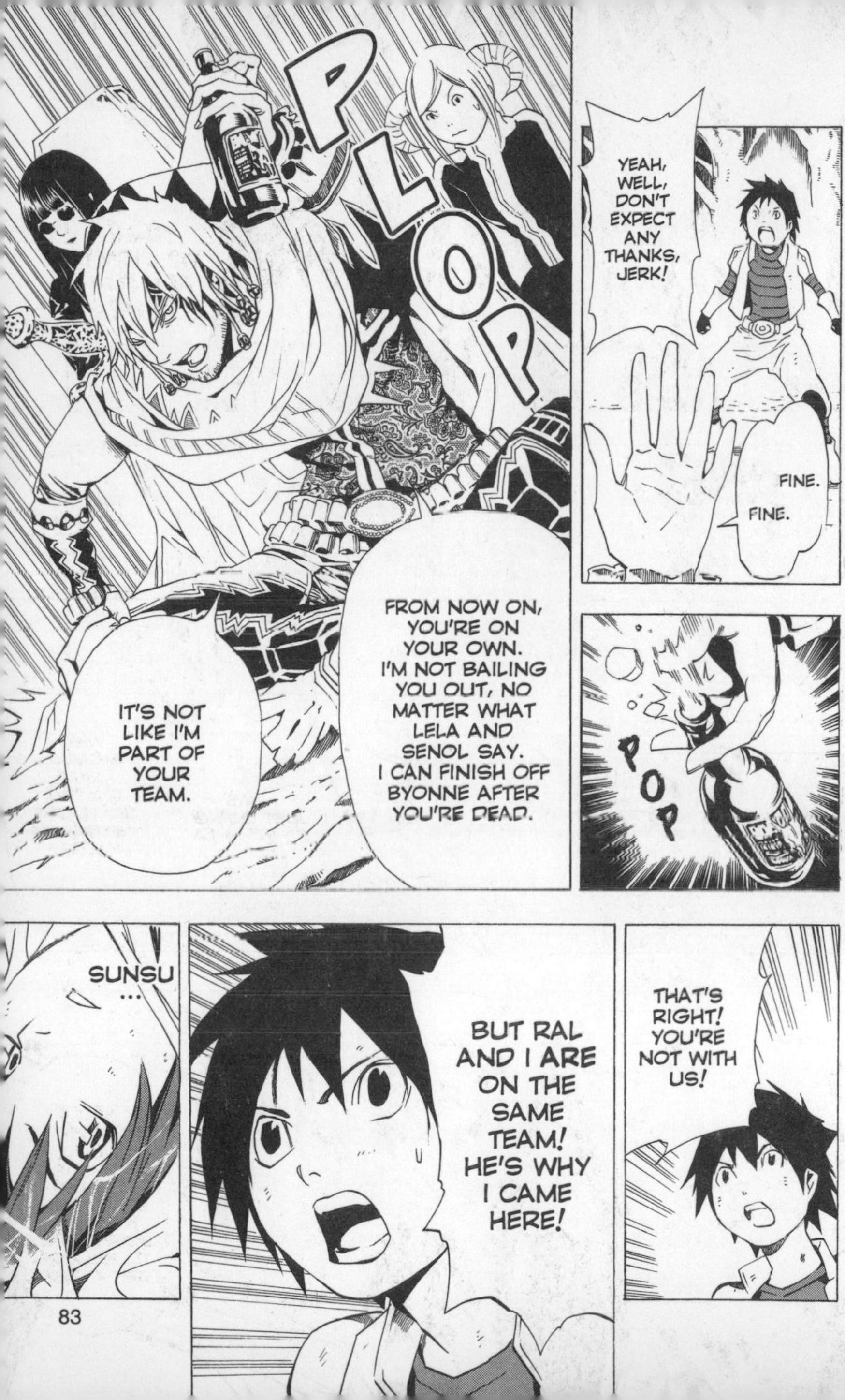
YEAH, WELL, DON'T EXPECT ANY THANKS, JERK!
FINE. FINE.
POP
PLOP
FROM NOW ON, YOU'RE ON YOUR OWN. I'M NOT BAILING YOU OUT, NO MATTER WHAT LELA AND SENOL SAY. I CAN FINISH OFF BYONNE AFTER YOU'RE DEAD.
IT'S NOT LIKE I'M PART OF YOUR TEAM.
THAT'S RIGHT! YOU'RE NOT WITH US!
BUT RAL AND I ARE ON THE SAME TEAM! HE'S WHY I CAME HERE!
SUNSU ...

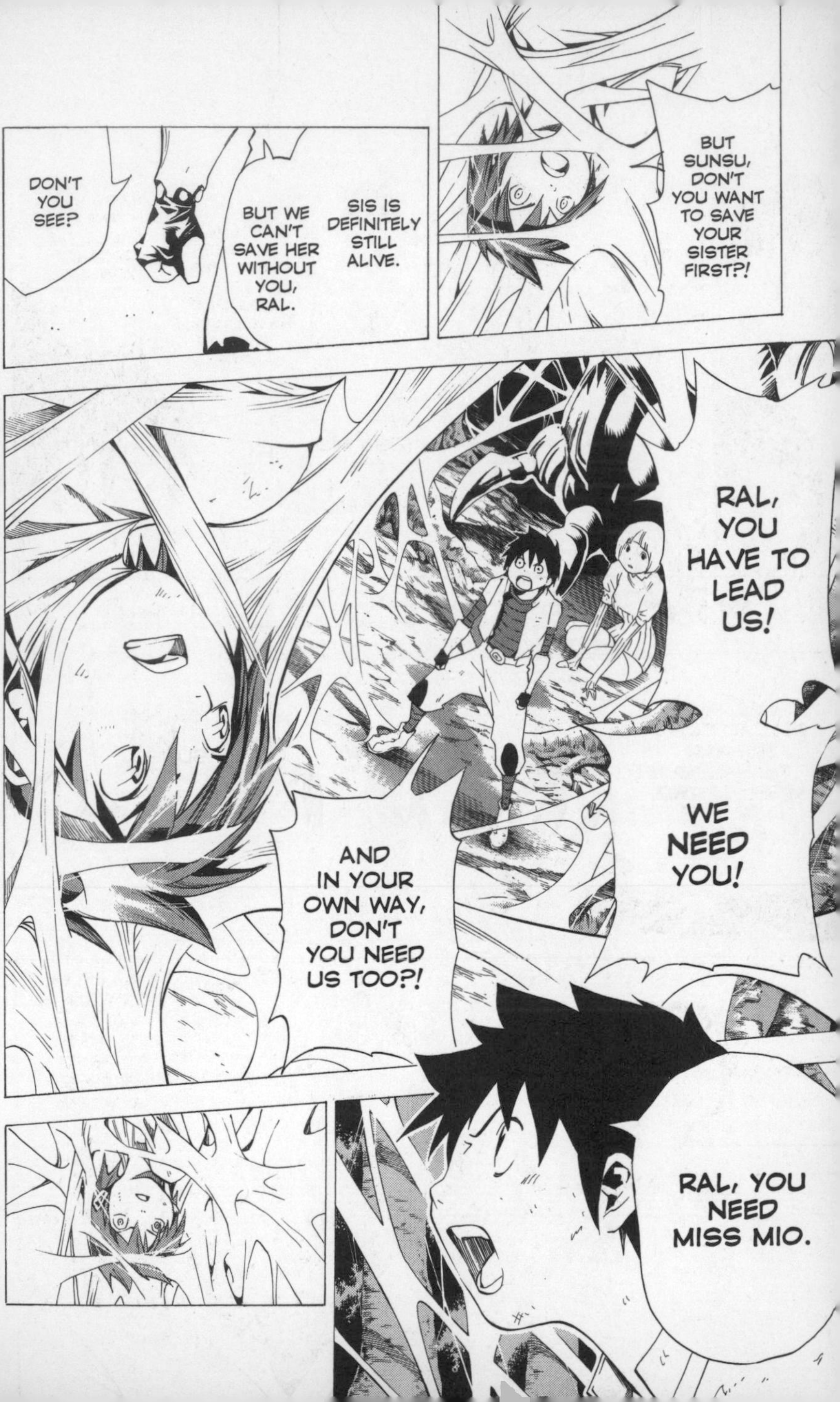
BUT SUNSU, DON'T YOU WANT TO SAVE YOUR SISTER FIRST?!
SIS IS DEFINITELY STILL ALIVE.
BUT WE CAN'T SAVE HER WITHOUT YOU, RAL.
DON'T YOU SEE?
RAL, YOU HAVE TO LEAD US!
WE NEED YOU!
AND IN YOUR OWN WAY, DON'T YOU NEED US TOO?!
RAL, YOU NEED MISS MIO.

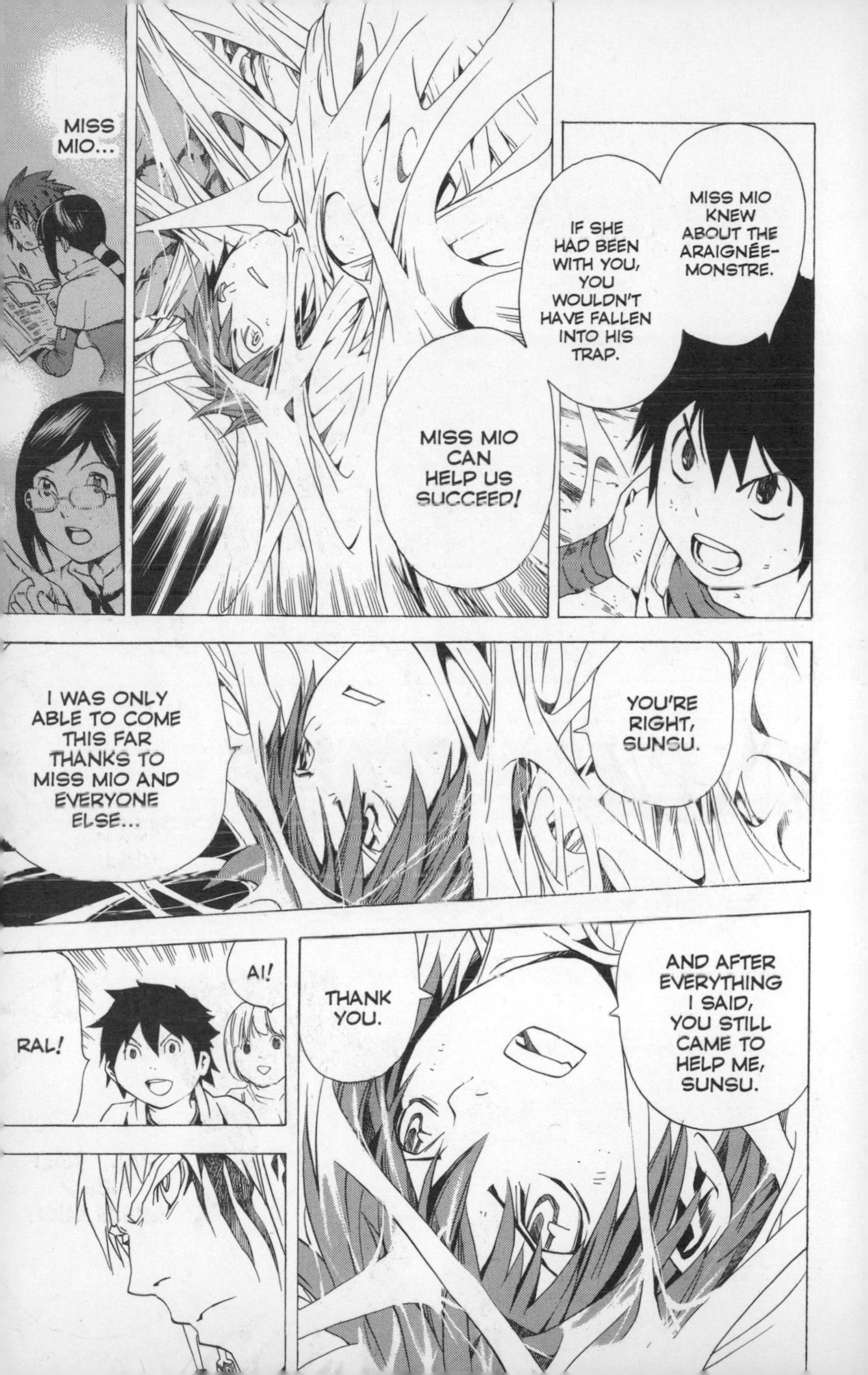
MISS MIO KNEW ABOUT THE ARAIGNÉE-MONSTRE.
IF SHE HAD BEEN WITH YOU, YOU WOULDN'T HAVE FALLEN INTO HIS TRAP.
MISS MIO CAN HELP US SUCCEED!
MISS MIO...
YOU'RE RIGHT, SUNSU.
I WAS ONLY ABLE TO COME THIS FAR THANKS TO MISS MIO AND EVERYONE ELSE...
AND AFTER EVERYTHING I SAID, YOU STILL CAME TO HELP ME, SUNSU.
THANK YOU.
AI!
RAL!

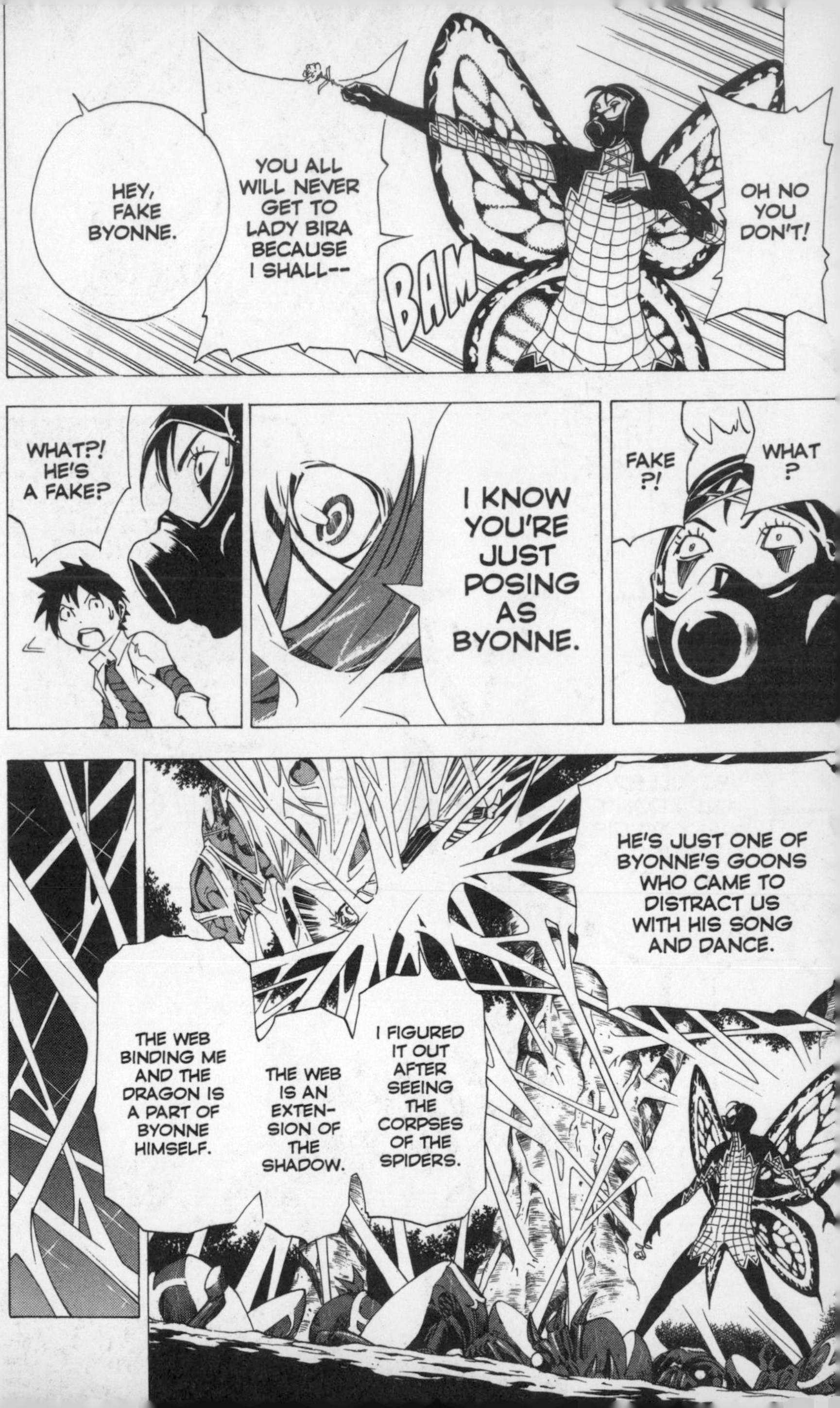
OH NO YOU DON'T!
BAM
YOU ALL WILL NEVER GET TO LADY BIRA BECAUSE I SHALL--
HEY, FAKE BYONNE.
WHAT ?
FAKE ?!
I KNOW YOU'RE JUST POSING AS BYONNE.
WHAT?! HE'S A FAKE?
HE'S JUST ONE OF BYONNE'S GOONS WHO CAME TO DISTRACT US WITH HIS SONG AND DANCE.
I FIGURED IT OUT AFTER SEEING THE CORPSES OF THE SPIDERS.
THE WEB IS AN EXTEN-SION OF THE SHADOW.
THE WEB BINDING ME AND THE DRAGON IS A PART OF BYONNE HIMSELF.

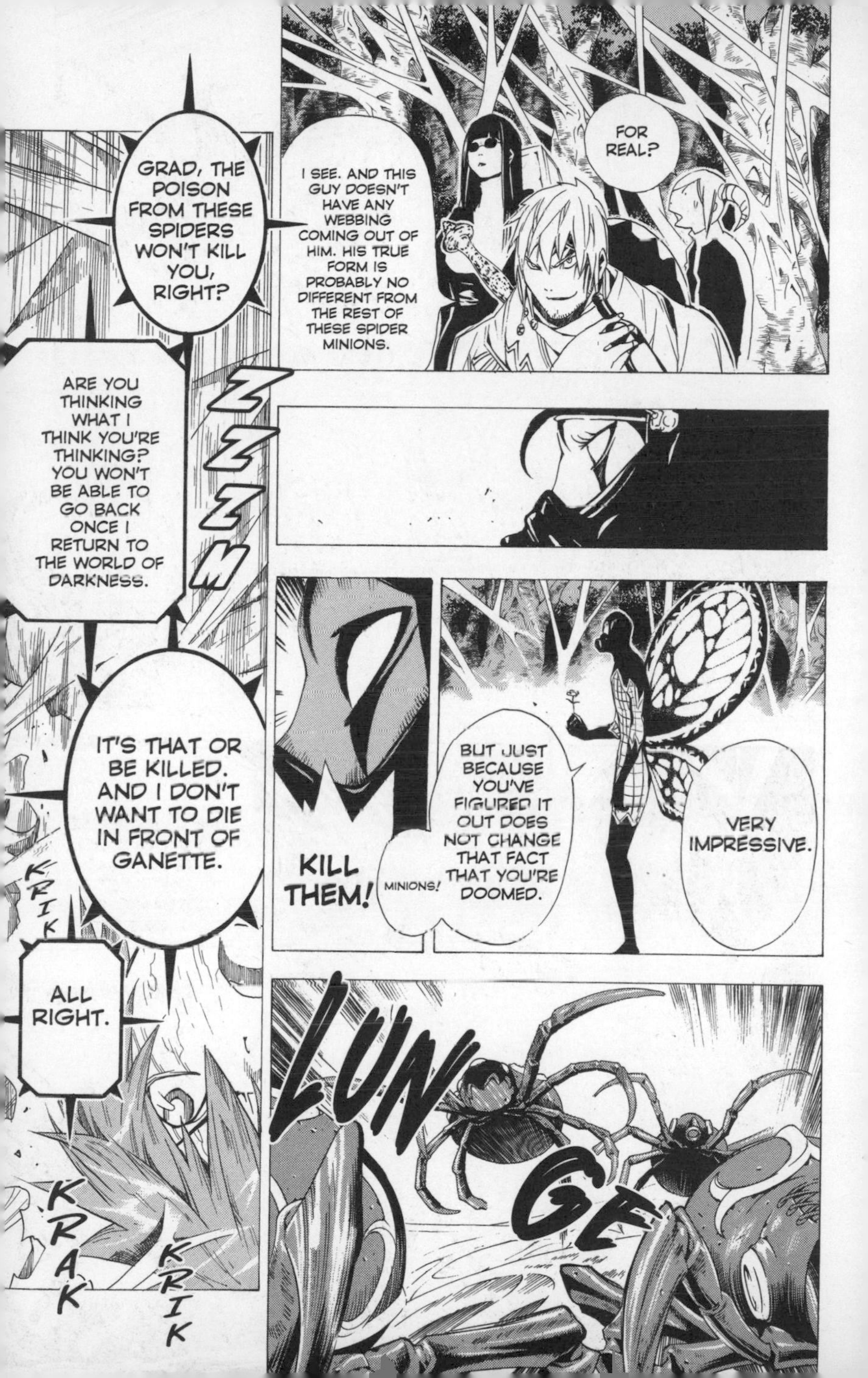
FOR REAL?
I SEE. AND THIS GUY DOESN'T HAVE ANY WEBBING COMING OUT OF HIM. HIS TRUE FORM IS PROBABLY NO DIFFERENT FROM THE REST OF THESE SPIDER MINIONS.
VERY IMPRESSIVE.
BUT JUST BECAUSE YOU'VE FIGURED IT OUT DOES NOT CHANGE THAT FACT THAT YOU'RE DOOMED.
MINIONS!
KILL THEM!
LUNGE
GRAD, THE POISON FROM THESE SPIDERS WON'T KILL YOU, RIGHT?
ZZZM
ARE YOU THINKING WHAT I THINK YOU'RE THINKING? YOU WON'T BE ABLE TO GO BACK ONCE I RETURN TO THE WORLD OF DARKNESS.
IT'S THAT OR BE KILLED. AND I DON'T WANT TO DIE IN FRONT OF GANETTE.
KRIK
ALL RIGHT.
KRAK
KRIK

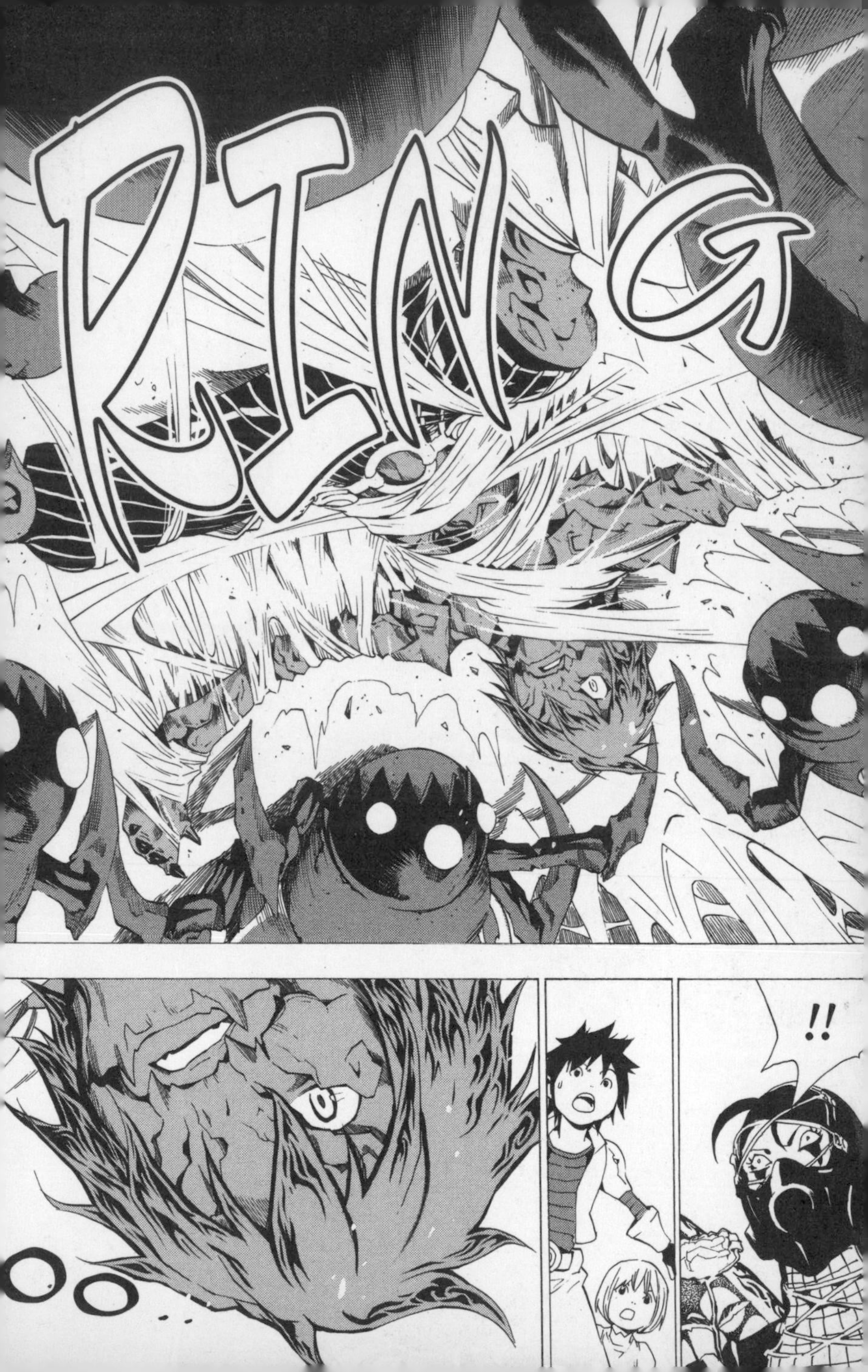
RING
!!
OO...

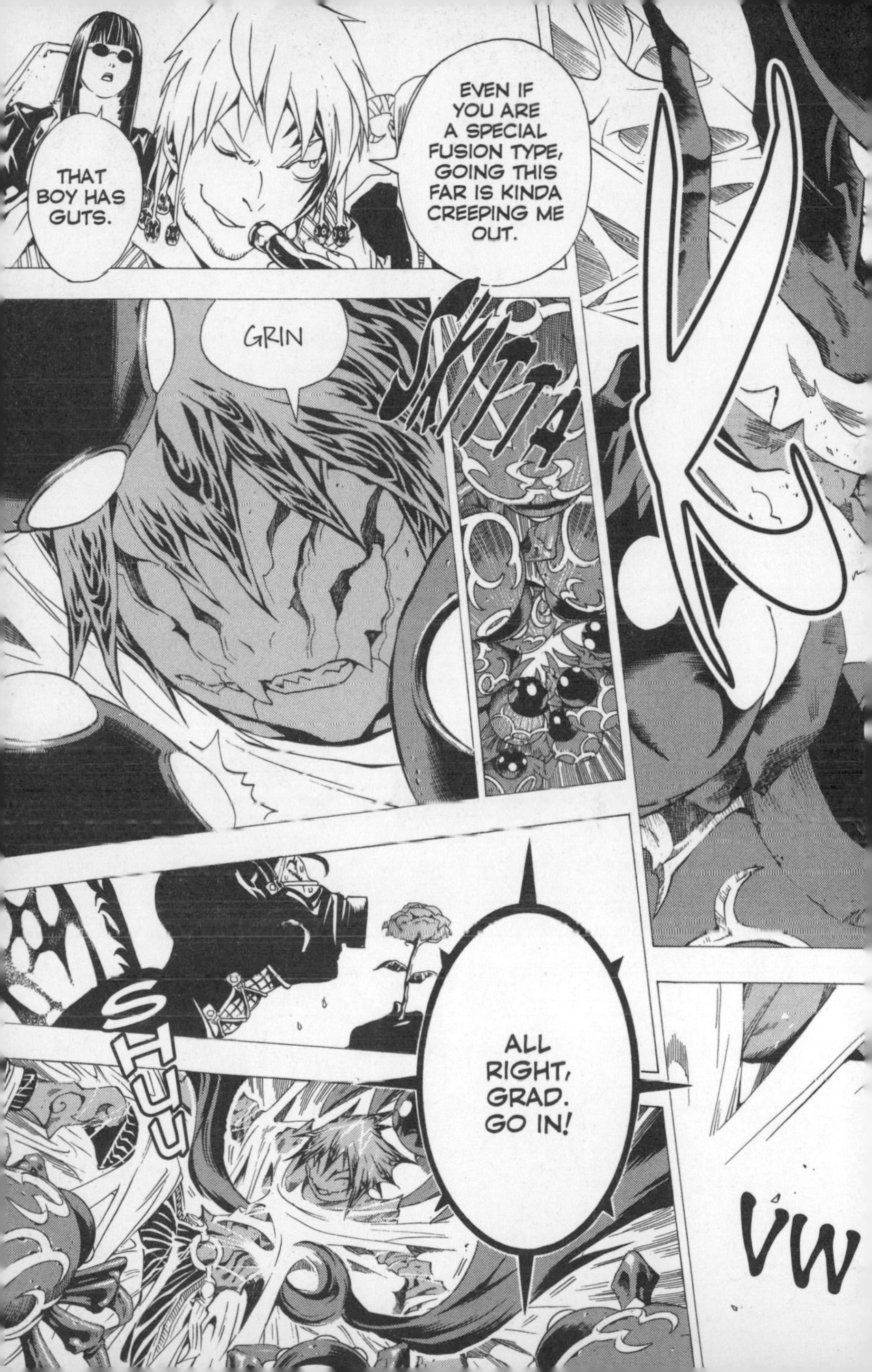
EVEN IF YOU ARE A SPECIAL FUSION TYPE, GOING THIS FAR IS KINDA CREEPING ME OUT.
THAT BOY HAS GUTS.
SHATA
GRIN
VW
ALL RIGHT, GRAD. GO IN!
SHUUU

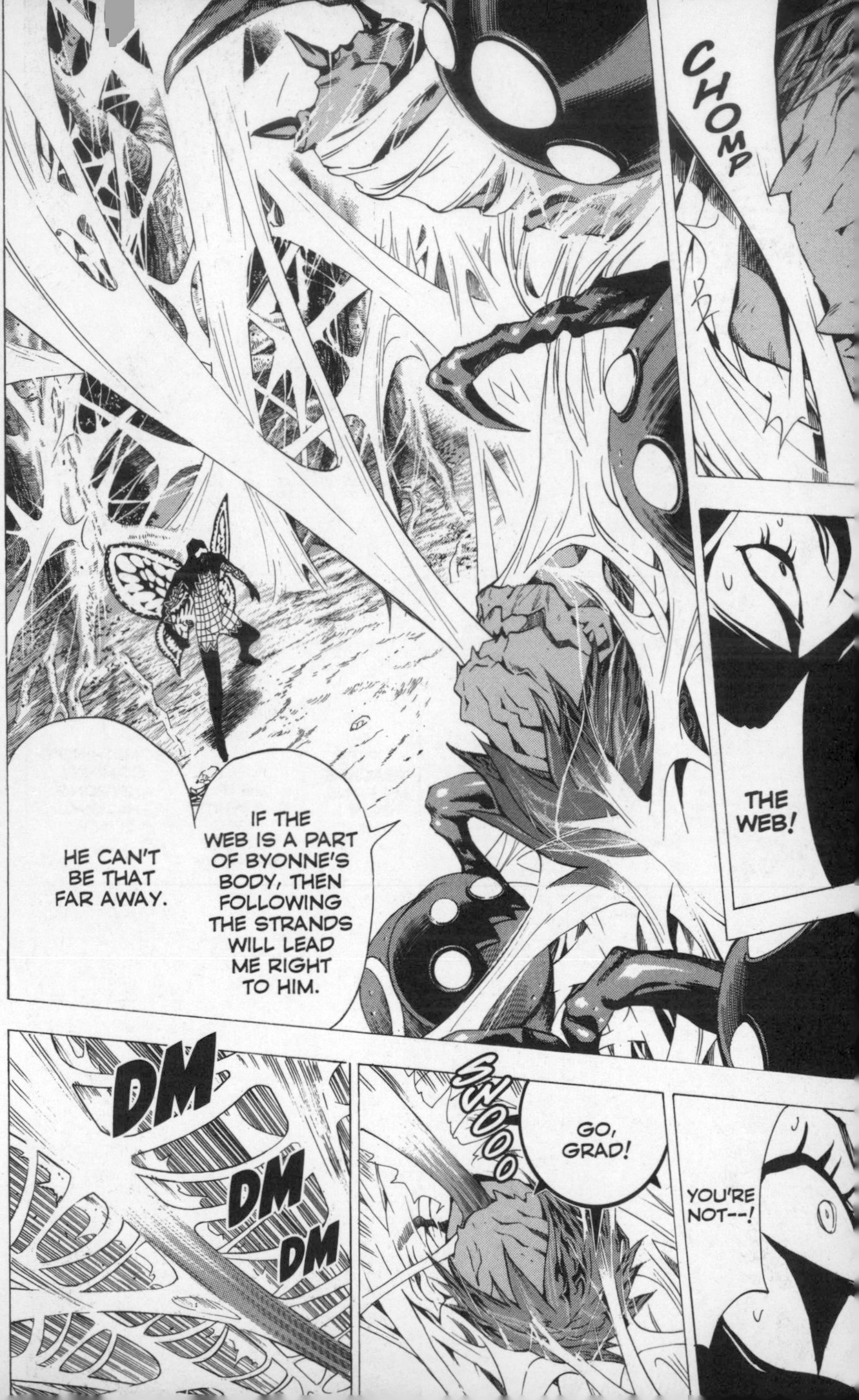
CHOMP
THE WEB!
IF THE WEB IS A PART OF BYONNE'S BODY, THEN FOLLOWING THE STRANDS WILL LEAD ME RIGHT TO HIM.
HE CAN'T BE THAT FAR AWAY.
YOU'RE NOT--!
SWOOO
GO, GRAD!
DM
DM
DM

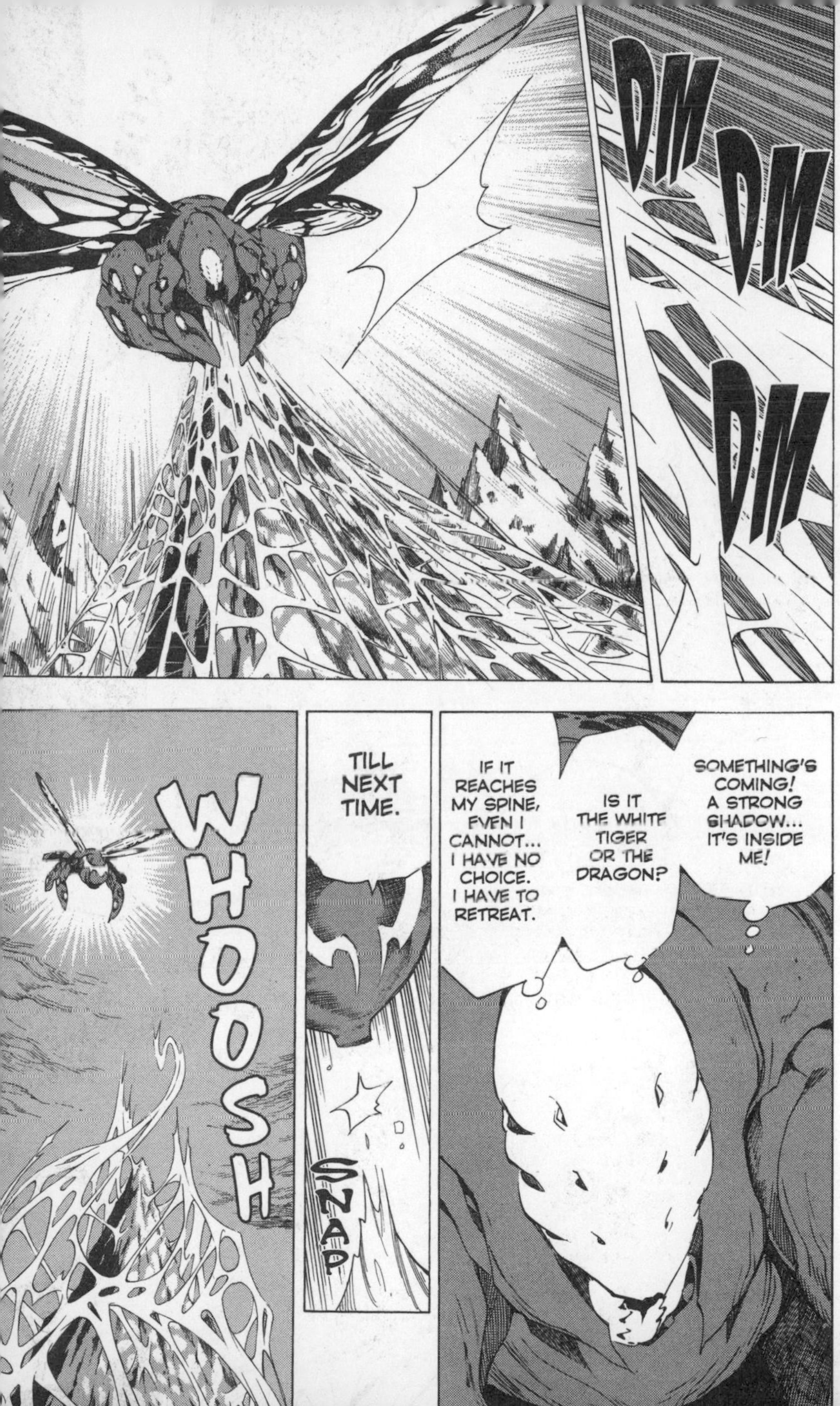
DM
DM
DM
SOMETHING'S COMING! A STRONG SHADOW... IT'S INSIDE ME!
IS IT THE WHITE TIGER OR THE DRAGON?
IF IT REACHES MY SPINE, EVEN I CANNOT... I HAVE NO CHOICE. I HAVE TO RETREAT.
TILL NEXT TIME.
SNAP
WHOOSH

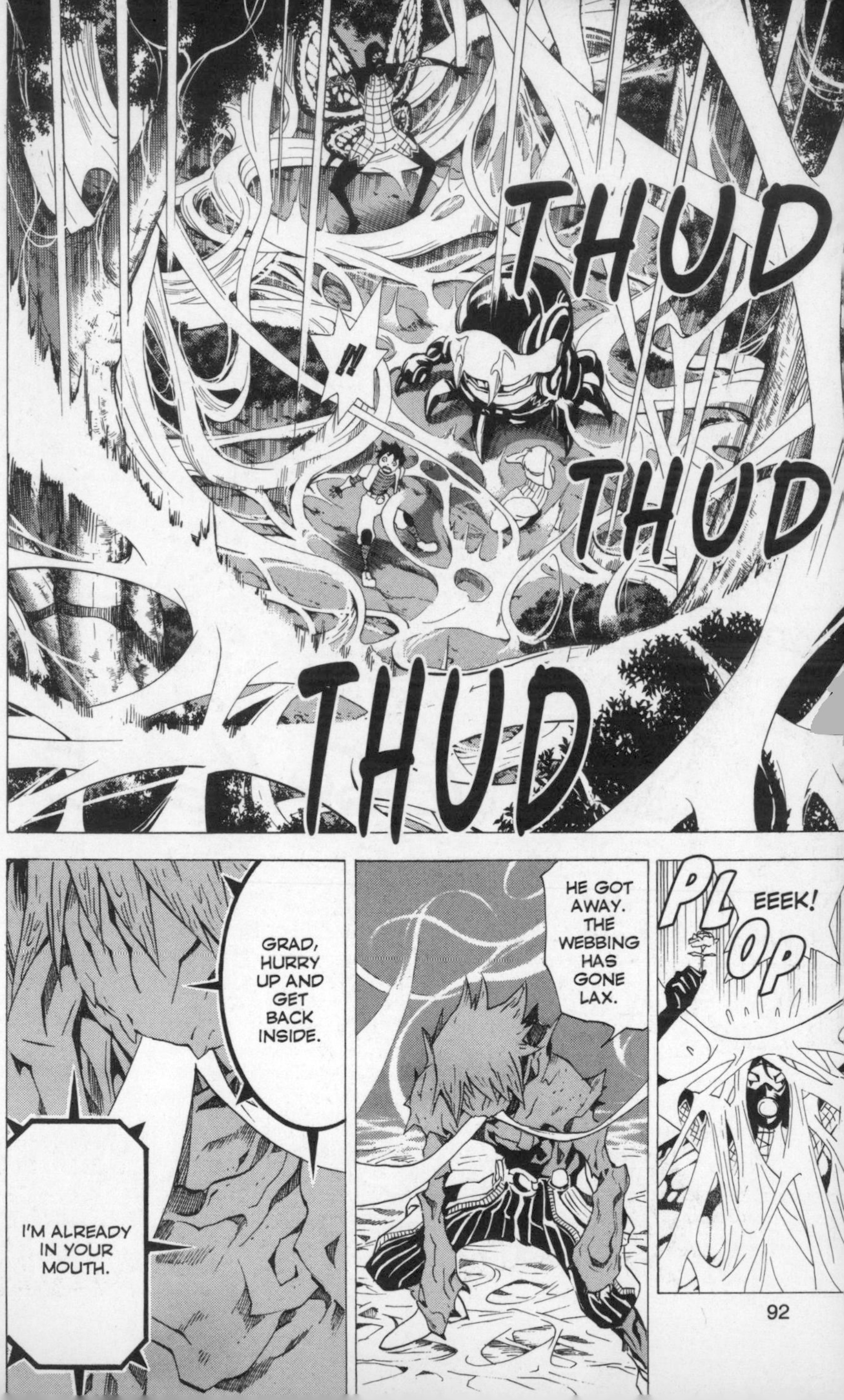

!!
THUD
THUD
THUD
PLOP
EEEK!
HE GOT AWAY. THE WEBBING HAS GONE LAX.
GRAD, HURRY UP AND GET BACK INSIDE.
I'M ALREADY IN YOUR MOUTH.

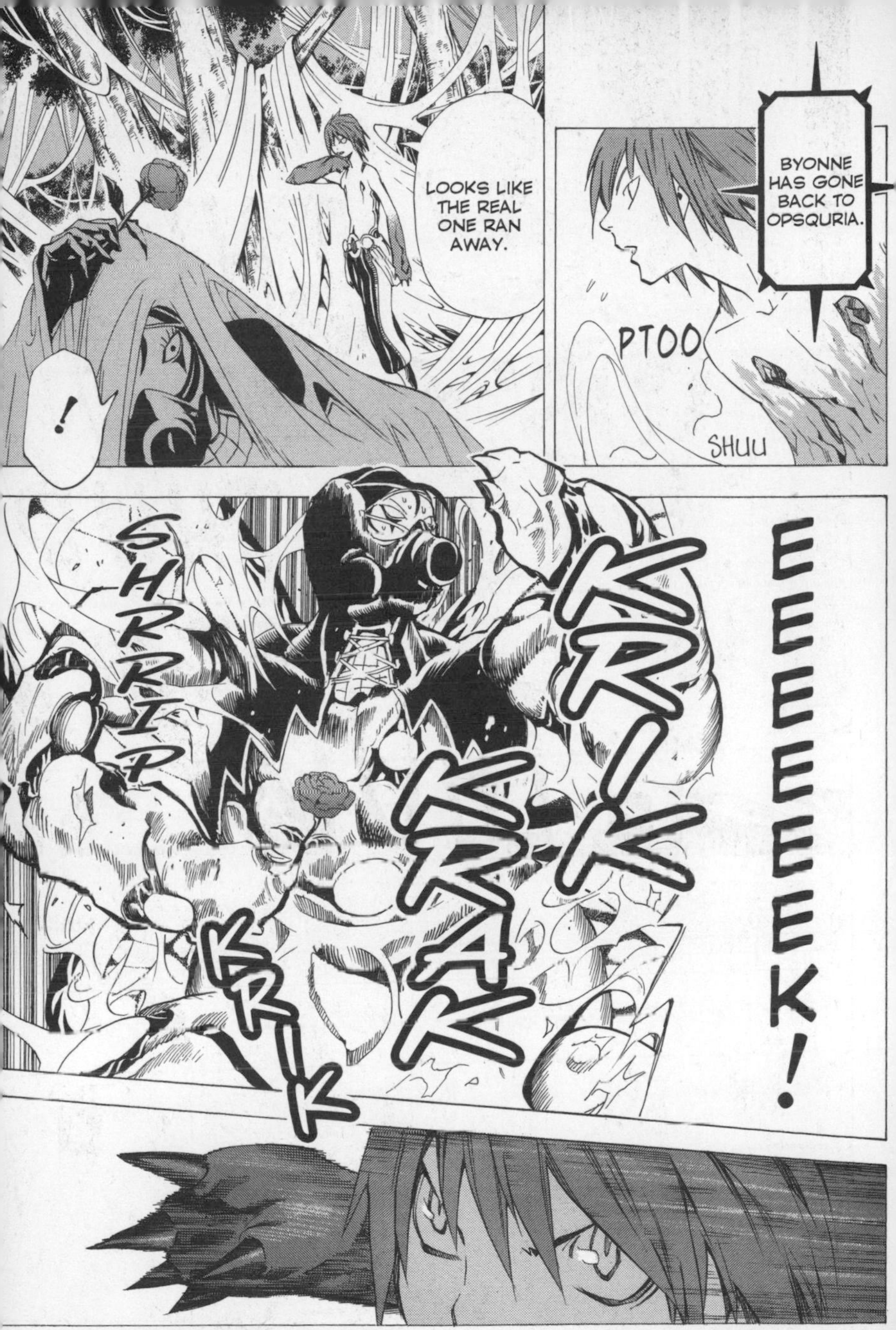
BYONNE HAS GONE BACK TO OPSQURIA.
PTOO
SHUU
LOOKS LIKE THE REAL ONE RAN AWAY.
!
EEEEEEK!
KRI-K KRAK
KRI-K
SHRRIP

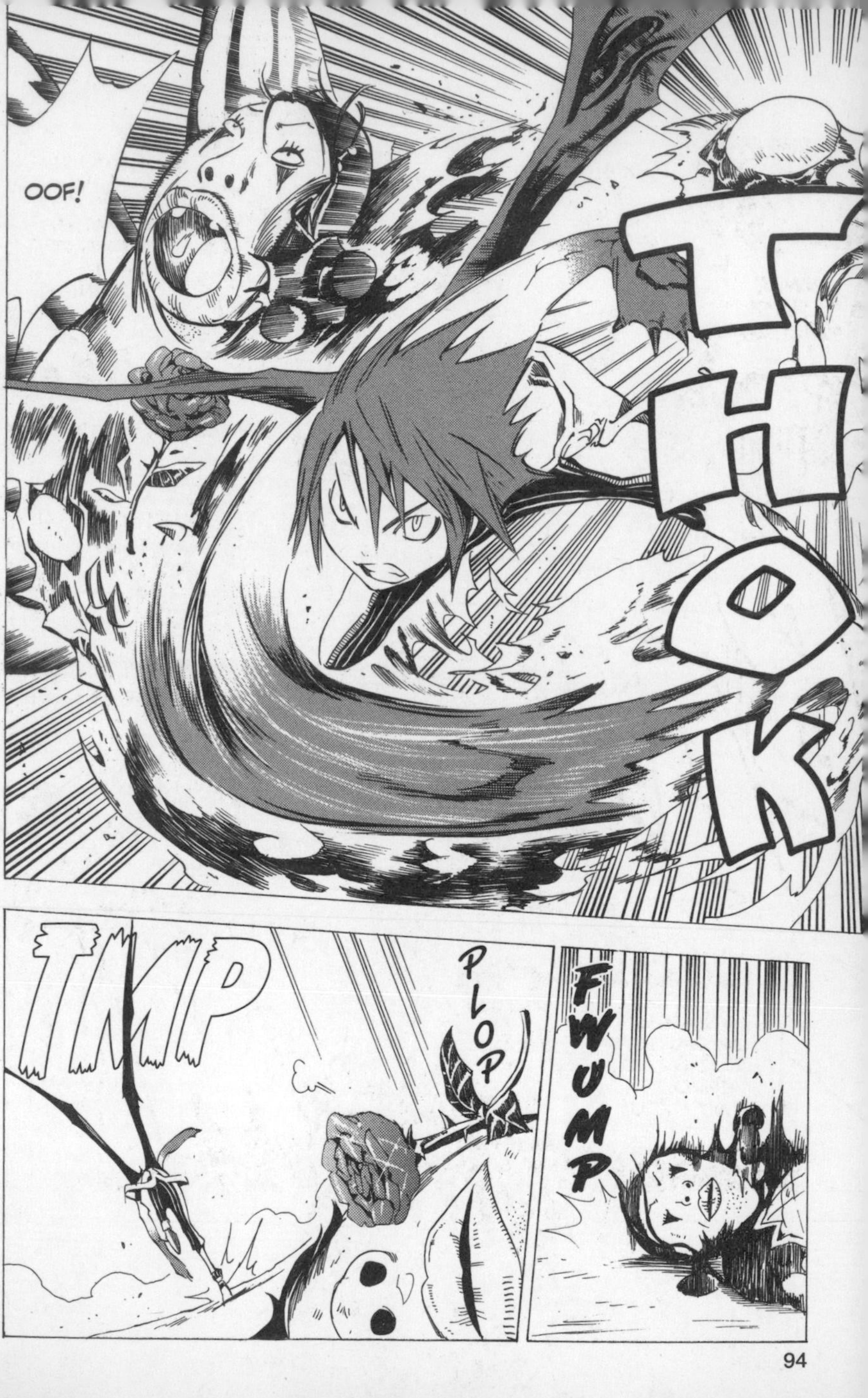
THOK
OOF!
FWUMP
PLOP
TMP

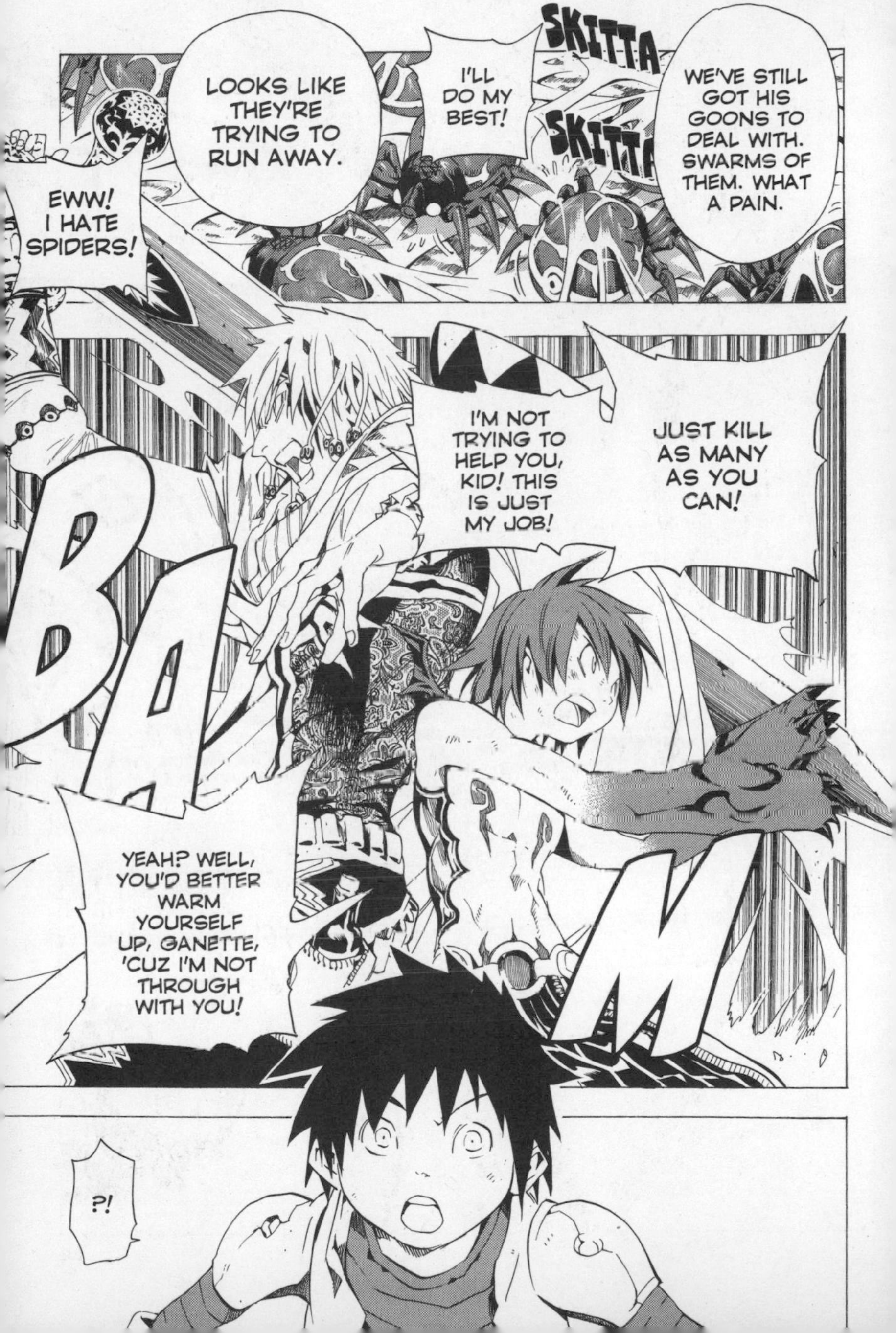
WE'VE STILL GOT HIS GOONS TO DEAL WITH. SWARMS OF THEM. WHAT A PAIN.
SKITTA
SKITTA
I'LL DO MY BEST!
LOOKS LIKE THEY'RE TRYING TO RUN AWAY.
EWW! I HATE SPIDERS!
JUST KILL AS MANY AS YOU CAN!
I'M NOT TRYING TO HELP YOU, KID! THIS IS JUST MY JOB!
BAM
YEAH? WELL, YOU'D BETTER WARM YOURSELF UP, GANETTE, 'CUZ I'M NOT THROUGH WITH YOU!
?!

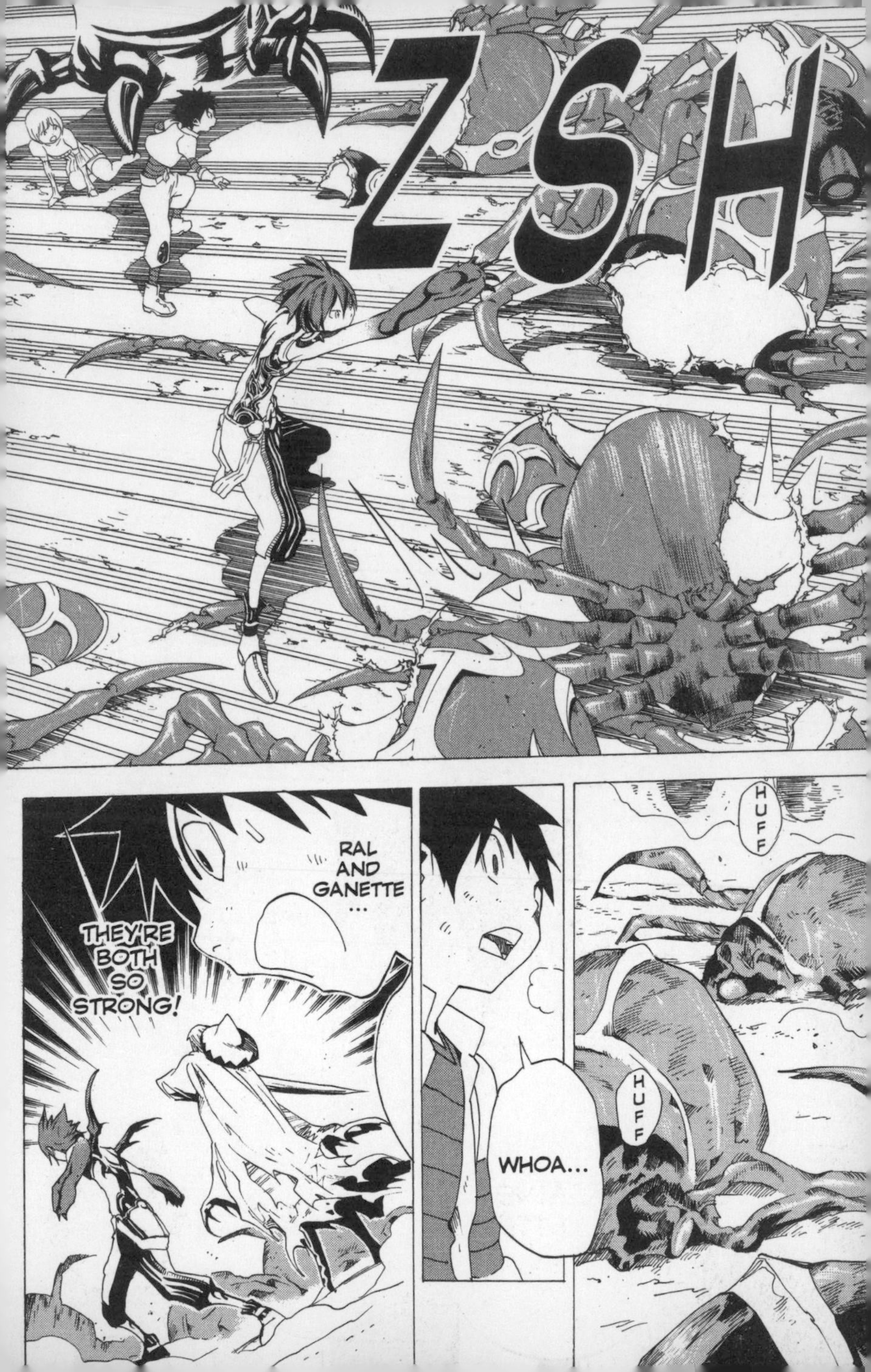
ZSH
HUFF
HUFF
WHOA...
RAL AND GANETTE...
THEY'RE BOTH SO STRONG!

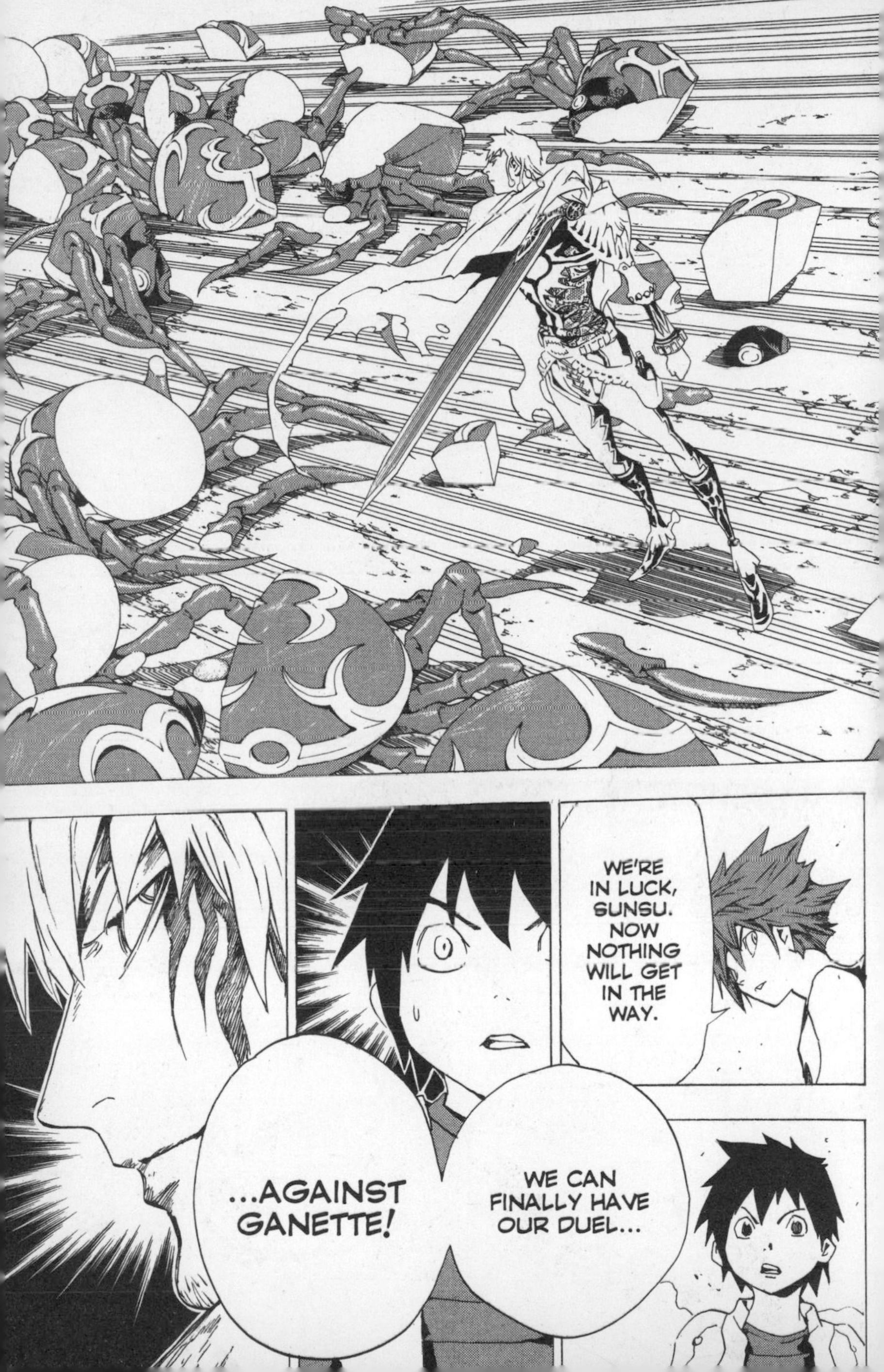
WE'RE IN LUCK, SUNSU. NOW NOTHING WILL GET IN THE WAY.
WE CAN FINALLY HAVE OUR DUEL...
...AGAINST GANETTE!

Ral Ω Grad

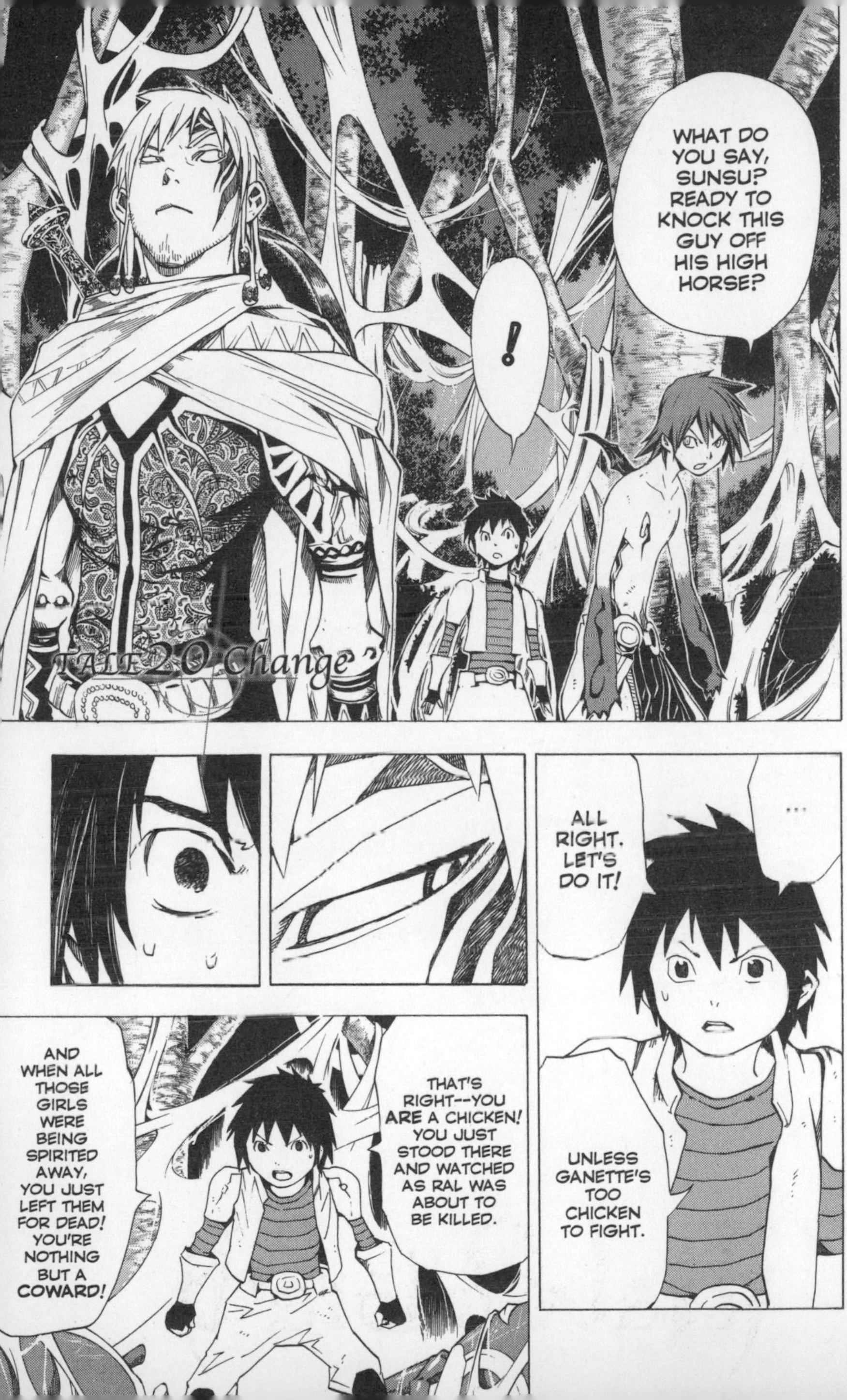
WHAT DO YOU SAY, SUNSU? READY TO KNOCK THIS GUY OFF HIS HIGH HORSE?
!
TALE 20 Change
...
ALL RIGHT. LET'S DO IT!
UNLESS GANETTE'S TOO CHICKEN TO FIGHT.
THAT'S RIGHT--YOU ARE A CHICKEN! YOU JUST STOOD THERE AND WATCHED AS RAL WAS ABOUT TO BE KILLED.
AND WHEN ALL THOSE GIRLS WERE BEING SPIRITED AWAY, YOU JUST LEFT THEM FOR DEAD! YOU'RE NOTHING BUT A COWARD!

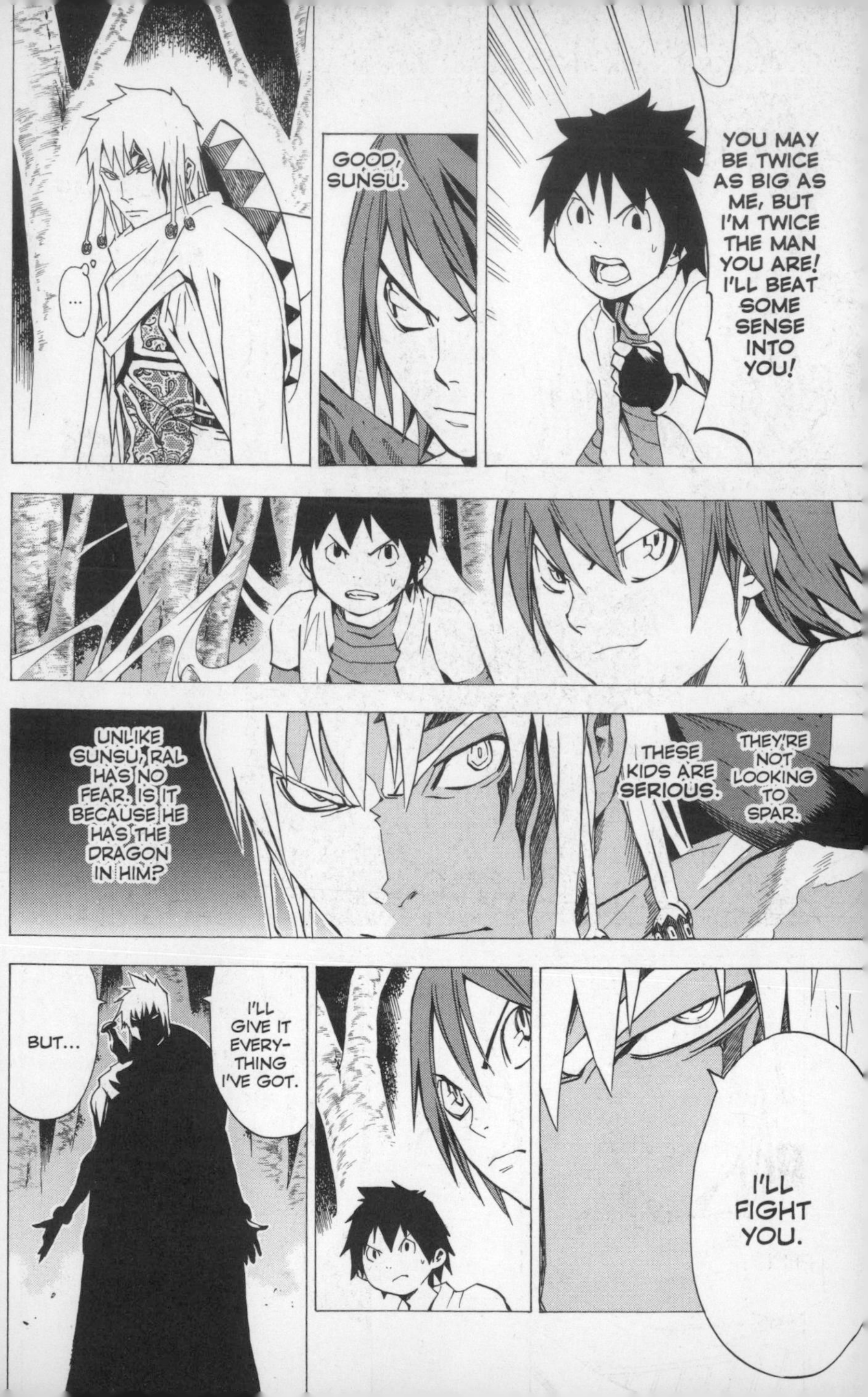
YOU MAY BE TWICE AS BIG AS ME, BUT I'M TWICE THE MAN YOU ARE! I'LL BEAT SOME SENSE INTO YOU!
GOOD, SUNSU.
...
THEY'RE NOT LOOKING TO SPAR.
THESE KIDS ARE SERIOUS.
UNLIKE SUNSU, RAL HAS NO FEAR. IS IT BECAUSE HE HAS THE DRAGON IN HIM?
I'LL FIGHT YOU.
I'LL GIVE IT EVERYTHING I'VE GOT.
BUT...

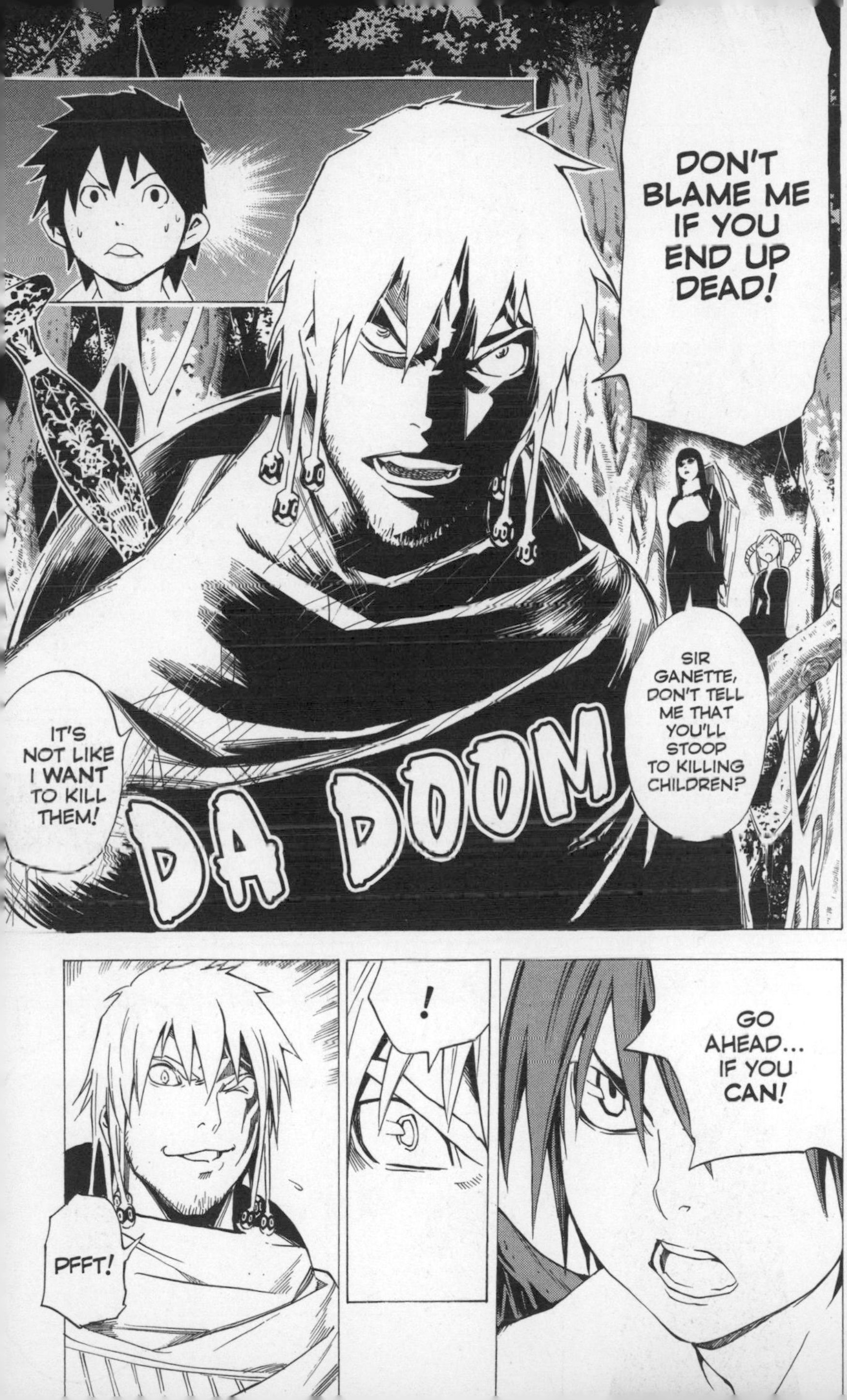
DON'T BLAME ME IF YOU END UP DEAD!
SIR GANETTE, DON'T TELL ME THAT YOU'LL STOOP TO KILLING CHILDREN?
DA DOOM
IT'S NOT LIKE I WANT TO KILL THEM!
GO AHEAD... IF YOU CAN!
!
PFFT!

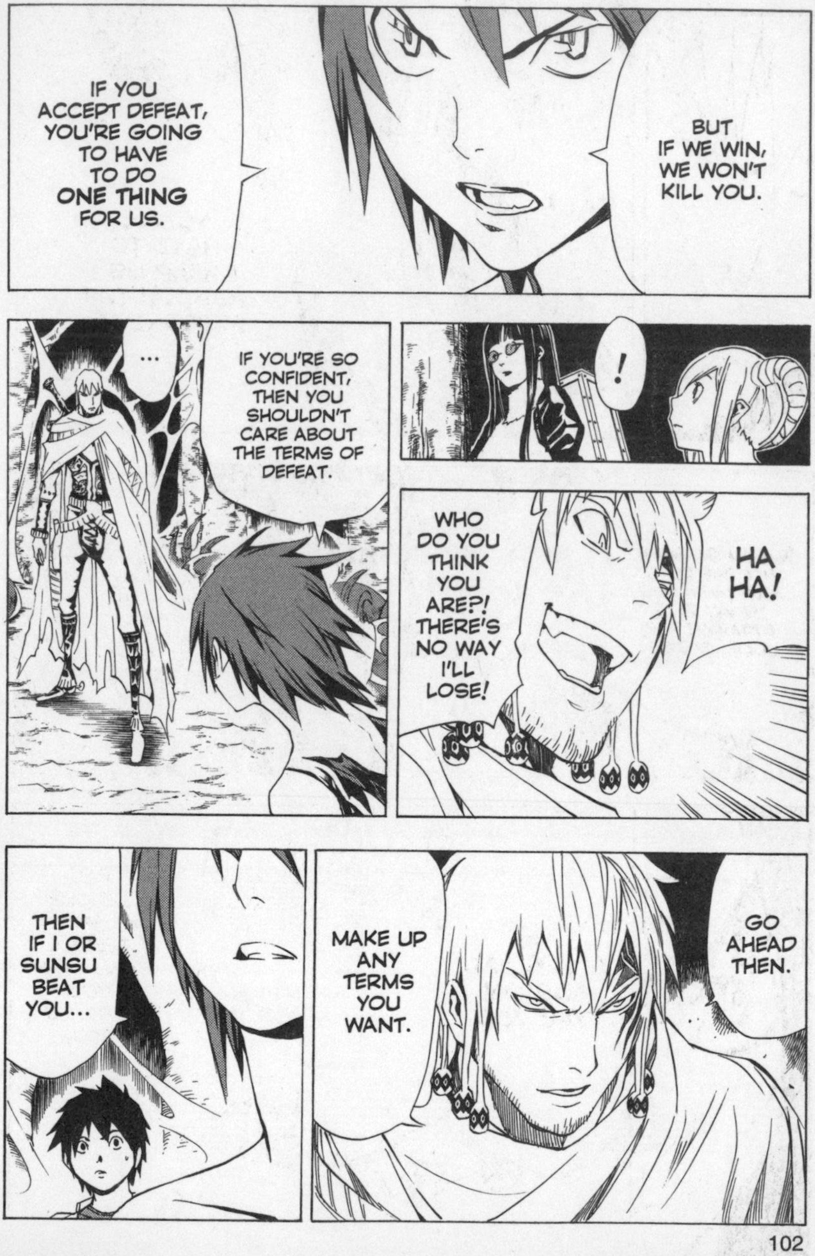
BUT IF WE WIN, WE WON'T KILL YOU.
IF YOU ACCEPT DEFEAT, YOU'RE GOING TO HAVE TO DO ONE THING FOR US.
!
HA HA!
WHO DO YOU THINK YOU ARE?! THERE'S NO WAY I'LL LOSE!
IF YOU'RE SO CONFIDENT, THEN YOU SHOULDN'T CARE ABOUT THE TERMS OF DEFEAT.
...
GO AHEAD THEN.
MAKE UP ANY TERMS YOU WANT.
THEN IF I OR SUNSU BEAT YOU...

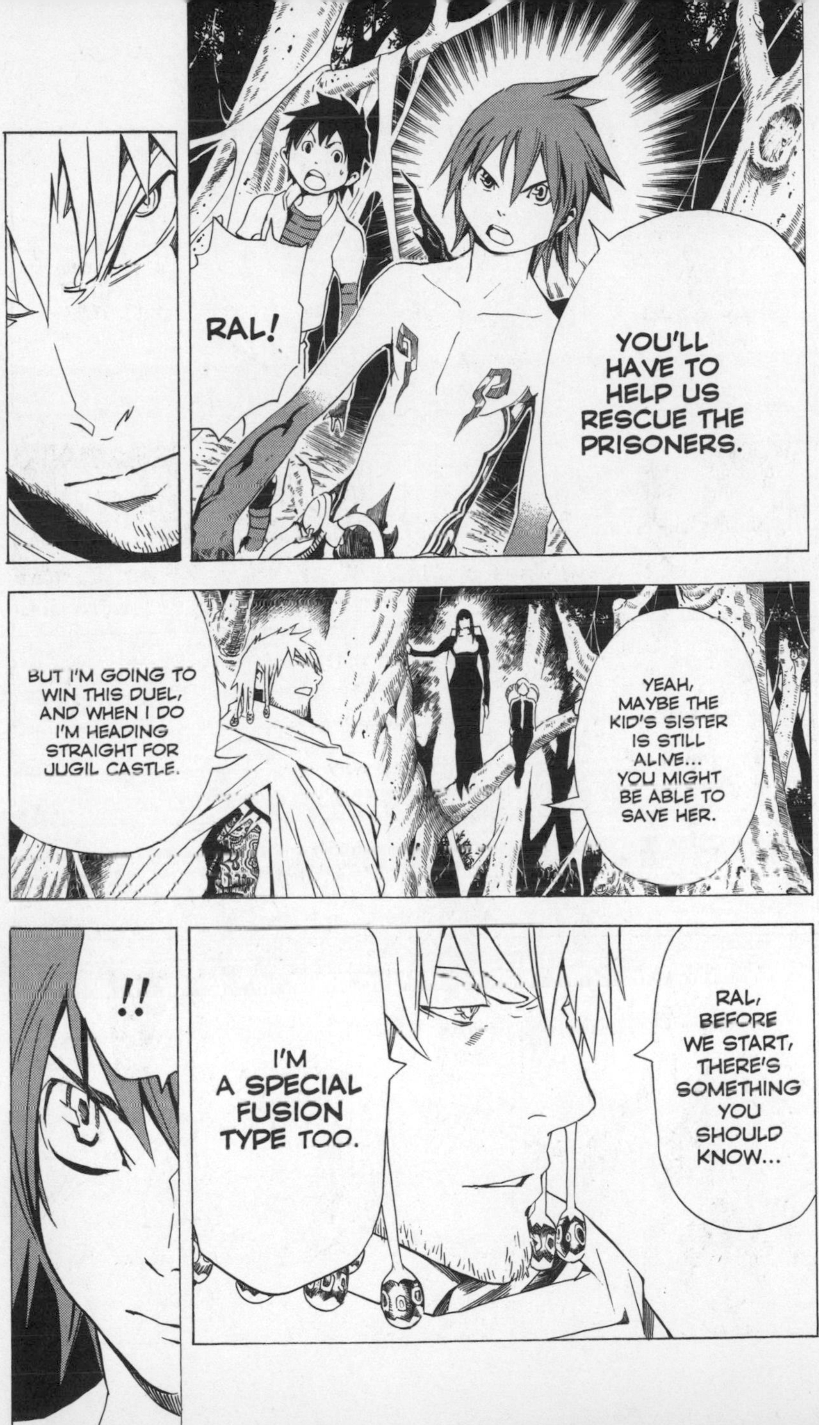
YOU'LL HAVE TO HELP US RESCUE THE PRISONERS.
RAL!
YEAH, MAYBE THE KID'S SISTER IS STILL ALIVE... YOU MIGHT BE ABLE TO SAVE HER.
BUT I'M GOING TO WIN THIS DUEL, AND WHEN I DO I'M HEADING STRAIGHT FOR JUGIL CASTLE.
RAL, BEFORE WE START, THERE'S SOMETHING YOU SHOULD KNOW...
I'M A SPECIAL FUSION TYPE TOO.
!!

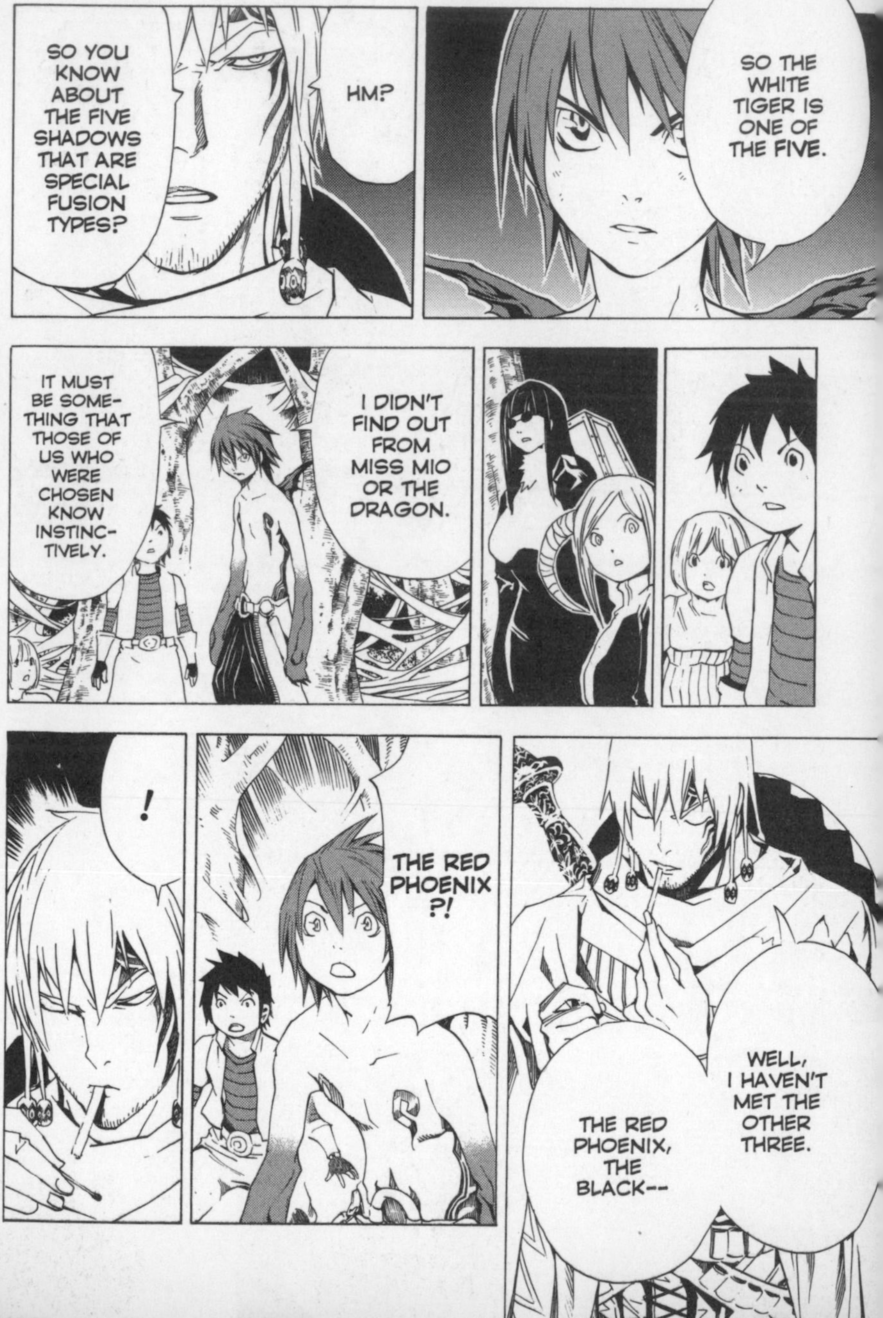
SO THE WHITE TIGER IS ONE OF THE FIVE.
HM?
SO YOU KNOW ABOUT THE FIVE SHADOWS THAT ARE SPECIAL FUSION TYPES?
I DIDN'T FIND OUT FROM MISS MIO OR THE DRAGON.
IT MUST BE SOME-THING THAT THOSE OF US WHO WERE CHOSEN KNOW INSTINC-TIVELY.
WELL, I HAVEN'T MET THE OTHER THREE.
THE RED PHOENIX, THE BLACK--
THE RED PHOENIX ?!
!

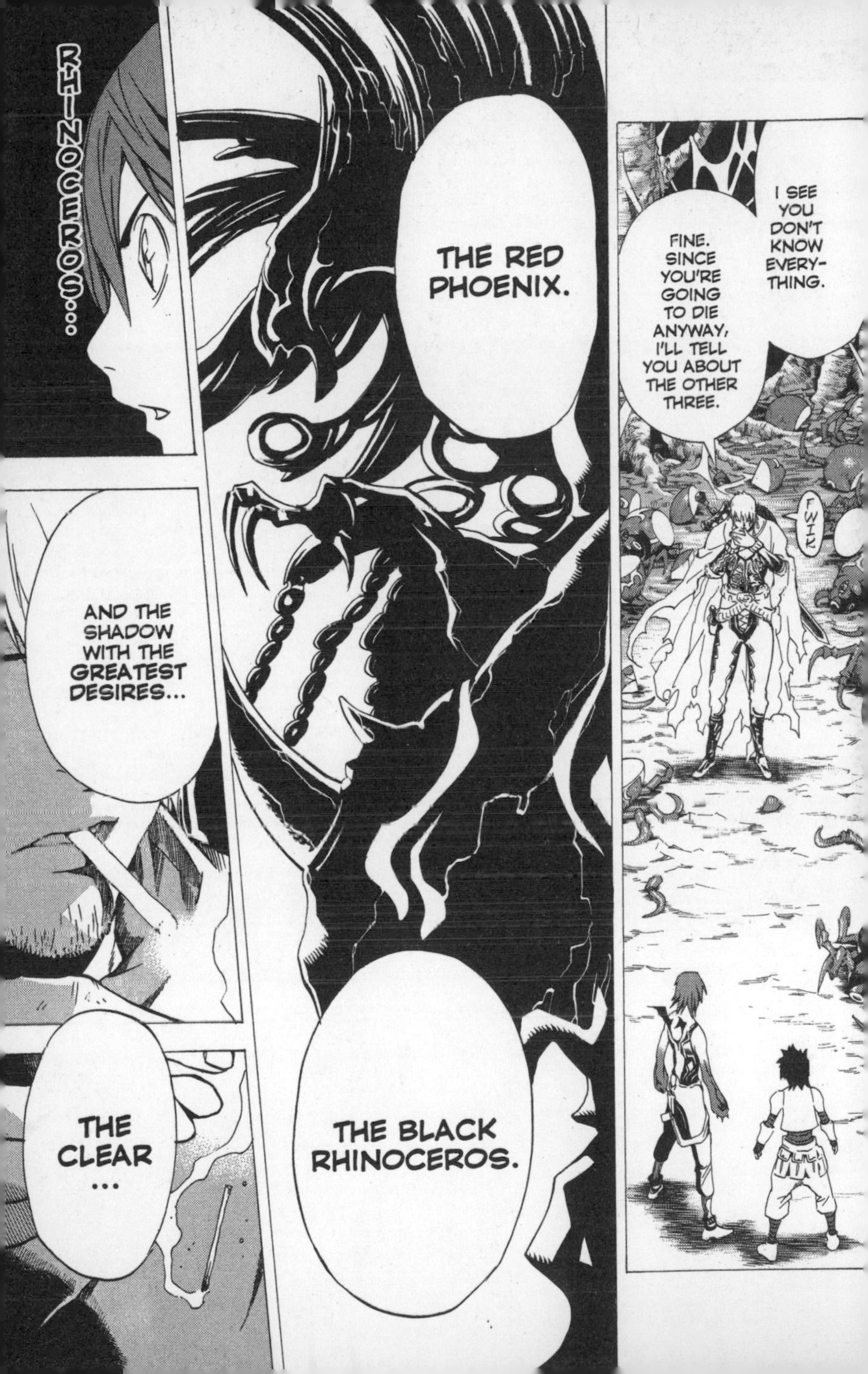
I SEE YOU DON'T KNOW EVERY-THING.
FINE. SINCE YOU'RE GOING TO DIE ANYWAY, I'LL TELL YOU ABOUT THE OTHER THREE.
FWIK
THE RED PHOENIX.
THE BLACK RHINOCEROS.
RHINOCEROS...
AND THE SHADOW WITH THE GREATEST DESIRES...
THE CLEAR ...

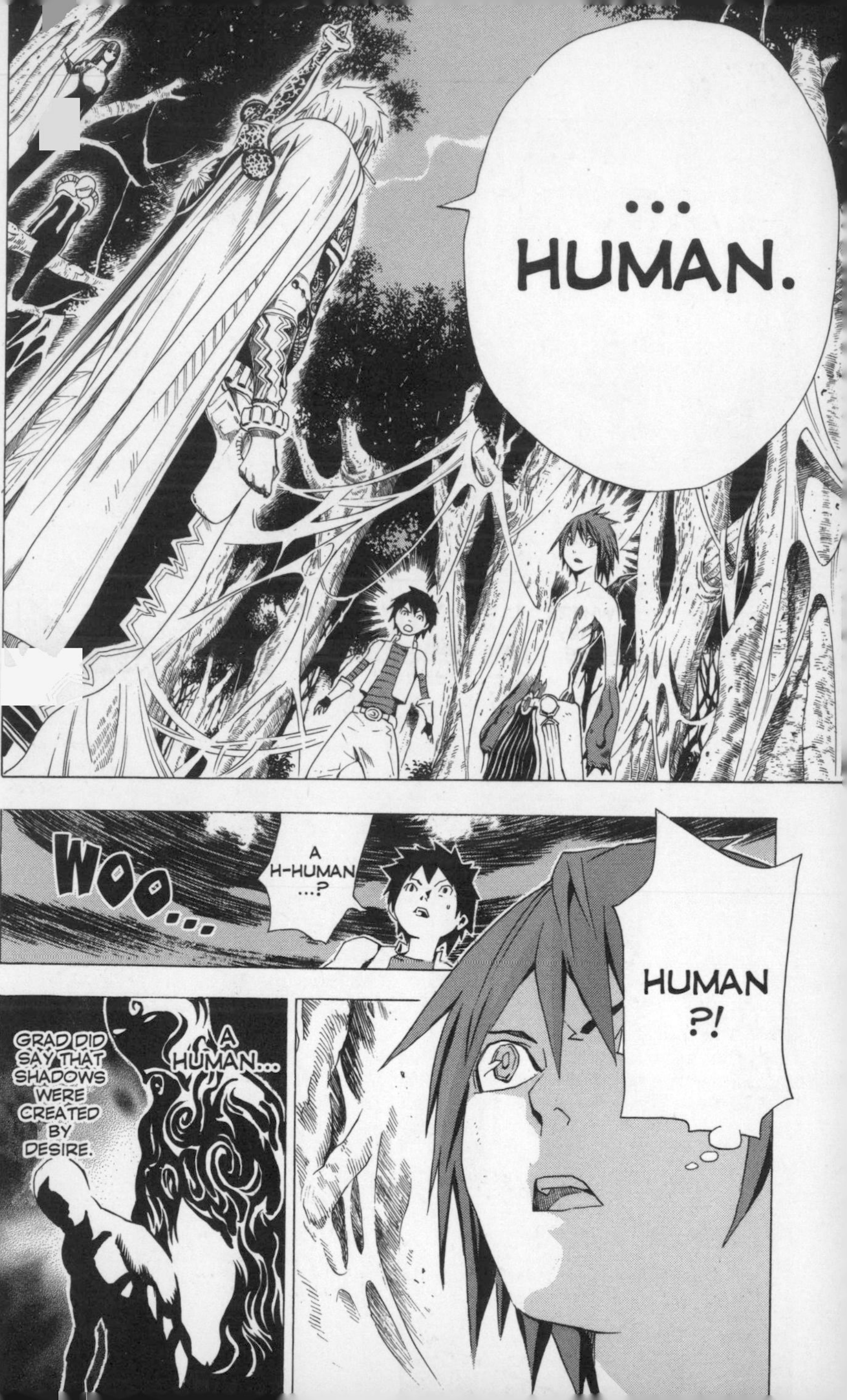

... HUMAN.
WOO...
A H-HUMAN ...?
HUMAN ?!
A HUMAN...
GRAD DID SAY THAT SHADOWS WERE CREATED BY DESIRE.

READ THIS WAY

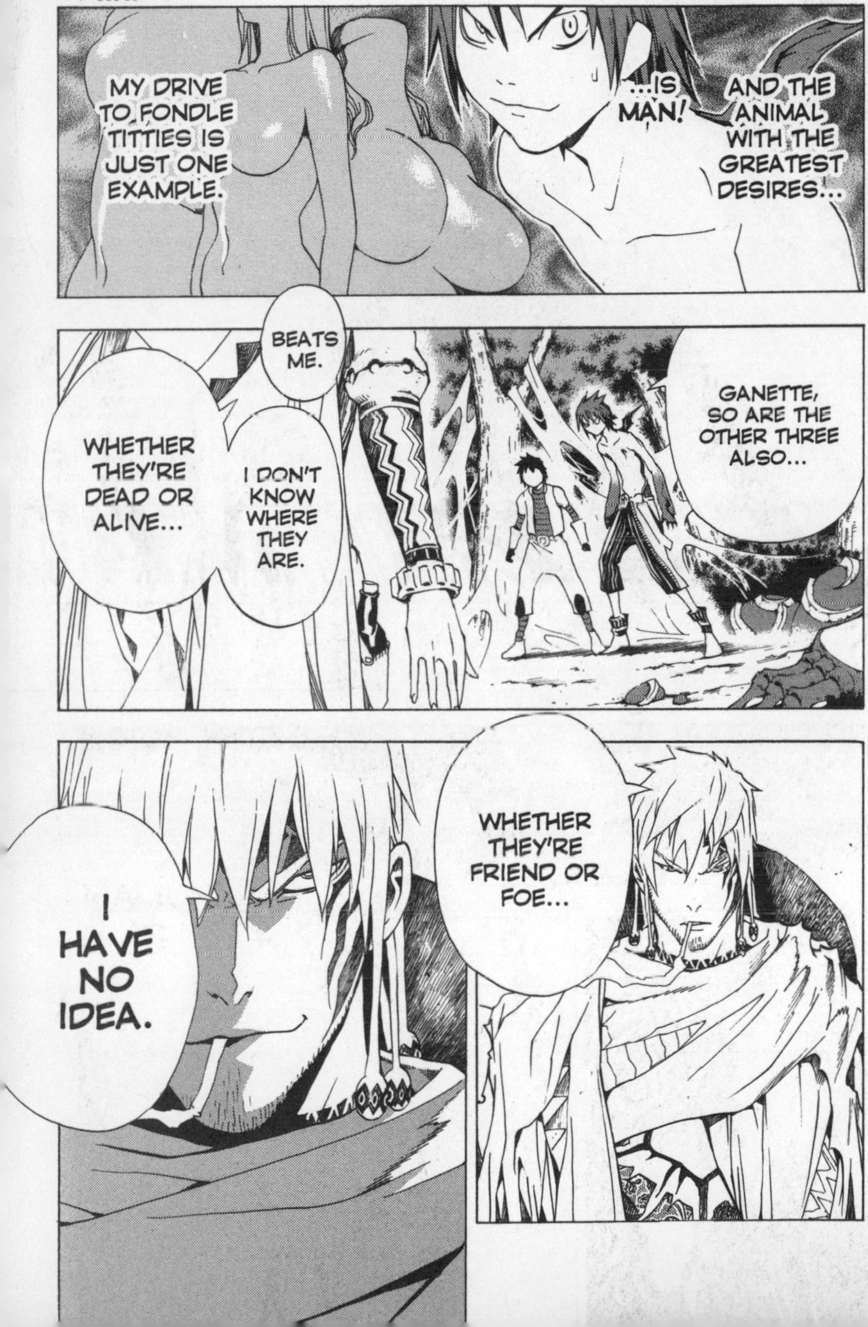

AND THE ANIMAL WITH THE GREATEST DESIRES...
...IS MAN!
MY DRIVE TO FONDLE TITTIES IS JUST ONE EXAMPLE.
GANETTE, SO ARE THE OTHER THREE ALSO...
BEATS ME.
I DON'T KNOW WHERE THEY ARE.
WHETHER THEY'RE DEAD OR ALIVE...
WHETHER THEY'RE FRIEND OR FOE...
I HAVE NO IDEA.

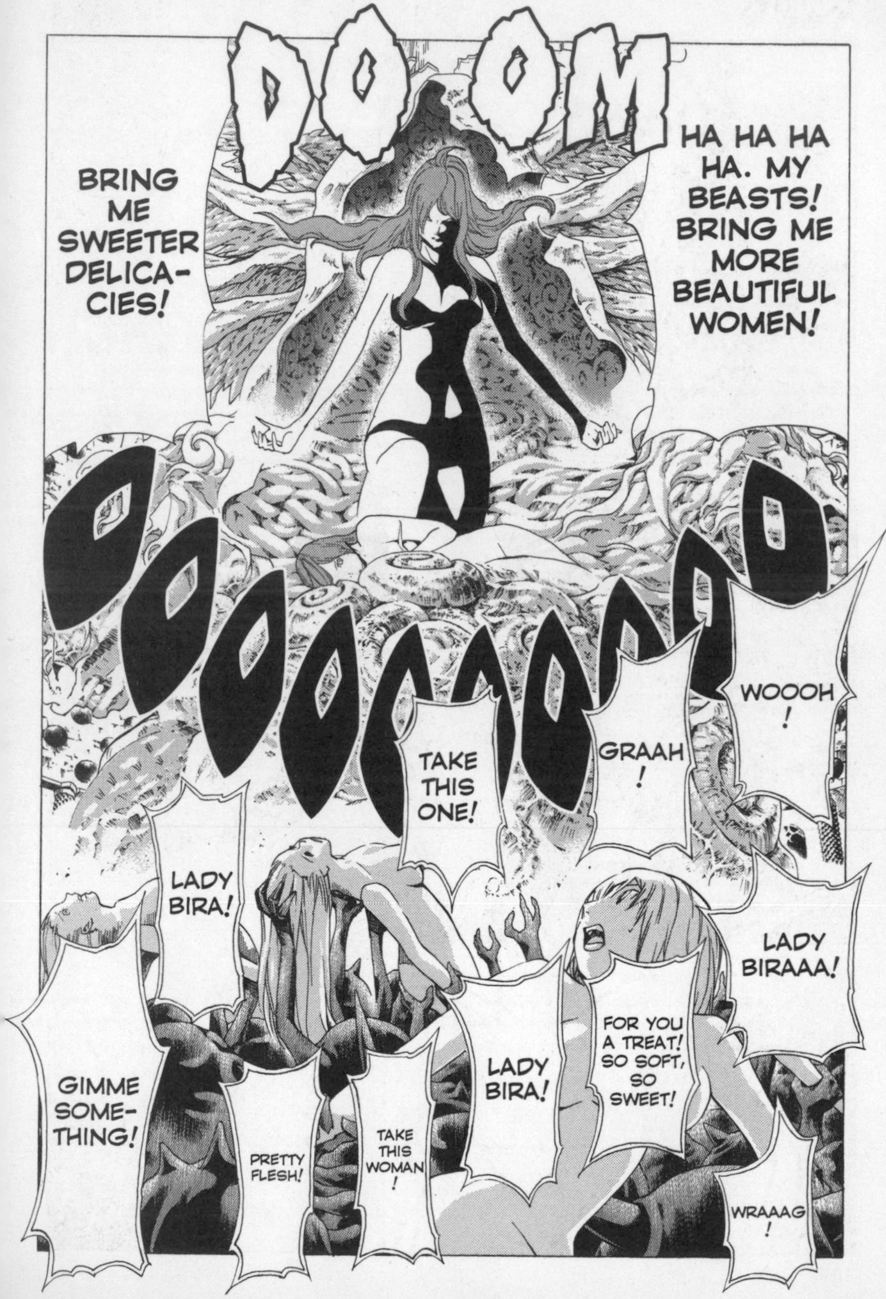
DO-OM
HA HA HA HA. MY BEASTS! BRING ME MORE BEAUTIFUL WOMEN!
BRING ME SWEETER DELICA-CIES!
WOOOH!
GRAAH!
TAKE THIS ONE!
LADY BIRAAA!
LADY BIRA!
WRAAAG!
FOR YOU A TREAT! SO SOFT, SO SWEET!
LADY BIRA!
TAKE THIS WOMAN!
PRETTY FLESH!
GIMME SOME-THING!

READ THIS WAY

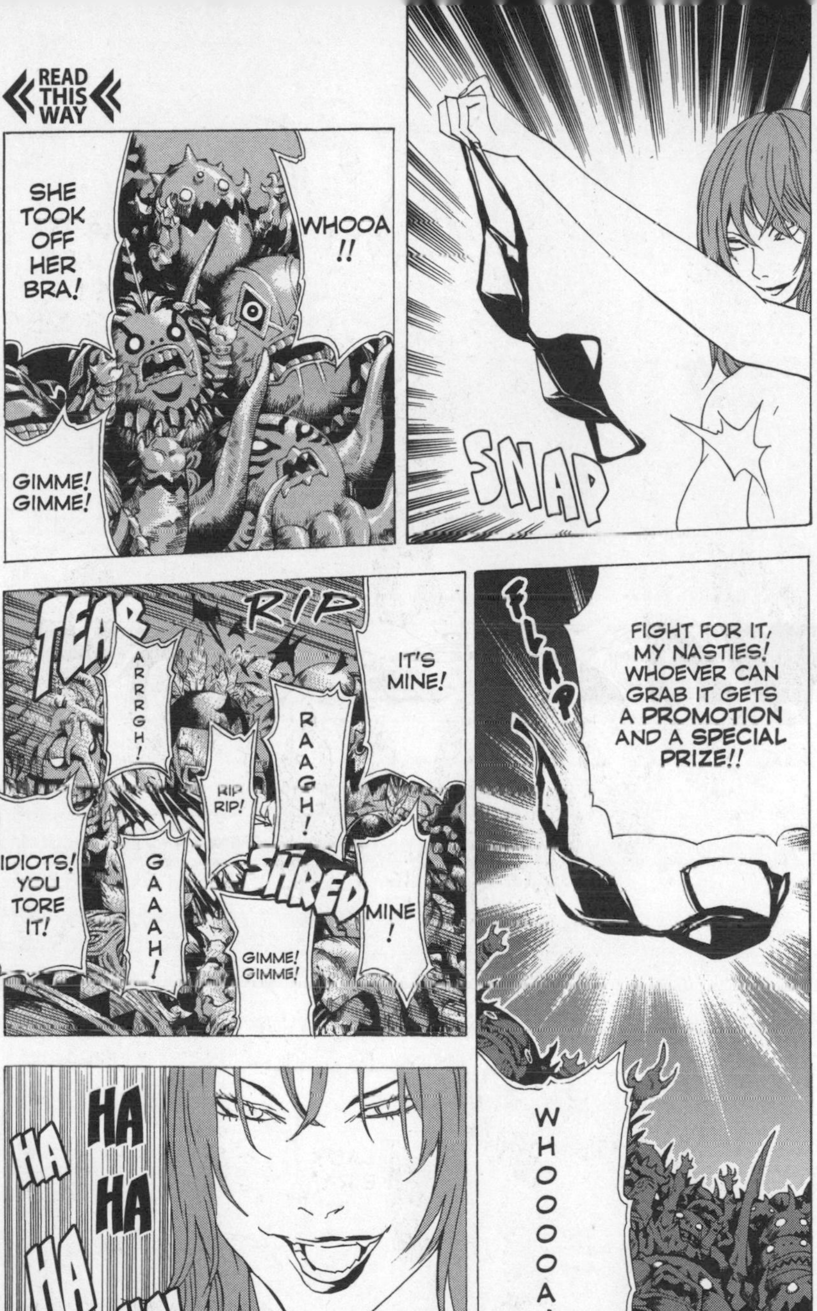
SNAP
WHOOA!!
SHE TOOK OFF HER BRA!
GIMME! GIMME!
FLAAP
FIGHT FOR IT, MY NASTIES! WHOEVER CAN GRAB IT GETS A PROMOTION AND A SPECIAL PRIZE!!
WHOOOOOA!
RIP
IT'S MINE!
TEAR
ARRRGH!
RAAGH!
RIP RIP!
MINE!
SHRED
GIMME! GIMME!
GAAAH!
IDIOTS! YOU TORE IT!
HA HA HA HA HA HA!

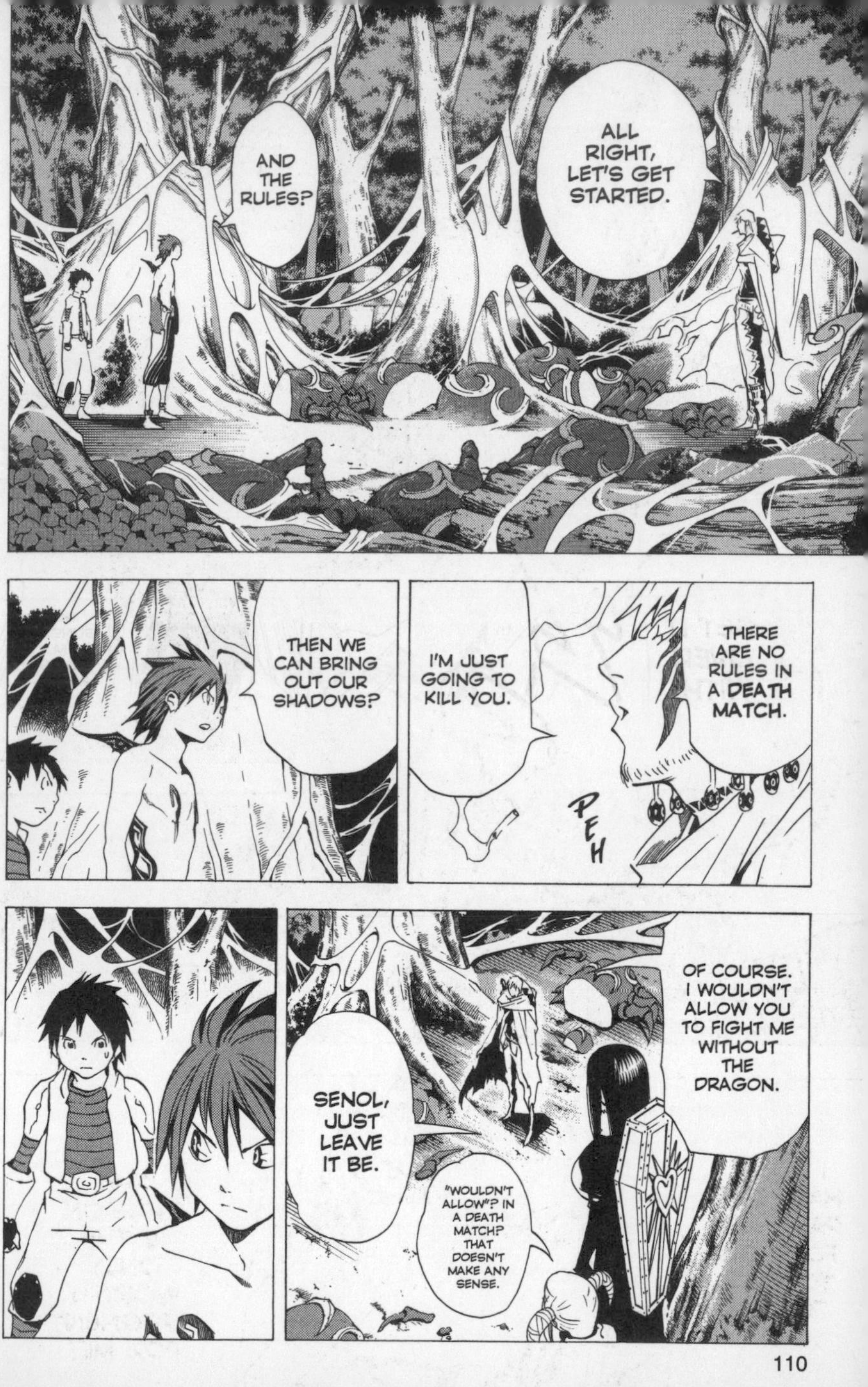
ALL RIGHT, LET'S GET STARTED.
AND THE RULES?
THERE ARE NO RULES IN A DEATH MATCH.
PEH
I'M JUST GOING TO KILL YOU.
THEN WE CAN BRING OUT OUR SHADOWS?
OF COURSE. I WOULDN'T ALLOW YOU TO FIGHT ME WITHOUT THE DRAGON.
SENOL, JUST LEAVE IT BE.
"WOULDN'T ALLOW"? IN A DEATH MATCH? THAT DOESN'T MAKE ANY SENSE.

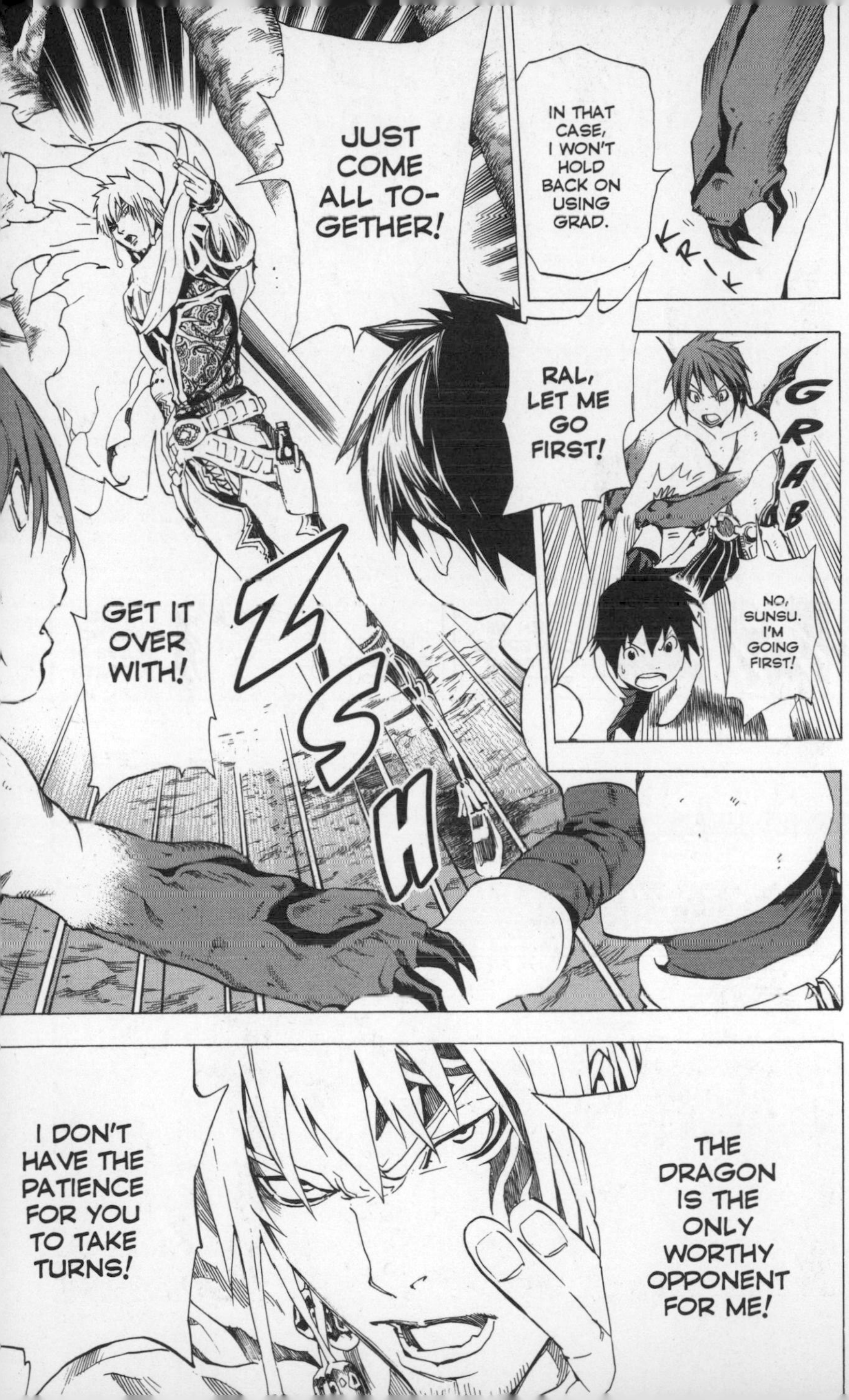
IN THAT CASE, I WON'T HOLD BACK ON USING GRAD.
KRIK
RAL, LET ME GO FIRST!
GRAB
NO, SUNSU. I'M GOING FIRST!
JUST COME ALL TOGETHER!
GET IT OVER WITH!
ZSSH
THE DRAGON IS THE ONLY WORTHY OPPONENT FOR ME!
I DON'T HAVE THE PATIENCE FOR YOU TO TAKE TURNS!

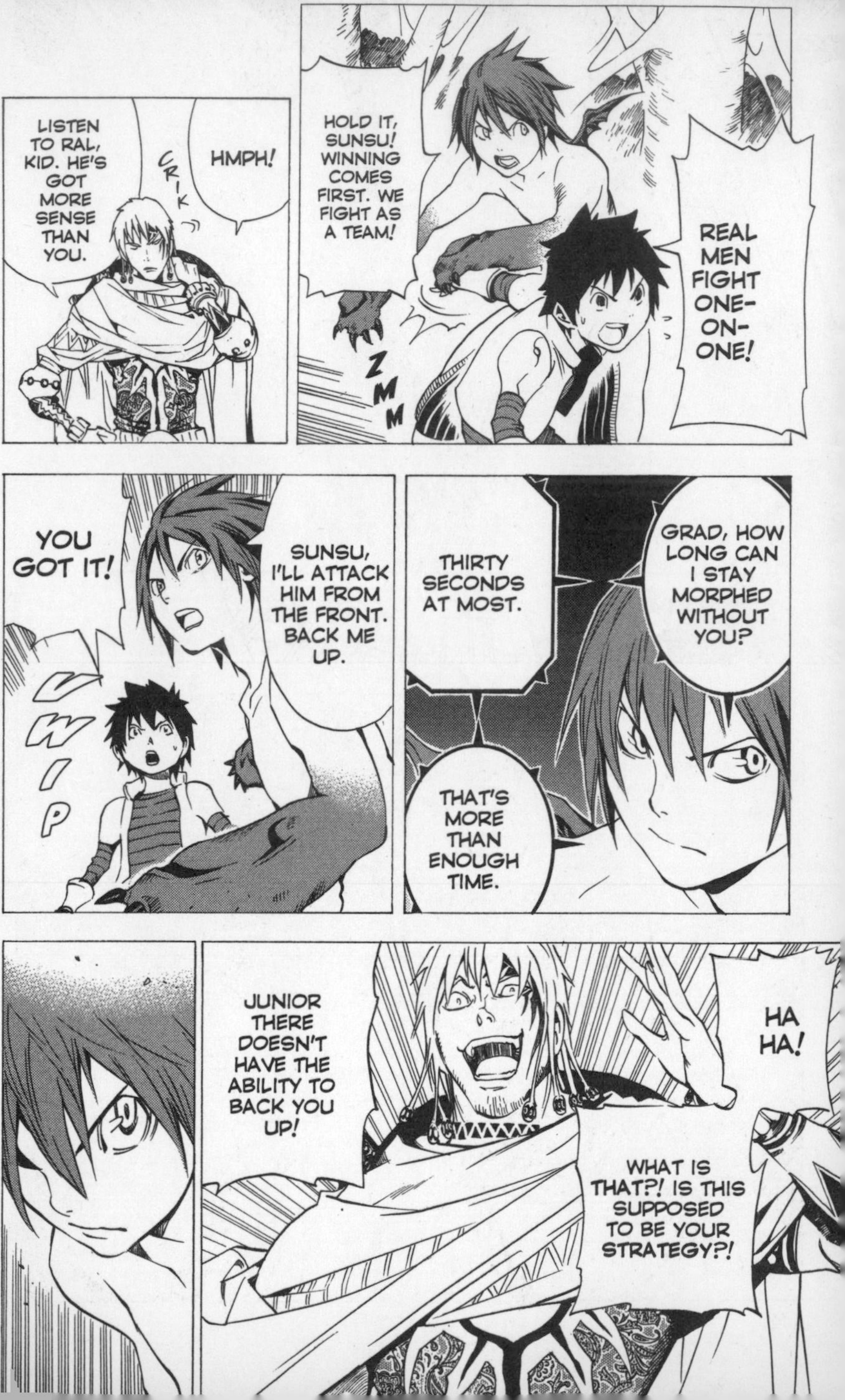
REAL MEN FIGHT ONE-ON-ONE!
ZMM
HOLD IT, SUNSU! WINNING COMES FIRST. WE FIGHT AS A TEAM!
HMPH!
CRIK
LISTEN TO RAL, KID. HE'S GOT MORE SENSE THAN YOU.
GRAD, HOW LONG CAN I STAY MORPHED WITHOUT YOU?
THIRTY SECONDS AT MOST.
THAT'S MORE THAN ENOUGH TIME.
SUNSU, I'LL ATTACK HIM FROM THE FRONT. BACK ME UP.
YOU GOT IT!
WHIP
HA HA!
JUNIOR THERE DOESN'T HAVE THE ABILITY TO BACK YOU UP!
WHAT IS THAT?! IS THIS SUPPOSED TO BE YOUR STRATEGY?!

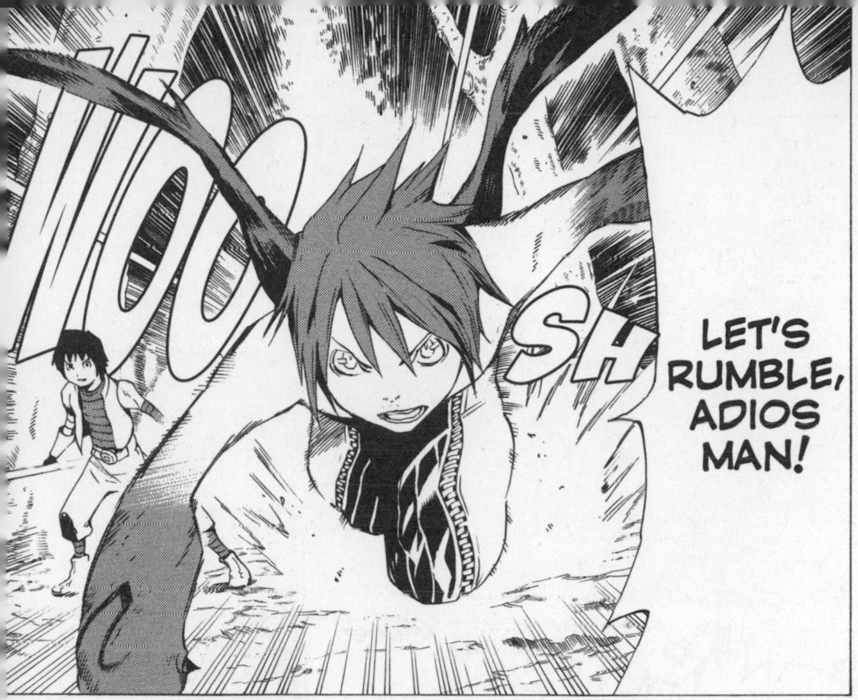
WHOOSH
LET'S RUMBLE, ADIOS MAN!

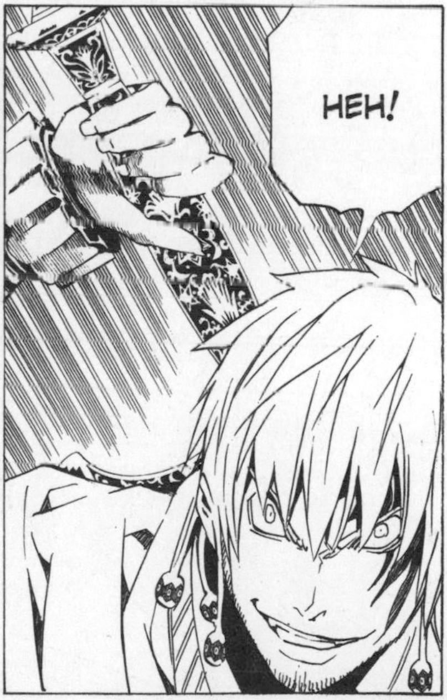
HEH!

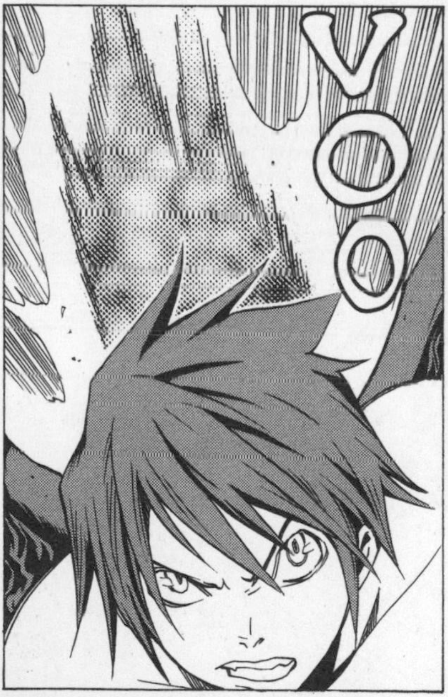
VOOO

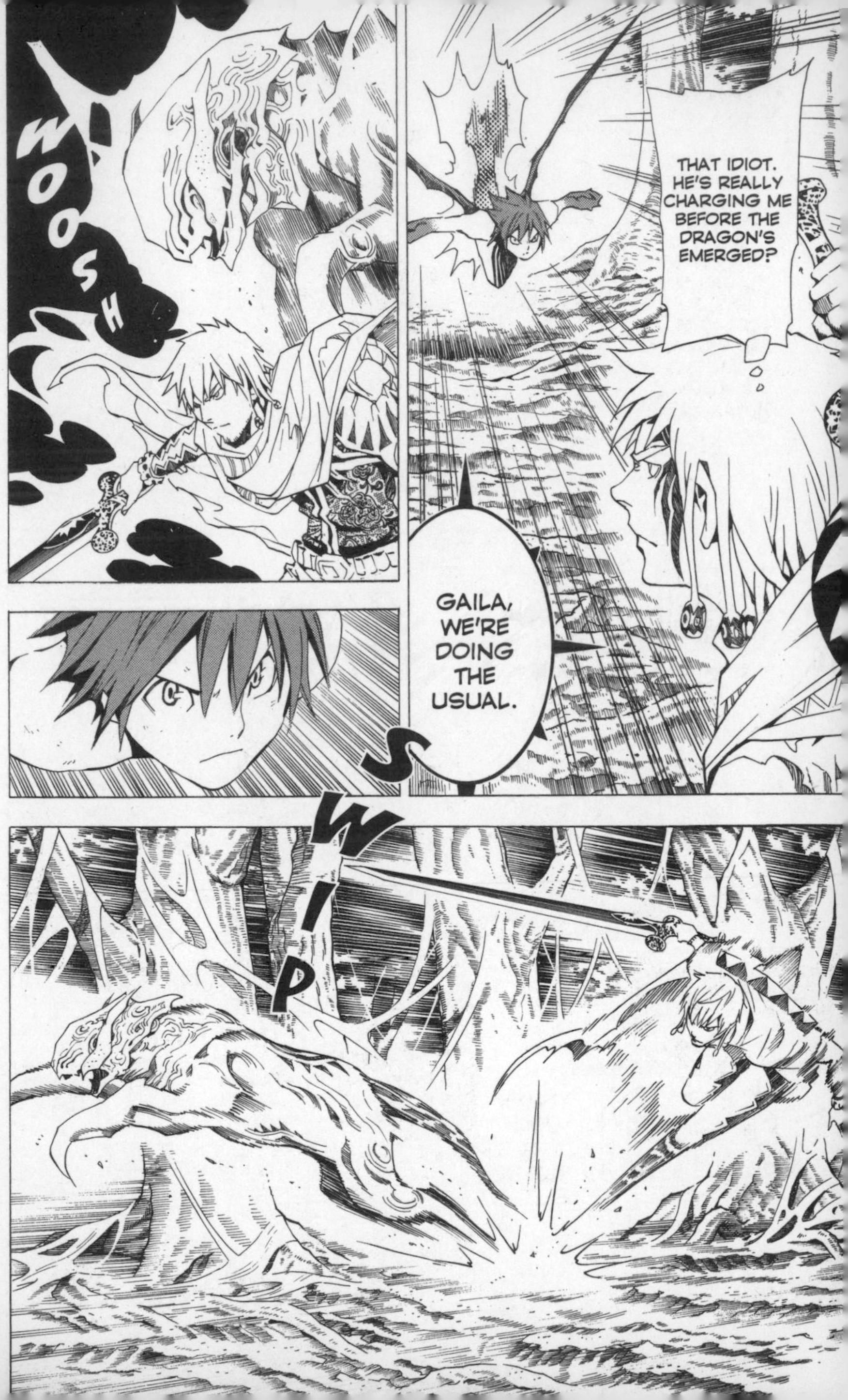
THAT IDIOT. HE'S REALLY CHARGING ME BEFORE THE DRAGON'S EMERGED?
GAILA, WE'RE DOING THE USUAL.
WOOSH
SWIP

READ THIS WAY

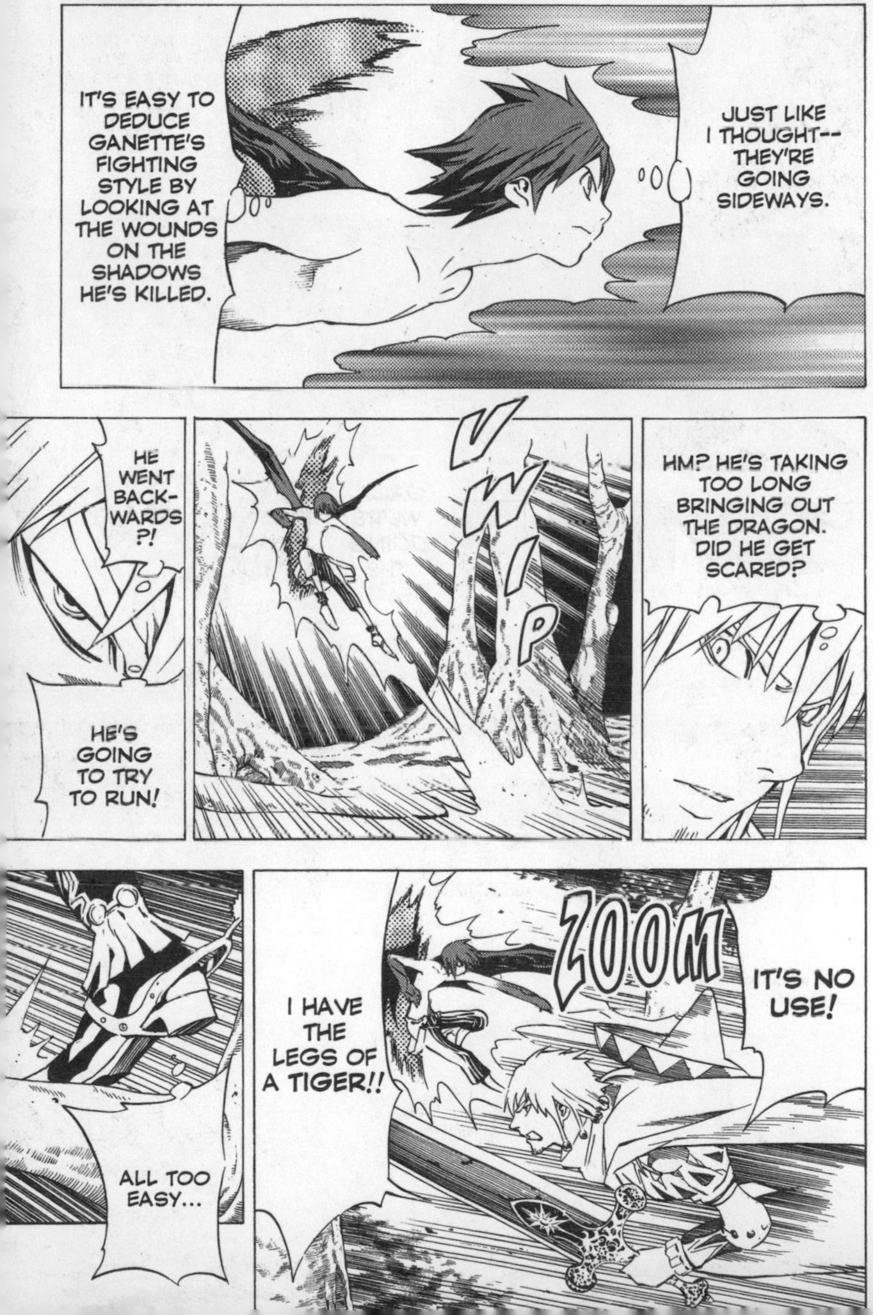
JUST LIKE I THOUGHT-- THEY'RE GOING SIDEWAYS.
IT'S EASY TO DEDUCE GANETTE'S FIGHTING STYLE BY LOOKING AT THE WOUNDS ON THE SHADOWS HE'S KILLED.
HM? HE'S TAKING TOO LONG BRINGING OUT THE DRAGON. DID HE GET SCARED?
WHIP
HE WENT BACKWARDS?!
HE'S GOING TO TRY TO RUN!
ZOOM
IT'S NO USE!
I HAVE THE LEGS OF A TIGER!!
ALL TOO EASY...

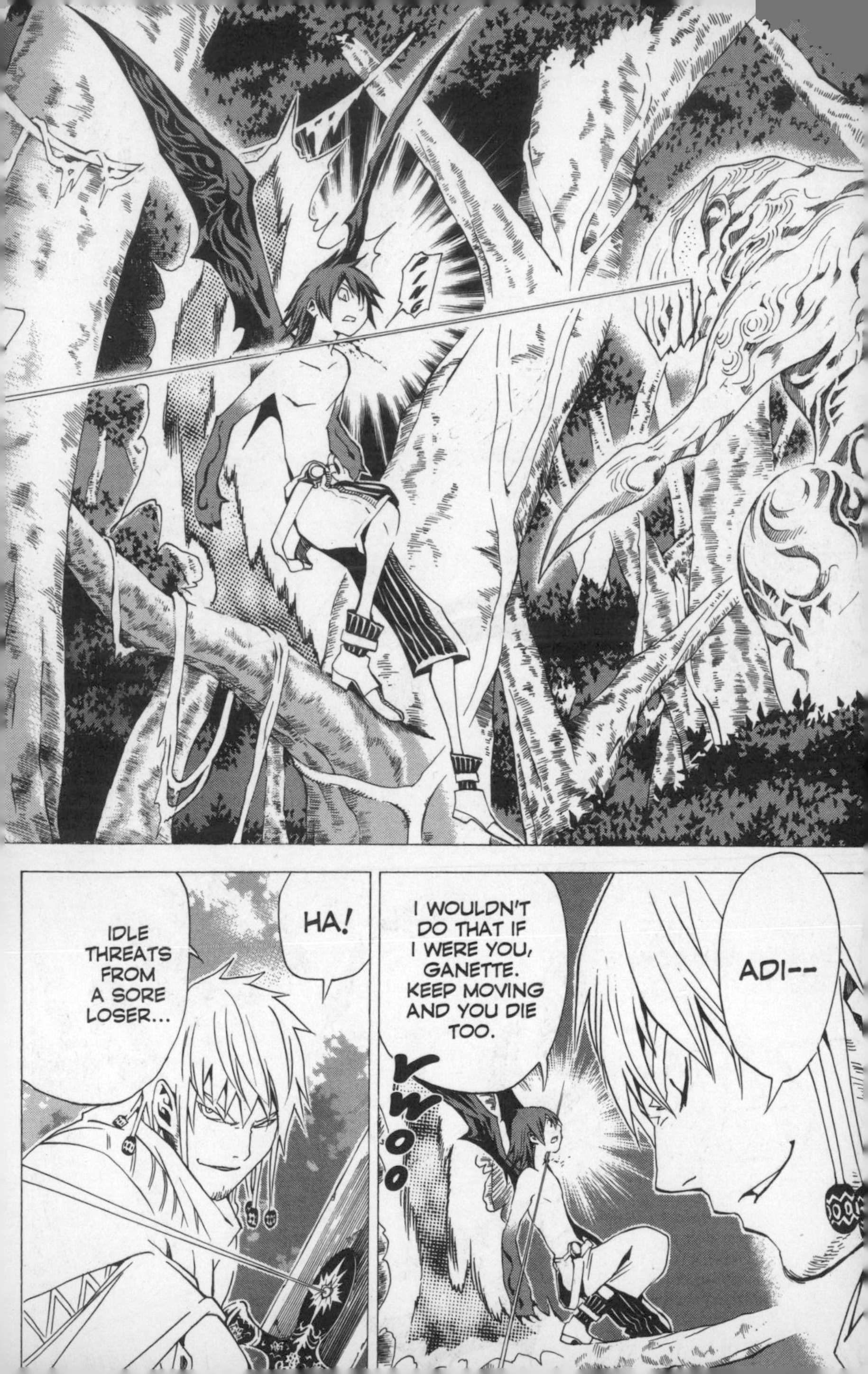
PING
ADI--
I WOULDN'T DO THAT IF I WERE YOU, GANETTE. KEEP MOVING AND YOU DIE TOO.
VWOO
HA!
IDLE THREATS FROM A SORE LOSER...

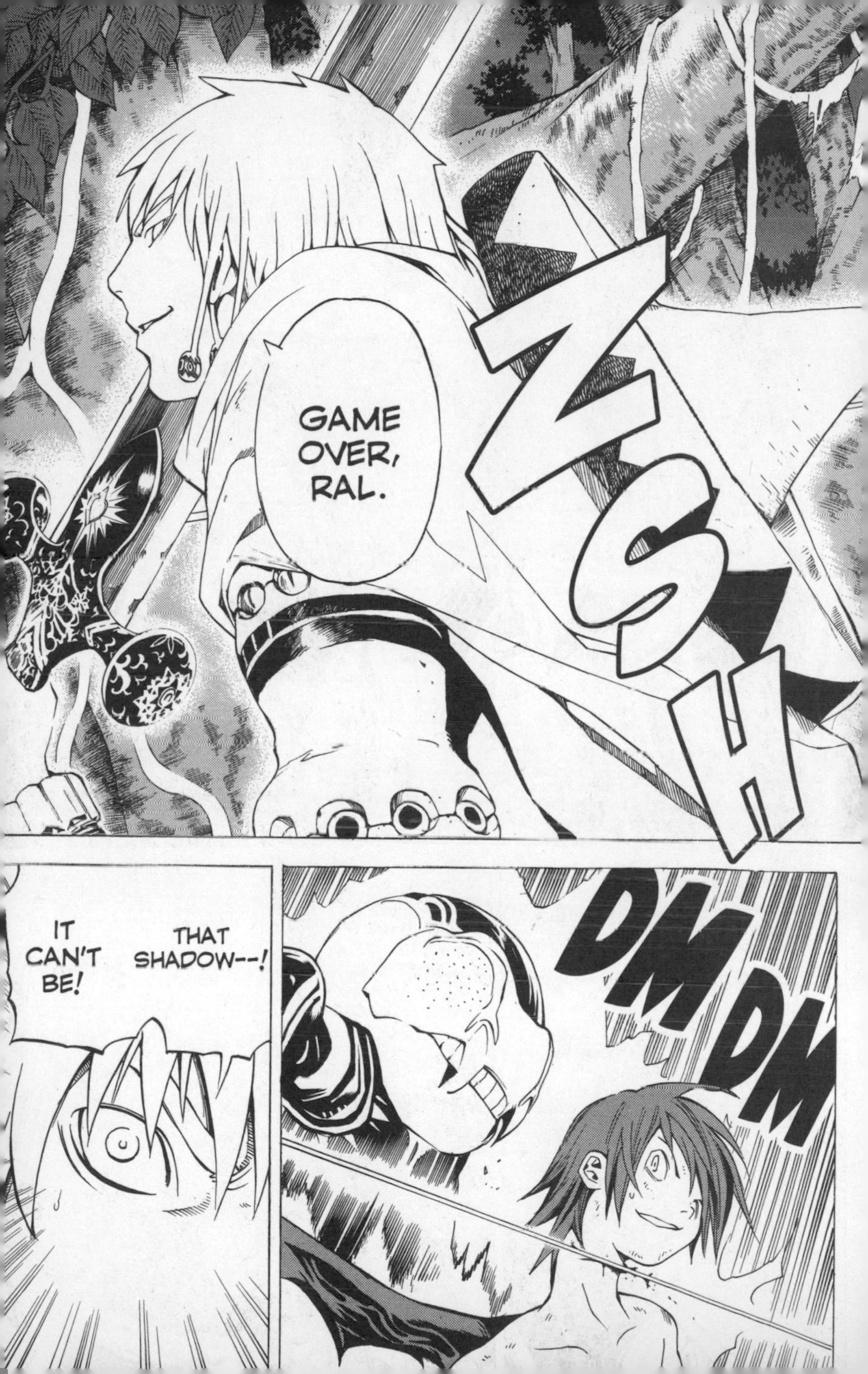
GAME OVER, RAL.
ZSH
DM DM DM
THAT SHADOW--!
IT CAN'T BE!

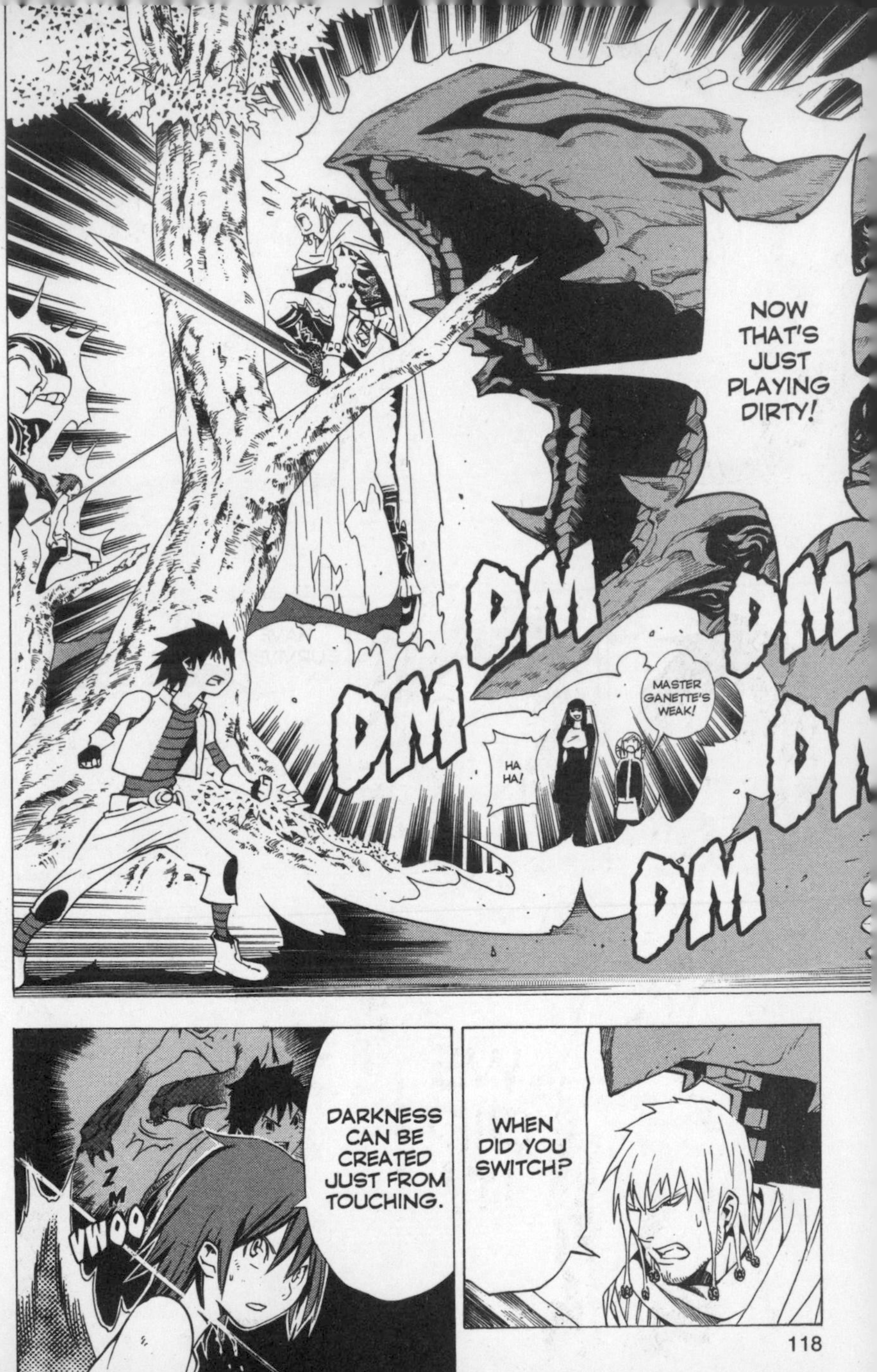
NOW THAT'S JUST PLAYING DIRTY!
DM DM DM DM DM DM
MASTER GANETTE'S WEAK!
HA HA!
WHEN DID YOU SWITCH?
DARKNESS CAN BE CREATED JUST FROM TOUCHING.
ZMVWOO

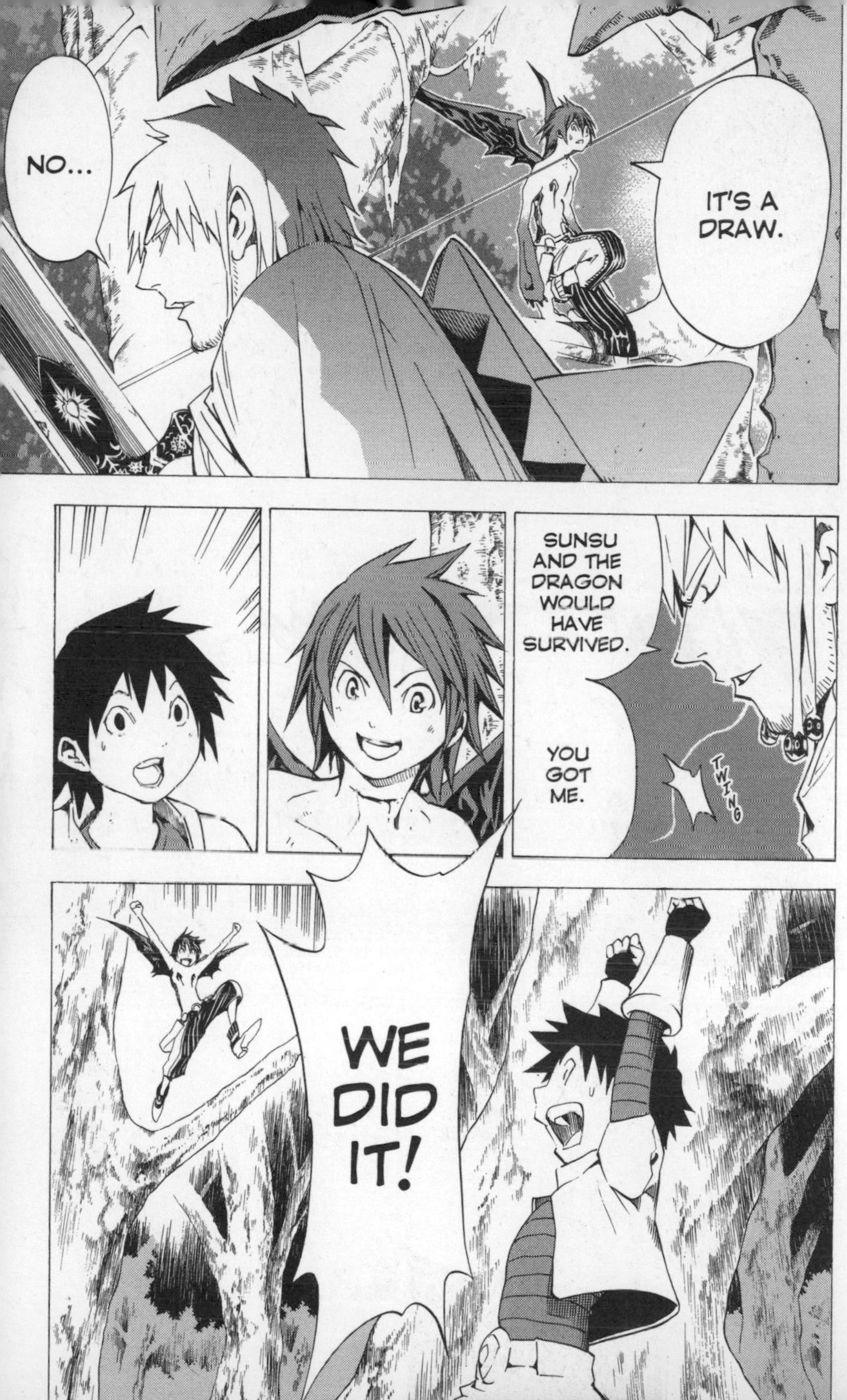
IT'S A DRAW.
NO...
SUNSU AND THE DRAGON WOULD HAVE SURVIVED.
YOU GOT ME.
TWING
WE DID IT!

RalΩGrad

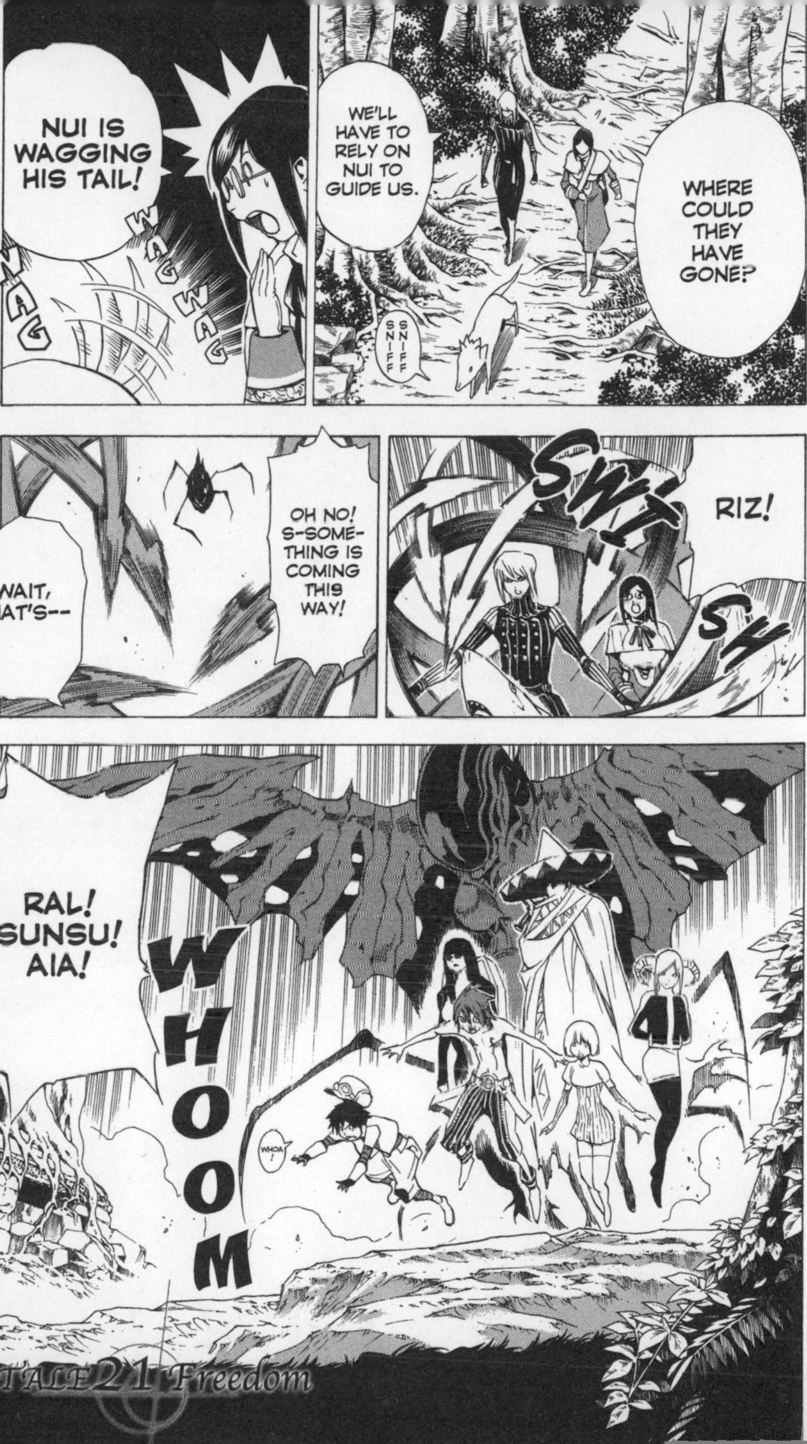
WHERE COULD THEY HAVE GONE?
WE'LL HAVE TO RELY ON NUI TO GUIDE US.
SNIFF SNIFF
NUI IS WAGGING HIS TAIL!
WAG WAG WAG
SWISH
RIZ!
OH NO! S-SOMETHING IS COMING THIS WAY!
WAIT, THAT'S--
RAL! SUNSU! AIA!
WHOOM
WHOA!
TALE 21 Freedom

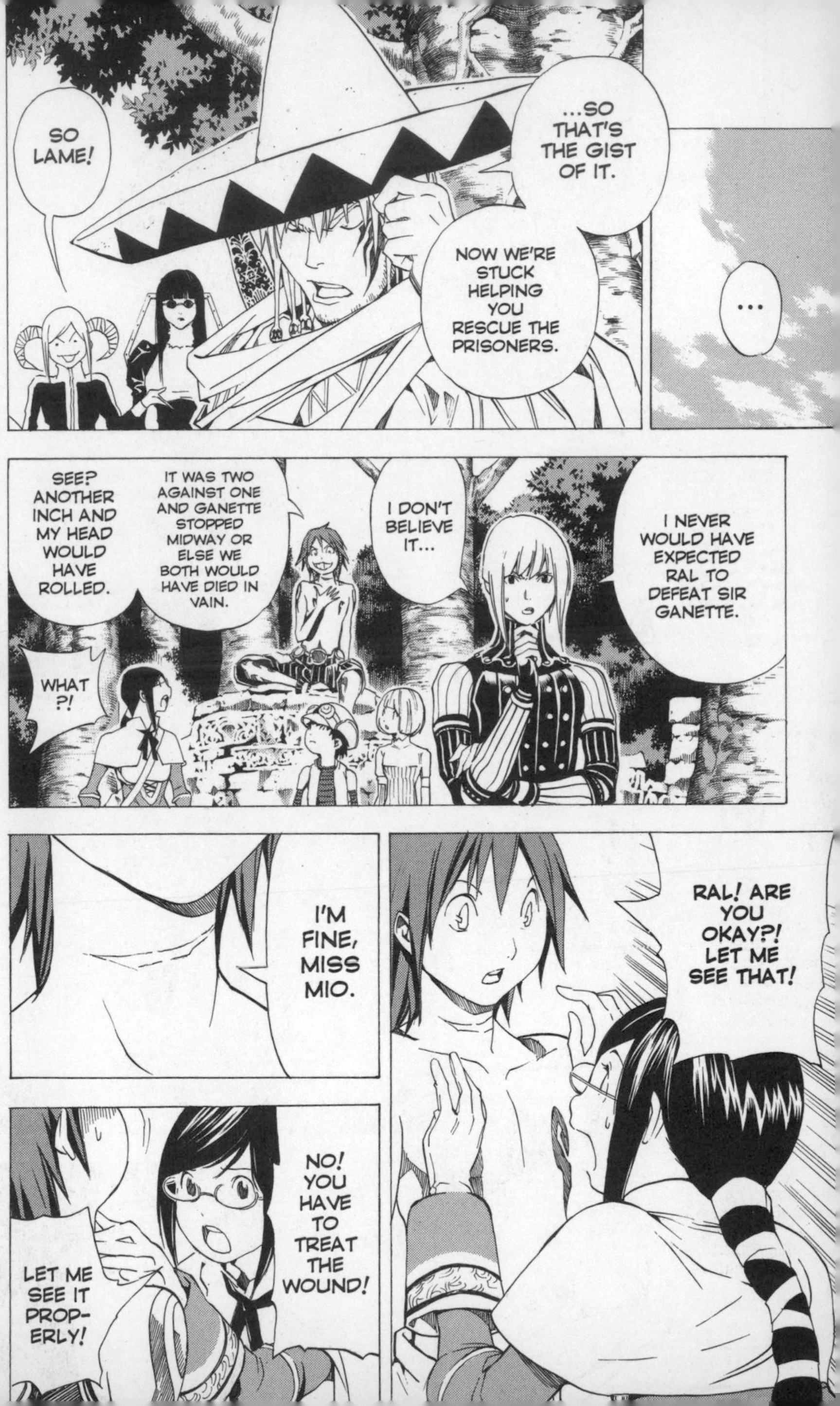
...
...SO THAT'S THE GIST OF IT.
NOW WE'RE STUCK HELPING YOU RESCUE THE PRISONERS.
SO LAME!
I NEVER WOULD HAVE EXPECTED RAL TO DEFEAT SIR GANETTE.
I DON'T BELIEVE IT...
IT WAS TWO AGAINST ONE AND GANETTE STOPPED MIDWAY OR ELSE WE BOTH WOULD HAVE DIED IN VAIN.
SEE? ANOTHER INCH AND MY HEAD WOULD HAVE ROLLED.
WHAT?!
RAL! ARE YOU OKAY?! LET ME SEE THAT!
I'M FINE, MISS MIO.
NO! YOU HAVE TO TREAT THE WOUND!
LET ME SEE IT PROPERLY!

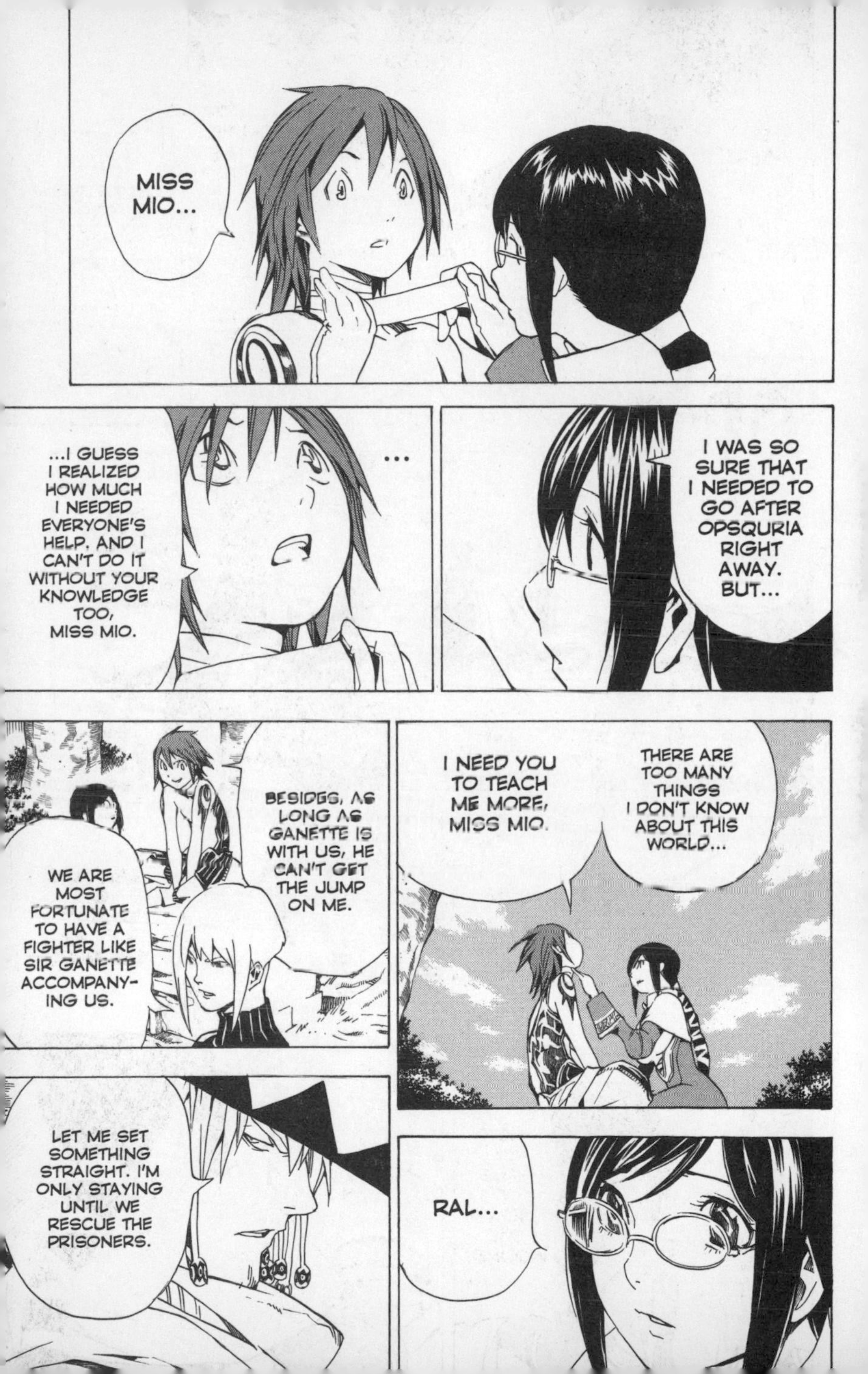
MISS MIO...
I WAS SO SURE THAT I NEEDED TO GO AFTER OPSQURIA RIGHT AWAY. BUT...
...
...I GUESS I REALIZED HOW MUCH I NEEDED EVERYONE'S HELP. AND I CAN'T DO IT WITHOUT YOUR KNOWLEDGE TOO, MISS MIO.
THERE ARE TOO MANY THINGS I DON'T KNOW ABOUT THIS WORLD...
I NEED YOU TO TEACH ME MORE, MISS MIO.
RAL...
BESIDES, AS LONG AS GANETTE IS WITH US, HE CAN'T GET THE JUMP ON ME.
WE ARE MOST FORTUNATE TO HAVE A FIGHTER LIKE SIR GANETTE ACCOMPANYING US.
LET ME SET SOMETHING STRAIGHT. I'M ONLY STAYING UNTIL WE RESCUE THE PRISONERS.

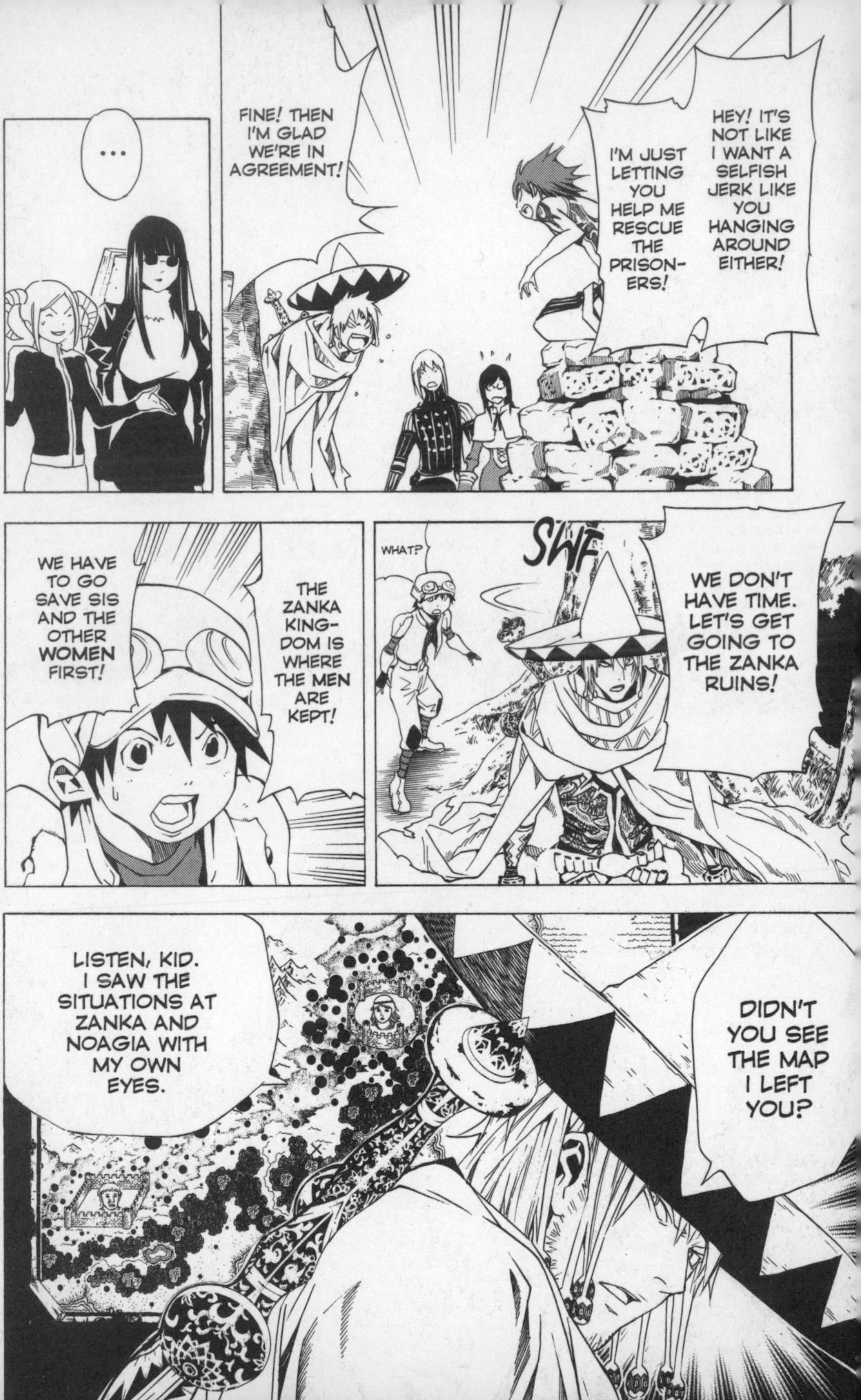
HEY! IT'S NOT LIKE I WANT A SELFISH JERK LIKE YOU HANGING AROUND EITHER!
I'M JUST LETTING YOU HELP ME RESCUE THE PRISON-ERS!
FINE! THEN I'M GLAD WE'RE IN AGREEMENT!
...
WE DON'T HAVE TIME. LET'S GET GOING TO THE ZANKA RUINS!
SWF
WHAT?
THE ZANKA KING-DOM IS WHERE THE MEN ARE KEPT!
WE HAVE TO GO SAVE SIS AND THE OTHER WOMEN FIRST!
DIDN'T YOU SEE THE MAP I LEFT YOU?
LISTEN, KID. I SAW THE SITUATIONS AT ZANKA AND NOAGIA WITH MY OWN EYES.

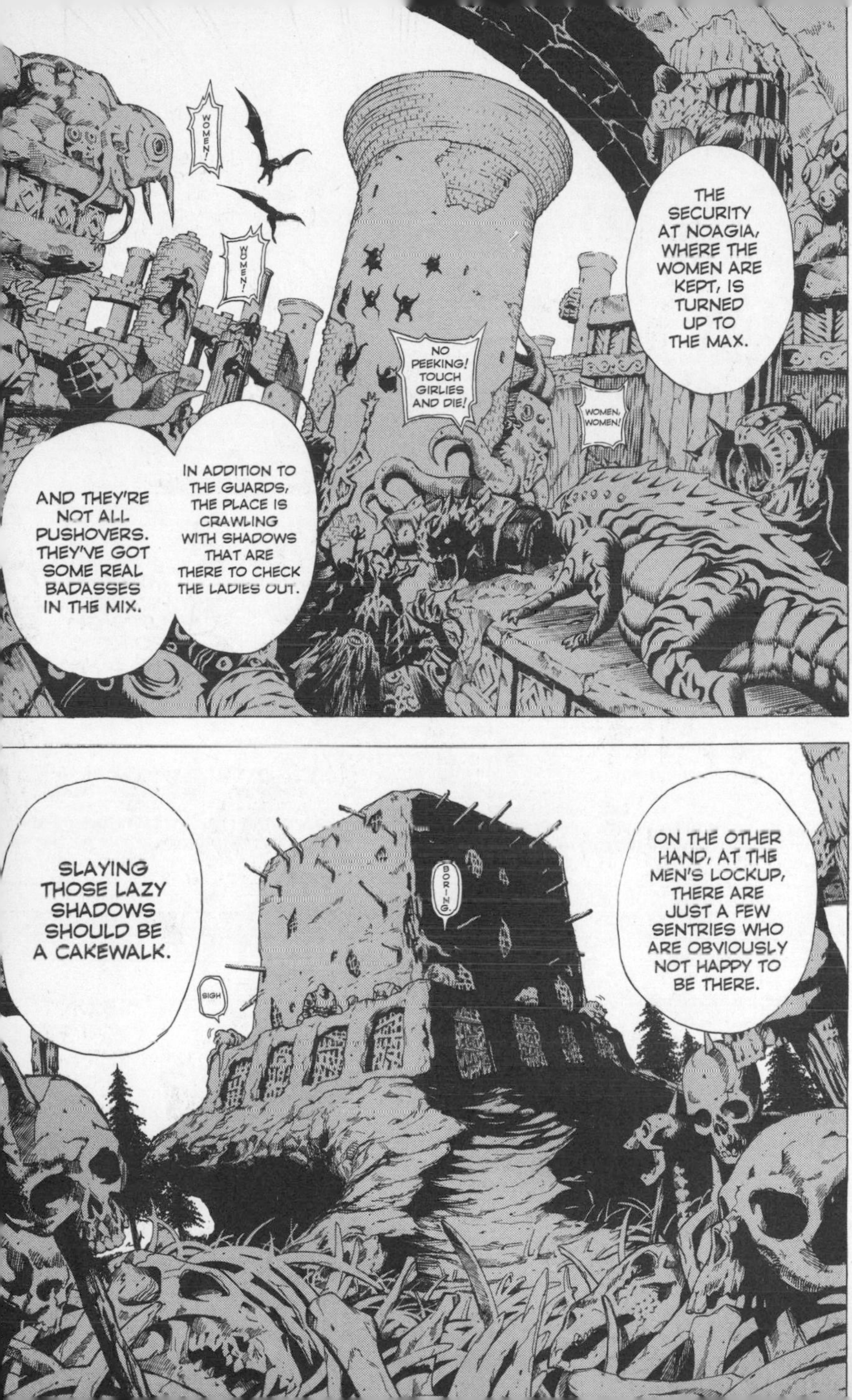
THE SECURITY AT NOAGIA, WHERE THE WOMEN ARE KEPT, IS TURNED UP TO THE MAX.
WOMEN!
WOMEN!
NO PEEKING! TOUCH GIRLIES AND DIE!
WOMEN, WOMEN!
IN ADDITION TO THE GUARDS, THE PLACE IS CRAWLING WITH SHADOWS THAT ARE THERE TO CHECK THE LADIES OUT.
AND THEY'RE NOT ALL PUSHOVERS. THEY'VE GOT SOME REAL BADASSES IN THE MIX.
ON THE OTHER HAND, AT THE MEN'S LOCKUP, THERE ARE JUST A FEW SENTRIES WHO ARE OBVIOUSLY NOT HAPPY TO BE THERE.
BORING.
SIGH
SLAYING THOSE LAZY SHADOWS SHOULD BE A CAKEWALK.

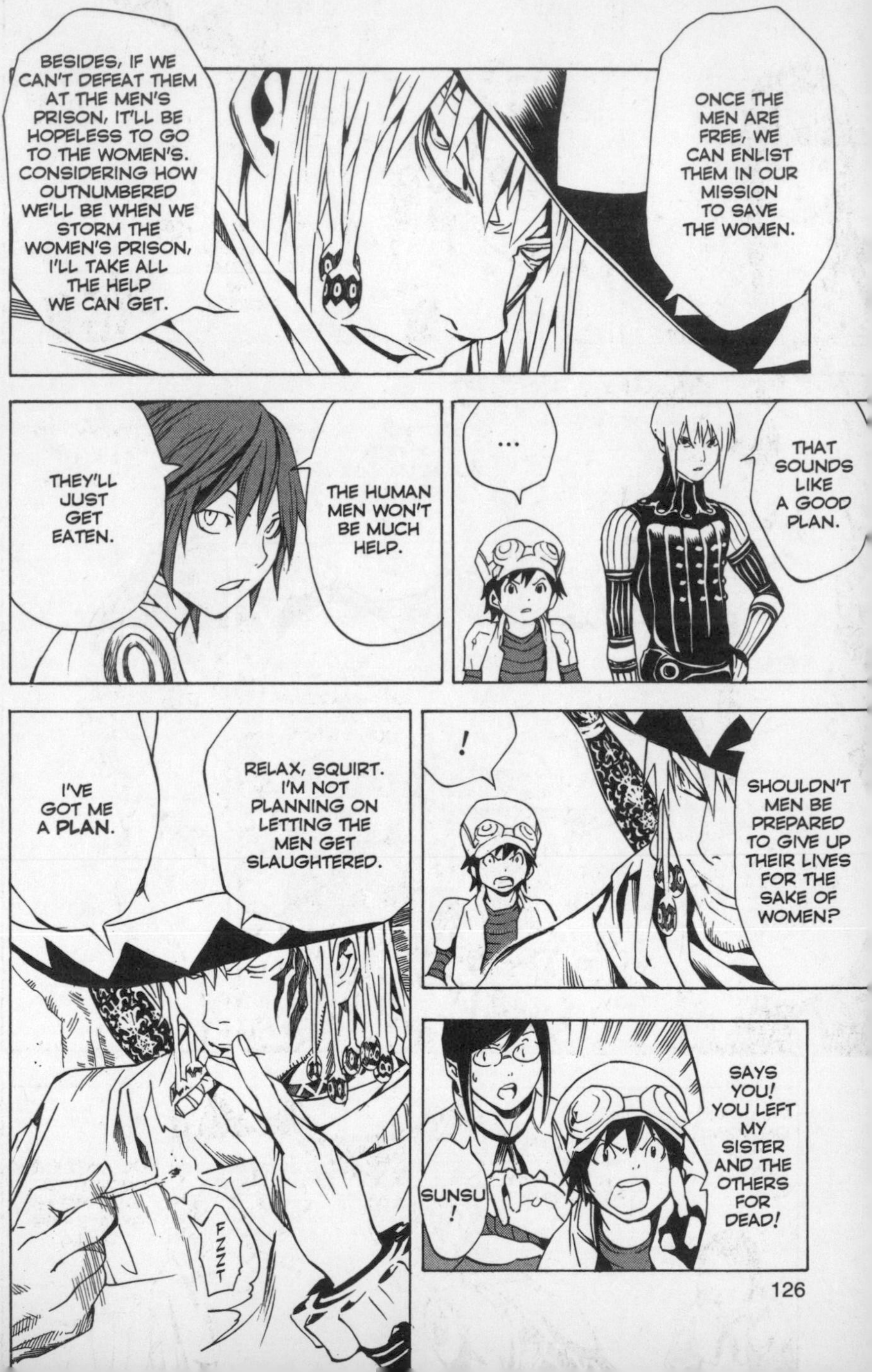
ONCE THE MEN ARE FREE, WE CAN ENLIST THEM IN OUR MISSION TO SAVE THE WOMEN.
BESIDES, IF WE CAN'T DEFEAT THEM AT THE MEN'S PRISON, IT'LL BE HOPELESS TO GO TO THE WOMEN'S. CONSIDERING HOW OUTNUMBERED WE'LL BE WHEN WE STORM THE WOMEN'S PRISON, I'LL TAKE ALL THE HELP WE CAN GET.
THAT SOUNDS LIKE A GOOD PLAN.
...
THE HUMAN MEN WON'T BE MUCH HELP.
THEY'LL JUST GET EATEN.
SHOULDN'T MEN BE PREPARED TO GIVE UP THEIR LIVES FOR THE SAKE OF WOMEN?
!
SAYS YOU! YOU LEFT MY SISTER AND THE OTHERS FOR DEAD!
SUNSU!
RELAX, SQUIRT. I'M NOT PLANNING ON LETTING THE MEN GET SLAUGHTERED.
I'VE GOT ME A **PLAN**.
FZZT

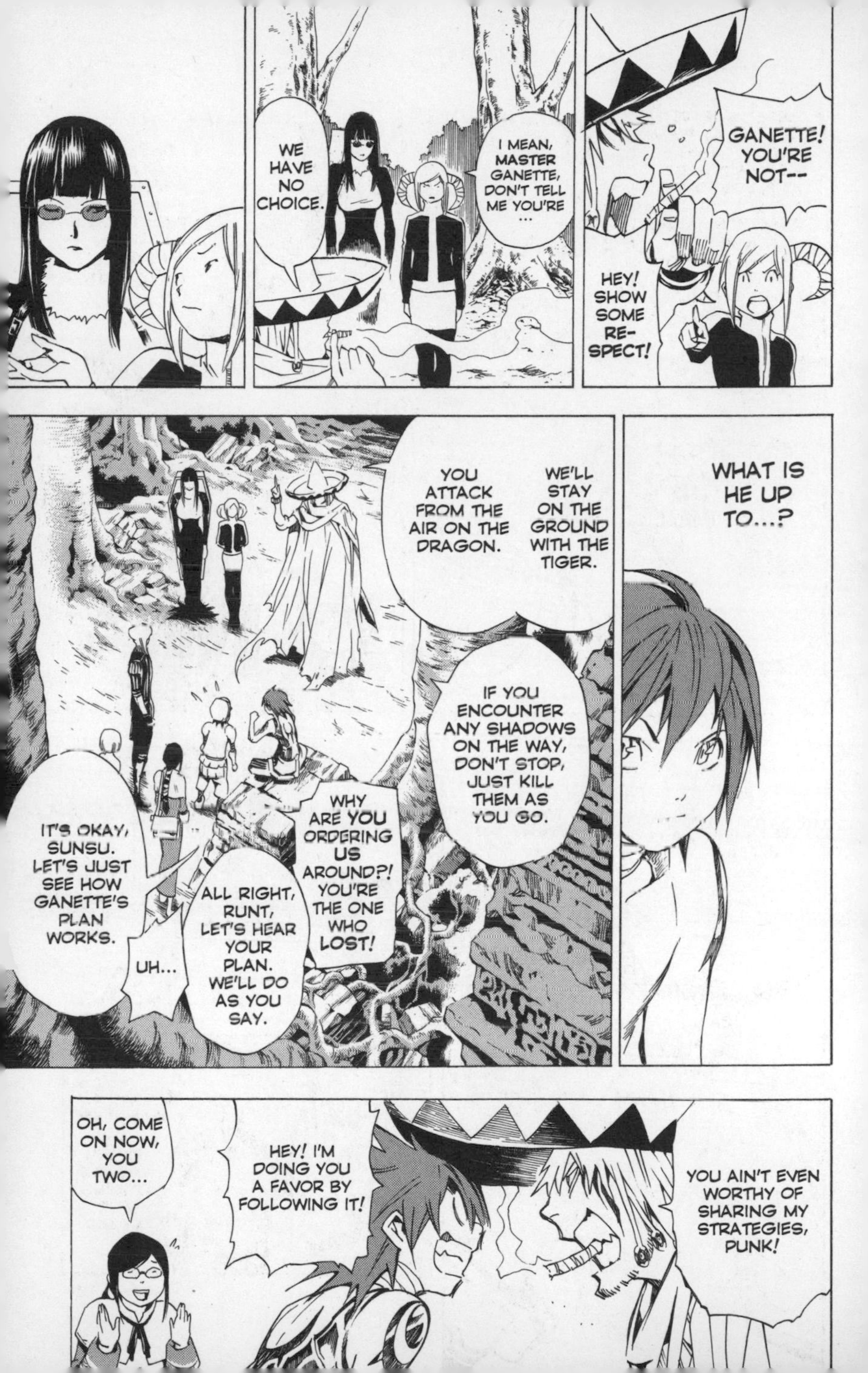
GANETTE! YOU'RE NOT--
HEY! SHOW SOME RE-SPECT!
I MEAN, MASTER GANETTE, DON'T TELL ME YOU'RE ...
WE HAVE NO CHOICE.
WHAT IS HE UP TO...?
WE'LL STAY ON THE GROUND WITH THE TIGER.
YOU ATTACK FROM THE AIR ON THE DRAGON.
IF YOU ENCOUNTER ANY SHADOWS ON THE WAY, DON'T STOP, JUST KILL THEM AS YOU GO.
WHY ARE YOU ORDERING US AROUND?! YOU'RE THE ONE WHO LOST!
ALL RIGHT, RUNT, LET'S HEAR YOUR PLAN. WE'LL DO AS YOU SAY.
IT'S OKAY, SUNSU. LET'S JUST SEE HOW GANETTE'S PLAN WORKS.
UH...
YOU AIN'T EVEN WORTHY OF SHARING MY STRATEGIES, PUNK!
HEY! I'M DOING YOU A FAVOR BY FOLLOWING IT!
OH, COME ON NOW, YOU TWO...

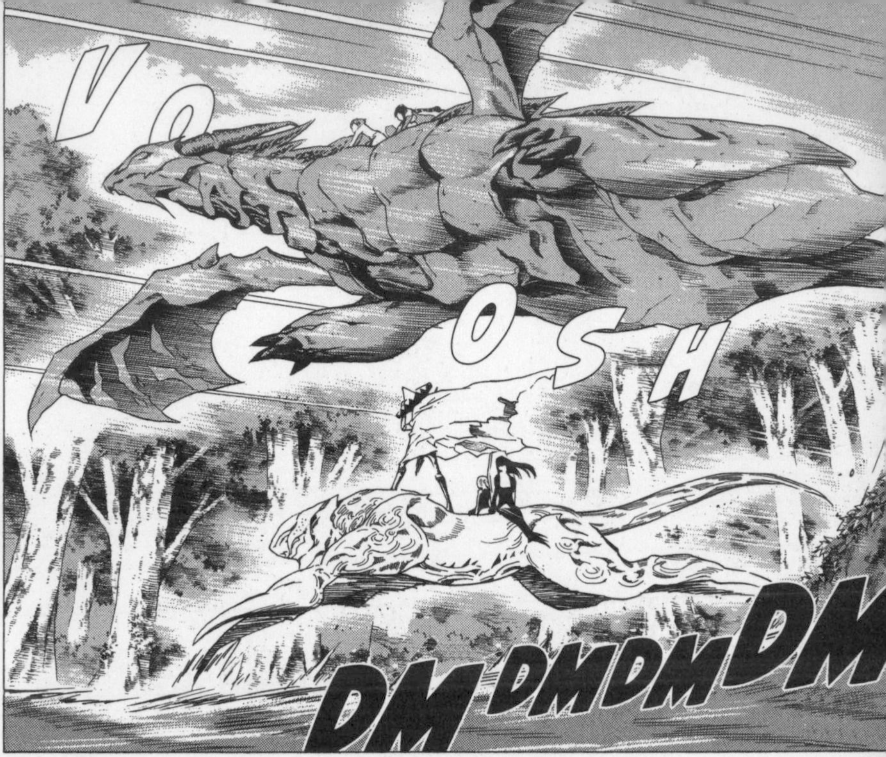
VOOSH
DMDMDMDMDM
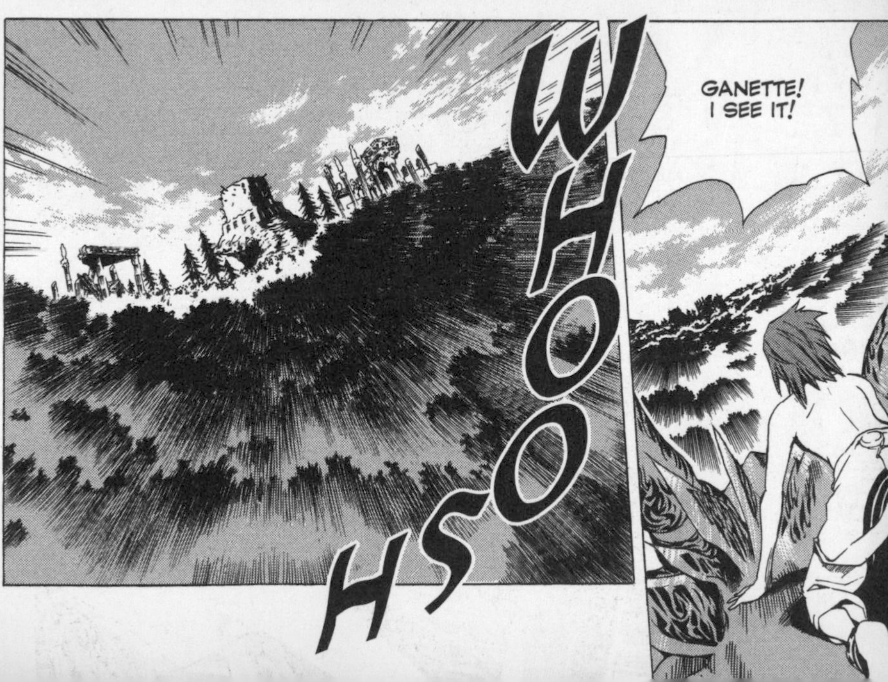
GANETTE! I SEE IT!
WHOOOOSH

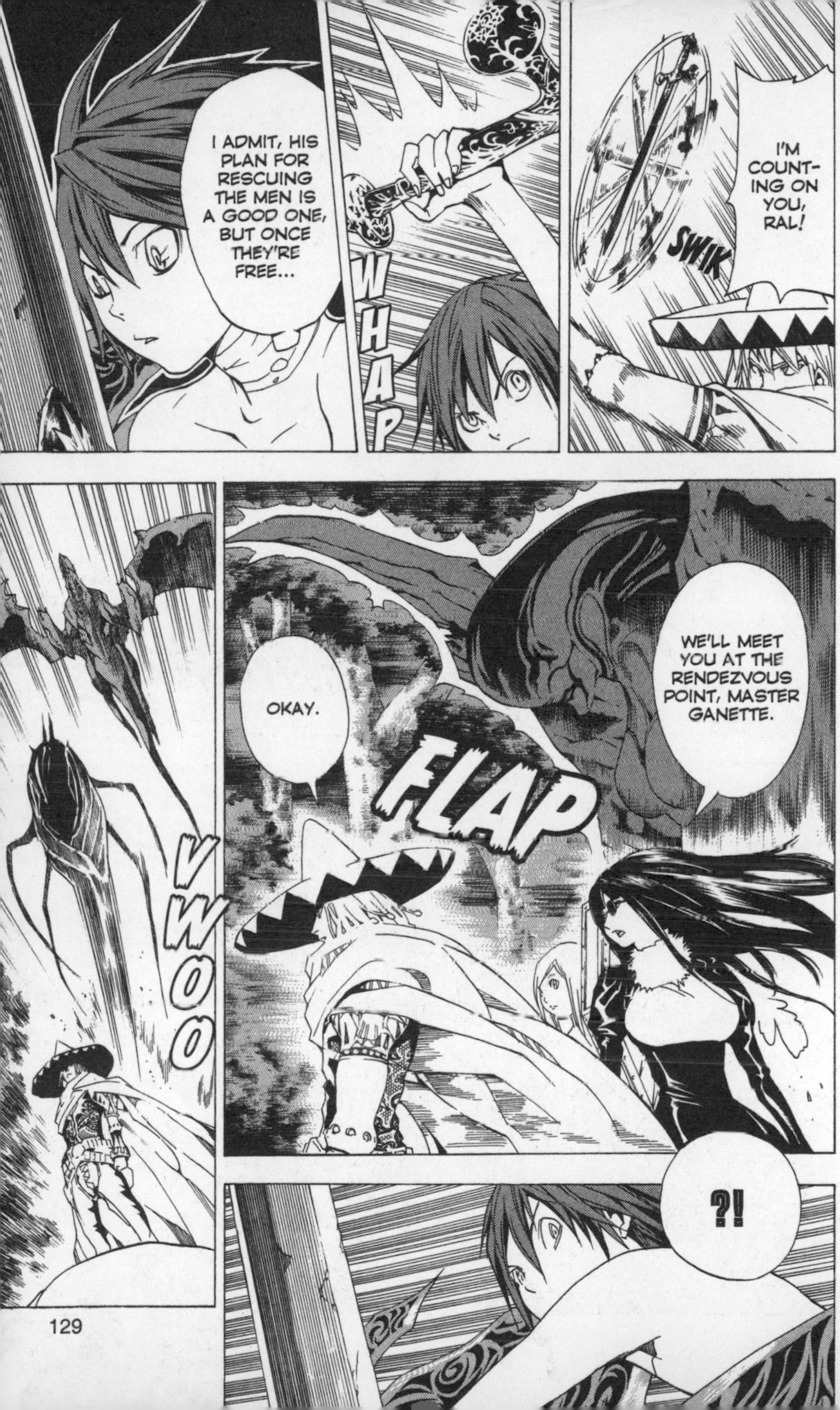
I'M COUNTING ON YOU, RAL!
SWIK
WHAP
I ADMIT, HIS PLAN FOR RESCUING THE MEN IS A GOOD ONE, BUT ONCE THEY'RE FREE...
WE'LL MEET YOU AT THE RENDEZVOUS POINT, MASTER GANETTE.
OKAY.
FLAP
?!
VWOO

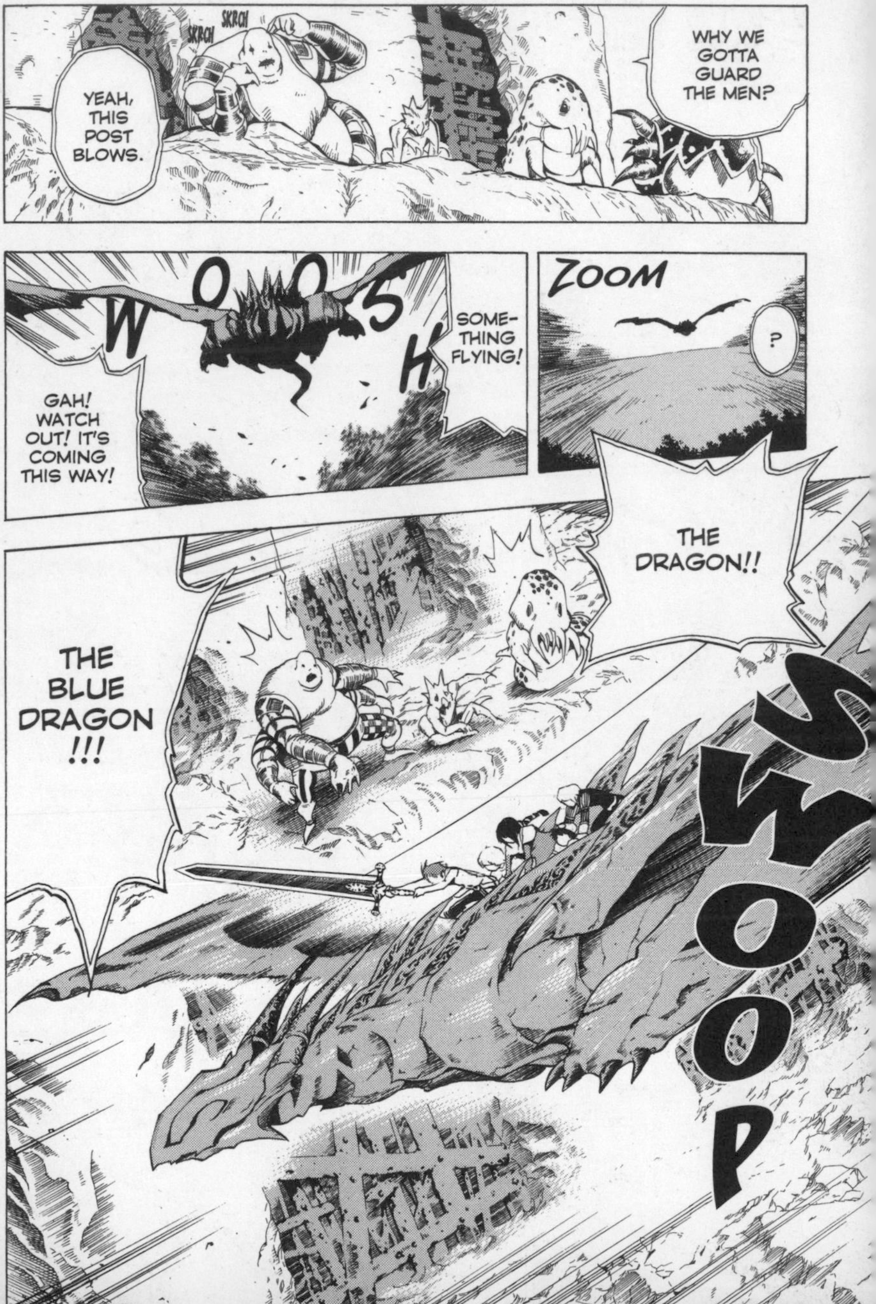
WHY WE GOTTA GUARD THE MEN?
SKRCH
SKRCH
YEAH, THIS POST BLOWS.
ZOOM
?
SOME-THING FLYING!
WOOSH
GAH! WATCH OUT! IT'S COMING THIS WAY!
THE DRAGON!!
SWOOP
THE BLUE DRAGON!!!

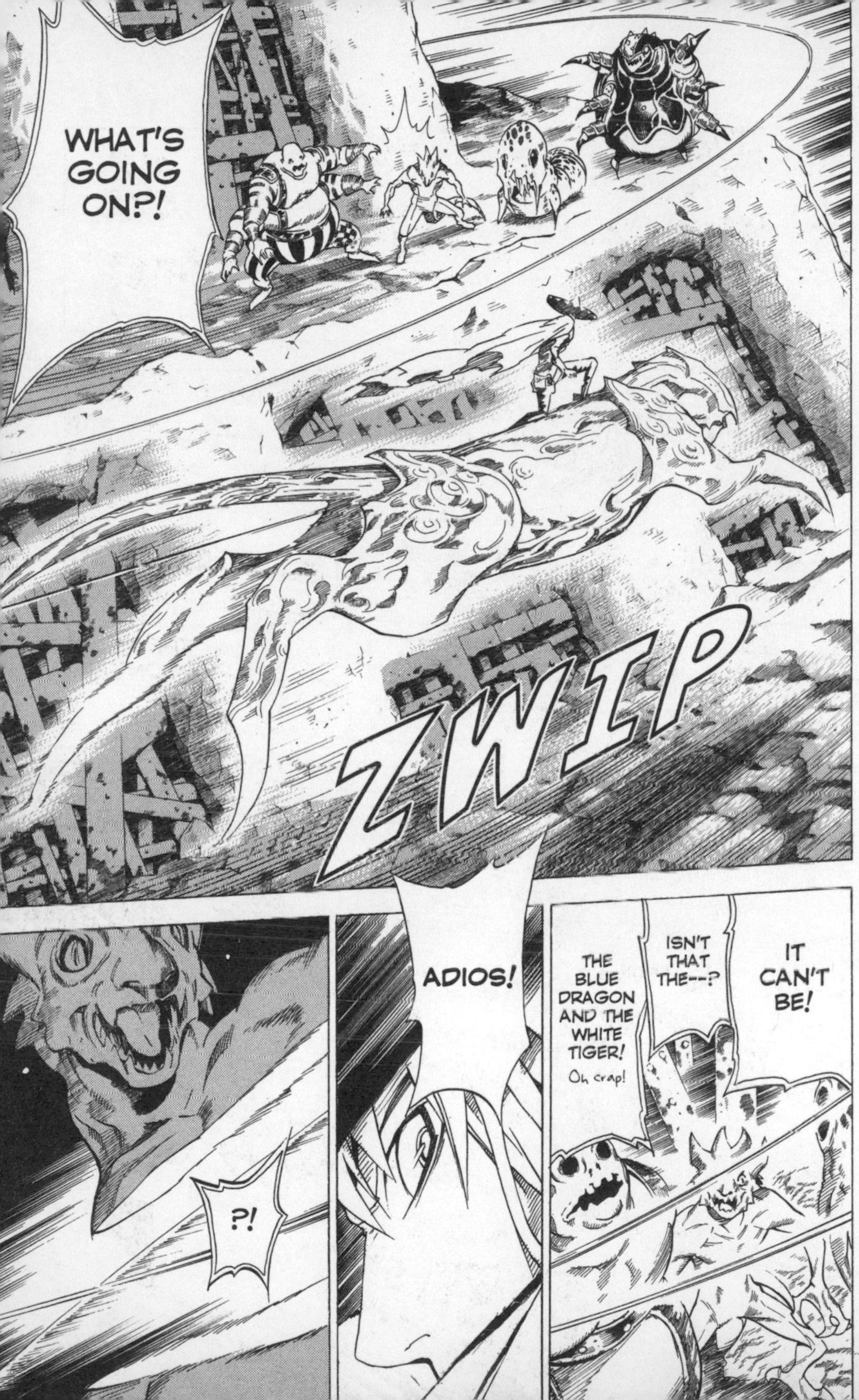
WHAT'S GOING ON?!
ZWIP
IT CAN'T BE!
ISN'T THAT THE--?
THE BLUE DRAGON AND THE WHITE TIGER!
Oh crap!
ADIOS!
?!

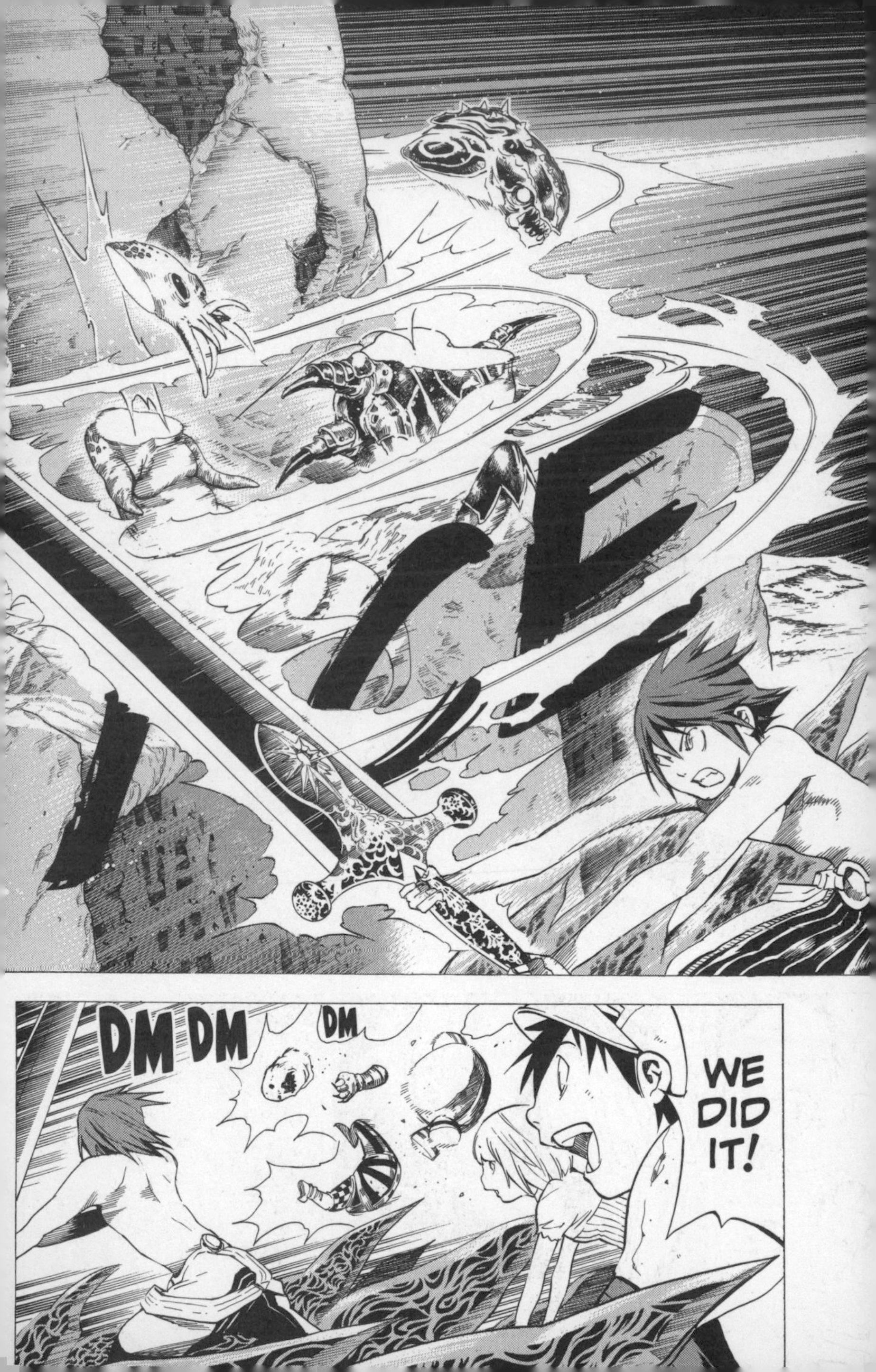
WE DID IT!
DM DM DM

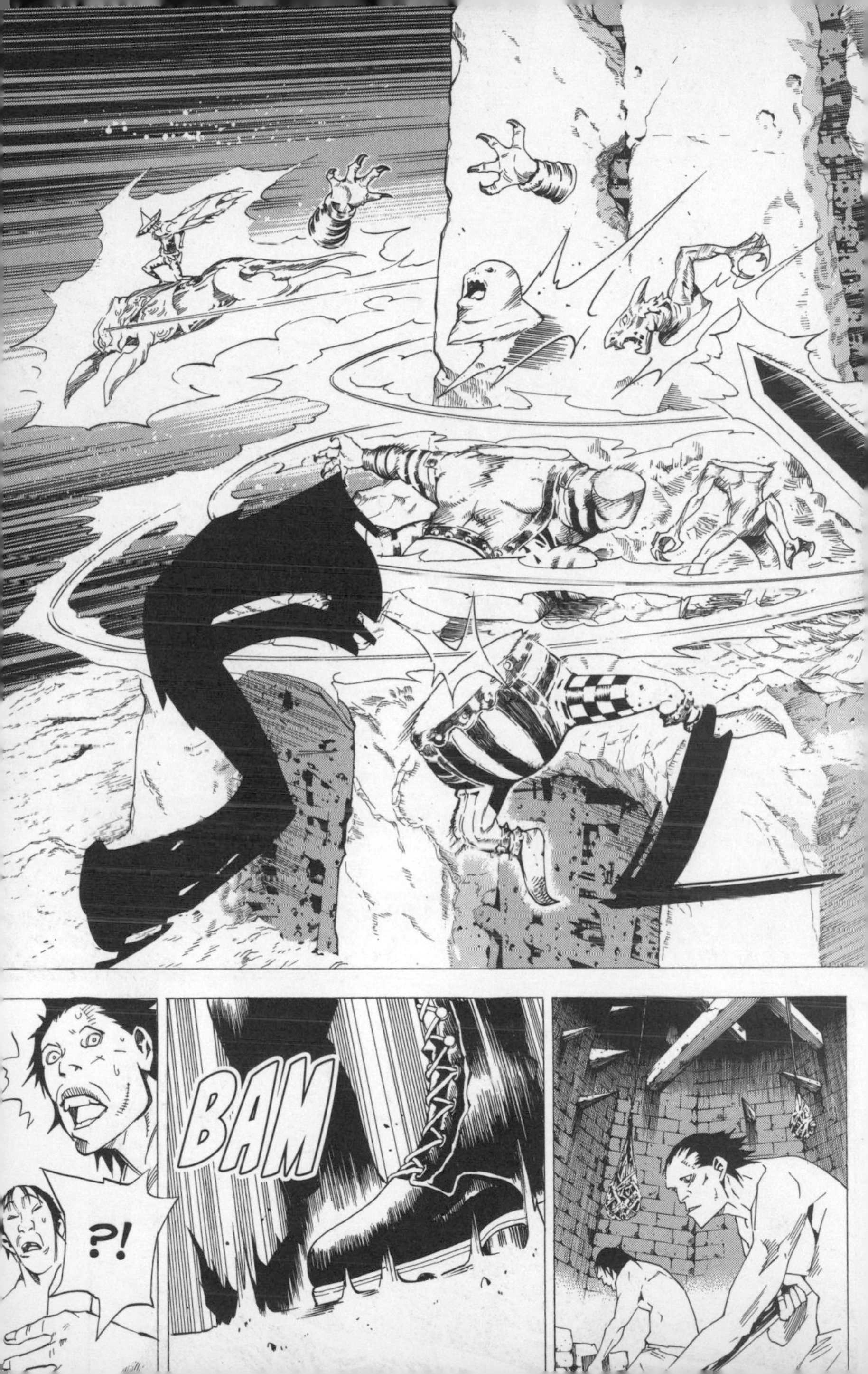
BAM
?!

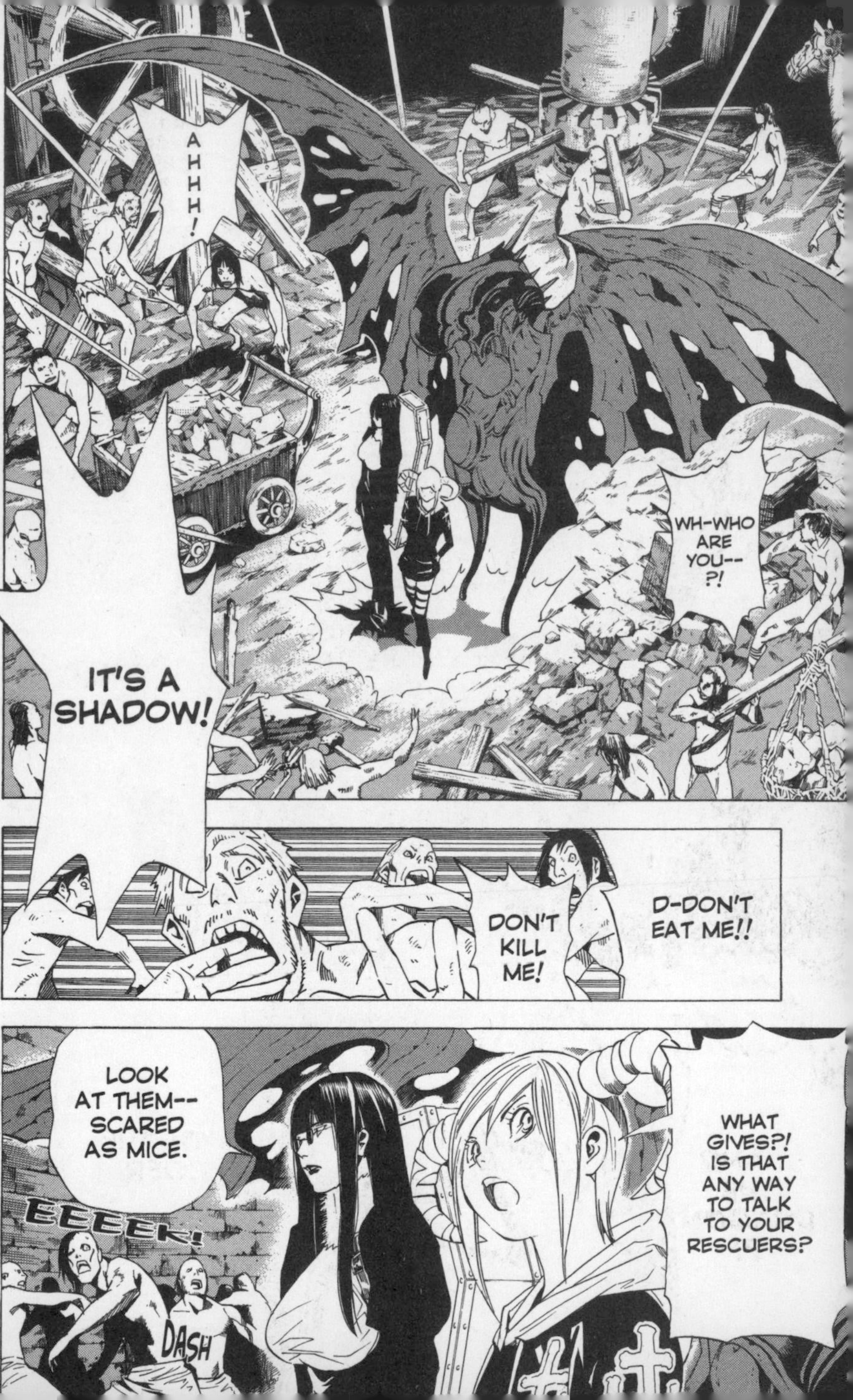
WH-WHO ARE YOU--?!
AHHH!
IT'S A SHADOW!
D-DON'T EAT ME!!
DON'T KILL ME!
WHAT GIVES?! IS THAT ANY WAY TO TALK TO YOUR RESCUERS?
LOOK AT THEM--SCARED AS MICE.
EEEEK!
DASH

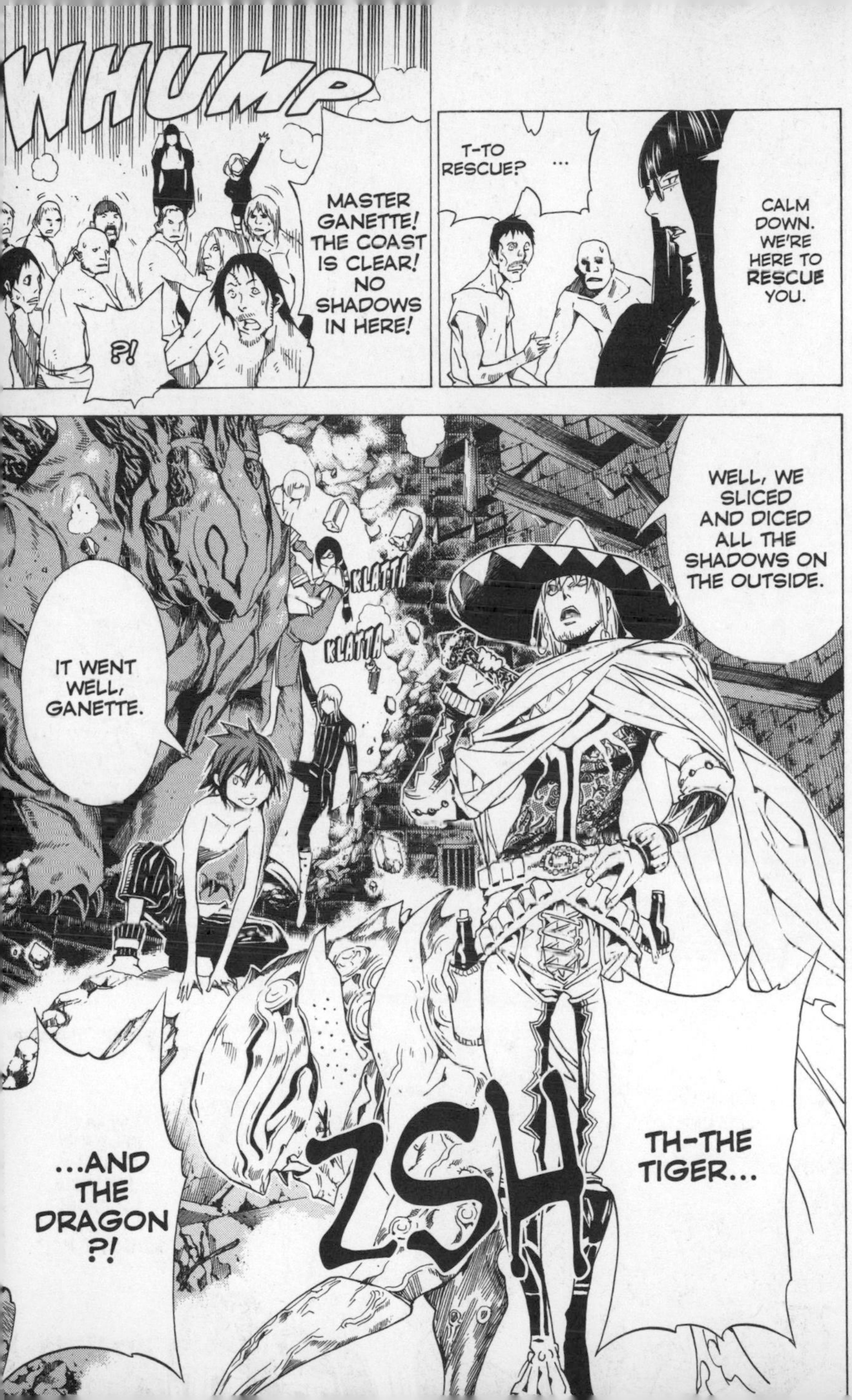
CALM DOWN. WE'RE HERE TO RESCUE YOU.
T-TO RESCUE?
...
WHUMP
MASTER GANETTE! THE COAST IS CLEAR! NO SHADOWS IN HERE!
?!
WELL, WE SLICED AND DICED ALL THE SHADOWS ON THE OUTSIDE.
KLATTA
KLATTA
IT WENT WELL, GANETTE.
TH-THE TIGER...
ZSH
...AND THE DRAGON ?!

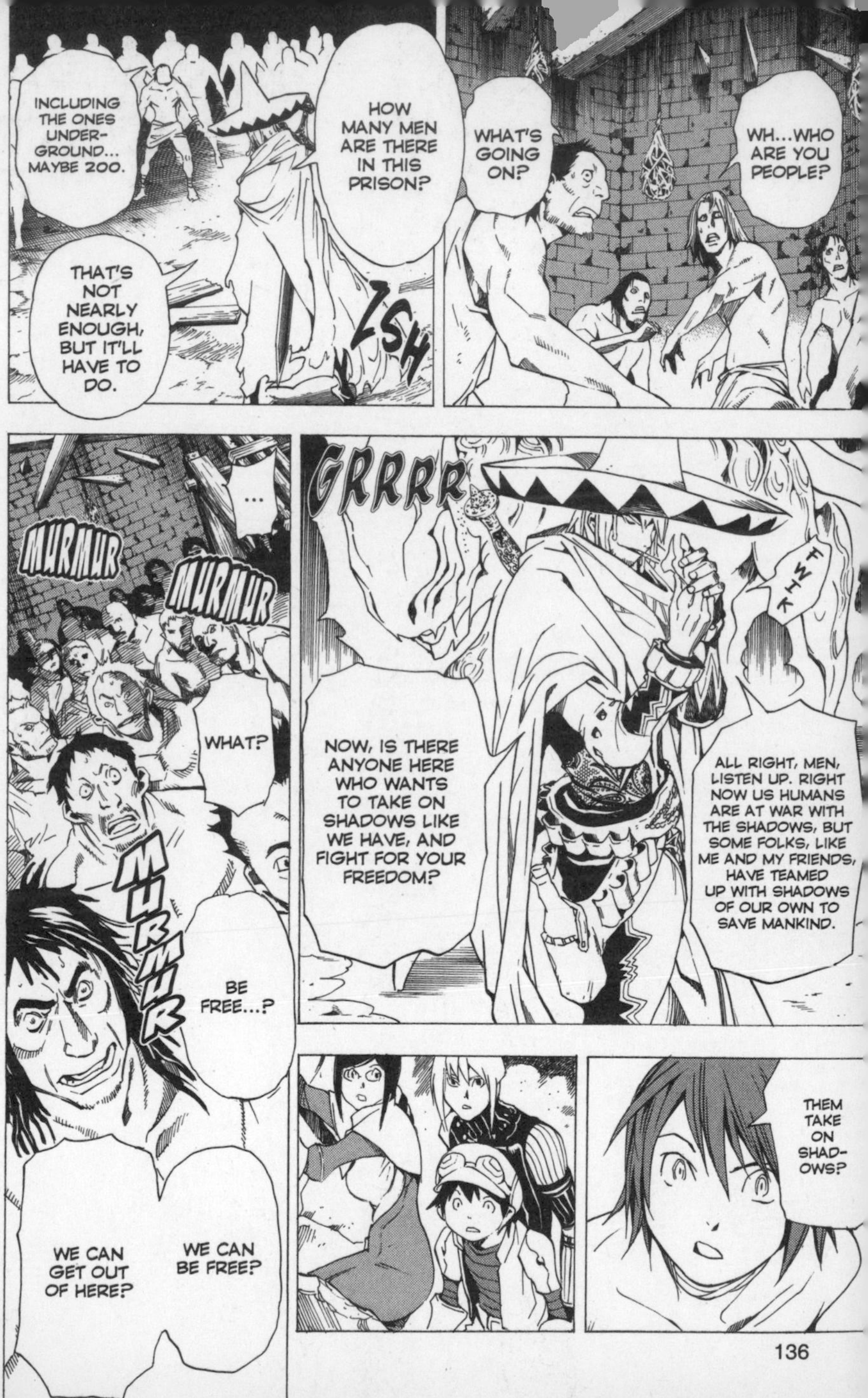
WH...WHO ARE YOU PEOPLE?
WHAT'S GOING ON?
HOW MANY MEN ARE THERE IN THIS PRISON?
INCLUDING THE ONES UNDERGROUND... MAYBE 200.
ZSH
THAT'S NOT NEARLY ENOUGH, BUT IT'LL HAVE TO DO.
GRRRR
FWIK
ALL RIGHT, MEN, LISTEN UP. RIGHT NOW US HUMANS ARE AT WAR WITH THE SHADOWS, BUT SOME FOLKS, LIKE ME AND MY FRIENDS, HAVE TEAMED UP WITH SHADOWS OF OUR OWN TO SAVE MANKIND.
NOW, IS THERE ANYONE HERE WHO WANTS TO TAKE ON SHADOWS LIKE WE HAVE, AND FIGHT FOR YOUR FREEDOM?
THEM TAKE ON SHADOWS?
...
MURMUR
MURMUR
WHAT?
MURMUR
BE FREE...?
WE CAN BE FREE?
WE CAN GET OUT OF HERE?

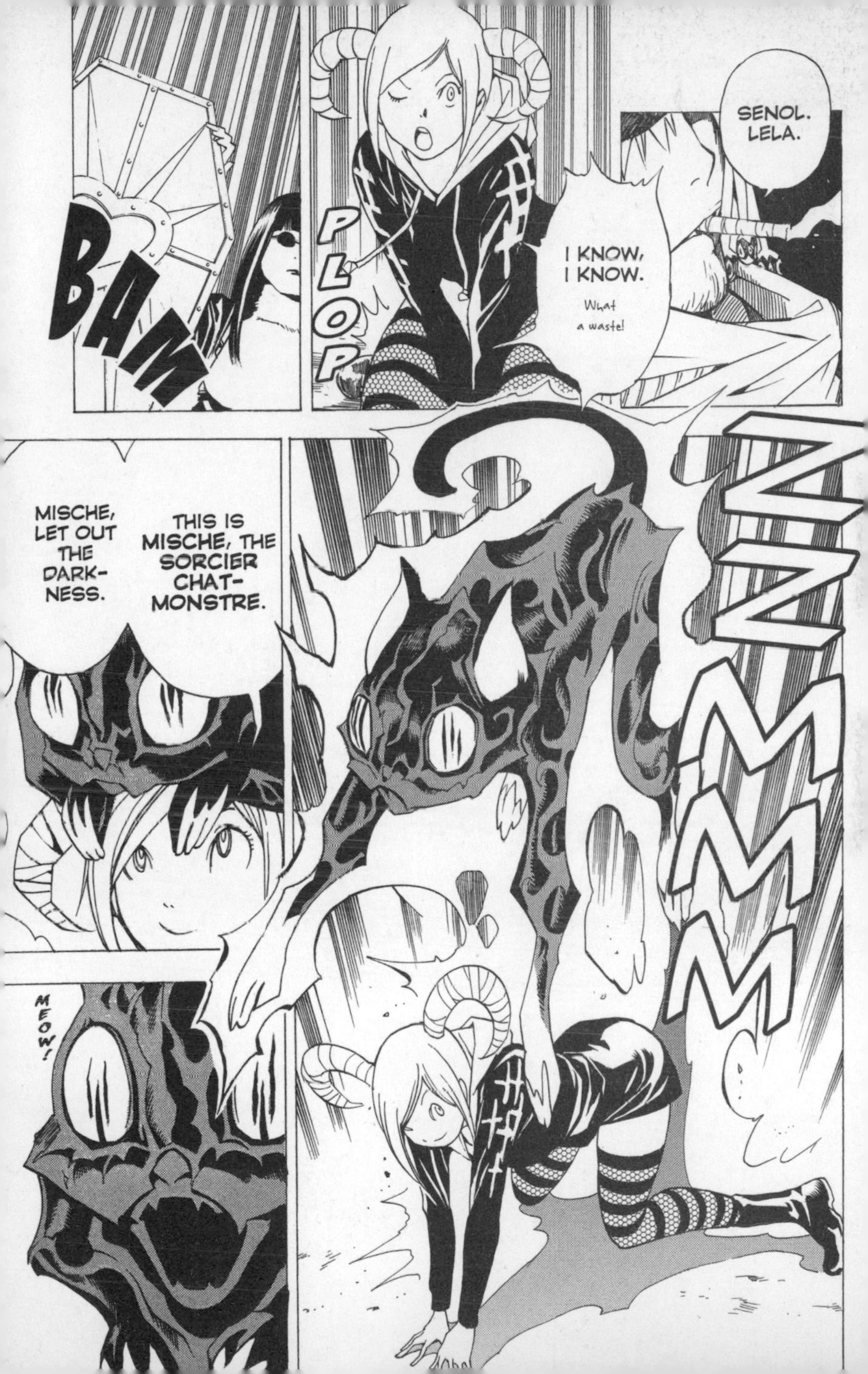
SENOL. LELA.
I KNOW, I KNOW.
What a waste!
PLOP
BAM
ZMMMM
THIS IS MISCHE, THE SORCIER CHAT-MONSTRE.
MISCHE, LET OUT THE DARKNESS.
MEOW!

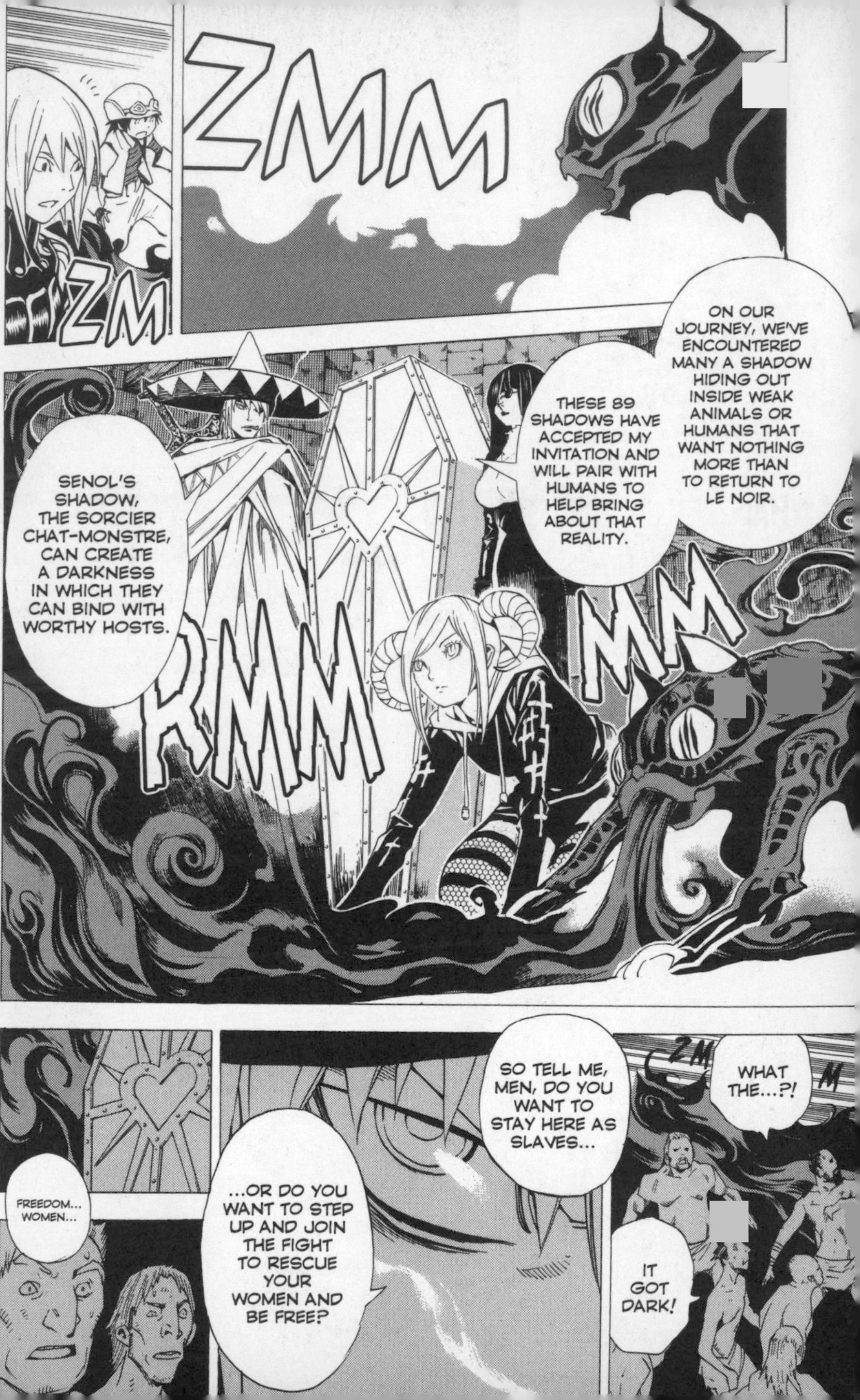
ZMM
ZM
ON OUR JOURNEY, WE'VE ENCOUNTERED MANY A SHADOW HIDING OUT INSIDE WEAK ANIMALS OR HUMANS THAT WANT NOTHING MORE THAN TO RETURN TO LE NOIR.
THESE 89 SHADOWS HAVE ACCEPTED MY INVITATION AND WILL PAIR WITH HUMANS TO HELP BRING ABOUT THAT REALITY.
SENOL'S SHADOW, THE SORCIER CHAT-MONSTRE, CAN CREATE A DARKNESS IN WHICH THEY CAN BIND WITH WORTHY HOSTS.
MM
RMMM
ZM
M
WHAT THE...?!
IT GOT DARK!
SO TELL ME, MEN, DO YOU WANT TO STAY HERE AS SLAVES...
...OR DO YOU WANT TO STEP UP AND JOIN THE FIGHT TO RESCUE YOUR WOMEN AND BE FREE?
FREEDOM... WOMEN...

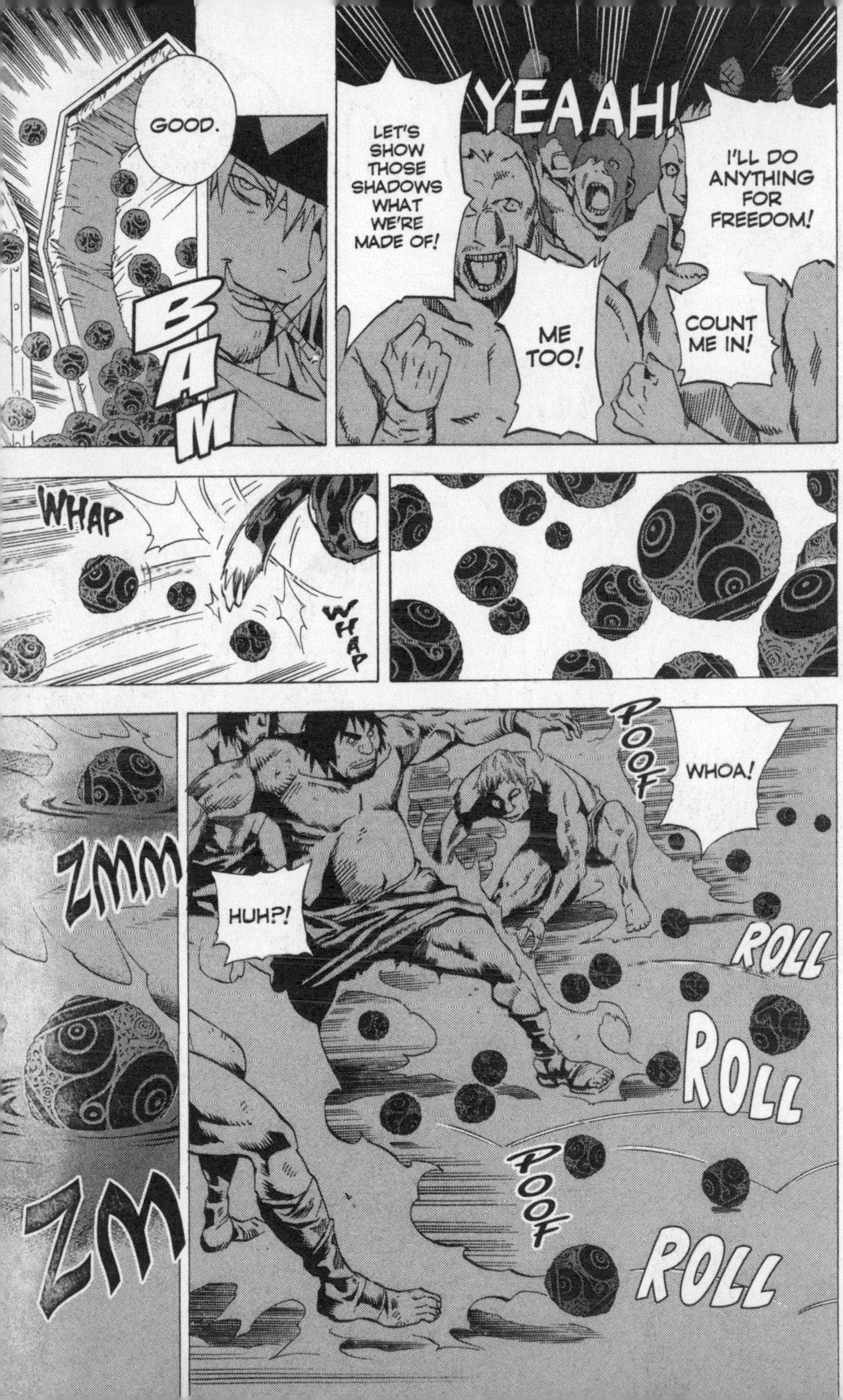
YEAAH!
I'LL DO ANYTHING FOR FREEDOM!
LET'S SHOW THOSE SHADOWS WHAT WE'RE MADE OF!
COUNT ME IN!
ME TOO!
GOOD.
BAM
WHAP
WHAP
POOF
WHOA!
HUH?!
ROLL
ROLL
POOF
ROLL
ZMM
ZM

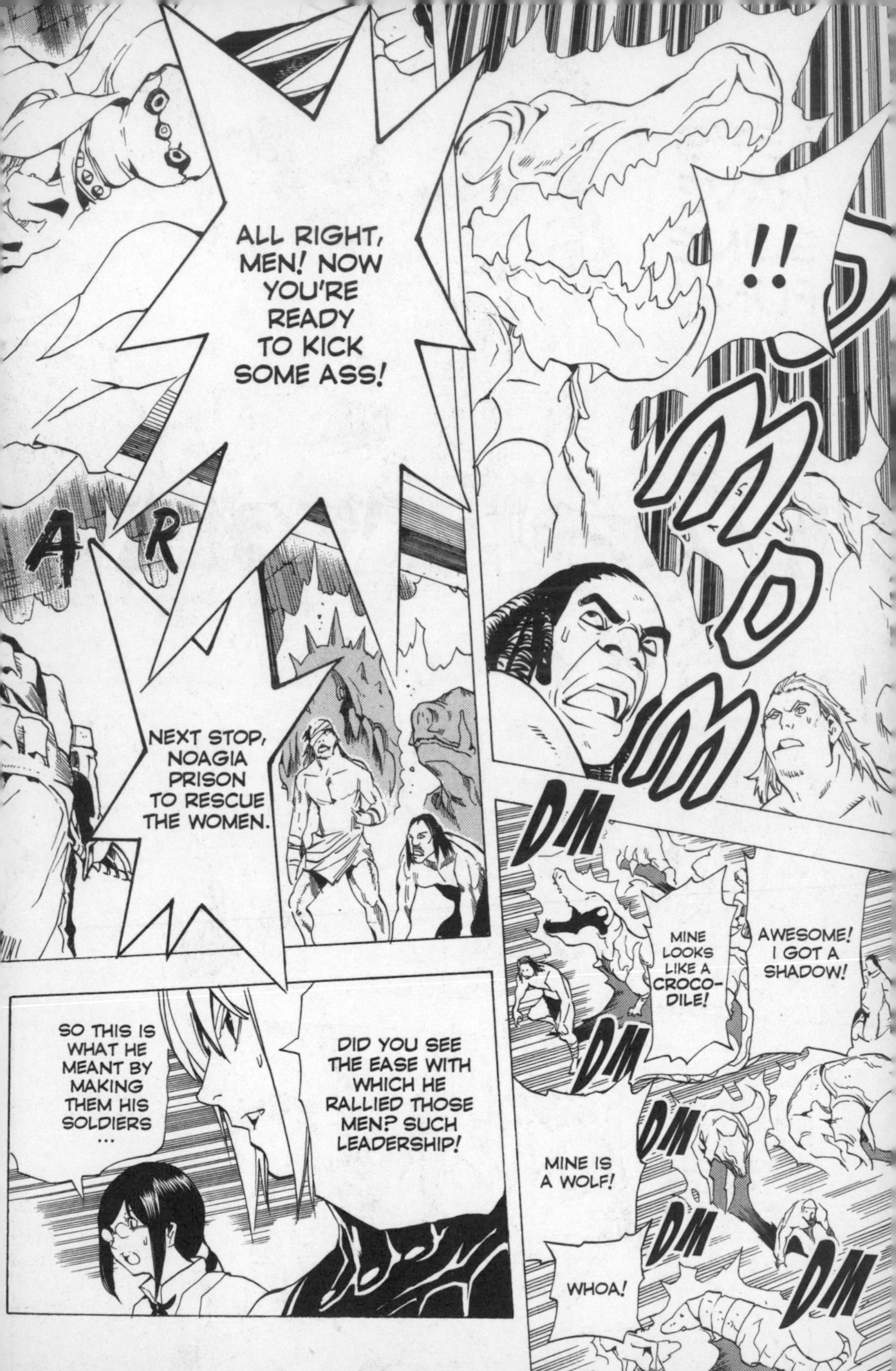
!!
ALL RIGHT, MEN! NOW YOU'RE READY TO KICK SOME ASS!
NEXT STOP, NOAGIA PRISON TO RESCUE THE WOMEN.
DM
AWESOME! I GOT A SHADOW!
MINE LOOKS LIKE A CROCO-DILE!
DM
DM
MINE IS A WOLF!
DM
DM
WHOA!
DID YOU SEE THE EASE WITH WHICH HE RALLIED THOSE MEN? SUCH LEADERSHIP!
SO THIS IS WHAT HE MEANT BY MAKING THEM HIS SOLDIERS ...

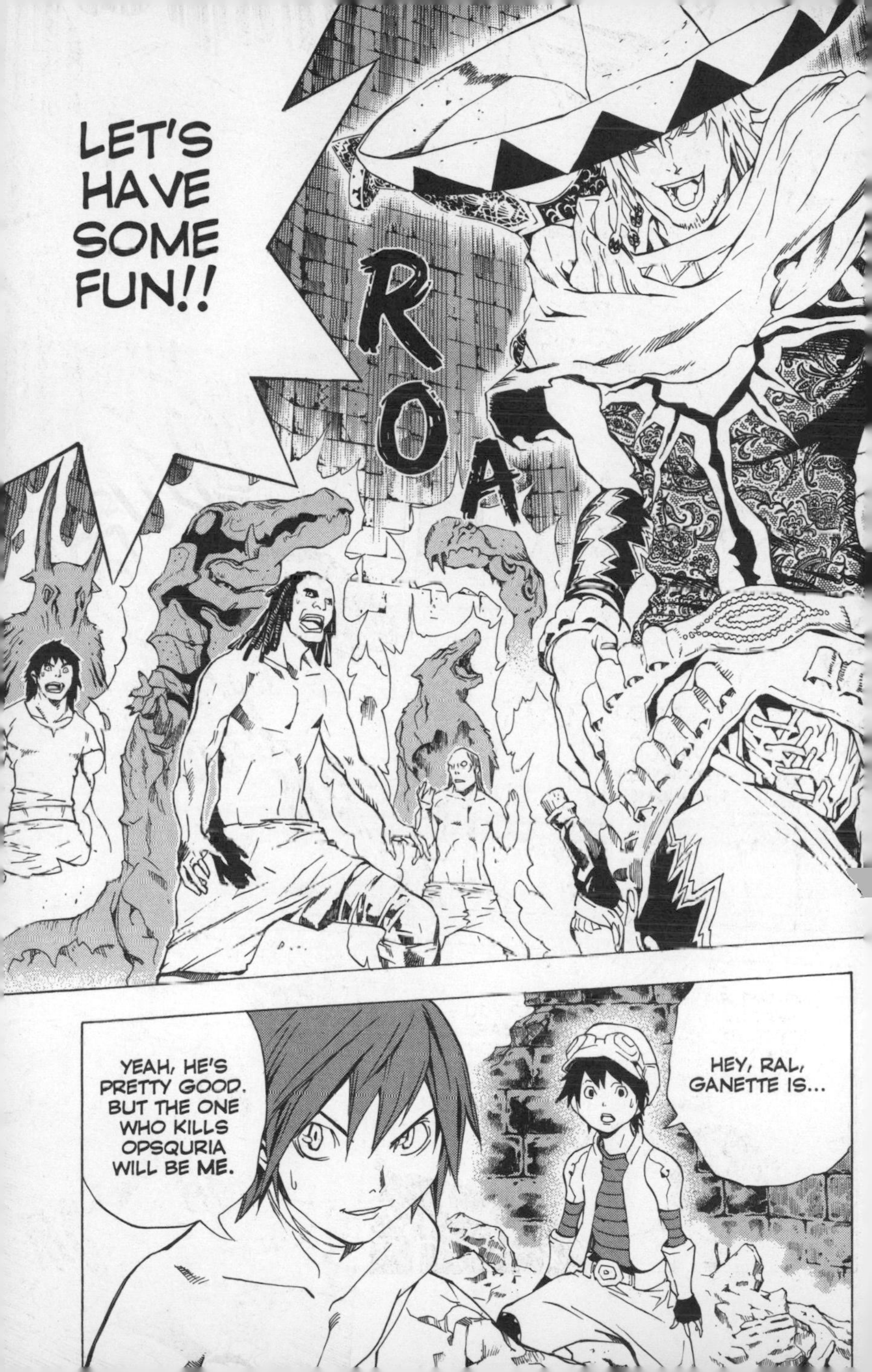
LET'S HAVE SOME FUN!!
ROA
HEY, RAL, GANETTE IS...
YEAH, HE'S PRETTY GOOD. BUT THE ONE WHO KILLS OPSQURIA WILL BE ME.

RalΩGrad

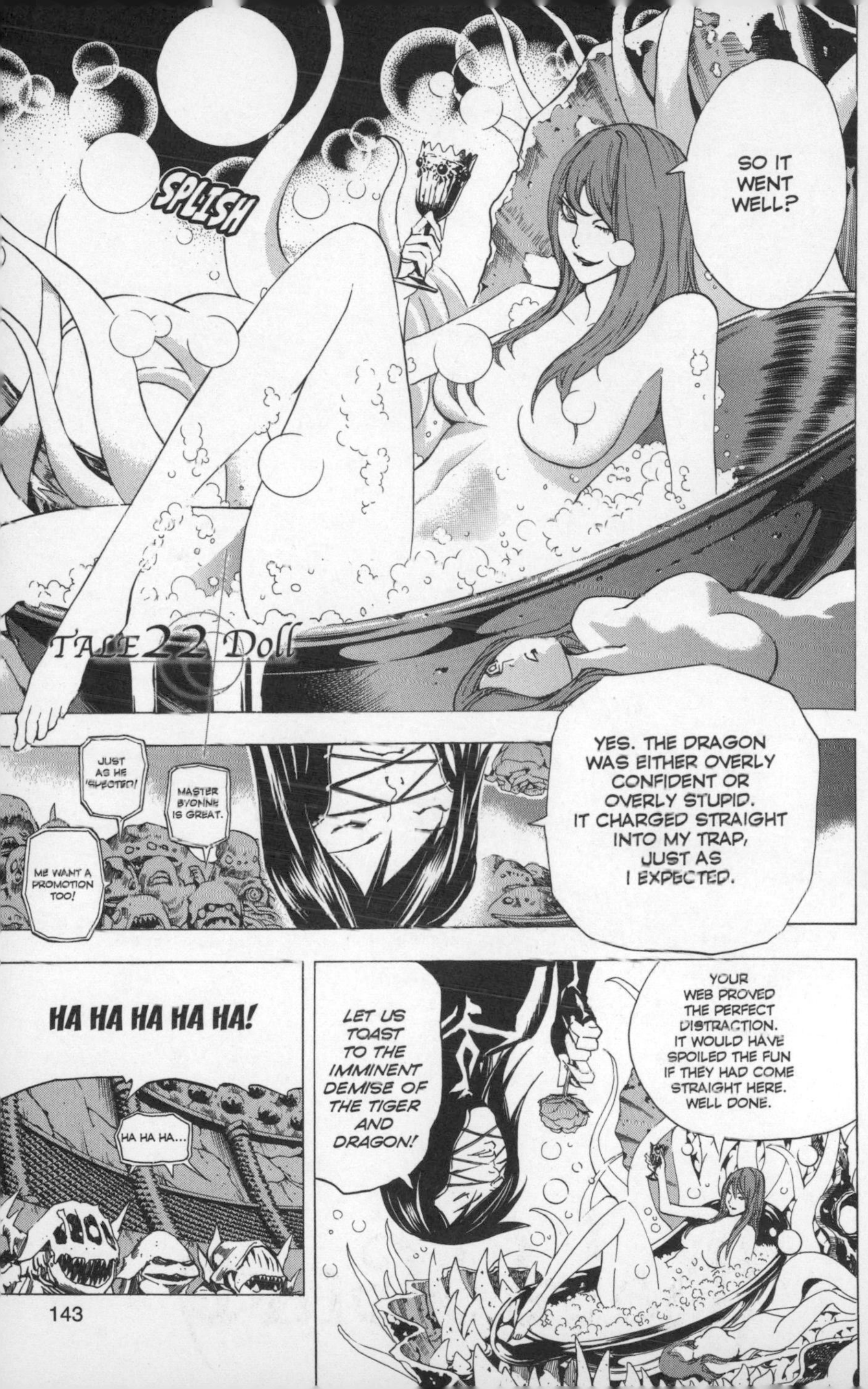
SPLISH
SO IT WENT WELL?
TALE 22 Doll
YES. THE DRAGON WAS EITHER OVERLY CONFIDENT OR OVERLY STUPID. IT CHARGED STRAIGHT INTO MY TRAP, JUST AS I EXPECTED.
MASTER BYONNE IS GREAT.
JUST AS HE 'SPECTED!
ME WANT A PROMOTION TOO!
YOUR WEB PROVED THE PERFECT DISTRACTION. IT WOULD HAVE SPOILED THE FUN IF THEY HAD COME STRAIGHT HERE. WELL DONE.
LET US TOAST TO THE IMMINENT DEMISE OF THE TIGER AND DRAGON!
HA HA HA HA HA!
HA HA HA...

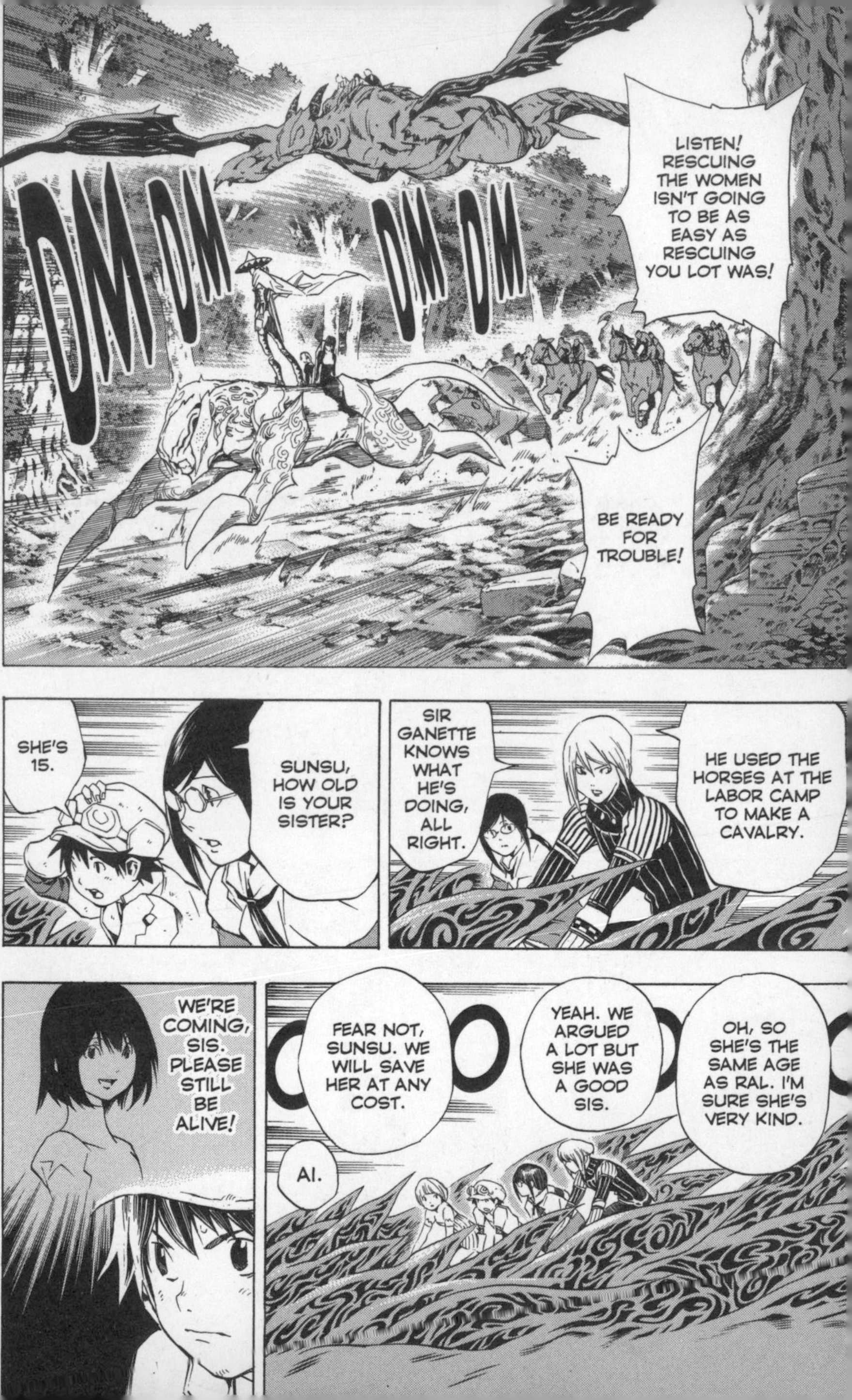
LISTEN! RESCUING THE WOMEN ISN'T GOING TO BE AS EASY AS RESCUING YOU LOT WAS!
DM DM
DM DM
BE READY FOR TROUBLE!
HE USED THE HORSES AT THE LABOR CAMP TO MAKE A CAVALRY.
SIR GANETTE KNOWS WHAT HE'S DOING, ALL RIGHT.
SUNSU, HOW OLD IS YOUR SISTER?
SHE'S 15.
OH, SO SHE'S THE SAME AGE AS RAL. I'M SURE SHE'S VERY KIND.
YEAH. WE ARGUED A LOT BUT SHE WAS A GOOD SIS.
FEAR NOT, SUNSU. WE WILL SAVE HER AT ANY COST.
AI.
WE'RE COMING, SIS. PLEASE STILL BE ALIVE!

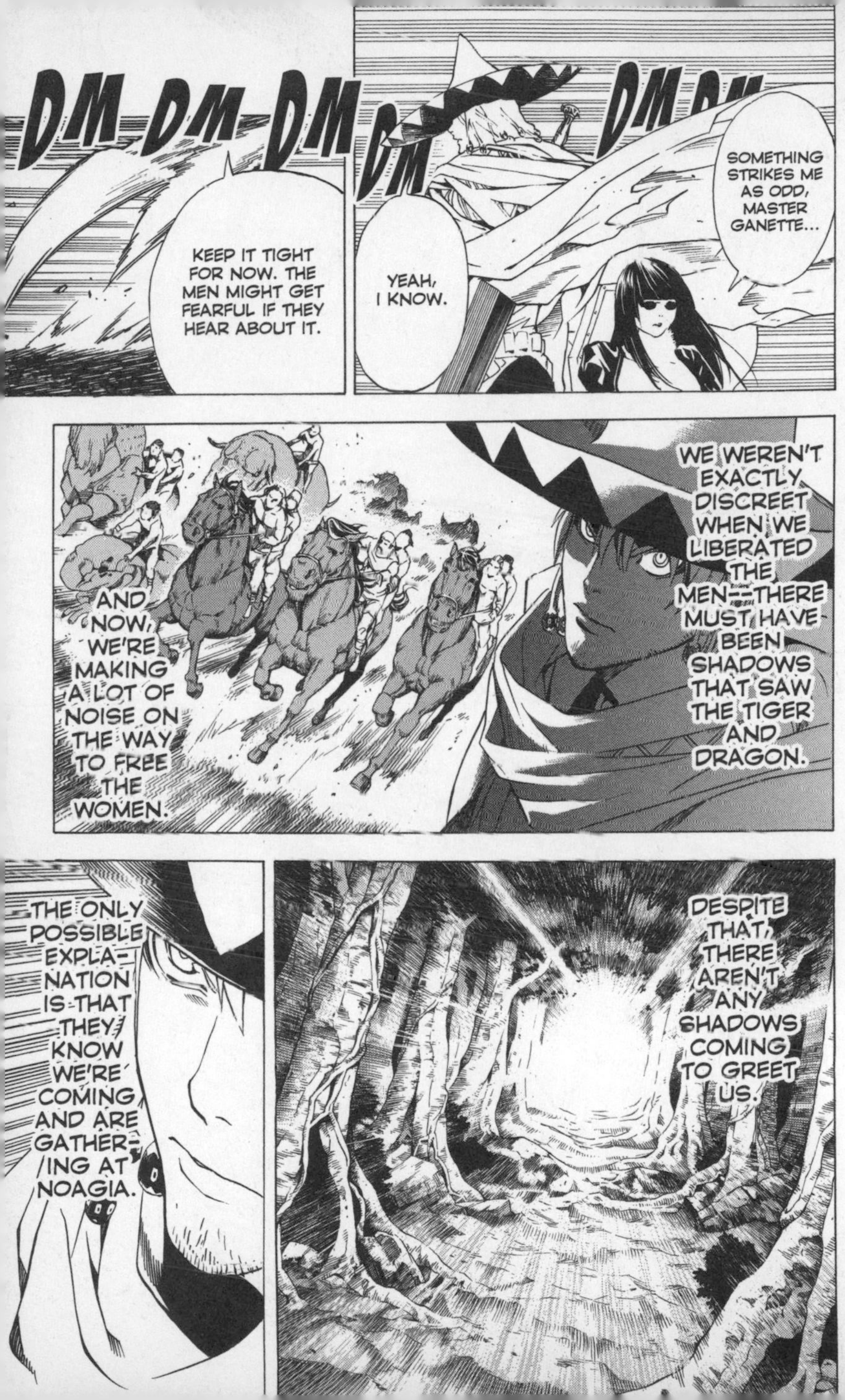
DM DM DM DM DM DM DM
SOMETHING STRIKES ME AS ODD, MASTER GANETTE...
YEAH, I KNOW.
KEEP IT TIGHT FOR NOW. THE MEN MIGHT GET FEARFUL IF THEY HEAR ABOUT IT.
WE WEREN'T EXACTLY DISCREET WHEN WE LIBERATED THE MEN--THERE MUST HAVE BEEN SHADOWS THAT SAW THE TIGER AND DRAGON.
AND NOW, WE'RE MAKING A LOT OF NOISE ON THE WAY TO FREE THE WOMEN.
DESPITE THAT, THERE AREN'T ANY SHADOWS COMING TO GREET US.
THE ONLY POSSIBLE EXPLANATION IS THAT THEY KNOW WE'RE COMING AND ARE GATHERING AT NOAGIA.

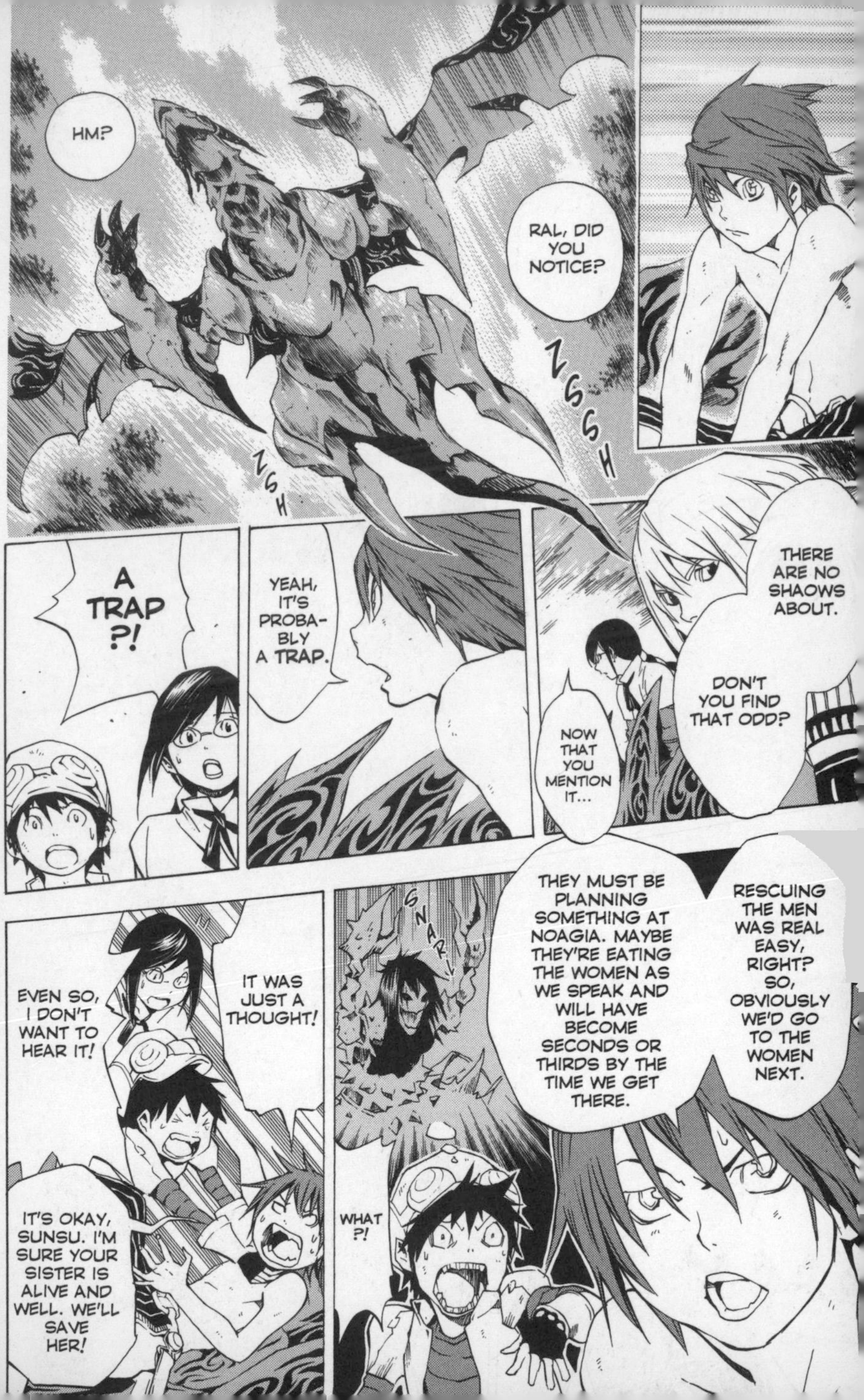
RAL, DID YOU NOTICE?
ZSSSH
HM?
ZSH
THERE ARE NO SHAOWS ABOUT.
DON'T YOU FIND THAT ODD?
NOW THAT YOU MENTION IT...
YEAH, IT'S PROBA-BLY A TRAP.
A TRAP?!
RESCUING THE MEN WAS REAL EASY, RIGHT? SO, OBVIOUSLY WE'D GO TO THE WOMEN NEXT.
THEY MUST BE PLANNING SOMETHING AT NOAGIA. MAYBE THEY'RE EATING THE WOMEN AS WE SPEAK AND WILL HAVE BECOME SECONDS OR THIRDS BY THE TIME WE GET THERE.
SNAR!
WHAT?!
IT WAS JUST A THOUGHT!
EVEN SO, I DON'T WANT TO HEAR IT!
IT'S OKAY, SUNSU. I'M SURE YOUR SISTER IS ALIVE AND WELL. WE'LL SAVE HER!

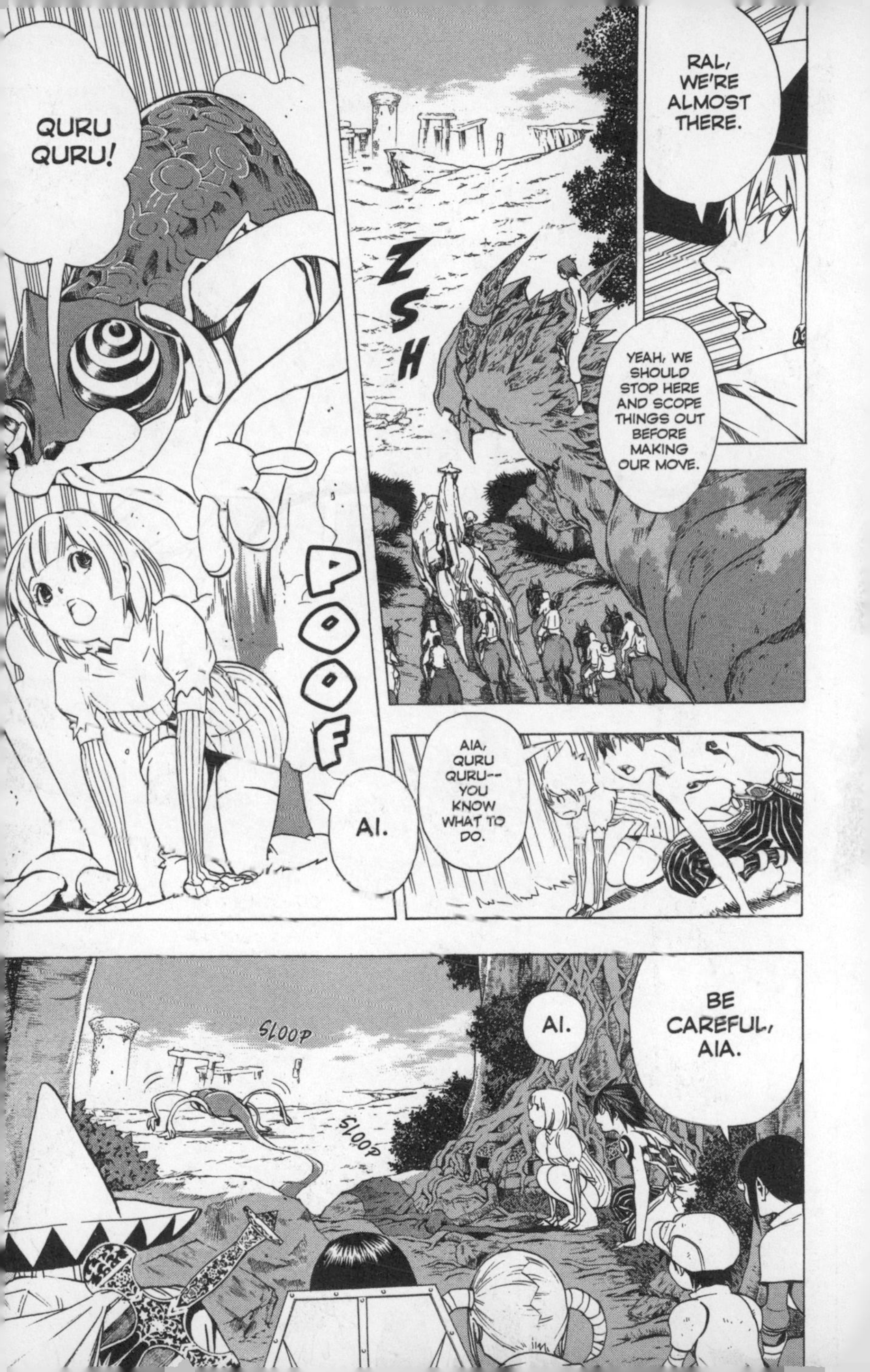
RAL, WE'RE ALMOST THERE.
ZSH
YEAH, WE SHOULD STOP HERE AND SCOPE THINGS OUT BEFORE MAKING OUR MOVE.
AIA, QURU QURU-- YOU KNOW WHAT TO DO.
AI.
QURU QURU!
POOF
BE CAREFUL, AIA.
AI.
SLOOP
SLOOP

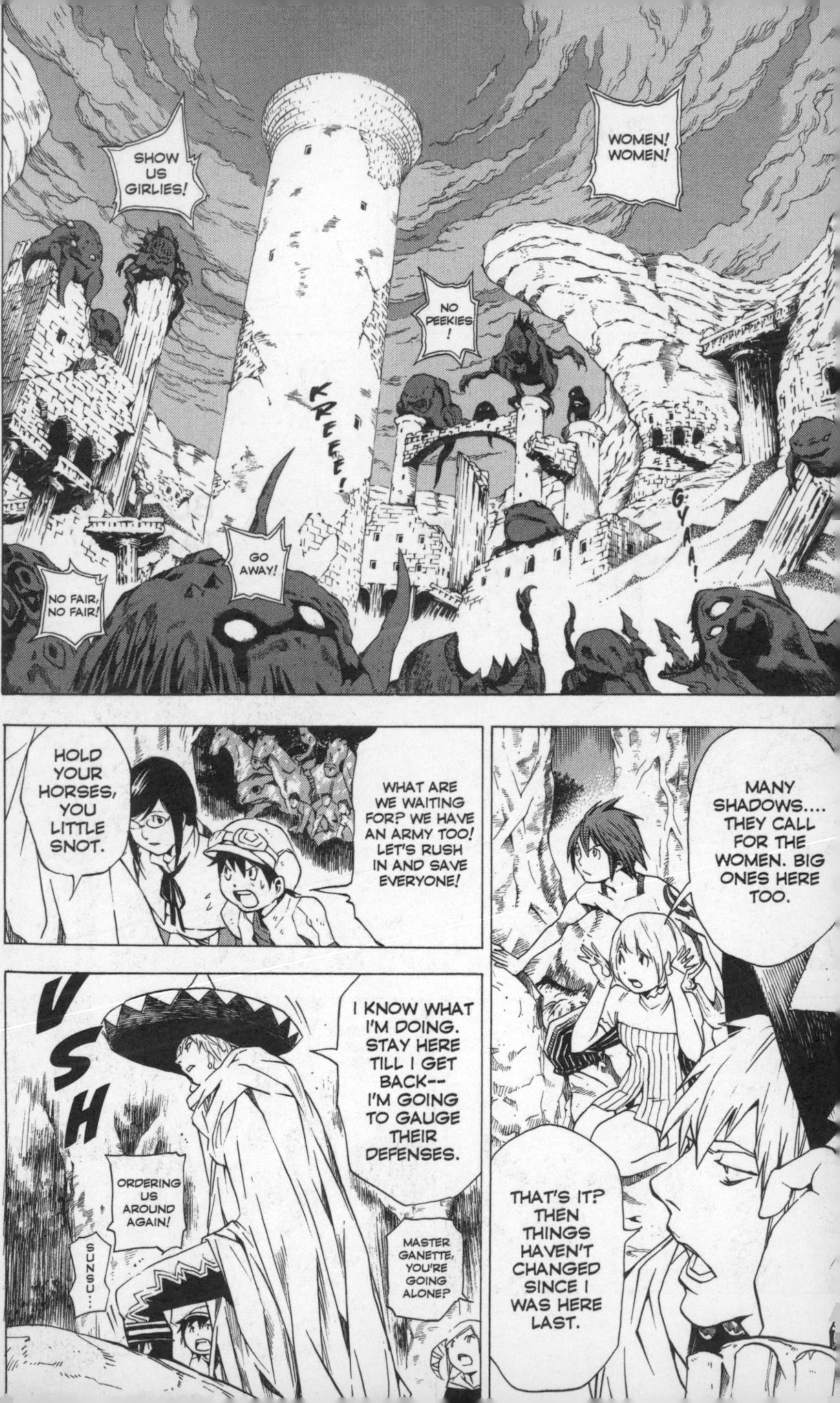
WOMEN! WOMEN!
SHOW US GIRLIES!
NO PEEKIES!
KREEE!
GYAA!
GO AWAY!
NO FAIR, NO FAIR!
MANY SHADOWS.... THEY CALL FOR THE WOMEN. BIG ONES HERE TOO.
THAT'S IT? THEN THINGS HAVEN'T CHANGED SINCE I WAS HERE LAST.
WHAT ARE WE WAITING FOR? WE HAVE AN ARMY TOO! LET'S RUSH IN AND SAVE EVERYONE!
HOLD YOUR HORSES, YOU LITTLE SNOT.
I KNOW WHAT I'M DOING. STAY HERE TILL I GET BACK-- I'M GOING TO GAUGE THEIR DEFENSES.
VSH
ORDERING US AROUND AGAIN!
MASTER GANETTE, YOU'RE GOING ALONE?
SUNSU...

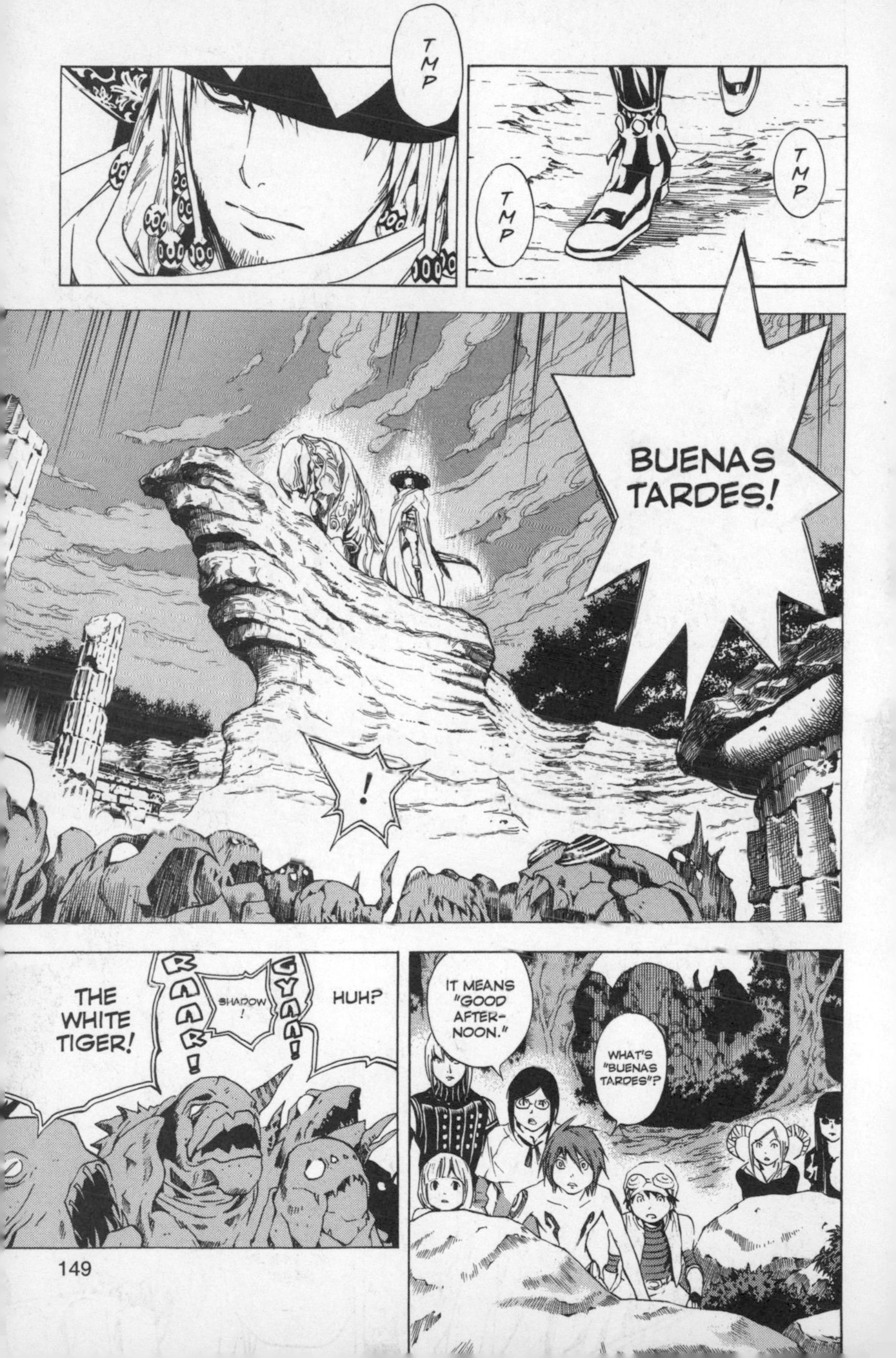
TMP
TMP
TMP
BUENAS TARDES!
!
WHAT'S "BUENAS TARDES"?
IT MEANS "GOOD AFTER-NOON."
HUH?
GYAAA!
SHADOW!
RAAAR!
THE WHITE TIGER!

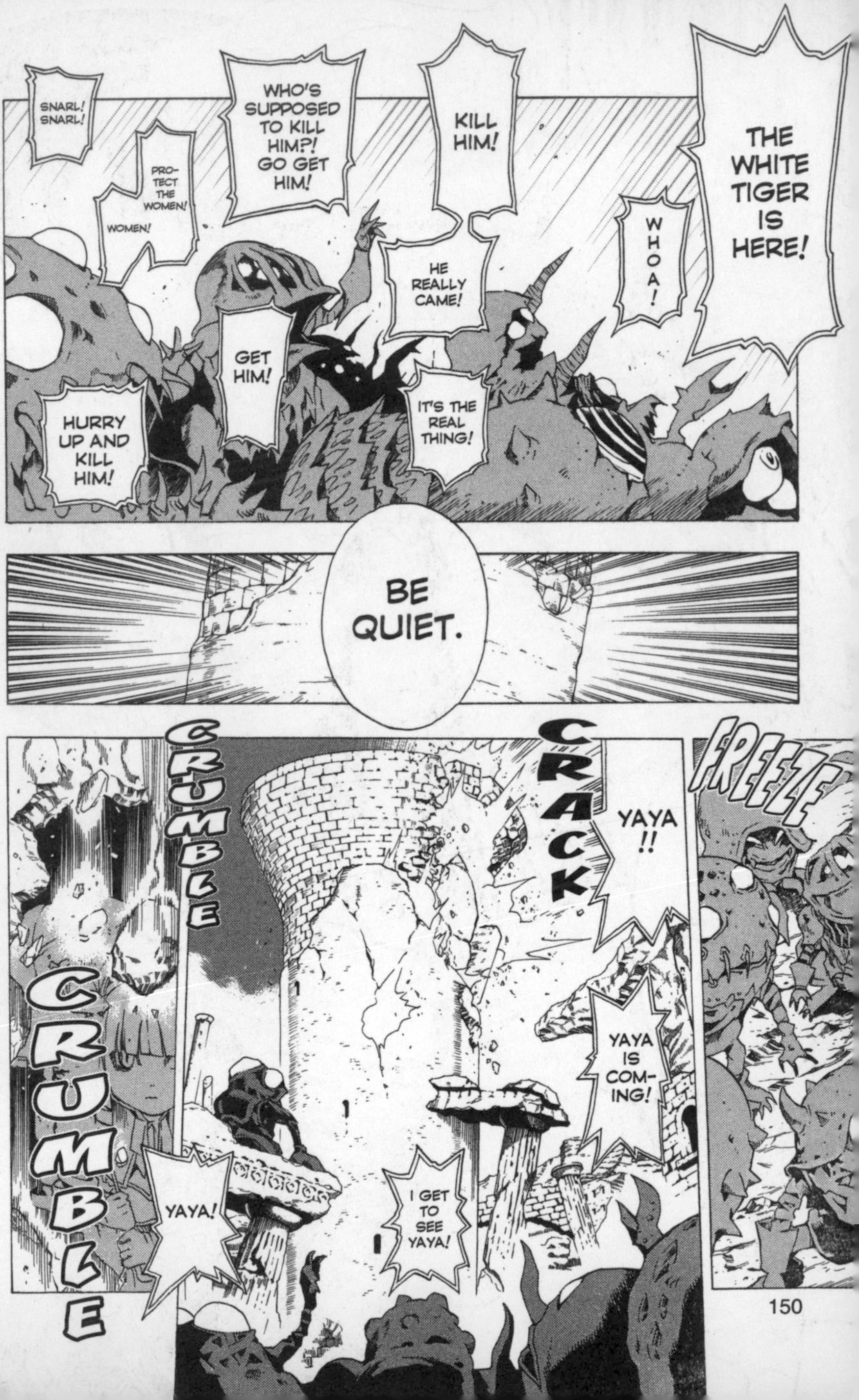
THE WHITE TIGER IS HERE!
WHOA!
KILL HIM!
WHO'S SUPPOSED TO KILL HIM?! GO GET HIM!
SNARL! SNARL!
PRO-TECT THE WOMEN!
WOMEN!
HE REALLY CAME!
IT'S THE REAL THING!
GET HIM!
HURRY UP AND KILL HIM!
BE QUIET.
FREEZE
CRACK
YAYA !!
CRUMBLE
YAYA IS COM-ING!
I GET TO SEE YAYA!
YAYA!
CRUMBLE

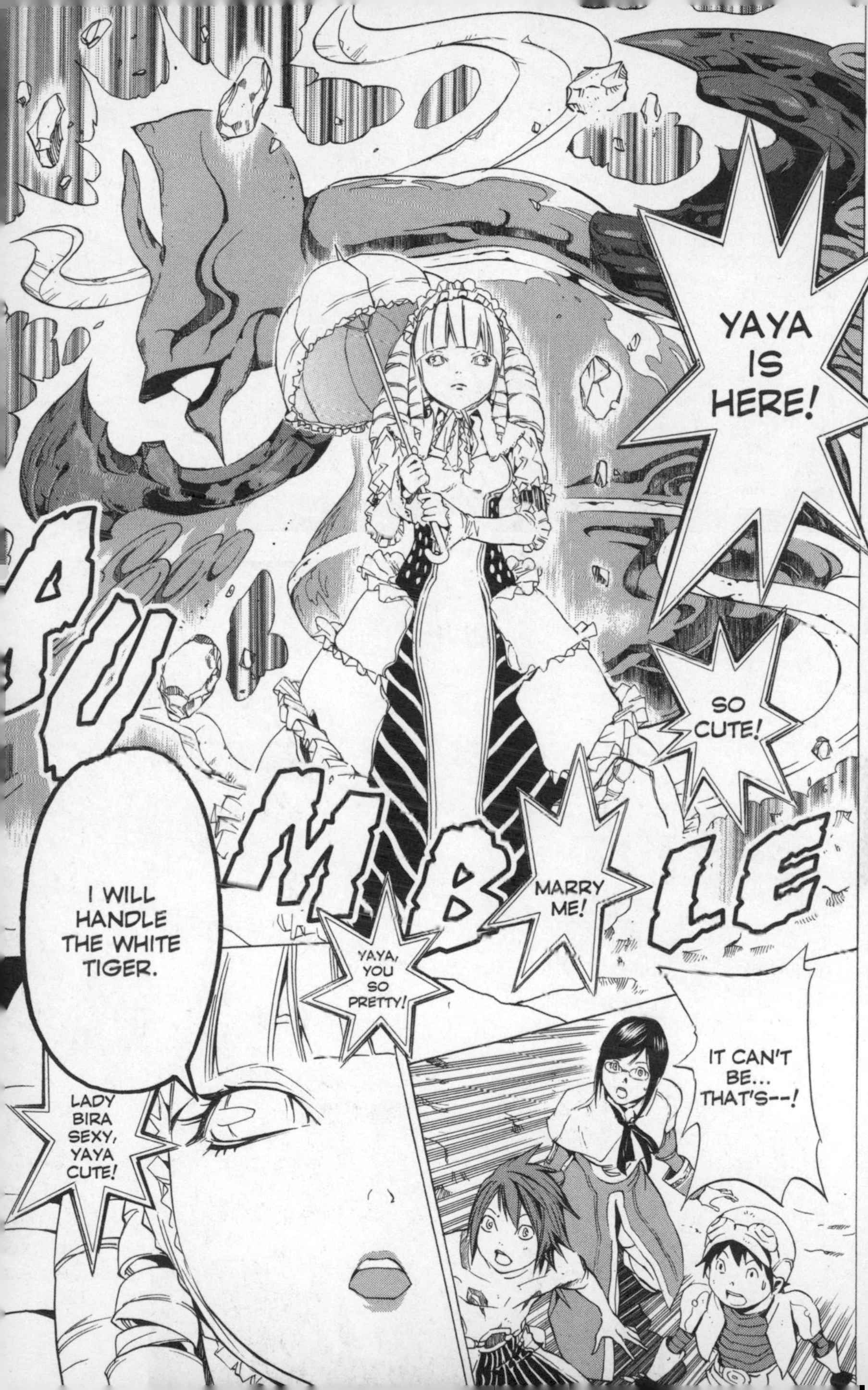
YAYA IS HERE!
SO CUTE!
MARRY ME!
YAYA, YOU SO PRETTY!
I WILL HANDLE THE WHITE TIGER.
IT CAN'T BE... THAT'S--!
LADY BIRA SEXY, YAYA CUTE!

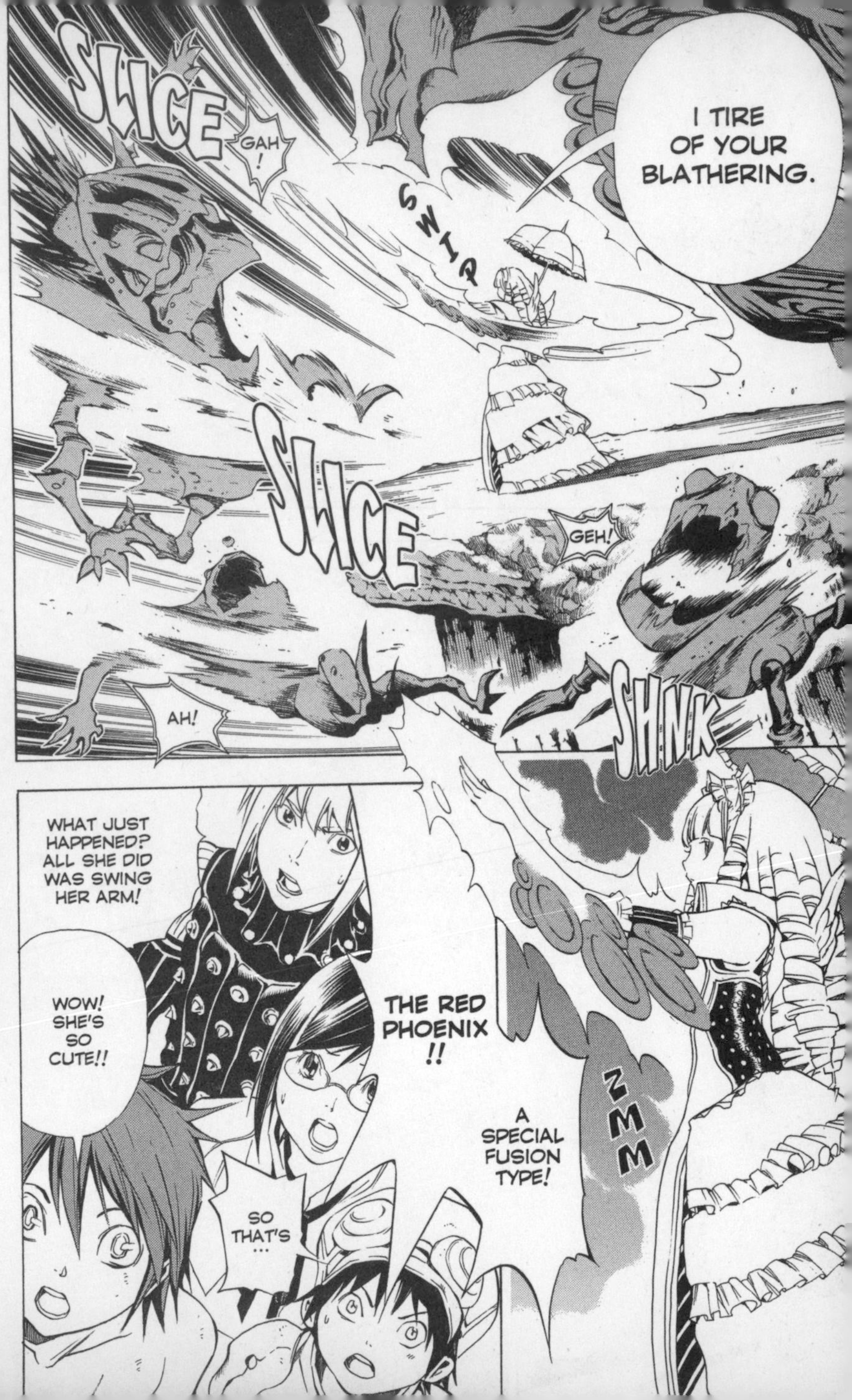
I TIRE OF YOUR BLATHERING.
SWIP
SLICE
GAH!
SLICE
GEH!
SHNK
AH!
ZMM
THE RED PHOENIX!!
A SPECIAL FUSION TYPE!
WHAT JUST HAPPENED? ALL SHE DID WAS SWING HER ARM!
WOW! SHE'S SO CUTE!!
SO THAT'S...

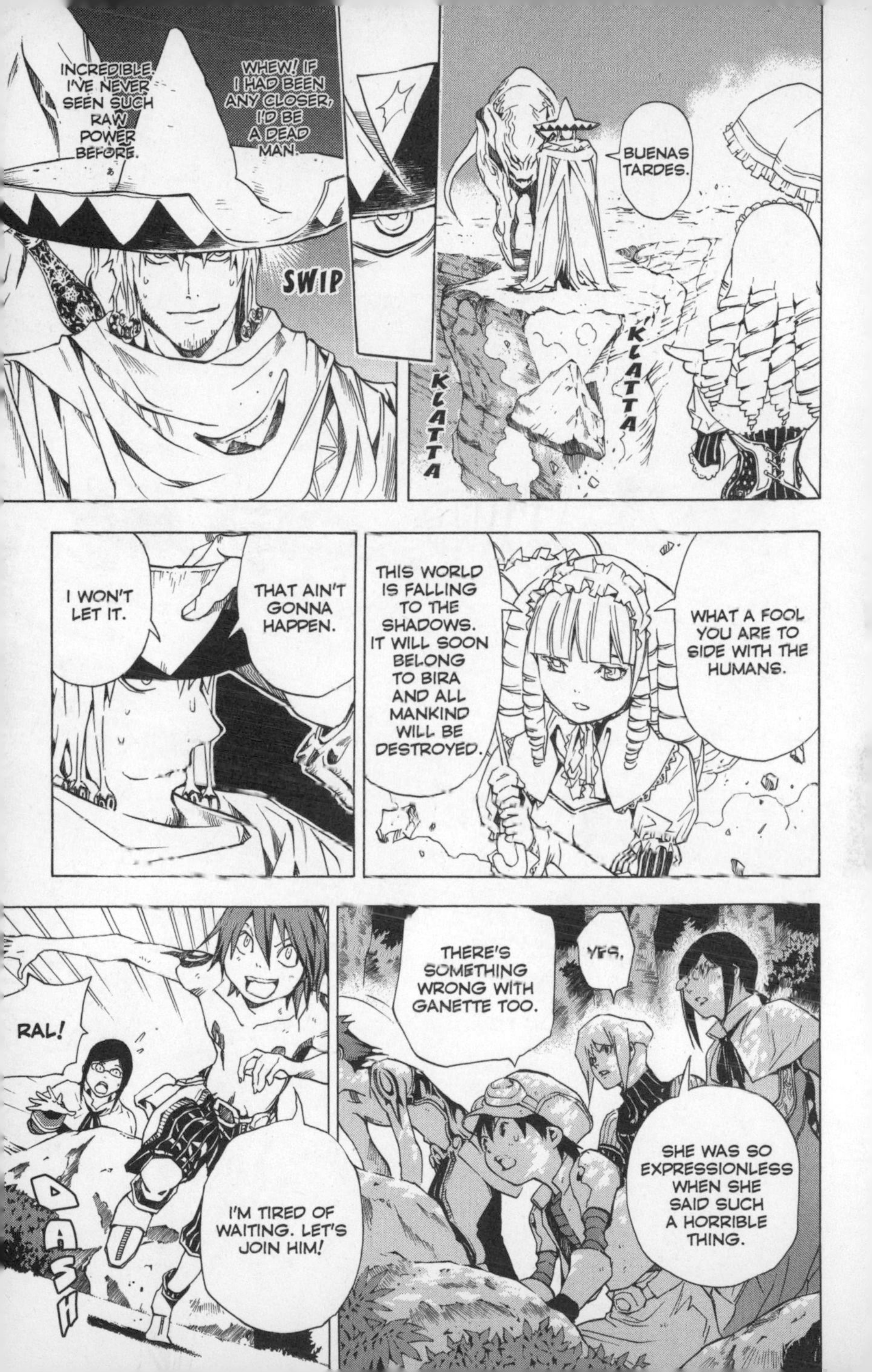
BUENAS TARDES.
KLATTA
KLATTA
WHEW! IF I HAD BEEN ANY CLOSER, I'D BE A DEAD MAN.
INCREDIBLE. I'VE NEVER SEEN SUCH RAW POWER BEFORE.
SWIP
WHAT A FOOL YOU ARE TO SIDE WITH THE HUMANS.
THIS WORLD IS FALLING TO THE SHADOWS. IT WILL SOON BELONG TO BIRA AND ALL MANKIND WILL BE DESTROYED.
THAT AIN'T GONNA HAPPEN.
I WON'T LET IT.
YES.
THERE'S SOMETHING WRONG WITH GANETTE TOO.
SHE WAS SO EXPRESSIONLESS WHEN SHE SAID SUCH A HORRIBLE THING.
RAL!
I'M TIRED OF WAITING. LET'S JOIN HIM!
DASH

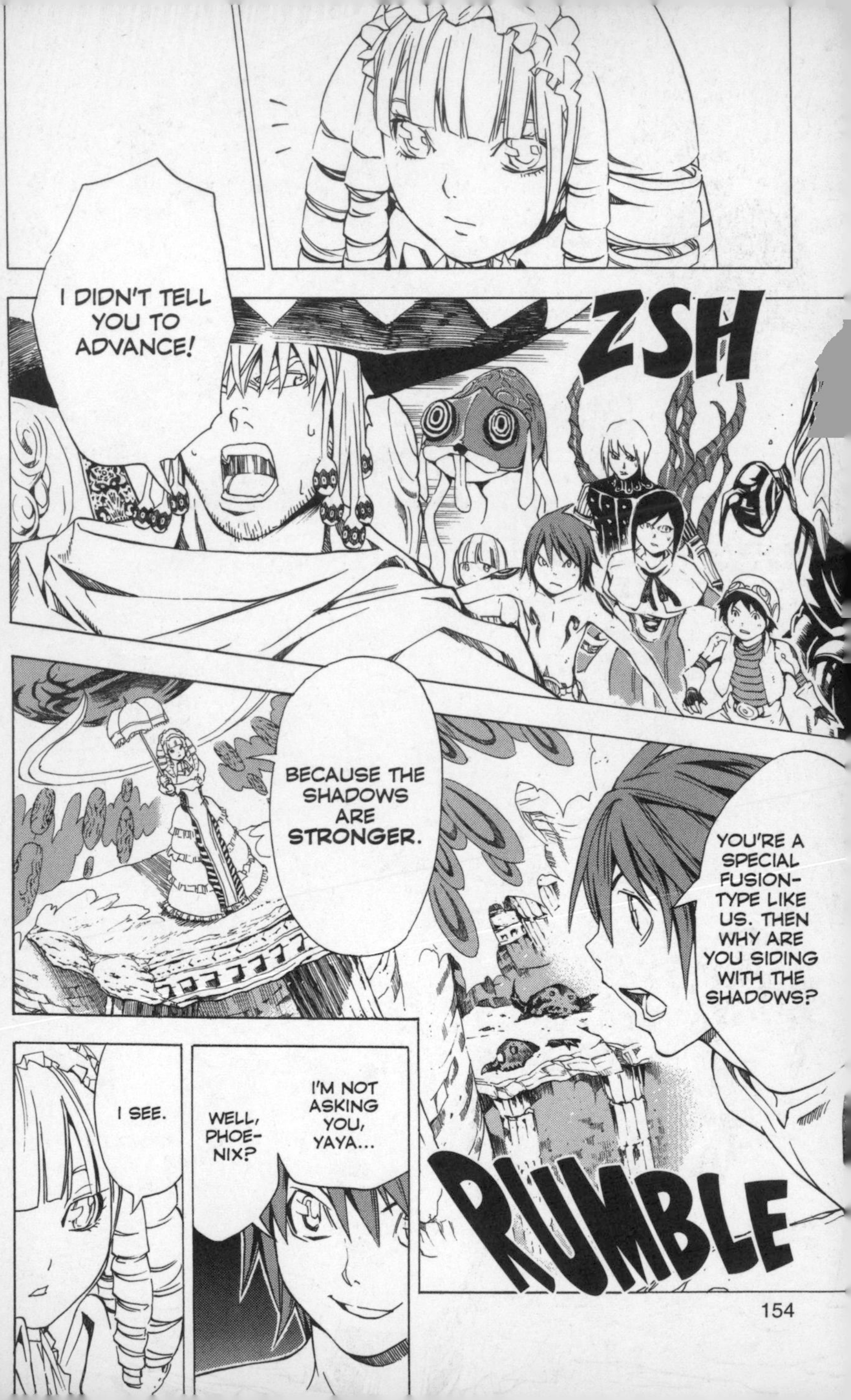
ZSH
I DIDN'T TELL YOU TO ADVANCE!
YOU'RE A SPECIAL FUSION-TYPE LIKE US. THEN WHY ARE YOU SIDING WITH THE SHADOWS?
BECAUSE THE SHADOWS ARE STRONGER.
RUMBLE
I'M NOT ASKING YOU, YAYA...
WELL, PHOE-NIX?
I SEE.

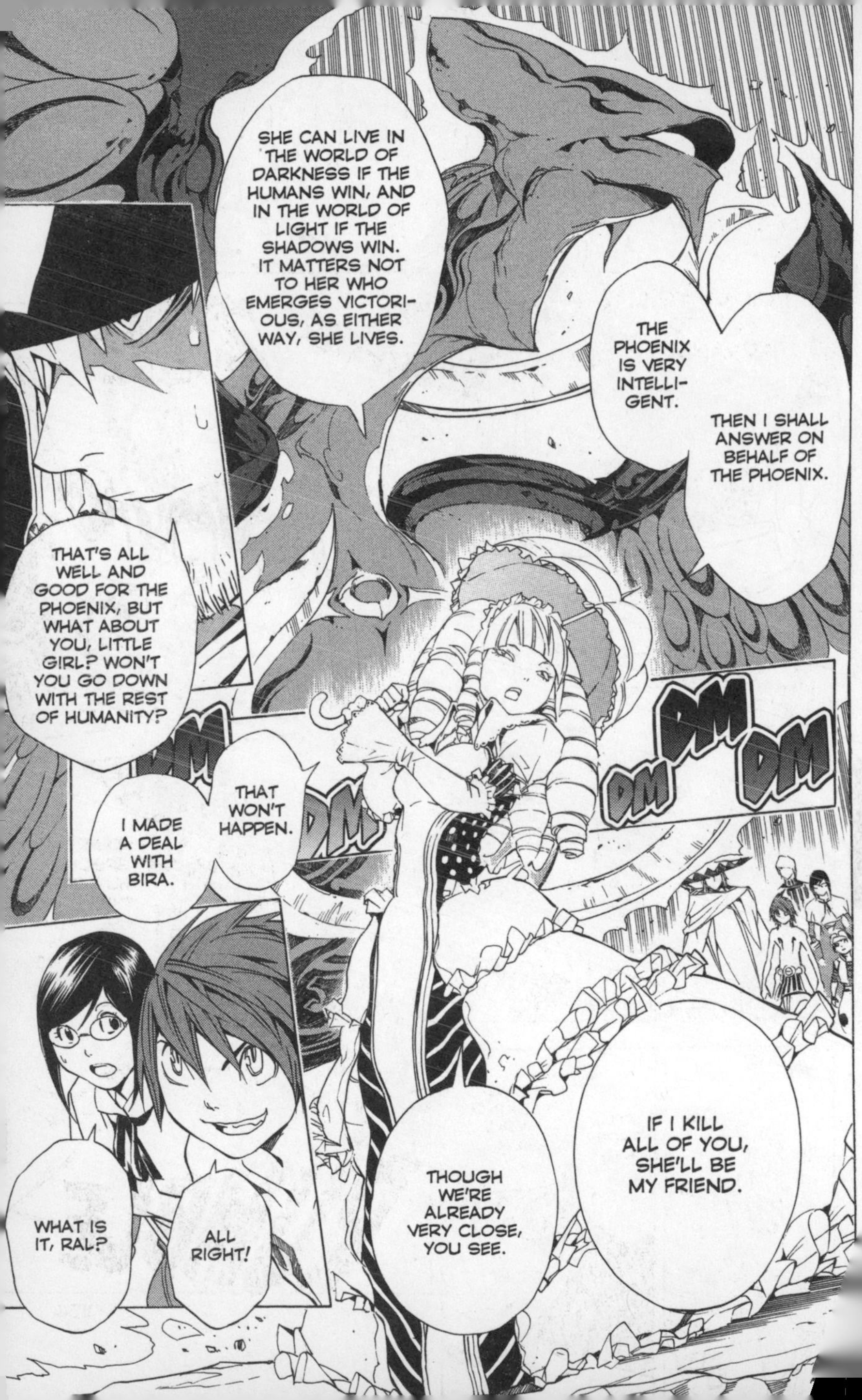
THEN I SHALL ANSWER ON BEHALF OF THE PHOENIX.
THE PHOENIX IS VERY INTELLIGENT.
SHE CAN LIVE IN THE WORLD OF DARKNESS IF THE HUMANS WIN, AND IN THE WORLD OF LIGHT IF THE SHADOWS WIN. IT MATTERS NOT TO HER WHO EMERGES VICTORIOUS, AS EITHER WAY, SHE LIVES.
THAT'S ALL WELL AND GOOD FOR THE PHOENIX, BUT WHAT ABOUT YOU, LITTLE GIRL? WON'T YOU GO DOWN WITH THE REST OF HUMANITY?
DM DM DM DM
THAT WON'T HAPPEN.
I MADE A DEAL WITH BIRA.
DM DM
IF I KILL ALL OF YOU, SHE'LL BE MY FRIEND.
THOUGH WE'RE ALREADY VERY CLOSE, YOU SEE.
ALL RIGHT!
WHAT IS IT, RAL?

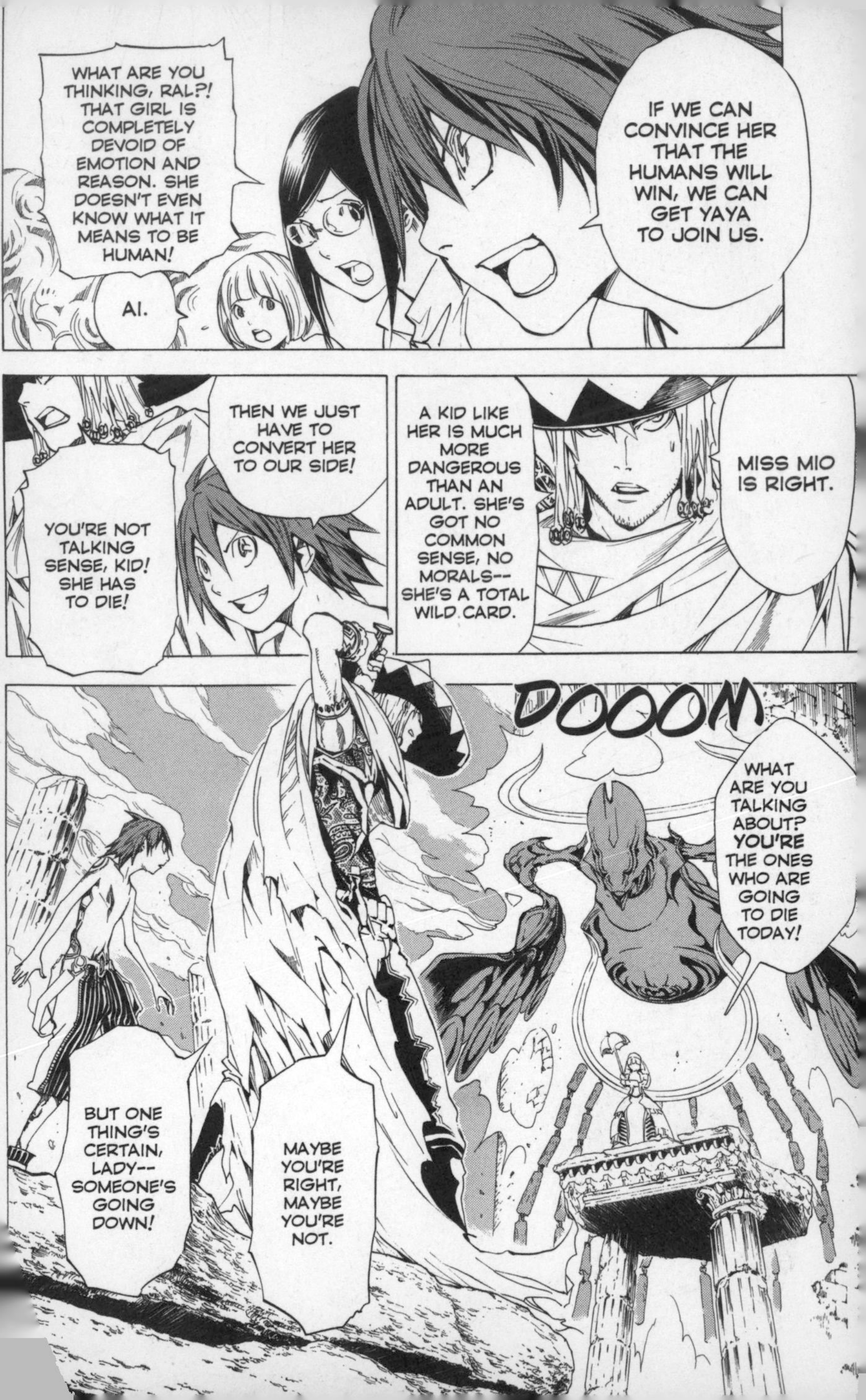
IF WE CAN CONVINCE HER THAT THE HUMANS WILL WIN, WE CAN GET YAYA TO JOIN US.
WHAT ARE YOU THINKING, RAL?! THAT GIRL IS COMPLETELY DEVOID OF EMOTION AND REASON. SHE DOESN'T EVEN KNOW WHAT IT MEANS TO BE HUMAN!
AI.
MISS MIO IS RIGHT.
A KID LIKE HER IS MUCH MORE DANGEROUS THAN AN ADULT. SHE'S GOT NO COMMON SENSE, NO MORALS-- SHE'S A TOTAL WILD CARD.
THEN WE JUST HAVE TO CONVERT HER TO OUR SIDE!
YOU'RE NOT TALKING SENSE, KID! SHE HAS TO DIE!
DOOOM
WHAT ARE YOU TALKING ABOUT? YOU'RE THE ONES WHO ARE GOING TO DIE TODAY!
MAYBE YOU'RE RIGHT, MAYBE YOU'RE NOT.
BUT ONE THING'S CERTAIN, LADY-- SOMEONE'S GOING DOWN!

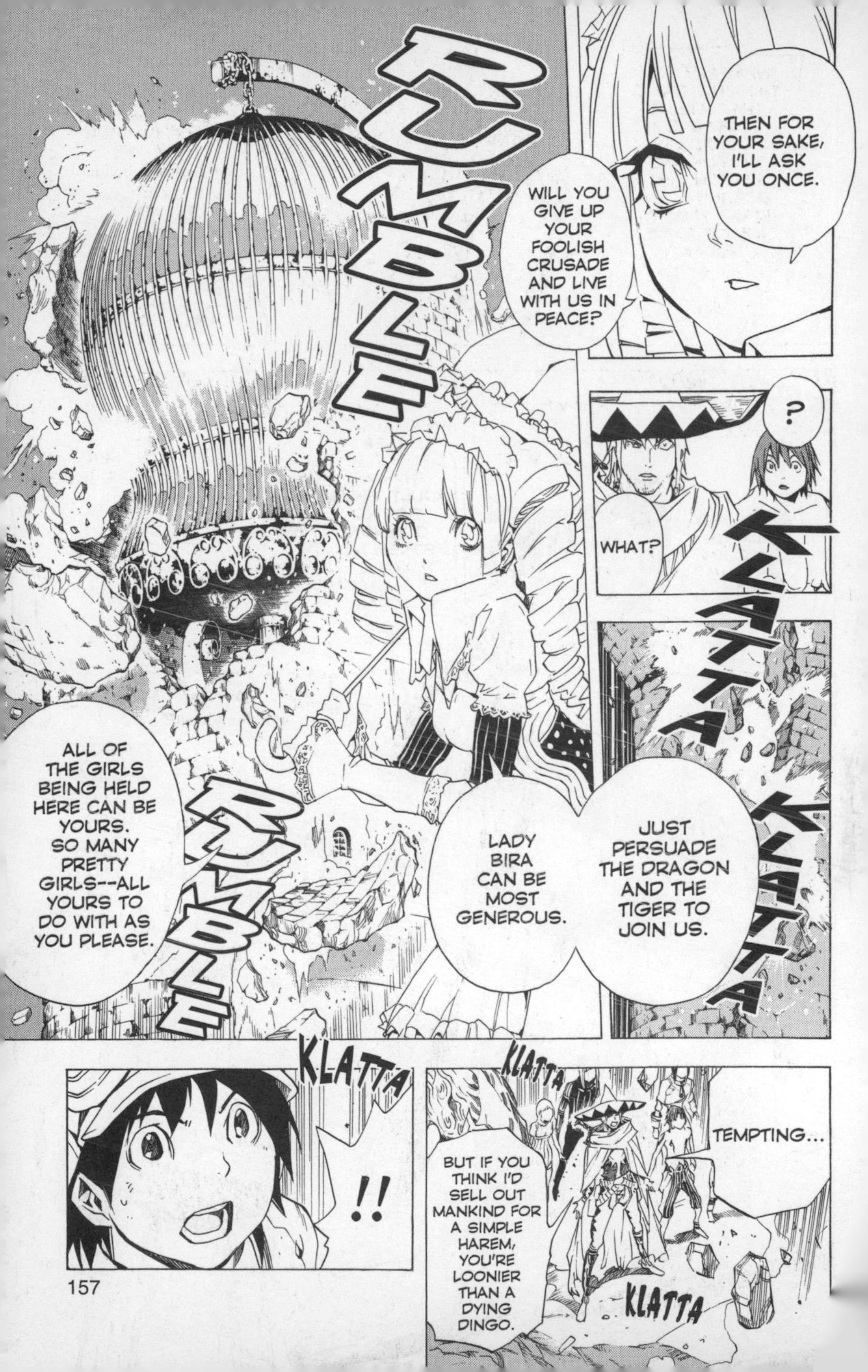
THEN FOR YOUR SAKE, I'LL ASK YOU ONCE.
WILL YOU GIVE UP YOUR FOOLISH CRUSADE AND LIVE WITH US IN PEACE?
?
WHAT?
KLATTA
KLATTA
JUST PERSUADE THE DRAGON AND THE TIGER TO JOIN US.
RUMBLE
LADY BIRA CAN BE MOST GENEROUS.
ALL OF THE GIRLS BEING HELD HERE CAN BE YOURS. SO MANY PRETTY GIRLS--ALL YOURS TO DO WITH AS YOU PLEASE.
RUMBLE
KLATTA
TEMPTING...
BUT IF YOU THINK I'D SELL OUT MANKIND FOR A SIMPLE HAREM, YOU'RE LOONIER THAN A DYING DINGO.
KLATTA
KLATTA
!!

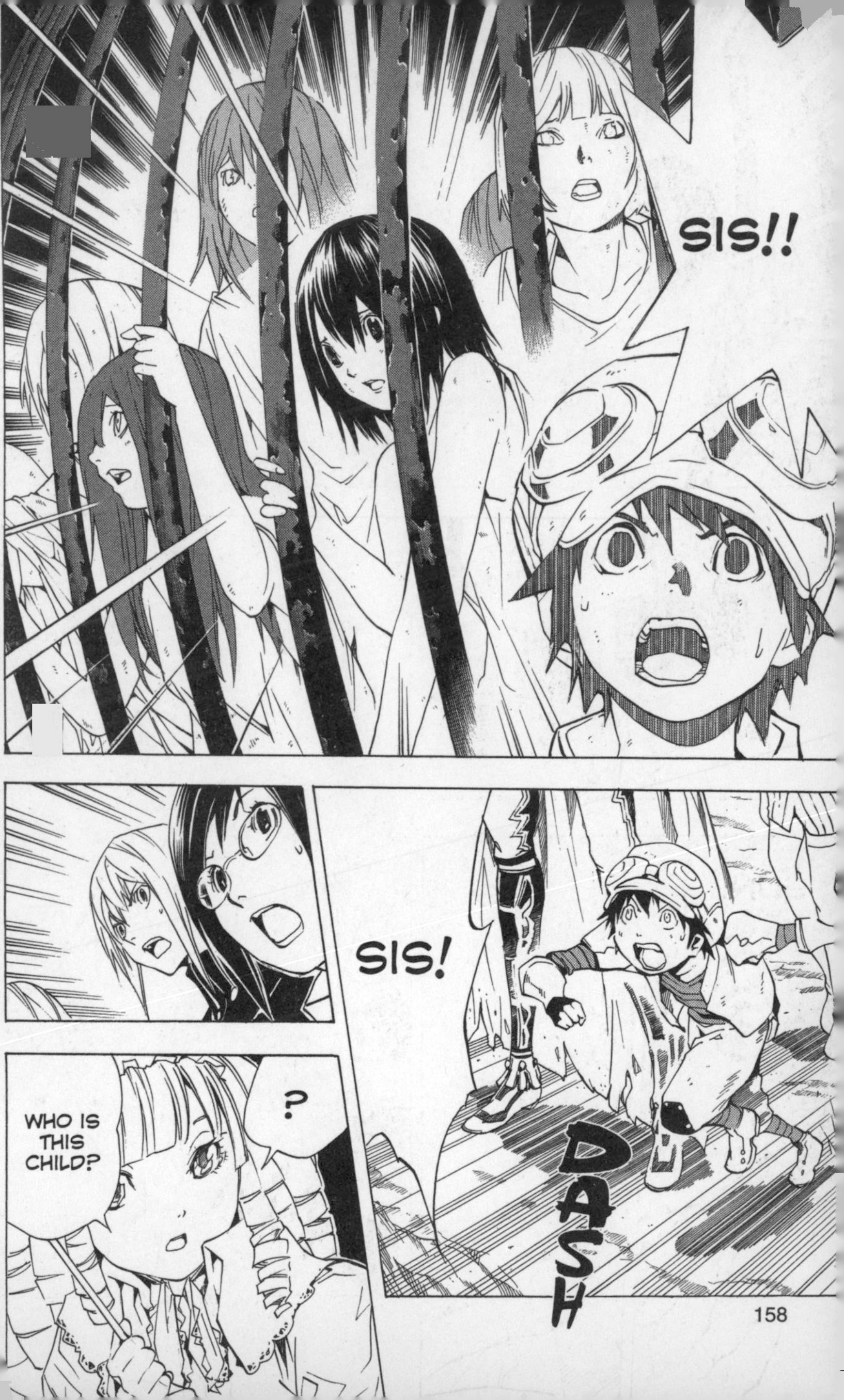
SIS!!
SIS!
DASH
?
WHO IS THIS CHILD?

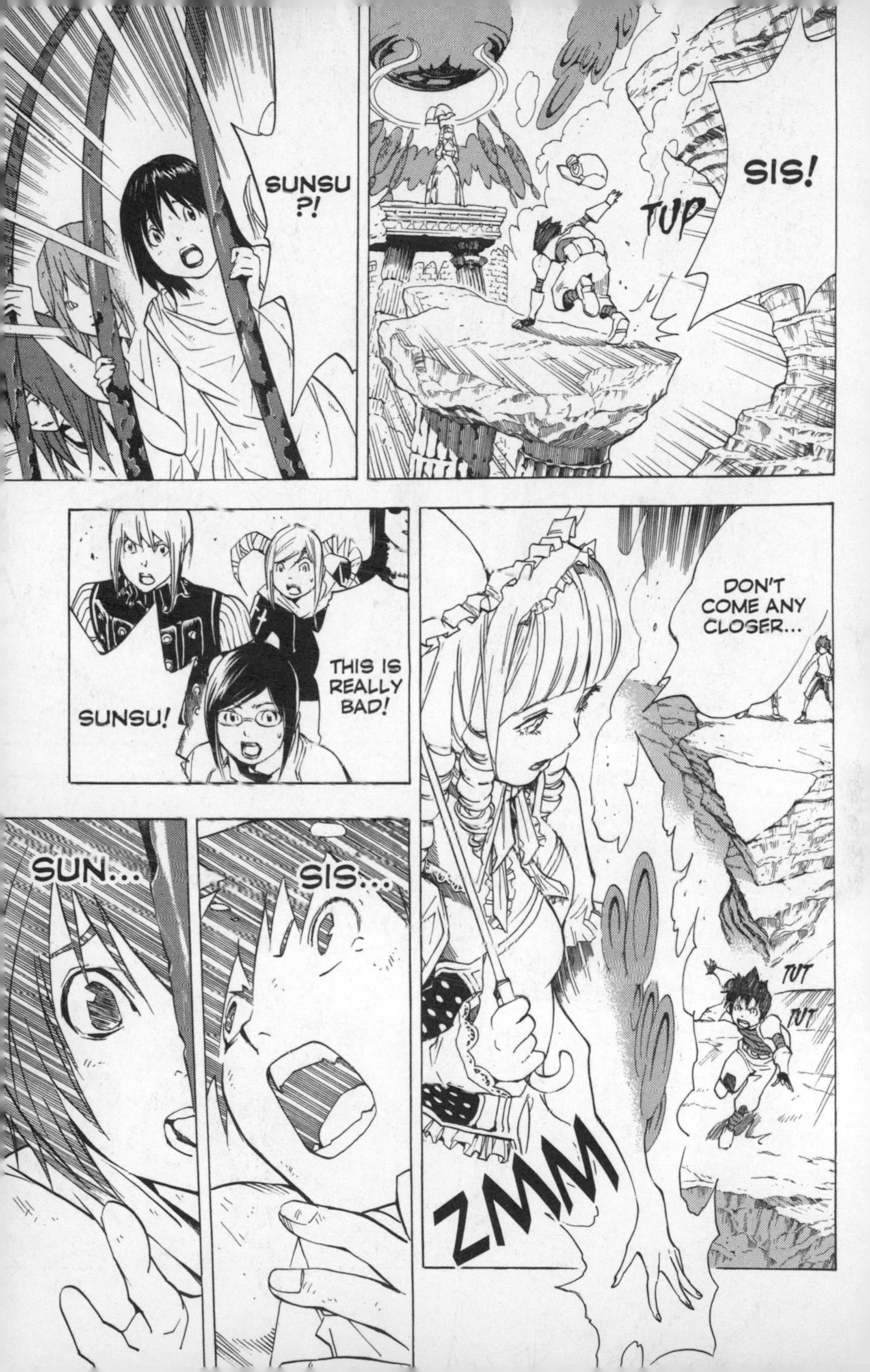
SIS!
TUP
SUNSU ?!
DON'T COME ANY CLOSER...
TUT
TUT
ZMM
THIS IS REALLY BAD!
SUNSU!
SIS...
SUN...

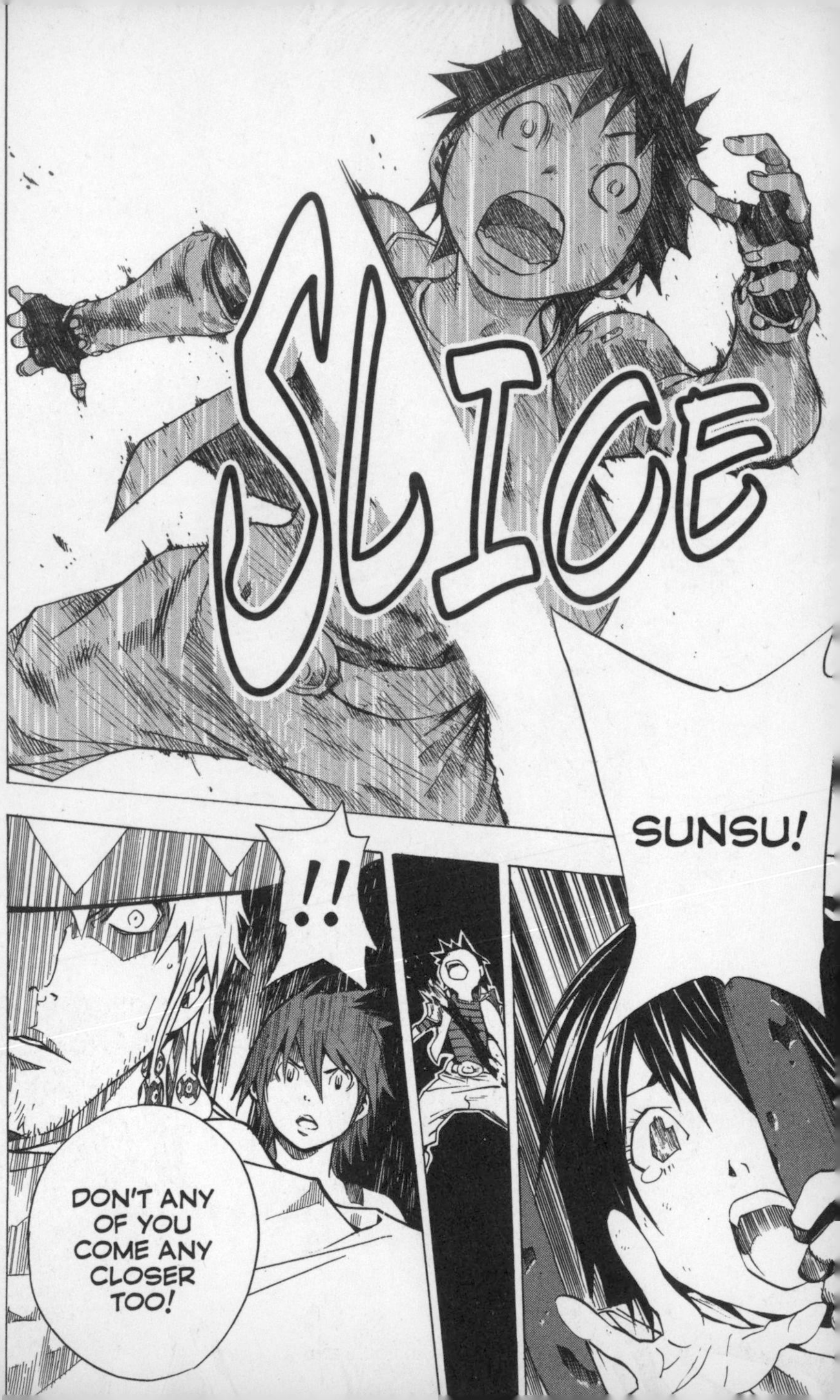
SLICE
SUNSU!
!!
DON'T ANY OF YOU COME ANY CLOSER TOO!

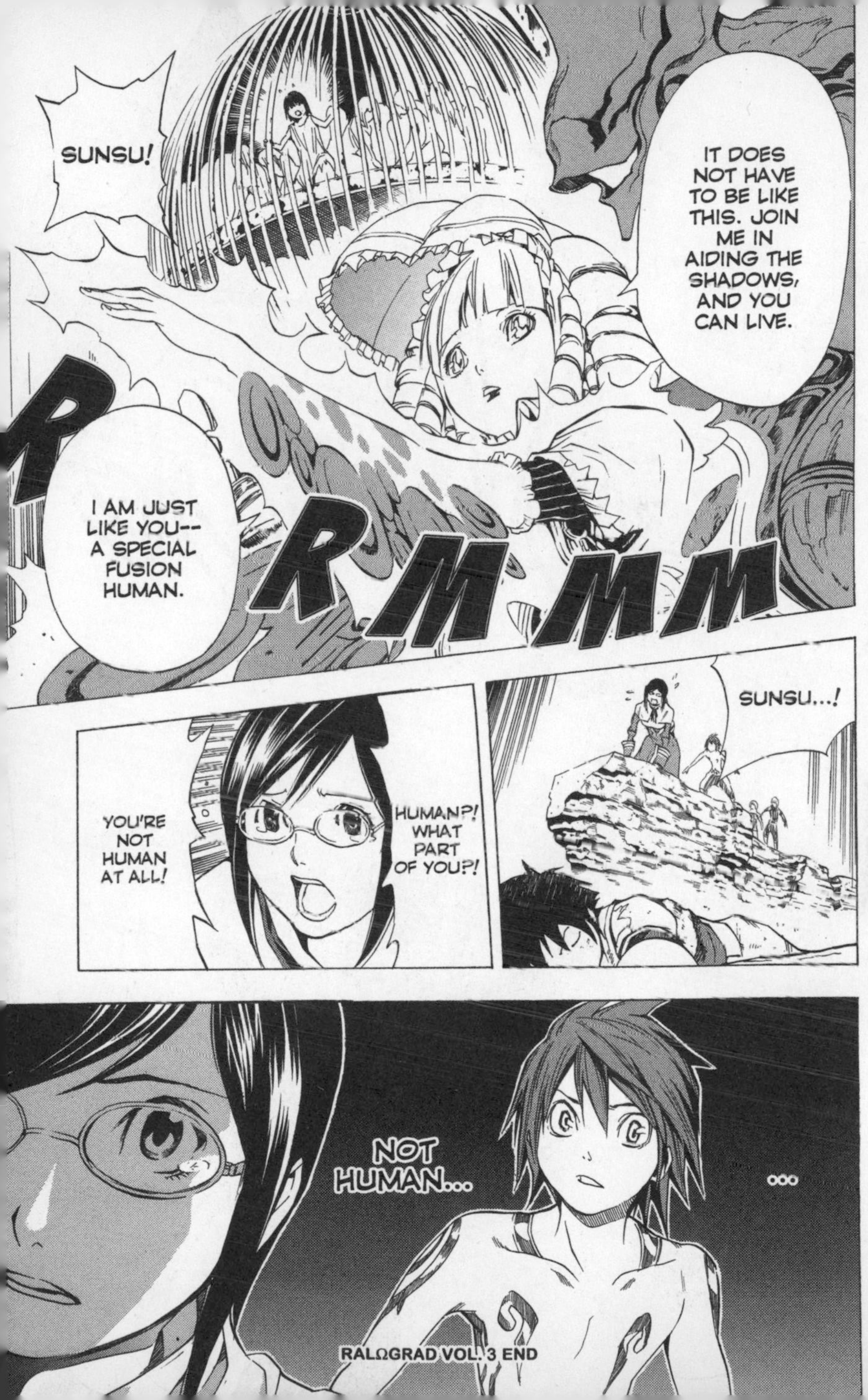
IT DOES NOT HAVE TO BE LIKE THIS. JOIN ME IN AIDING THE SHADOWS, AND YOU CAN LIVE.
SUNSU!
RRMMMM
I AM JUST LIKE YOU-- A SPECIAL FUSION HUMAN.
SUNSU...!
HUMAN?! WHAT PART OF YOU?!
YOU'RE NOT HUMAN AT ALL!
...
NOT HUMAN...
RALΩGRAD VOL. 3 END

DEATH NOTE 13

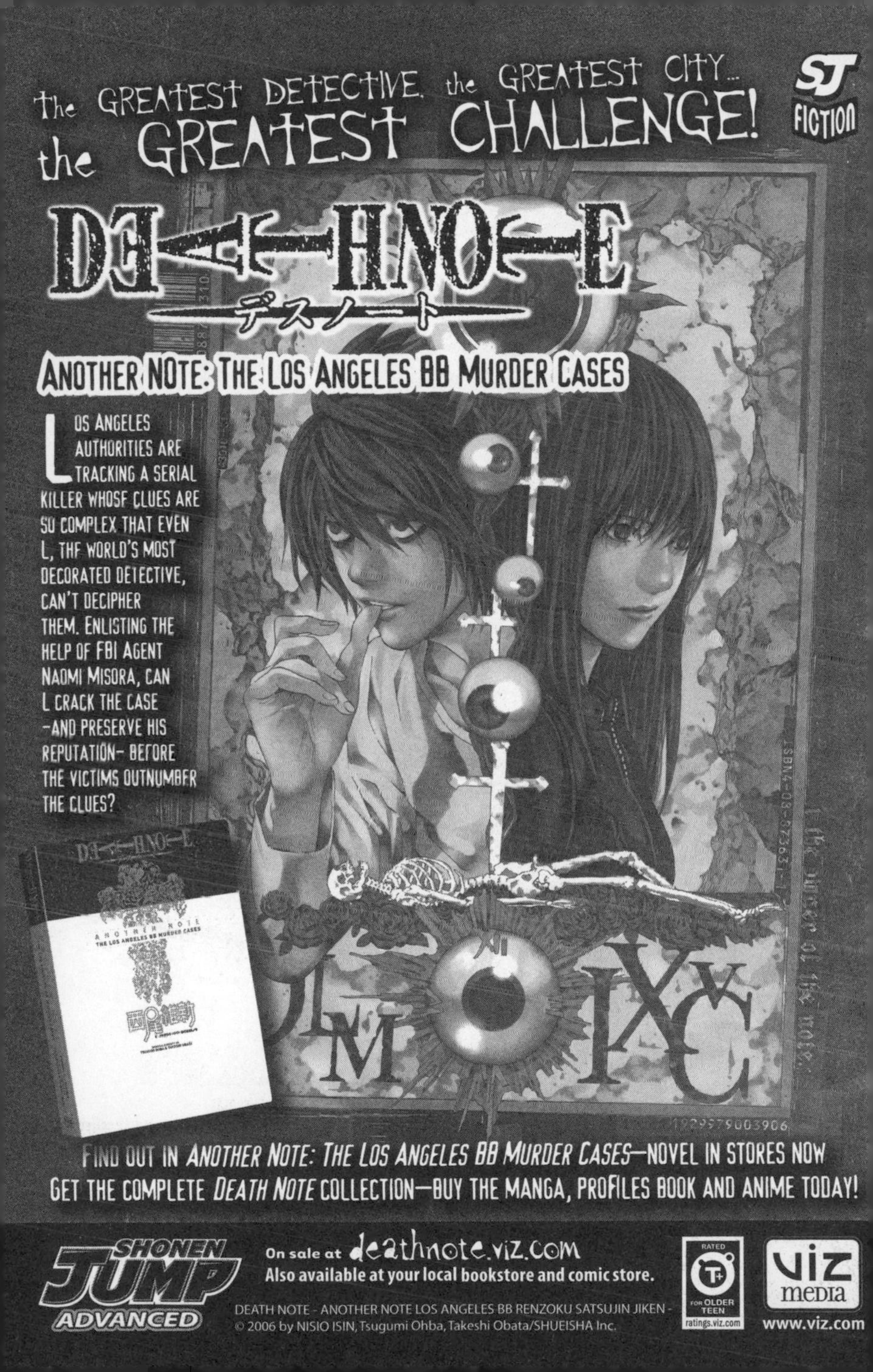

the GREATEST DETECTIVE, the GREATEST CITY...
the GREATEST CHALLENGE!
SJ FICTION
DEATH NOTE
デスノート
ANOTHER NOTE: THE LOS ANGELES BB MURDER CASES
LOS ANGELES AUTHORITIES ARE TRACKING A SERIAL KILLER WHOSE CLUES ARE SO COMPLEX THAT EVEN L, THE WORLD'S MOST DECORATED DETECTIVE, CAN'T DECIPHER THEM. ENLISTING THE HELP OF FBI AGENT NAOMI MISORA, CAN L CRACK THE CASE —AND PRESERVE HIS REPUTATION— BEFORE THE VICTIMS OUTNUMBER THE CLUES?
ANOTHER NOTE
THE LOS ANGELES BB MURDER CASES
FIND OUT IN *ANOTHER NOTE: THE LOS ANGELES BB MURDER CASES*—NOVEL IN STORES NOW
GET THE COMPLETE *DEATH NOTE* COLLECTION—BUY THE MANGA, PROFILES BOOK AND ANIME TODAY!
SHONEN JUMP ADVANCED
On sale at deathnote.viz.com
Also available at your local bookstore and comic store.
DEATH NOTE - ANOTHER NOTE LOS ANGELES BB RENZOKU SATSUJIN JIKEN - © 2006 by NISIO ISIN, Tsugumi Ohba, Takeshi Obata/SHUEISHA Inc.
RATED T+ FOR OLDER TEEN
ratings.viz.com
viz media
www.viz.com

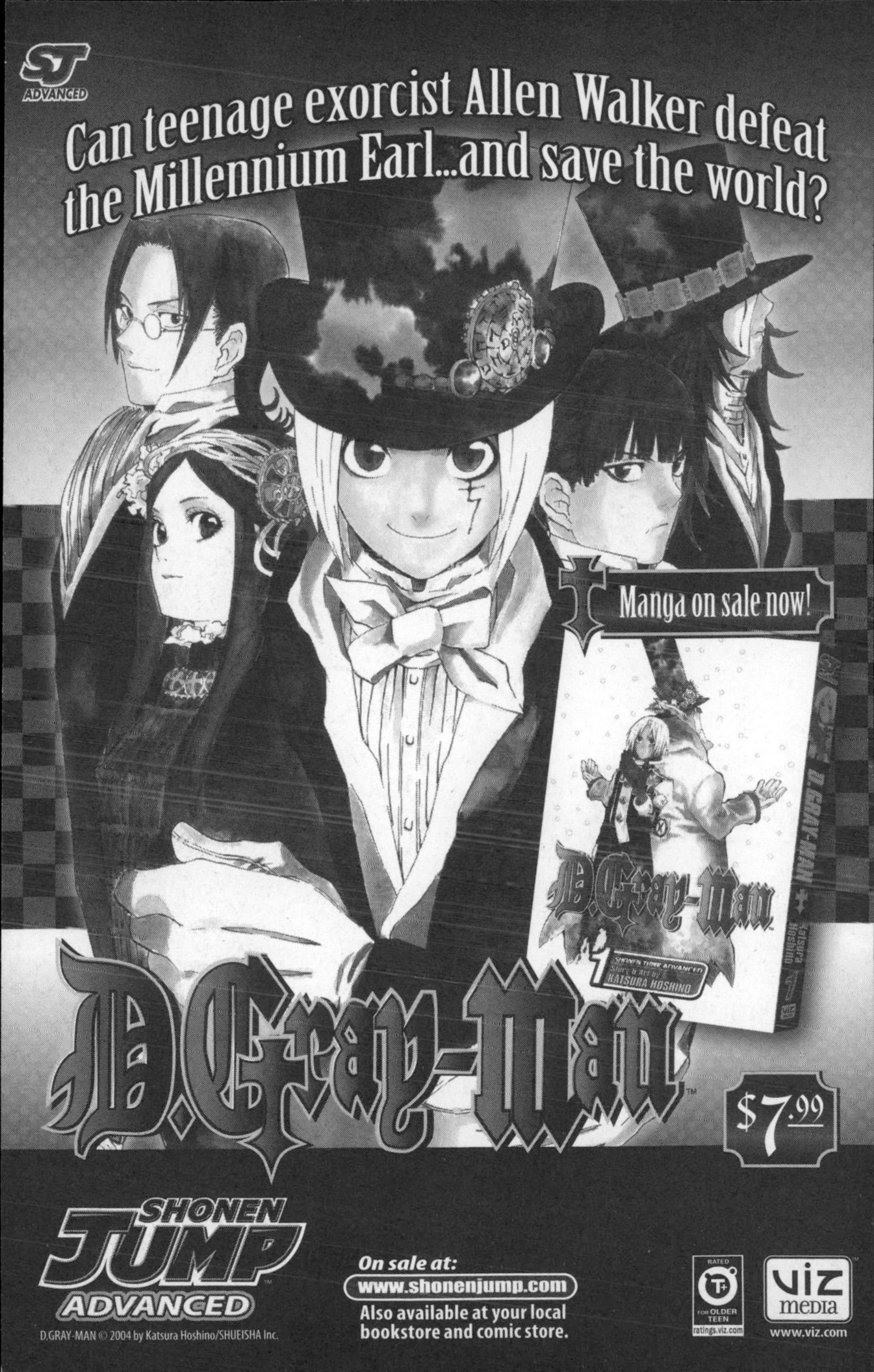
SJ ADVANCED
Can teenage exorcist Allen Walker defeat the Millennium Earl...and save the world?
Manga on sale now!
D.Gray-man
1 SHONEN JUMP ADVANCED
Story & Art by KATSURA HOSHINO
D.Gray-man™
$7.99
SHONEN JUMP ADVANCED
On sale at:
www.shonenjump.com
Also available at your local bookstore and comic store.
RATED T+ FOR OLDER TEEN
ratings.viz.com
viz media
www.viz.com
D.GRAY-MAN © 2004 by Katsura Hoshino/SHUEISHA Inc.

Tell us what you think about SHONEN JUMP manga!

Our survey is now available online.
Go to: **www.SHONENJUMP.com/mangasurvey**

Help us make our product offering better!

Save **50% OFF** the cover price!